This book, which celebrates the bicentenary of Edward Gibbon's death, examines Gibbon's interpretations of empire, and the intellectual context in which he formulated them, against a background of the eighteenth- and late twentieth-century knowledge of late antiquity and the Middle Ages.

Gibbon's ideas of empire, his understanding of monarchy and the balance of power, his sources and working methods, the structure of the *History of the decline and fall of the Roman Empire*, his attitude towards the barbarians, the contrasting treatments of the eastern and western Empires, his appreciation of past civilizations and their material remains, his audience and their reactions – contemporary and Victorian – to his text are considered in the light of the latest research on eighteenth-century intellectual history on the one hand and on late antiquity, Byzantium and the Middle Ages on the other. The book breaks new ground, in taking the form of a dialogue between experts on the fields about which Gibbon himself wrote and eighteenth-century intellectual historians.

EDWARD GIBBON AND EMPIRE

EDWARD GIBBON
AND EMPIRE

EDITED BY

ROSAMOND MCKITTERICK

University of Cambridge

AND

ROLAND QUINAULT

University of North London

CAMBRIDGE
UNIVERSITY PRESS

Published by the Press Syndicate of the University of Cambridge
The Pitt Building, Trumpington Street, Cambridge CB2 1RP
40 West 20th Street, New York, NY 10011-4211, USA
10 Stamford Road, Oakleigh, Melbourne 3166, Australia

First published 1997

Printed in Great Britain at the University Press, Cambridge

A catalogue record for this book is available from the British Library

Library of Congress cataloguing in publication data
Edward Gibbon and empire / edited by Rosamond McKitterick
and Roland Quinault.
p.   cm.
Includes index.
ISBN 0 521 49724 8 (hc)
1. Gibbon, Edward, 1737–1794 – Views on Rome. 2. Historians – Great
Britain – Biography. 3. Rome – History – Empire 30 BC–476 AD
– Historiography. 4. Byzantine Empire – Historiography. 5. Great
Britain – Intellectual life – 18th century. 6. Scholars – Great
Britain – Attitudes. 7. Gibbon, Edward, 1737–1794. History of the
decline and fall of the Roman Empire. I. McKitterick, Rosamond.
II. Quinault, Roland E.
DG206.G6E38 1997 937'.06 – dc20   96–2411   CIP

ISBN 0 521 49724 8 hardback

In memory of Angus McIntyre

Contents

Contributors

JEREMY BLACK Professor of History, University of Exeter

T. S. BROWN Reader in History, University of Edinburgh

ANTHONY BRYER Professor of Byzantine History, Centre for Byzantine, Ottoman and Modern Greek Studies, University of Birmingham

J. W. BURROW Professor of European Thought in the University of Oxford and Fellow of Balliol College

AVERIL CAMERON Warden of Keble College, Oxford

PETER GHOSH Lecturer in Modern History, University of Oxford and Fellow of St Anne's College, Oxford

JAMES HOWARD-JOHNSTON Lecturer in Byzantine Studies, University of Oxford

ROSAMOND MCKITTERICK Reader in Early Medieval European History, University of Cambridge and Fellow of Newnham College

JOHN MATTHEWS Professor of Roman History, Yale University

ROLAND QUINAULT Reader in History, University of North London

JOHN ROBERTSON Lecturer in Modern History, University of Oxford and Fellow of St Hugh's College

JONATHAN SHEPARD Lecturer in Russian History, University of Cambridge and Fellow of Peterhouse

DAVID WOMERSLEY Lecturer in English and Fellow of Jesus College, Oxford

IAN WOOD Professor of Early Medieval History, University of Leeds

Preface

This book began in January 1994 as a conference under the auspices of the Royal Historical Society as part of the bicentenary celebrations of the death of Edward Gibbon. We wish to express our warmest thanks, first of all, to all who participated in the discussions at that gathering of late antique, medieval and modern historians, and most particularly to the contributors to this volume. We are, moreover, especially grateful to Rees Davies, President of the Royal Historical Society, and the Fellows for making the conference possible, and to Joy McCarthy for all her cheerfully efficient organization. The work of preparing the typescript for publication benefited from the assistance of Sheila Willson in the History Faculty Office, University of Cambridge, and the staff of the Cambridge University Library. We are indebted to William Davies and the staff of Cambridge University Press for seeing the book through the press, and most particularly to Katy Cooper for her meticulous copy-editing. We should also like to thank Alice Prochaska and her colleagues in the British Library for mounting the Bicentenary Exhibition of Gibboniana in January 1994.

It afforded particular pleasure that the conference was held in Magdalen College, Oxford, Gibbon's own college (despite his opinion of it). We shall long treasure the beautiful image of Magdalen meadow transformed into a lake, with the snow deep upon the ground. We are indebted to the President and Fellows of Magdalen College for their hospitality, and to Janie Cottis the College Archivist and Gerald Harriss for providing an exhibition of Magdalen Gibboniana while we were there. To Felicity Heal (who offered hospitality to the conference for a memorable evening at Jesus College) and to Lord Dacre of Glanton (who reminded us in his inimitable way of the philosophical dimension to Gibbon's historical thinking by way of a closing address at the conference) go our special thanks.

The final dinner of the conference was held in Magdalen College Hall. The after dinner address, on Gibbon at Magdalen, was delivered, with characteristic wit and grace, by our host on that occasion, Angus McIntyre (it has since been published in the *Magdalen College Record* for 1994). Angus had been an enthusiastic and benevolent participant in the discussions throughout the days we spent in Magdalen; his untimely death was a great grief to all who knew him. As a tribute to his scholarship, and in affection and gratitude, we dedicate this volume to his memory.

ROSAMOND MCKITTERICK AND ROLAND QUINAULT

Abbreviations

Autobiographies	*The autobiographies of Edward Gibbon*, ed. J. Murray (London, 1896)
Decline and fall	Edward Gibbon, *The history of the decline and fall of the Roman Empire*, 6 vols. (London, 1776–88)
Decline and fall, ed. Bury	Edward Gibbon, *The history of the decline and fall of the Roman Empire*, ed. J. B. Bury, 7 vols. (London, 1897–1901)
Decline and fall, ed. Bury (2)	Edward Gibbon, *The history of the decline and fall of the Roman Empire*, ed. J. B. Bury, 7 vols., 2nd edn (London, 1909–14)
Decline and fall, ed. Milman	Edward Gibbon, *The history of the decline and fall of the Roman Empire*, ed. H. H. Milman, 6 vols., 2nd edn (London, 1846)
Decline and fall, ed. Smeaton	Edward Gibbon, *The history of the decline and fall of the Roman Empire*, ed. Oliphant Smeaton, 6 vols. (London, 1910)
English essays	*The English essays of Edward Gibbon*, ed. P. B. Craddock (Oxford, 1972)
EHR	*English Historical Review*
Journal	*Gibbon's Journal to January 28th, 1763*, ed. D. M. Low (London, 1929)
Journal 2	*Journal à Lausanne, 18 août 1763– 19 avril 1764*, ed. G. A. Bonnard (Lausanne, 1945)
JRS	*Journal of Roman Studies*

Letters	*The letters of Edward Gibbon*, ed. J. R. E. Norton, 3 vols. (London, 1956)
Memoirs, ed. Bonnard	*Edward Gibbon. Memoirs of my life*, ed. G. A. Bonnard (London, 1966)
Miscellaneous works	*The miscellaneous works of Edward Gibbon, Esq.*, ed. John, Lord Sheffield, 5 vols. (London, 1814)
Norton, *Bibliography*	J. R. E. Norton, *A bibliography of the works of Edward Gibbon* (Oxford, 1940)

Introduction

Rosamond McKitterick and Roland Quinault

Why do we, or why should we continue to read Gibbon's *History of the decline and fall of the Roman Empire*? The many who still read Gibbon – a number surely set to rise further with the publication of David Womersley's new edition of *Decline and fall* – may do so for reasons which have little to do with Gibbon's subject or his historical method, but more for his superb wit and ruminative literary style and for his reputation as one of the finest of the historians produced by the European Enlightenment. Consequently, the new edition of *Decline and fall* was at first reviewed by modern rather than by classical or medieval historians.[1] Thus Jose Harris has observed that Gibbon's ability to speak to us now is 'not a consequence of his scholarship (which was often faulty) nor the authority of his historical judgment (which was often grotesquely biassed) but in the style of his writing, the high drama and human interest of his subject matter, and in the fact that many of the philosophical dilemmas which confront and engage him seem eerily familiar in the present day'. Gibbon remains 'part of the mental furniture of any reasonably literate person . . . his reputation has been given a series of shots in the arm by the rise of literary theory, the fashion for Europeanism, and the revival of academic interest in the history of civic humanist thought'.[2]

---

[1] One exception is the late antique historian Christopher Kelly in the *Pembroke College, Cambridge Society's Annual Gazette* 69 (1995), pp. 32–42.

[2] Jose Harris, 'Our sarcastic scholar', (review of David Womersley's edition of *Decline and fall*) in *The Times Higher Education Supplement* 30 June 1995. Contemporary admiration for Gibbon's achievement is most apparent amongst those historians who have attempted to write history on a Gibbonian scale, notably Felipe Fernandez-Armesto, *Millenium* (London, 1995). Compare Paul Johnson, 'Namier's icecream', and Anthony Pagden, 'The barbarian spirit: is the day of Empires coming to an end?', *The Times Literary Supplement* 29 September 1995 and Anthony Pagden, *Lords of all the world: ideologies of empire in Spain, Britain and France c. 1500–1800* (London, 1995).

These recent reviewers of *Decline and fall*, however, have not mentioned the coincidental renaissance of studies of late antiquity and the early Middle Ages in Europe and North America over the last thirty years – partly inspired by the work of scholars like Peter Brown, John Matthews and Michael Wallace-Hadrill. Yet this scholarship, together with the sheer importance and scope of Gibbon's subject, means that we cannot and should not ignore the details of Gibbon's history and regard it merely as a good read spiced with a dash of philosophy.[3] On the contrary, Gibbon established the terms of reference for the debate about the transformation of the Roman world and the emergence of medieval Europe. Although his vision of 'decline and fall' has now to be drastically revised in the light of the present generations of research, and although the validity of the concepts of 'barbarian' and 'Roman' are now seriously called into question, the debate is by no means resolved.

To read Gibbon in the late twentieth century, therefore, is also to engage with his subject matter. To understand him properly it is necessary to have knowledge of his historiographical and philosophical context.[4] Gibbon's *Decline and fall* needs to be considered, in other words, as a forceful interpretation of the period and not just for what it reveals of eighteenth-century intellectual attitudes. Style, contemporary ideas and the historical narrative cannot be separated. This volume of essays is structured, therefore, as a kind of dialogue examining particular portions of Gibbon's narrative, especially in his interpretations of empire and the intellectual context in which he formulated them, against a background of the eighteenth- and twentieth-century knowledge of late antiquity and the Middle Ages. Gibbon's ideas of empire, explored in so many different contexts in his work,[5] his understanding of monarchy and balance of power, his sources and

---

[3] As it has been alleged that Churchill did, see Quinault below, pp. 317 and 331.

[4] This was the theme of the 1976 Gibbon celebrations, published by G. Bowersock *et al.* (eds.), *Edward Gibbon and the decline and fall of the Roman Empire, Daedalus. Journal of the American Academy of Arts and Sciences* 105 (1976). See also K. Hammer and J. Voss (eds.), *Historische Forschung im 18. Jahrhundert*, Pariser Historische Studien 13 (Paris, 1988).

[5] On the later Roman, Byzantine, Carolingian, Seljuk, Ottoman and Mongol empires, see Matthews, Cameron, Shepard, Howard-Johnston, McKitterick and Bryer below, but Gibbon also encompasses the medieval German, Norman, Latin crusading empires, and the European empires of his own day.

working methods, the structure of the work, his attitude towards the 'barbarians', the contrasting treatments of the eastern and western Empires in *Decline and fall*, his appreciation of past civilizations and their material remains and his visual sense, his audience, and reactions – contemporary and modern – to his text, are considered in the light of modern research on eighteenth-century intellectual history on the one hand and on late antiquity, Byzantium and the Middle Ages on the other.

Such consideration is at both a general and a specific level, for we wish to stress the importance of understanding the concept of empire in a precise sense and within a specific context. While John Robertson explains Gibbon's choice of topic and elucidates his essential hostility towards the Roman Empire and Jeremy Black highlights the seam of classical analogy in its eighteenth-century context, such attitudes are also examined by Averil Cameron in the light of Gibbon's own specific focus on the Byzantine Emperor Justinian, by Ian Wood in relation to Merovingian Frankish rulers and by Tom Brown in considering Gibbon's interpretation of the reign of Theodoric the Ostrogoth in Italy. Similarly, Averil Cameron and Peter Ghosh are able to provide complementary interpretations, from two different perspectives, of the significance of the structure, methods and conceptual framework of *Decline and fall*, as well as the function of the 'General observations on the fall of the Roman Empire in the west' which concluded volume III of *Decline and fall*. An examination of Gibbon's sources and working methods throws into relief some of Gibbon's genius as well as his shortcomings, as is clear from the expositions by John Matthews, Jonathan Shepard, James Howard-Johnston, Anthony Bryer and Rosamond McKitterick.

The question of Gibbon's audience and the degree to which he was addressing a public familiar with at least the main events and heroes of his story, is a crucial one. David Womersley investigates the question of Gibbon's contemporary audience by means of a meticulous analysis of Gibbon's reaction to criticisms of his notorious chapters 15 and 16. He indicates how Gibbon under-estimated the strength of religious sentiment in his time as well as the appeal of his subject even in those quarters apparently most resistant to historical scholarship. Rosamond McKitterick tackles the question of the wider cultural understanding of late antiquity, Byzantium and early medieval Europe in the eighteenth century and the relevance and interest of particular segments of the past to eighteenth-century political thinking in Europe as a whole. The hermeneutic question of how Gibbon might have been read is also explored by Roland Quinault in relation to someone in a position to act on what he thought he had learnt from Gibbon, namely, Winston Churchill, who was wont to relate the Roman and British Empires in his own mind in consequence.

Many chapters in this book assess Gibbon as a scholar and fellow historian in relation to his sources, for it is by such analysis that the inclinations in his thinking can be made clear. John Matthews and Averil Cameron examine Gibbon's grasp of the techniques of source criticism in his use of the Augustan history and Procopius respectively. The consequences of ignoring whole categories of evidence are exposed by James Howard-Johnston in his study of Gibbon's notoriously cavalier treatment of the Byzantine middle period. Conversely, Anthony Bryer and Jonathan Shepard demonstrate how Gibbon was able to make innovative use of other primary material both in relation to the Mongols and Ottomans and in the chapters on the Slavs, Bulgars, Hungarians and Rus and the story of their retrospective conversion to Christianity. Gibbon's attitudes to some of the historiographical material he read and the degree to which he treated past histories as idiosyncratic interpretations of a comparable purpose to his own are elucidated by Ian Wood and Tom Brown, with reference to the Franks in Gaul and the Goths and Lombards in Italy. Although Gibbon concentrated on political and military events, he fully appreciated that empires are not merely narrow political and military constructs. He allowed room for technological prowess and economic vitality as essential foundations for military success. Gibbon's visual sense and his imagination, touched on by many of the papers in this volume, led him to interpret aspects of the art and architecture he had observed as potent symbols of imperial greatness in ways that have many contemporary resonances.

Gibbon criticism hitherto has largely focussed on the three volumes published in 1776. We have deliberately chosen to concentrate on volumes IV–VI, first published in 1788; that is, we have been most concerned with those chapters which comprise a series of portraits of nations external to Byzantium, as well as Byzantium itself. Our studies of these chapters and their implications offer new perspectives on Gibbon's preoccupations with the 'decline and fall' of Rome as a whole. We have followed Gibbon's own chronological course in the first portion of the book. We then take up the themes, referred to above, defined in the chapters by the Roman, Byzantine and medieval historians, and examine them in their eighteenth-century context as well. As John Robertson observes below, 'decline' is not synonymous with 'fall'. Gibbon's problem was as much one of the Empire's survival as its decay. Indeed, the contradictions of his work are a direct consequence of his charting the former as if it were the latter. This is particularly evident in his treatment of the German successor states as the destroyers of Roman ways, a view that cannot now be sustained. Although Gibbon acknowledged that many of his barbarian leaders laid the basis for a new political system, he failed to acknowledge how much there was that was Roman in that system. As is clear from the papers by Matthews, Wood, Shepard, Howard-Johnston and Bryer in particular, Gibbon's subtle intelligence led him many times to chart the development of particular institutions and states that implicitly, and sometimes explicitly (notably the famous chapter on Roman law)[6] contradicted his title.

The nub of the matter is contained in Gibbon's fourth volume: the 'extinction of the Western Empire AD 476'[7] in Gibbon's eyes was an immediate consequence of the action of the barbarian *magister militum* Odoacer in abolishing the 'useless and expensive office' of emperor. He describes the 'decay of the Roman spirit' in Odoacer's kingdom which, notwithstanding the prudence and success of Odoacer, 'exhibited the sad prospect of misery and desolation'.[8]

For many, with Gibbon, the deposition of the unfortunate Romulus Augustulus, the last Roman emperor in the west, who 'was made the instrument of his own disgrace',[9] can be seen as marking the point from which central political control over the western provinces of the Roman Empire officially ceased to be effective. Yet this is emphatically not the same as the 'fall of the Roman Empire', nor even a crucial phase in its 'decline'. Efficient propagandists in

---

[6] See McKitterick, below, p. 170.

[7] *Decline and fall*, ed. Bury, IV, p. 50. Some would prefer the demise of Julius Nepos in Dalmatia in 480 but see Gibbon's note 132, pp. 51–2 on the case for 479 and another set of Bury's 'implacable square brackets' insisting on 476.

[8] *Ibid.*, pp. 50 and 53.

[9] *Ibid.*, p. 50.

Justinian's eastern empire developed the notion that 476 was a decisive break.[10] To the population of Italy, however, the general Odoacer's military *coup d'état* no doubt seemed to herald merely another vacancy on the imperial throne, such as they had experienced many times over during the preceding century, while political and army factions manoeuvred for control. To at least one articulate Gallo-Roman aristocrat in fifth-century Provence, the triumph of Odoacer marked a definitive end to Roman political control in this region;[11] to Byzantine propagandists, moreover, it was a convenient justification for Justinian's wars of reconquest. Yet both were thinking in terms of specific political leadership.

Rome meant more than this. Indeed, it is one remarkable indication of how much more it meant that so many recent studies have been devoted to an examination of the process of transformation of the Roman world and the degree to which the western European successor states were heirs to Rome in terms of their political and administrative institutions, law, culture, religion and social organization.[12] In discussing the fragmentation of political leadership, the gradual changes in the character, status and objectives of the ruling personnel, the resurfacing of political and social identities at a local level and the transformation of the political configurations of the west, it is unfortunate that notions of 'decline and fall', first propagated by patristic theologians, adapted by Renaissance humanists and Protestant reformation scholars,

---

[10] See Walter Goffart, 'The theme of "The barbarian invasions" in later antique and modern historiography' in E. Chrysos and A. Schwarz (eds.), *Das Reich und die Barbaren*, Veröffentlichungen des Instituts für Österreichische Geschichtsforschung 29 (Vienna, 1989), pp. 87–107, and reprinted in Walter Goffart, *Rome's fall and after* (London, 1989), pp. 111–32, and general reflections in 'An empire unmade: Rome AD 300–600' in Goffart, *Rome's fall and after*, pp. 33–44; Brian Croke, 'AD 476: the manufacturing of a turning point', *Chiron* 13 (1983), pp. 81–119.

[11] Jill Harries, *Sidonius Apollinaris and the fall of Rome* (Oxford, 1995).

[12] See, for example, C. R. Whittaker, *Frontiers of the Roman Empire. A social and economic study* (Baltimore and London, 1994); Rosamond McKitterick (ed.), *Carolingian culture: emulation and innovation* (Cambridge, 1994); Ian Wood, *The Merovingian kingdoms, 450–751* (London, 1993); Chris Wickham, *Early medieval Italy* (London, 1983) and *Land and power. Studies in Italian and European social history, 400–1200*; Roger Collins, *Early medieval Spain* (2nd edn, London, 1995); Patrick Amory, *Ethnography and community in Ostrogothic Italy, AD 489–554*, Cambridge Studies in Medieval Life and Thought (Cambridge, 1996); G. Ausenda (ed.), *After Empire. Towards an ethnology of Europe's barbarians* (Woodbridge, 1995) and the volumes in preparation by members of the European Science Foundation's project: *The transformation of the Roman world: new approaches to the emergence of early medieval Europe.*

were taken up by Gibbon and his contemporaries.[13] They established not only disputes over alternative 'reasons' for the 'fall' of the Roman Empire, but also dichotomies between Roman and barbarian, civilized and primitive, insiders and outsiders, foreign invasions (the barbarians) versus internal weakness (corruption, social injustices, depopulation, economic decline).[14] As a consequence, preconceptions of 'barbarians' persist which are themselves, as Patrick Amory has established, inherited from the literary and artistic depictions of Graeco-Latin ethnography.[15] Such preconceptions have an observable influence on those who read Gibbon. We are only now learning, for example, to appreciate that the world, especially that of Italy and the Balkans between the fourth and seventh centuries, was one in which our distinctions between Roman and Goth or Roman and barbarian are simply irrelevant.[16] Even critical readings are still offered within the conceptual framework of the 'decline and fall' of an empire that Gibbon created with such magisterial literary artifice.

Yet a crucial distinction must be made between Gibbon's treatment of the various empires which absorbed his attention. Recent scholarship of Byzantium, for instance, has tended to corroborate and draw strength from Gibbon and to rehabilitate many of his negative judgments on the culture and polity of the empire. It has thus diverged widely from the best of the western medievalists' work. Although Gibbon stressed the weakness of the Byzantine state in the 'middle period', he also pointed out that before Heraclius, 'Give centuries of the decline and fall of the empire have already elapsed'.[17] His criticisms of the Byzantine emperors of this period are no more pungent than his comments on many of their Roman predecessors, from Commodus to Honorius. It is true, moreover, that Gibbon's skimpy account in chapter 48 of the emperors from Heraclius to the Latin conquest was a product of design, rather than disdain. It was not his 'intention to expatiate

---

[13] See Jean-Pierre Devroey, 'Les invasions barbares. Sentiments de défaite et mort des empires' in M. Vaïsse (ed.), *La Défaite. Études offertes à Annie Rey-Goldzeigner* (Rheims, 1994), pp. 9–18.

[14] Compare Peter Heather, 'The Huns and the end of the Roman Empire in western Europe', *EHR* 110 (1995), pp. 4–41 and *Goths and Romans 332–489* (Oxford, 1991) and John Drinkwater and Hugh Elton (eds.), *Fifth-century Gaul: a crisis of identity* (Cambridge, 1992).

[15] Amory, *Ethnography and community*.

[16] Notably in the light of Amory, *Ethnography and community*.

[17] *Decline and fall*, ed. Bury, v, p. 169.

with the same minuteness on the whole series of the Byzantine history. From the seventh to the eleventh centuries the obscure interval will be supplied by a concise narrative of such facts as may still appear either interesting or important.'[18] Nevertheless, the judgment of Byzantium as an obscure period, his selection of 'such facts as may appear either interesting or important' and what Howard-Johnston has referred to as his selective use of the sources, and his willingness to resort to short cuts if they were available (a willingness equally in evidence in Gibbon's pages on the western medieval empires after 800) are what has earned Gibbon criticism by subsequent Byzantinists. Despite his unjustifiable disparagement of the middle Byzantine period, cogently contested by Howard-Johnston below,[19] Gibbon, as Bryer and Shepard make clear, could be in many ways a lucid and quite sure-footed evaluator of his sources. It was, after all, Gibbon's interest in Byzantine and Muslim history, aroused on a visit to Mr Hoare's library at Stourhead in 1751 when he was still a boy,[20] which encouraged him to continue his *History* beyond the fall of the western Empire.

In publishing these papers we have been very conscious of our predecessors in the Royal Historical Society a century ago who held the first centenary celebration of Gibbon's achievement. Comparisons are inevitable. Victorian interest in Gibbon appears to have been stimulated not only by his skill as a story teller and a stylist, but also by his perceived views on topical issues such as imperial policy and religious uniformity. Gibbon had modestly expressed the hope 'that a hundred years hence I may still continue to be abused'.[21] For much of the century after his death in 1794,

---

[18] *Ibid.*, I, p. viii.

[19] Steven Runciman, 'Gibbon and Byzantium' in Bowersock, *Edward Gibbon*, pp. 103–9; and compare Freeman's complaint in 1888 that Gibbon had made the later Byzantine Empire appear ridiculous, W. R. W. Stephens, *The life and letters of Edward A. Freeman* (2 vols., London, 1895), vol. II, p. 380: Freeman to Goldwin Smith, 25 April 1888 with Frederic Harrison's Rede Lecture in Cambridge in 1900. Harrison claimed that the great achievement of modern Byzantinists was in removing the incubus of Gibbon's disdain: Martha S. Vogeler, *Frederic Harrison. The vocations of a positivist* (Oxford, 1984), p. 35. Even J. B. Bury believed that Gibbon had displayed a contemptuous attitude to the mid-Byzantine Empire.

[20] There he read the Continuation of Echard's *Roman History* when he was only fourteen: see *Autobiography*, p. 32.

[21] Walter Bagehot, *Literary studies*, ed. R. H. Hutton (2 vols., London, 1884), vol. II, p. 53.

Decline and fall remained a controversial text.[22] Gibbon's rude remarks about the dismal education he received at Magdalen were grist to the mill of the mid-Victorian university reformers, while his criticisms of the early church were welcomed by secularists, libertarians and Positivists. Thomas Carlyle, no less, lost his faith after reading *Decline and fall*. Indeed, a century after the first publication of *Decline and fall*, Gibbon was admired by many intellectuals who were much more critical of the *status quo* than he had ever been. Whereas Gibbon had been a conservative Whig who had supported Lord North's attempt to suppress American Independence and opposed the French Revolution, many of his Victorian admirers were radical liberals. A group of them, originally from Oxford, were responsible for celebrating the centenary of Gibbon's death in 1894 with a 'Gibbon commemoration'. The meeting and the volume which was its outcome were sponsored by the Royal Historical Society, under the presidency of M. E. Grant Duff, at the suggestion of Frederic Harrison, who also gave the main commemorative address. The Royal Historical Society established a special committee to organize the commemoration which included some of the principal luminaries of historical scholarship in Europe – Edward Acton, Frederick Maitland, Theodor Mommsen and Ernest Lavisse. The Prime Minister Lord Rosebery (a great admirer of Gibbon) and the President of Magdalen College were also on the Committee.

The *Commemoration* contained a sprinkling of conservatives, including George Prothero (later a president of the Royal Historical Society), several senior members of the Church of England and Henry Holroyd, third earl of Sheffield. The last named is best known as a patron of cricket, but he was also the grandson of Gibbon's friend and patron, Lord Sheffield, who had inherited most of Gibbon's papers and effects. His seat at Sheffield Park in Sussex was close to the country home of Frederic Harrison, who persuaded the third Lord Sheffield to become president of the Gibbon centenary committee and to loan his Gibboniana to the British Museum's Centenary Exhibition.[23] The exhibition generated public interest in the Gibbon papers which the earl subsequently

---

[22] On its publishing history see Norton's *Bibliography*; compare Brown and Quinault below.
[23] Royal Historical Society, *Proceedings of the Gibbon Commemoration 1794–1894* (London, 1985). See also R. A. Humphreys, *The Royal Historical Society 1868–1968* (London, 1969), pp. 24–5.

sold to the British Museum in 1895. Lord Sheffield wrote the preface to Richard Prothero's edition of *The private letters of Edward Gibbon*, published in 1896 by John Murray, who himself edited and published *The autobiographies of Edward Gibbon* in 1898. Thus both directly and indirectly the 1894 commemoration stimulated the scholarly study of Gibbon.

Frederic Harrison's role appears to have been crucial. He and two other members of the Gibbon commemoration committee – J. H. Bridges and E. S. Beesley – were Positivists who had been educated at Wadham College, Oxford, where they had been influenced by the Positivist tutor, Richard Congreve. Gibbon's sceptical attitude towards the early Christian church ensured him a place in the Positivist Calendar and *Decline and fall* a place in the Positivist library. Harrison did not, however, adopt a totally uncritical attitude towards Gibbon. He declared in his commemorative address:

We come to study Gibbon – not to praise him . . .
His monumental work still stands alone, in the colossal range of its proportions, and in the artistic symmetry of its execution. It has its blemishes, its limitations, we venture to add its misconceptions; it is not always sound in his philosophy; it is sometimes ungenerous and cynical. But withal it is beyond question the greatest monument of historical research united to imaginative art, of any age in any language.[24]

Who would endorse this today? It is for readers of Gibbon and of this volume to decide. Certainly when we gathered for the two hundredth anniversary meeting, again under the auspices of the Royal Historical Society, Gibbon's phrases at the end of chapter 33 seemed especially apt:

We imperceptibly advance from youth to age without observing the gradual, but incessant, change of human affairs; and even in our larger experience of history, the imagination is accustomed, by a perpetual series of causes and effects, to unite the most distant revolutions. But if the interval between two memorable eras could be instantly annihilated; if it were possible, after a momentary slumber of two hundred years, to display the *new* world to the eyes of a spectator who still retained a lively and recent impression of the *old* his surprise and his reflections would furnish the pleasing subject of a philosophical romance.[25]

---

[24] *Gibbon Commemoration*, p. 21.
[25] *Decline and fall*, ed. Bury, III, pp. 414–15 and compare John Matthews below, p. 13.

Not only does this passage emphasize the possible connections between the 'most distant revolutions'; it also serves to underline the inevitable differences in perspective on the part of an historian, whether in the eighteenth century, in the nineteenth or at the end of the twentieth, when assessing the Roman world and its transformation. It remains for our successors to make their own contributions in due course.

CHAPTER I

Gibbon and the later Roman
Empire: causes and circumstances

John Matthews

Having reached the surrender of Carthage to the Vandals in the year 439, Gibbon ended chapter 33 of *Decline and fall* by telling the 'memorable fable of the SEVEN SLEEPERS, whose imaginary date corresponds with the reign of the younger Theodosius and the conquest of Africa by the Vandals'.[1] Gibbon was not the last philosophic mind to feel the fascination of the story,[2] and that he was not the first is attested by his own erudite tracing of the legend and its variants from Syriac and Latin versions to the Koran and among Muslim nations from Bengal to Africa, even in the 'remote extremities of Scandinavia', not to mention the inscription of the saints' names in the Roman, Abyssinian and Russian calendars. It told of the martyrdom of seven young men of Ephesus under the emperor Decius by their immolation in a cave which was then blocked by stones. The young men fell asleep, and were wakened, it seemed after a few hours, when someone opened the cave and let in the sunlight. They sent one of their number to town to buy bread, but he found that he could no longer recognize the country; the main gate of Ephesus was, to his amazement, surmounted by a large cross. His odd dress and old-fashioned speech equally surprised an Ephesian baker, to whom the young man, in an episode that should interest numismatists, offered a coin of Decius as current exchange. The mystery was solved when it was discovered that it was not just a few hours but almost two hundred years since the young man and his companions had 'escaped from the rage of a pagan tyrant' to find themselves living, however briefly, under

---

[1] *Decline and fall*, ed. Bury, III, pp. 412–15.
[2] It forms the riveting opening sentence of Peter Brown's Carl Newell Jackson Lectures, *The making of late antiquity* (London, 1978): 'I wish I had been one of the Seven Sleepers of Ephesus'!

a Christian emperor. I say 'however briefly', because as soon as the seven young men had bestowed their benediction and told their story to their amazed hearers, they 'at the same instant peaceably expired'.

Gibbon assigned the interest of the fable to its 'genuine merit'; the immediate contrast between two ages so far apart would display what was surprising in the new world, to one with a still clear image of the old; 'his surprise and his reflections', wrote Gibbon, 'would furnish the pleasing subject of a philosophical romance'. It would however not constitute history, for that would be concerned, not with the dramatic contrast between two ages so presented, but with the process by which one became the other; the 'perpetual series of causes and effects' by which 'the imagination is accustomed to unite the most distant revolutions'.

The two hundred years between the reigns of Decius and Theodosius II were ideally placed to provide the materials for such imaginative reflection, for during this period,

the seat of government had been transported from Rome to a new city on the banks of the Thracian Bosphorus; and the abuse of military spirit had been suppressed by an artificial system of tame and ceremonious servitude. The throne of the persecuting Decius was filled by a succession of Christian and orthodox princes, who had extirpated the fabulous gods of antiquity; and the public devotion of the age was impatient to exalt the saints and martyrs of the Catholic church on the altars of Diana and Hercules. The union of the Roman empire was dissolved; its genius was humbled in the dust; and armies of unknown Barbarians, issuing from the frozen regions of the North, had established their victorious reign over the fairest provinces of Europe and Africa.[3]

Whether as history or romance, these two centuries did not however form a consistent framework for Gibbon's conception of the decline and fall of the Roman Empire. He had, famously, set its origins under the Antonine emperors of the second century, when the 'long peace and uniform government' of the Romans had 'introduced a slow and secret poison into the vitals of the empire ' – notably, in this passage, by the extinction of the fire of genius, and the evaporation of the military spirit among the populations of the Empire.[4] Gibbon's formal narrative begins with the sole reign of Commodus (180–92), which marked the end of this era of seductive

---

[3] *Decline and fall*, ed. Bury, III, p. 415. [4] *Ibid.*, I, p. 56.

but poisoned peace; but even this choice of starting point, as he wrote later in a possibly excessive fit of self-criticism (one has to begin somewhere), was a mistake now beyond retrieval. He should, he now claimed, have begun with the civil wars after the death of Nero, or even with the 'tyranny which succeeded the reign of Augustus'.[5] In the 'General observations on the fall of the Roman Empire in the west' with which he concluded chapter 38, he extended the framework still further, for he began this section by describing how Polybius had explained the strengths of the Roman constitution of the Republic to his Greek contemporaries of the second century BC. In Gibbon's powerful and evocative phrase, Polybius had 'opened to their view the deep foundations of the greatness of Rome', for those Greeks who erroneously believed that this greatness was the product, not of merit, but of Fortune.[6] The longer perspective is evoked in an episode narrated in chapter 30 of *Decline and fall*. When the senate was invited by the government of Ravenna to discuss the terms of peace offered by Alaric the Visigoth in 408, it was as if they (rather like the Seven Sleepers, except for the reversal of values of past over present) 'had been suddenly awakened from the dream of four hundred years':

They loudly declared, in regular speeches, or in tumultuary acclamations, that it was unworthy of the majesty of Rome to purchase a precarious and disgraceful truce from a Barbarian king; and that, in the judgment of a magnanimous people, the chance of ruin was always preferable to the certainty of dishonour.[7]

That 'tumult of virtue and freedom subsided', however, and the senate voted a ransom of 4,000 pounds of gold. The decline of Rome was not to be impeded by such occasional reminders of her once-great liberties.

Historical processes, the constructions of historians, are notoriously unstable phenomena; as their 'true causes' move back in time, so too their moments of accomplishment move forward. There is however a point beyond which a historical process may become so

---

[5] See for Gibbon's second thoughts on this matter (and adducing the parallel of Tacitus) G. W. Bowersock, 'Gibbon on civil war and rebellion in the decline of the Roman Empire', in G. W. Bowersock et al. (eds.), *Edward Gibbon and the decline and fall of the Roman Empire*; *Daedalus: Journal of the American Academy of Arts and Sciences* 3 (1976), pp. 63–71, at p. 63.

[6] *Decline and fall*, ed. Bury, IV, p. 160.

[7] *Ibid.*, III, p. 277.

extended that it cannot be examined with proper discrimination, and it has often been remarked that Gibbon's concept of 'decline and fall' is not particularly well-defined. He said as much himself, in a revealing passage of his *Memoirs*:

So flexible is the title of my history that the final era might be fixed at my own choice: and I long hesitated whether I should be content with the three Volumes, the fall of the Western Empire, which fulfilled my first engagement with the public[8]

– words which in part pick up very closely the postscript to the preface published with the appearance of volume III in 1781:

The entire History, which is now published, of the Decline and Fall of the Roman Empire in the West abundantly discharges my engagements with the Public. Perhaps their favourable opinion may encourage me to prosecute a work, which, however laborious it may seem, is the most agreeable occupation of my leisure hours.[9]

One might wonder, reading these words, about a historical construction that seems primarily designed to suit its author's leisure, but that is no doubt to do less than justice to Gibbon's literary modesty.

The point, if it is accepted, that Gibbon did not have an exactly formulated definition of 'decline and fall', is relevant to the 'General observations on the fall of the Roman Empire in the west',[10] and more broadly to the way in which the critic should approach Gibbon as an analytic historian of the later Empire. The 'General observations', taken as a whole, are not so much a positive statement of what Gibbon thought to be the causes of the decline of the Roman Empire, as a summary of what he thought he could take for granted, together with a specific wish to correct misunderstanding. Above all, they point to the future. As I just mentioned, they begin with a reference to Polybius as the writer who had made clear to Greek contemporaries the true character of the greatness of Rome. It may be no coincidence that the last clause of the narrative part of chapter 38, in the sentence immediately preceding the 'General observations', contains a reference to 'the history of the *Greek* emperors [who] may still afford a long series of instructive lessons and interesting revolutions'; but that is to look forward to

---

[8] *Memoirs*, ed. Bonnard, p. 164.
[9] *Decline and fall*, ed. Bury, I, p. vii.   [10] *Ibid.*, IV, pp. 160–9.

the second part of Gibbon's project, and does not fully connect the 'Observations' with the preceding text of a history from which they seem, to me and to others, to stand apart. One reason for this, obviously, is that the 'Observations' were actually drafted at an early stage, whether in summer/autumn of 1772 or, perhaps more likely, in summer 1773.[11] What Gibbon now says about the decline of Rome as 'the natural and inevitable effect of immoderate greatness' is less a positive attempt to offer an analysis of the phenomenon, than a prefiguring of the contrast with the states of modern Europe which form the second part of the 'Observations'. Indeed, in so far as anything needed explaining, Gibbon thought it was not the fall, but the rise, of Rome that 'may deserve, as a singular prodigy, the reflection of a philosophic mind'.[12] He meant, of course, that it had already deserved the reflection of a philosophic mind – that of Montesquieu.[13] The story of the ruin of Rome, Gibbon wrote in 1772 or 1773, was 'simple and obvious'. Whether this is so or not, Gibbon did not go into that question here; except that in his opinion that 'as *time or accident* [my italics] had removed the artificial supports, the stupendous fabric yielded to the pressure of its own weight', we have re-entered the dimensions of the memorable fable of the Seven Sleepers of Ephesus. There, as we saw, Gibbon noted the distinction between seeing two worlds juxtaposed without transition, and the tracing of the series of causes and effects – 'time or accident' – by which the two were connected.

Next in the 'Observations' come two points of correction. It might be thought, said Gibbon, that the foundation of Constantinople was a material factor in the decline of the west, but Gibbon thought that not to be so; 'The foundation of Constantinople more essentially contributed to the preservation of the East than to the ruin of the West' – again looking forward to the still notional second half of *Decline and fall*. So too one might think that the 'introduction, or at least the abuse, of Christianity had some influence on the decline and fall of the Roman empire'. Gibbon conceded the force of the argument but offered in return

---

[11] Patricia B. Craddock, *Edward Gibbon, luminous historian, 1772–1794* (Baltimore, 1989), p. 8; for 1772, P. R. Ghosh, 'Gibbon's dark ages: some remarks on the genesis of the *Decline and fall*', *JRS* 73 (1983), pp. 1–23, at pp. 18–19.

[12] *Decline and fall*, ed. Bury, IV, p. 161.

[13] Craddock, *Edward Gibbon, luminous historian*, p. 9.

the contribution of 'eighteen hundred pulpits' to the lawful obedience of the people of the Roman world, and the mollifying effects of Christianity on the ferocious temper of its barbarian conquerors. These two factors are often seen as contributory factors in the decline of the Roman Empire, but, in this passage at least, Gibbon denied this, to him commonplace, interpretation.

All of this – drafted before Gibbon published even volume I of *Decline and fall* – is certainly more observation than systematic analysis, and his reader may be misled if he mistakes one for the other. Gibbon now moved on to modern Europe, in order to explain how its sovereign states, individually modest in size and improved by a level of scientific invention that made them collectively immune from barbarian conquest, might hope to avoid the fate of the Roman Empire. Now, the editions of Gibbon that most present-day readers have at their disposal fail, in their arrangement of volumes, to bring out the impact of the 'Observations' in the economy of *Decline and fall*. They stand, not indeterminately between chapters 38 and 39 in the middle of volume IV of Bury's edition (to take the most obvious example), but emphatically at the end of the first three volumes of the original publication, bringing to an end what Gibbon thought would satisfy his 'first engagement with the public'. The narrative text preceding the 'Observations' ends with the reference to the 'Greek emperors' who would form the second part of his work, and the beginning of chapter 39 is deliberately composed as a new start to a new volume and instalment. The 'Observations' themselves end, in a gracious footnote added to the final version, with praise of the five voyages of exploration (the voyages of James Cook) 'undertaken by the command of his present Majesty', who had also, 'adapting his benefactions to the different stages of society' founded a school of painting in his capital, and 'introduced to the islands of the South Sea the vegetables and animals most useful to human life'.[14] One is reminded here of that earlier footnote, to a description of the dietary habits of the barbarian folk of Roman Britain, expressing the 'pleasing hope that New Zealand may produce, in some future age, the Hume of the Southern Hemisphere' – in the form possibly,

---

[14] *Decline and fall*, ed. Bury, IV, p. 169 n. 15; Craddock, *Edward Gibbon, luminous historian*, p. 13. The 'five voyages' of exploration take us down to 1776; similarly note 8 of the 'Observations' on the 'political situation' of the American colonies.

as he himself hinted with characteristic sly subtlety, of that distinctly Gibbonian New Zealander, Sir Ronald Syme.[15]

In his famous essay on Tolstoy's view of history, Sir Isaiah Berlin used a fragment of the Greek poet Archilochus to suggest 'one of the deepest differences which divide writers and thinkers, and, it may be, human beings in general'; *'The fox knows many things, but the hedgehog knows one big thing'*. Some people, like the hedgehog, know one big thing – 'a single, universal organizing principle in terms of which alone all that they are and say has significance'.[16] Others, like the fox, know many things; 'their thought is scattered or diffuse, moving on many levels, seizing upon the essence of a vast variety of experiences and objects for what they are, without, consciously or unconsciously, seeking to fit them into, or exclude them from, any one unchanging, all-embracing . . . unitary inner vision'. Among Berlin's examples, Dante is a hedgehog, Shakespeare a fox; Plato a hedgehog, Aristotle a fox. Herodotus is an obvious fox, Thucydides, whom Berlin happens not to mention, a prime case for identification as a hedgehog;[17] and so on. Tolstoy, Berlin proposes, believed himself to be a hedgehog, but was in fact a fox, and it may be that a similar misidentification sometimes affects readers of Gibbon. I am not sure that I would agree with G. W. Bowersock, that Gibbon's problem 'consisted in the continuing search for a single secret cause', and then that 'It is unclear why Gibbon's concept of the philosophic spirit kept driving him to find a secret poison, a single hidden cause to explain the whole story of Rome's decline.'[18] The question can certainly be posed differently. Gibbon, as Momigliano wrote with delightful humour which I remember much appealing to me as a graduate student of late Roman history, 'must not be made responsible for the D.Phil. candidate's dream of sleeping beauty: somewhere in the wood the true cause of the

---

[15] *Decline and fall*, ed. Bury, III, p. 44 and R. Syme, *Ammianus and the Historia Augusta* (Oxford, 1968), p. 22 n. 3. Gibbon's original context is the alleged cannibalism of the Attacotti: 'If, in the neighbourhood of the commercial and literary town of Glasgow, a race of cannibals has really existed, we may contemplate in the period of Scottish history, the opposite extremes of savage and civilized life. Such reflections tend to enlarge the circle of our ideas; and to encourage the pleasing hope', etc.

[16] Isaiah Berlin, *The hedgehog and the fox: an essay on Tolstoy's view of history* (London, 1953 and reprinted London, 1967), p. 1.

[17] See however Simon Hornblower, *Thucydides* (Baltimore, 1987), p. 145.

[18] Bowersock, 'Gibbon on civil war', p. 67. In going on, however, to hazard the guess that the explanation may 'once again have been Gibbon's great evil genius, Tacitus', Bowersock satisfactorily counts Tacitus among the hedgehogs!

decline and fall of the Roman empire lies hidden and only awaits to be reawakened by him, the lucky D.Phil. candidate'. To Gibbon on the other hand, 'the decline and fall of Rome suggested a picture of new societies, laws, customs, superstitions, something to be described in its various stages rather than to be deduced from certain premises'.[19] To adapt this to the literary zoology of Sir Isaiah Berlin, Gibbon was a fox – erudite, imaginative, universal, someone who, in his own words, 'by reading and reflection, multiplies his own experience, and lives in distant ages and remote countries'.[20]

Gibbon says as much on the first page of *Decline and fall* and, given this clue, in many other passages. Even the full title of his work, *The history of the decline and fall of the Roman Empire* – not, as he might have taken over from Montesquieu, *Considerations on the decline and fall . . .* – is in itself revealing, and at the end of the very first paragraph of his work Gibbon spells out the implications of this:

It is the design of this and of the two succeeding chapters, to describe the prosperous condition of [the Antonines'] empire; and afterwards, from the death of Marcus Antoninus, to *deduce the most important circumstances* of its decline and fall.[21]

– that is, not to explain or analyze, but to describe and bring out the most important circumstances of a known phenomenon. The notions of 'decline and fall', of a 'declining empire' and so on, as well as the physical metaphors aptly noted by Bowersock, like the 'secret poison', the 'wounds of civil discord' affecting the Roman Empire like a human body,[22] recur throughout the text without doing more than provide reminders of what the book is about; they do not and are not meant to *explain* it. The historian's task is to 'unite the most distant revolutions' by a 'perpetual series of causes and effects', not to expatiate upon the 'pleasing romance' provided by the juxtaposition of two ages; this is what Gibbon means by 'deducing the most important circumstances' of the decline and fall of the Roman Empire, and this too is what is meant in the 'General observations',

---

[19] Arnaldo Momigliano, 'Gibbon's contribution to historical method', in his *Studies in Historiography* (London, 1966), pp. 40–55, at pp. 49–50.

[20] *Decline and fall*, ed. Bury, I, p. 218.

[21] *Ibid.*, I, p. 1 (my italics).

[22] Bowersock, 'Gibbon on civil war', pp. 63–4; the metaphors occur 'in contexts which rarely represent the historian's most profound thought', but show him rather in the grip of his own literary style.

in Gibbon's reference to the way in which 'time or accident' had
removed the artificial supports of the Roman Empire. All this is at
one with the emphasis placed by Momigliano and others (from
Byron onwards) on Gibbon's immense erudition, and with the
first words of the 'Advertisement to the notes', which in the first
printing of volume I appeared at the end of the volume and not at
the bottom of the page: 'Diligence and accuracy', wrote Gibbon,
'are the only merits which an historical writer may ascribe to
himself; if any merit indeed can be assumed from the performance
of an indispensable duty.'[23] Contrast the *philosophe* Voltaire, for
whom details in history were 'the vermin that kills great works' – or,
to put it otherwise: 'Details which lead to nothing are in history
what baggage is to an army, impedimenta; for we must look at
things in large, for the reason that the human mind is small and
sinks under the weight of trivial encumbrances.'[24] Self-evidently, no
good historian will spend time on details that lead to nothing
(although this may not always be clear at the outset); but no more
than an army (as Europe was about to see with a vengeance) can
history function without impedimenta.

For Gibbon therefore, the fall of the Roman Empire, itself no
mystery, was to be described in the sequence of circumstances,
sometimes accidental, by which it came about. Not surprisingly,
there were many moments at which something relevant to the
process came to pass and, therefore, many moments to which
Gibbon seems to assign the decisive influence. These passages
come with a certain similarity of expression which can give the
reader the impression, when he puts them side by side (that is,
when he ignores the hundreds of pages that may lie between them),
that Gibbon is contradicting himself, or allowing himself the
constant luxury of hedging his bets by invoking ever new and
shifting 'immediate causes'. Having located the infusion of 'secret
poison' into the Roman Empire as early as the time of the
Antonines, it would be surprising if Gibbon had found no
'important circumstance' of the decline of Rome before the fourth
century, but the first significant moment occurs only under the
emperor Septimius Severus, with his unleashing of the power and
privileges of the army. So chapter 5 ends emphatically, that

---

[23] *Decline and fall*, ed. Bury, I, p. ix.
[24] In the spirit of Voltaire, I have mislaid this reference.

'Posterity, who experienced the fatal effect of [Severus'] maxims and example, justly considered him as the principal author of the decline of the Roman Empire.'[25] Bowersock considered that Gibbon had forced himself into this 'remarkable opinion' by his obsession with a 'secret cause for the whole decline of Rome'. I have expressed my doubts already about this obsession, but should add in support of Bowersock that, whatever its origin in Gibbon's mind, his view about the contribution of Severus would not be widely accepted today. It might still be agreed that Severus and his dynasty saw significant changes in the military organization of the Roman Empire, but if so, this would not be in the terms laid down by Gibbon, but with reference to the pressures on the frontiers of the Empire going back at least to the time of Marcus Aurelius.[26]

Gibbon's narrative of the third century is from a technical point of view the weakest part of his treatment of the Roman Empire, largely because of his reliance on the set of imperial biographies known as the 'Augustan History', a text of which he perceived the difficulties without drawing their consequences. (It was, indeed, in his understanding of the principles of source criticism that lay Gibbon's most obvious technical weakness, as was pointed out by an early German reviewer.[27]) The reign of Constantine might next seem to offer great opportunities for one tracing the circumstances of the decline and fall of the Roman Empire. Various aspects of the reign – the founding of a new Rome, the recruitment of barbarians, the adoption and encouragement of Christianity – were all features in Gibbon's conception of the process of decline; while the manner in which the 'abuse of military spirit had been suppressed by an artificial system of tame and ceremonious servitude', as he wrote in commentary on the Seven Sleepers of Ephesus, formed the subject of the imposing chapter 17, in which Gibbon described the political system of Constantine and his successors, using sources from the time of Constantine himself down to the publication of the Theodosian Code in 438. Gibbon did not however adopt an especially critical approach to Constantine, even though one was already formulated by hostile pagan writers of the fourth and fifth

---

[25] *Decline and fall*, ed. Bury, I, p. 125.
[26] See, for example, R. MacMullen, *Soldier and civilian in the later Roman Empire* (Cambridge, Mass., 1963); J. B. Campbell, *The emperor and the Roman Army, 31 BC–AD 235* (Oxford, 1984).
[27] Momigliano, 'Gibbon's contribution', p. 40.

centuries. Though he wrote of his description as 'amusing the fancy by the singular picture of a great empire, and illustrating the secret and internal causes of its rapid decay',[28] he regarded the actual decline of the empire (i.e. the *circumstances* of its decline) as beginning only after the strong emperors of the fourth century. The reforms of Constantine strengthened it and, at the price of a further suppression of liberty and independence, maintained its institutions for several generations.

In what must be admitted to be a rather inconsequential fashion, the emperor Julian is said to be responsible, in some measure, for the triumph and the calamities of the Empire, not, as we would expect and as Gibbon's admired Ammianus clearly concedes, because of the disastrous losses on the Persian campaign which he had undertaken, but because, fatally wounded in the course of the campaign, he neglected to nominate a successor.[29] More significantly, Julian's religious fanaticism and other-worldly intellectualism might seem to stand against him, but in Gibbon's words the emperor 'could break from the dream of superstition to arm himself for battle; and, after vanquishing in the field the enemies of Rome, he calmly retired to his tent, to dictate the wise and salutary laws of an empire, or to indulge his genius in the elegant pursuits of literature and philosophy'.[30] Despite the unreality of this picture, Gibbon's emphasis on the value of action marks him, as it seems to me to mark Ammianus Marcellinus, as an essentially classical historian.[31]

Valens, who lost the battle of Hadrianople to the Goths, is a straightforward case. From his reign, wrote Gibbon, may justly be dated the 'disastrous period of the fall of the Roman empire',[32] a point of view forcibly endorsed in a footnote, the last in chapter 26, criticizing Montesquieu for a most serious historical error in asserting that the Goths had left the Roman territory after the battle. The error was inexcusable, wrote Gibbon in one of his rare direct denunciations of a scholar, 'since it disguises the principal and immediate cause of the fall of the Western empire of Rome'.[33] Yet again, at the end of the reign of Theodosius, Gibbon wrote,

---

[28] *Decline and fall*, ed. Bury, II, p. 158.
[29] *Ibid.*, II, p. 517.   [30] *Ibid.*, II, p. 441.
[31] *The Roman Empire of Ammianus* (London, 1989), pp. 471–2.
[32] *Decline and fall*, ed. Bury, III, p. 70.   [33] *Ibid.*, III, p. 132 n. 143.

after the military writer Vegetius, that it was the pusillanimous indolence of the soldiery that might be considered as the 'immediate cause of the downfall of the empire'.[34] Here J. B. Bury, in one of what Peter Brown calls his 'implacable square brackets', cites the later doubts of Otto Seeck as to the dating of Vegetius, adding soberly that 'the work is by no means critical or trustworthy'. This is perfectly true, though on the question of dating, it happens that more recent scholarship has (on balance, rather than decisively) favoured Gibbon's view.[35] After the reign of Theodosius, who like Constantine receives a surprisingly warm endorsement from Gibbon, a series of inactive, feeble emperors both in east and west failed to assert the initiatives of their predecessors and delegated military control to barbarian war-lords. Of one of these emperors, Honorius, Gibbon wrote with magnificent sarcasm that since, in the course of a busy and interesting narrative, he might possibly forget to mention the death of such a prince when it occurred, he would take the precaution of observing at this place (under the year 413) that he survived the last siege of Rome by about thirteen years.[36]

Taking this select list of immediate or proximate causes as a systematic account of the reasons for the decline and fall of the western Empire, we might concede that it is a somewhat assorted collection, with a broad conception, both in time and character, of what counts as an 'immediate cause'. This is, however, a serious objection only if we regard Gibbon as one of Sir Isaiah Berlin's hedgehogs, such as would be forced into self-contradiction by an obsession with a single cause for the decline and fall of the Roman Empire. But, as Momigliano said in a passage quoted earlier, for Gibbon the decline and fall of Rome suggested a much more complex and varied picture of 'new societies, laws, customs, superstitions, something to be described in its various stages rather than to be deduced from certain premises'.[37]

---

[34] *Ibid.*, III, p. 187.

[35] *Ibid.*, III, p. 132 n. 128; on Vegetius see now N. P. Milner, *Vegetius: Epitome of Military Science* (Liverpool, 1993), pp. xxi–xxix on the author and time of writing.

[36] *Decline and fall*, ed. Bury, III, pp. 339–40; cf. III, p. 239 (the last words of chapter 29): 'In the eventful history of a reign of twenty-eight years, it will seldom be necessary to mention the name of the emperor Honorius.'

[37] Above, n. 19.

To convey this complex and varied picture, Gibbon established his account not only upon the narratives that would trace the 'most important circumstances' of the decline of the Roman Empire, but upon the digressions that are, in themselves, a monument to Gibbon's multifarious learning, and to his debt to the historians of the classical world. In reading *Decline and fall*, it is just as important to grasp the interrelations of these with each other, as with the narrative chapters that frame them. Chapters 8 and 9 on the Persians and the Germanic peoples respectively, should be taken with the vivid pages within chapter 26 on the manners of the pastoral nations, and with chapter 34 on the history of the Huns – in the course of which Gibbon's conception, at least of the *indirect* causes of the fall of the Roman Empire, extends to the frontiers of China.[38] Chapters 15 and 16, on the character of Roman religion, the early advances of Christianity and its persecutions by the Roman government, should be taken, not only with the delayed chapter 37 on the monastic life and the conversion to Christianity of the barbarian peoples; they also go with the long chapter 21 on the persecution of heresy and, by extension, with the descriptions of the pagan policies of Julian in chapter 23 and of the end of paganism in chapter 28. With the large section of chapter 31 on the society, population and physical extent of Rome, we should connect the earlier description of the foundation of Constantinople in the first part of chapter 17. The four chapters on Constantine (17–18, 20–1) form a substantial monograph on that emperor, taking within themselves the form of narrative and digressions largely because Gibbon deliberately segregated civil and ecclesiastical affairs in his narrative. This was a tactical, not a strategic segregation, one of the most notable features of Gibbon's writing being its extraordinary assimilation within one framework of all types of source and all subjects.

No arrangement of a large literary structure is ever perfect and there are, it must be said, some awkwardnesses in Gibbon's arrangement of his digressions. He remarks that the account of the monastic movement (chapter 37) is 'purposely delayed', but does

---

[38] Cf. Bury's discussion of the identity of the Hiong-Nou (*vel sim.*) of the Chinese sources, at *Decline and fall*, ed. Bury, III, pp. 493–4. Gibbon's discussion is in his chapter 26 (III, pp. 81–7 with n. 27). See Matthews, *The Roman Empire of Ammianus*, pp. 488 n. 26, 533 n. 95.

not say why this should be, with an account that begins with St Antony and proceeds into the fourth and fifth centuries but is placed after the accession of Theodoric the Ostrogoth in 493. Perhaps the explanation lies in the second half of the chapter, on the conversion of the barbarians, but this does not really belong to it, and the effect is to delay the point at which it is needed, an account that is clearly relevant to Gibbon's conception of the religious history of the fourth century. The description of the city of Rome and its society is offered in the context of the sieges of the city by Alaric in 408 and 410, but its material is taken explicitly (in the form of an extended translation) from Ammianus Marcellinus, whose account is contextually located quite differently, and in fact begins with an explanation of the eternity of Rome.[39]

More significantly, the location of the digression on Roman law in the time of Justinian (chapter 44) defers that important subject to the second part of Gibbon's 'engagement with the public', and means that Gibbon cannot give to it due recognition in its proper place, as a component of the liberties and rights of the Romans in earlier centuries. This is important, since most modern historians, like ancient ones, would look to the law as a restraint on the tyranny of those emperors in whose hands Gibbon laid much responsibility for the decline and fall of the Roman Empire.[40] He obliquely concedes in its narrative context the significance of the classical jurists of the Severan period; a fuller reflection, based on the Digest of Justinian and its sources, might reasonably ask whether the temper of the Severan (and, indeed, the Tetrarchic) Age was not so much militaristic as juristic. And, for some reason, in his account of Roman law under Justinian, Gibbon pays hardly any attention to the earlier codification of Theodosius II, the subject of the scholarly work of Godefroy that was so much admired by him.[41] In his *Memoirs* Gibbon described the Theodosian Code, with Godefroy's commentary, as 'a work of history, rather than of Jurisprudence',[42] which in no way allays one's surprise that he made so little reference to it in his account of Roman jurisprudence, and that this

[39] Ammianus Marcellinus, 14. 6.3–26 ed. and trans. J. C. Rolfe, *Ammiani Marcellini Rerum Gestarum libri qui supersunt* (London and Cambridge, Mass., 1971), pp. 36–63.
[40] Cf. Matthews, *The Roman Empire of Ammianus*, pp. 250–2.
[41] See Tony Honoré, *Emperors and lawyers* (London, 1981; 2nd edn, Oxford, 1994).
[42] On the classical jurists see *Decline and fall*, ed. Bury, I, pp. 134–5, 153, and on the Theodosian Code, *Memoirs*, ed. Bonnard, p. 147.

subject as a whole did not take its place in the history of the Roman Empire in its own right. It is a paradox that in Gibbon's text as it stands, one reads about the foundation of barbarian legal systems (in chapter 38) before one reads about Roman law itself; and that, on a literal interpretation of Gibbon's words mentioned earlier, if he had failed to proceed beyond the first three volumes of his history he would not have discussed the subject at all. It is one of the ways in which, as will be pursued below, Gibbon tended to follow the disposition of his sources. The Digest was edited under Justinian, so that is where, despite its massive relevance to the earlier period, he located the digression that grew out of it.

This is not the place for a systematic account of the ways in which modern scholarship has superseded Gibbon's methods and conclusions. J. B. Bury's introduction to his edition has a review of how this stood at the very end of the nineteenth century, after a hundred years of scientific scholarship since Gibbon's time. By the end of the nineteenth century Gibbon's texts had largely been replaced by critical editions – though one would be hard pressed to find an occasion on which any conclusion drawn by him was vitiated by a false reading in a text, and Gibbon made more use than most modern scholars of the great commentaries of seventeenth- and eighteenth-century editors, some of them unsurpassed to this day.[43] There is affection as well as irony in Gibbon's admiration of the great editor of the Greek patristic writer of the fourth century, John Chrysostom – this was Father Montfaucon, 'who, by the command of his Benedictine superiors, was compelled to execute the laborious edition of St Chrysostom, in thirteen volumes in folio (Paris, 1738)'[44] – and of the learned Tillemont, 'who compiles the lives of the saints with incredible patience and religious accuracy. He has minutely searched the voluminous works of Chrysostom himself!'[45] This was the Tillemont, 'whose inimitable accuracy', according to a famous phrase in the Memoirs, 'almost assumes the character of Genius'.[46]

Gibbon knew nothing of the developed sciences of numismatics and epigraphy, and was unable to exploit these sources as a modern

---

[43] Cf. A. H. M. Jones, *The later Roman Empire* (Oxford, 1964), p. vii; these editions are a 'mine of curious information'.

[44] *Decline and fall*, ed. Bury, III, p. 358 n. 1.

[45] *Ibid.*, III, p. 374 n. 41.   [46] *Memoirs*, ed. Bonnard, p. 147.

historian uses them, as the base of his method and to assert his freedom from the influence of literary texts;[47] for this, one needs the systematic collections, such as the *Corpus* of Latin inscriptions initiated by Mommsen and its Greek equivalents. Yet Gibbon knew how to illuminate his theme from this material as it stood. He was aware that the 'majestic ruins that are still scattered over Italy and the provinces' were usually the products not directly of imperial policy but of local munificence by the leading citizens of the empire, citing the inscription of the 'stupendous bridge at Alcantara' as proof that it was 'thrown over the Tagus by the contribution of a few Lusitanian communities', and quoting the tenth book of the letters of the younger Pliny to show the competitive rivalries of local communities of Asia Minor.[48] The same passage and others show Gibbon's appreciation of the possibilities of archaeology, at least in terms of an awareness of the standing ruins and surviving artefacts of the Roman period – especially when one adds the reminder that the idea of writing *Decline and fall* first came to his mind while reflecting on the ruins of Rome, and that his first idea was to write a history of the city rather than of the empire as such.[49] It is not irrelevant to add that the very year, 1764, of Gibbon's famous (though somewhat redrafted)[50] musings on the Capitol was that of the discovery of the Great Theatre at Pompeii. Nine years earlier, in his French *Journal* of the tour of Switzerland which he undertook from 21 September to 20 October 1755, the eighteen-year-old Gibbon noted the ruins of Avenches in words curiously reminiscent of those of Ammianus Marcellinus, who was later to mean so much to the historian of the later Roman empire: 'a en juger par les ruines il a du avoir été fort grand et fort beau', he there wrote of a town that was 'bien plus considérable autrefois qu'il n'est aujourdhuy', mentioning columns, remains of walls, a small amphitheatre, and a bath-house mosaic discovered just four years earlier.[51]

---

[47] See on this theme Momigliano, 'Ancient history and the antiquarian', in *Studies in Historiography*, pp. 1–39, at p. 13.

[48] *Decline and fall*, ed. Bury, I, p. 44.

[49] *Memoirs*, ed. Bonnard, p. 136; 'But my original plan was circumscribed to the decay of the City, rather than of the Empire', etc.

[50] See Bonnard, pp. 304–5, for the various drafts of this passage of the *Memoirs*.

[51] Edward Gibbon, *Journal de mon voyage dans quelques endroits de la Suisse*, 1755, in G. R. de Beer, G. A. Bonnard, and L. Junod (eds.), *Miscellanea Gibboniana* (Lausanne, 1952), p. 66; cf. Ammianus Marcellinus, ed. Rolfe, 15.11.12, p. 191; 'Aventicum, desertam quidem

Papyrology was a science of the future when Gibbon wrote, and indeed still was so when Bury added his survey of scholarly developments since Gibbon's day. The 'stately and populous city of Oxyrinchus' (as Gibbon spells it) does gain a single mention in his text, as a place of twelve churches, and of ten thousand female and twenty thousand male adherents of the monastic profession;[52] but neither Gibbon nor anyone else could have anticipated the historical riches that lay hidden within this efflorescence of misguided piety. As for the technique of prosopography, that too lay beyond Gibbon's grasp as a developed method, but that he would have seen its possibilities is clear. In describing the proclamation of Pertinax after the death of Commodus, he set out in detail the earlier military career of the new emperor as 'expressive of the form of government and manners of his age',[53] and later, describing the late Roman state as established by Constantine, explicitly paralleled this (with cross-reference) with the career of a late Roman court official, Mallius Theodorus, as it is known from a poem of Claudian.[54] In the implications of these two passages lurk the unborn souls of the *Prosopographia Imperii Romani* and the *Prosopography of the later Roman Empire* respectively.

As we saw earlier, a more rigorous use of the principles of source criticism, to the extent that it was available to him, might have saved Gibbon from the largely fictitious narrative, based on the *Historia Augusta*, which he provides of the history of the third century (from the reigns of Elagabalus and Alexander Severus to the immediate predecessors of Diocletian). If he had fully appreciated that the fifth-century historian Zosimus was essentially an abbreviated paraphrase of the later fourth-century pagan historian Eunapius he might have come up with an answer to the chronological problem of the conversion of Constantine, and his

civitatem, sed non ignobilem quondam, ut aedificia semiruta nunc usque demonstrant.' The resemblance is coincidental, or due to the identity of subject-matter; the *Memoirs* place Gibbon's reading of Ammianus long after the composition of the *Journal* (below, p. 29). For the journey, Patricia B. Craddock, *Young Gibbon: gentleman of letters* (Baltimore, 1982), pp. 79–85.

[52] *Decline and fall*, ed. Bury, IV, p. 60.

[53] *Ibid.*, I, p. 97 n. 47.

[54] *Ibid.*, II, p. 173 n. 127; Bury adds at this point that 'Inscriptions supply us with more illustrations of official careers under the Constantinian monarchy. The career of Caelius Saturninus (*Corpus Inscriptionum Latinarum* 6, 1704) occasioned an important study by Mommsen', etc.

description of the luxury of the Romans in the time of Theodosius might have appeared to him as the propaganda that it is. This, to be sure, would have undermined what he here has to say about 'the progress of luxury amidst the misfortunes and terrors of a sinking nation', especially since it is immediately followed by the dubious judgment on the pusillanimous character of the soldiery derived from Vegetius which I mentioned earlier.[55] On the other hand, where there are no relevant advances in technique since Gibbon's day, and where the sources he used can still be understood as he read them, his judgments are often still highly pertinent. To take just three examples, Gibbon's assessment of Constantine the Great is not only extraordinarily full and well documented but presents an emperor closer to the modern conception than some that have appeared in the meantime. His explicit appreciation of the impact upon the Goths of the invention of writing as the vehicle of their translated Bible has observations relevant to modern discussions of literacy and the role of a culture based on a book.[56] His judgment of the ascetic movement of the fourth and fifth centuries is as waspish as only Gibbon can be, but many will judge it closer to the truth than some of the neo-fundamentalist hagiography of our own time.

In general, and it can be a strength and a weakness, Gibbon tended to follow the grain of his literary sources. He did so consciously, relying on his judgment of their value. He thereby produces a marvellous account, derived from a famous fragment of Priscus, of a Byzantine embassy to the court of Attila the Hun, and his account of the history of the third quarter of the fourth century, from Constantine II to Valentinian and Valens, is constantly underpinned, not only by the information but by the judgment and correctives of Ammianus Marcellinus, whom he rightly admired. At the same time, his equally famous criticisms of Ammianus' literary

---

[55] *Decline and fall*, ed. Bury, iii, pp. 186–7.
[56] *Ibid.*, iv, p. 79; 'They received, at the same time, the use of letters, so essential to a religion whose doctrines are contained in a sacred book, and, while they studied the divine truth, their minds were insensibly enlarged by the distant view of history, of nature, of the arts, and of society'; cf. *ibid.*, i, p. 218, cited above. p. 19 (of the early Germans' ignorance of letters). See also William V. Harris, *Ancient literacy* (Cambridge, Mass., 1989) and Alan Bowman and Greg Woolf, *Literacy and power in the ancient world* (Cambridge, UK, 1994).

style suggest an inference relevant to the way in which Gibbon conceived of the historical character of his subject.[57]

The extent to which the formation of Gibbon's conception of the decline and fall of the Roman Empire is bound up with a judgment of the quality of its literary sources is implicit in the description given in the *Memoirs* of his early reading of classical texts:

> The Classics, as low as Tacitus, the younger Pliny, and Juvenal, were my old and familiar companions. I insensibly plunged into the ocean of the Augustan History; and in the descending series I investigated, with my pen almost always in my hand, the original records, both Greek and Latin, from Dion Cassius to Ammianus Marcellinus, from the reign of Trajan to the last age of the Western Caesars.[58]

We should not make too much in this passage, taken alone, of Gibbon's language of descent through the ages. People commonly use phrases like 'down to the present day' without, at least consciously, thinking of a process of decline (though they may also say 'up to the present day'). But other passages also suggest that Gibbon's concept of 'decline and fall' should not be seen as a specifically studied analytical tool, but more as an *attitude* embedded in his classical culture and the use he made of it. I can best illustrate this by citing three of Gibbon's opinions on literary and artistic movements of late antiquity, taking first his judgment on late Roman philosophy, especially the movement of the 'New Platonists':

> The *declining age of learning and of mankind* is marked, however, by the rise and rapid progress of the new Platonists. The school of Alexandria silenced those of Athens; and the ancient sects enrolled themselves under the banners of the more fashionable teachers, who recommended their system by the novelty of their method and the austerity of their manners. Several of these masters . . . were men of profound thought and intense application; but, by mistaking the true object of philosophy, their labours contributed much less to improve than to corrupt the human understanding.[59]

---

[57] *Ibid.*, III, p. 122; 'It is not without the most sincere regret that I must now take leave of an accurate and faithful guide, who has composed the history of his own times without indulging the prejudices and passions which usually affect the mind of a contemporary', cf. p. 116 n. 100; 'Zosimus, whom we are now reduced to cherish'. At p. 111 n. 93 admiration for Ammianus is tempered by 'the vices of his style, the disorder and perplexity of his narrative'.

[58] *Memoirs*, ed. Bonnard, pp. 146–7.

[59] *Decline and fall*, ed. Bury, I, p. 392.

Gibbon took a similarly negative view of the visual arts of late antiquity, as he saw them exemplified on the arch of Constantine at Rome (*c.* 315). The arch, wrote Gibbon,

still remains a melancholy proof of the *decline of the arts*, and a singular testimony of the meanest vanity. As it was not possible to find in the capital of the empire a sculptor who was capable of adorning that public monument, the arch of Trajan, without any respect either for his memory or the rules of propriety, was stripped of its most elegant figures. The difference of times and persons, of actions and characters, was totally disregarded. The Parthian captives appear prostrate at the feet of a prince who never carried his arms beyond the Euphrates; and curious antiquarians can still discover the head of Trajan on the trophies of Constantine. The new ornaments which it was necessary to introduce between the vacancies of ancient sculpture are executed in the rudest and most unskilful manner.[60]

As for the literary arts of late antiquity, the popularity of the poems of Ausonius seemed to Gibbon to 'condemn the taste of his age', one particular production being dismissed as a 'servile and insipid piece of flattery'.[61] In sharp contrast stands his judgment of Claudian, a poet of altogether more classic virtues:

In the *decline of arts and of empire*, a native of Egypt, who had received the education of a Greek, assumed, in a mature age, the familiar use and absolute command of the Latin language, soared above the heads of his feeble contemporaries, and placed himself, after an interval of three hundred years, among the poets of ancient Rome.[62]

Gibbon omitted to remark, as he might, on the fact that both the greatest Latin poet and the greatest Latin historian of late antiquity originated in the Greek east, Claudian from Alexandria and Ammianus Marcellinus from Syrian Antioch.[63] His preference for Claudian over other late classical poets was clearly because he most seemed to resemble the poets of the Silver Age.

Gibbon did not ask whether there might have been positive aspects to the developments which he saw in late classical philosophy, art, and poetry, nor did he wonder what changes in the sensitivities and self-perceptions of men might have taken place to

---

[60] *Ibid.*, I, pp. 423–4. [61] *Ibid.*, III, p. 134 nn. 1–2.
[62] *Ibid.*, III, p. 284.
[63] At p. 122 nn. 116–17 Gibbon touches in passing, but does not stress, Ammianus's origin in the Greek east. See now John Matthews, 'The origin of Ammianus', *Classical Quarterly* 44 (1994), pp. 252–69, confirming his Antiochene origin.

explain these developments (such changes would, after all, themselves not stand outside but form part of a concept of social and political decline). In a way that has long survived Gibbon, late Roman culture was judged by the standards of an earlier period, and these standards were as much aesthetic as historical. Particularly telling are those recurring phrases which I have shown in italics, 'the *declining age of learning and of mankind* . . . ', 'the *decline of arts and of empire* . . . '. If these phrases are at all significant, Gibbon conceived the nature of the artistic and literary culture of a society as fundamental to an evaluation of that society in *all* its aspects, and saw the relationship between the two, the arts and society, as a very intimate one; if, indeed, he consciously distinguished them at all. Gibbon took a standpoint from which a judgment of the culture of late antiquity led him, as he might have said, insensibly, to a corresponding judgment of the decline of society and its government. Not surprisingly, it is in the fields of late Roman literary and artistic style, and of later Roman religion and philosophy, that some of the most interesting recent advances have been made, as historians have looked for more positive appreciations of what Gibbon, and many after him, perceived in such negative terms. The new ornaments added to the arch of Constantine may have been 'executed in the rudest and most unskilful manner'; but this cannot be said of the mosaics of Ravenna, which display some of the same stylistic characteristics.[64]

In the last resort, however, it must be remembered that, although Gibbon's history was one of decline and fall, it was in the very long term an optimistic work. The effects of that great revolution were still felt in the world of Gibbon's day, but modern Europe, as he explained in the 'General observations' – drafted, as we have seen, before he had published any of *Decline and fall* – was well placed to avoid the same fate. I will say no more about this (it is far from my field), except in conclusion to illustrate the theme from one of Gibbon's characteristically precise footnotes, and to adduce a passage of his text. Describing the submission of the Alamanni to Clovis the Frank, Gibbon had occasion to mention

---

[64] From this more recent work I cite just one book, for its freshness and sophistication, and for the positive adventure of its interpretation; Michael Roberts, *The jeweled style: poetry and poetics in late antiquity* (Ithaca and London, 1989); chapter 3 is on 'Poetry and the visual arts'. Roberts begins his critique by assembling modern approbations of Gibbon's judgment of Ausonius, quoted above. The arch of Constantine is discussed, pp. 91–2.

the 'vestige of stately Vindonissa [that] may still be discovered in the fertile and populous valley of the Aar'.[65] At this point a marginal note adds '[Windisch]' to denote the spot at which the early Romans had established a legionary fortress, and at the foot of the page appears one of Gibbon's luminous notes:

Within the ancient walls of Vindonissa, the castle of Habsburg, the abbey of Königsfeld, and the town of Bruck, have successively arisen. The philosophic traveller may compare the monuments of Roman conquest, of feudal or Austrian tyranny, of monkish superstition, and of industrious freedom. If he be truly a philosopher he will applaud the merit and happiness of his own times.[66]

In chapter 34 on the wars of Attila with the Romans, Gibbon had described the unique resistance offered by 'the firmness of a single town', the obscure Azimus in Illyrian Thrace. Organizing its own resistance, the town held out against Attila and induced him to make an agreement, even deceiving him when he asked for the return of captives by asserting that they had already killed them. Delegating to the casuists the morality of this deception, Gibbon asserted that every soldier and every statesman 'must acknowledge that, if the race of the Azimuntines had been encouraged and multiplied, the Barbarians would have ceased to trample on the majesty of the empire'.[67] Here for Gibbon was a model for his times – one for every 'soldier and statesman' – as it should have been a model for its own; a community whose sense of liberty had borne the weight of the 'stupendous fabric' of the political power of Rome, and expressed in action the spirit of industrious freedom.

[65] *Decline and fall*, ed. Bury, IV, p. 104.
[66] The eighteen-year-old Gibbon (was he already a 'philosophic traveller'?) had visited Bruck (or Brugg) twice in the course of the tour of Switzerland of September–October 1755 mentioned in the *Memoirs* (ed. Bonnard, pp. 79–80) and described in the French *Journal* (above, n. 51). He will have passed it on the way from Aarau to Baden on 28 September, and he spent the night of 6 October there on the return journey (*Journal*, pp. 20–1, 39).
[67] *Decline and fall*, ed. Bury, III, p. 432.

CHAPTER 2

Gibbon and Justinian

Averil Cameron

The portrayal of the reign of Justinian in Gibbon's *History* has not up to now received the attention it deserves, whether in terms of its presentation of one of the most brilliant periods covered in the work, or in relation to its function within the structure of the *Decline and fall* in its final form. Did Gibbon consider Justinian to be as 'Roman' as the emperor himself claimed to be? How did he make the narrative of the reconquest of the west fit his own account of the end of the western empire which precedes it? Where did Gibbon find his material, and how far was it possible for him to escape from the influence of Procopius, the contemporary historian who was at once Justinian's eulogist and his most savage critic? Many such questions suggest themselves, but while Gibbon's interest in Belisarius, Justinian's general and Procopius' hero, has been well noted, as has his fascination with the flamboyant empress Theodora, neither his use of Procopius as a main source nor the structural importance of this part of the *Decline and fall*, has been fully explored.

Two features of Gibbon's method in the *History* that have received a good deal of scholarly attention are highly relevant here too: these are his focus on certain individual characters – Julian the Apostate is one – and his use of certain ancient writers as major sources. Into the latter category fall two of his main sources and influences, Tacitus for the early Empire and Ammianus Marcellinus for the fourth century. When Gibbon can follow a full and detailed account he does so, while always interposing his own judgments based on other reading or critical perception.[1] As for the characters,

---

[1] See on Tacitus and Ammianus, David Womersley, *The transformation of 'The decline and fall of the Roman Empire'*, Cambridge Studies in Eighteenth-Century English Literature and Thought 1 (Cambridge, 1988), chs. 6 and 11.

Gibbon will, when he can, hang his narrative around a focal point – Augustus, say, or Constantine. This partly depended on his own reading: he emphasizes himself how important had been the early reading of a life of the emperor Julian, even though he later prepared more systematically for the *History* by reading or rereading the Greek and Latin historians of the Empire, 'from the reign of Trajan to the last age of the western Caesars', and mostly in the original.[2] These aspects, both of his preparation and his narrative technique, are significant for the present subject too. What does Gibbon do in his *History*, we shall ask, with the figure of Justinian, and how did he exploit the works of Procopius for the task?

It is a matter of some interest to know at what stage Gibbon was first introduced to the age of Justinian. In 1753, after the lonely youth had succumbed, as he describes it, to Roman Catholicism and had had to leave Oxford, his father decided to remove him from further dangerous influences and put him in the hands of a sober Protestant, indeed Calvinist, instructor at Lausanne. The sixteen-year-old Gibbon, whose five-year stay in Lausanne had little of the comfort and social advantages enjoyed by such sons of the English aristocracy as travelled on the Continent, or even of his own later Grand Tour, was brought back within eighteen months to suitable Protestantism (his Catholic opinions 'disappeared like a dream').[3] Equally important, however, was the return and development of his love of reading after the sloth of Oxford; he returned, at the age of nineteen, to serious study of Greek, including Homer, Xenophon and Herodotus, though he confesses that having to look up so many words in the dictionary was something of a strain, and that he found it a relief to return to Latin.[4]

In fact, Gibbon had already been initiated into the Age of Justinian when he was very young. Even before he went up to Oxford at the age of fourteen he had been reading Procopius – 'greedily devouring a ragged Procopius of the last century'.[5] This was a translation, presumably of the *Wars*: Gibbon did not absorb

---

[2] E. Gibbon, *Memoirs of my life and writings*, ed. G. B. Hill (London, 1900), pp. 181–2.
[3] *Ibid.*, p. 90.
[4] *Ibid.*, pp. 94–5; he returned again to Greek, neglected since leaving Lausanne, while at Buriton in the summer of 1762, when he finished the *Iliad* and read other works, including some Strabo (*ibid.*, pp. 141–2).
[5] *Ibid.*, p. 42.

much Greek at school, and defended his reliance on translations at this stage on the grounds that his own would have been far inferior to those already published by experts. He turned back deliberately to Procopius when he came to write the *History*: 'Procopius and Agathias [this time in the original Greek] supplied the events and even the characters' for the reign of Justinian.[6] This was in fact the last part in the *History* for which he could follow an ancient source in such detail. His relation to Procopius, and the methods which he followed in his use of the latter's material, are essential elements in his presentation of Justinian.

First, however, the sections on this period need to be placed in their context in the composition of the work as a whole. Again Gibbon himself is our guide. When he began his account of 'Roman decay', he tells us, he had no very clear idea of its contents, structure or chronological scope; although his first reading took him as far as the Theodosian Code, he did not as yet think in terms of twenty years' work or of what he calls 'six quartos'. Both the title of the work and the date at which the Empire 'fell' were as yet unclear to him, as was the proper literary style for such a history, defined by him later as 'the middle tone between a dull chronicle and a rhetorical declamation'.[7] In the event three volumes had been published by 1781, covering the first thirty-eight chapters and concluding with the 'General observations on the fall of the Roman Empire in the west';[8] the chronological divide came after accounts of the invasions in Gaul, Spain and Britain, and before he would have reached the reign of Zeno in the east. He had finished his fourth volume, containing his account of Justinian's reign, before returning to Lausanne in 1783, and the rest followed, after a year's interruption, in the years up to 1787, when the last words were written there, on 27 June of that year. At Lausanne he had a library of more than two thousand volumes in addition to what he could find in other nearby libraries, and while there he worked solidly at the *History* on a daily basis.

---

[6] *Ibid.*, p. 213.   [7] *Ibid.*, pp. 181, 189.

[8] The composition of the 'General observations' is dated by Gibbon in the *Memoirs* to before 1774, though the accuracy of this statement has been challenged; such an early date would of course be important for the understanding of the genesis of the *History*. For discussion see P. R. Ghosh, 'Gibbon's dark ages; some remarks on the genesis of the *Decline and fall*', *JRS* 73 (1983), pp. 1–23; also his 'Gibbon observed', *JRS* 81 (1991), pp. 132–56.

The narrative of Justinian's reign was continued as far as that
of Heraclius, after which he inserted a chapter on the history of
Christological controversy and the divisions of the eastern church
(chapter 47). Only then did he reach the Byzantine section proper,
with the famous chapter on Mahomet and Arabia and with the
whole remaining history of Byzantium compressed into a rapid
survey, written on a vastly more compressed scale than the earlier
Roman chapters.[9] Gibbon explains his reasons: the patient reader
would find intolerable a detailed narrative of the remaining eight
hundred years of decline, with their uniform and dreary history. It
would be more profitable and more interesting to present in turn
each of the new peoples to whom the torch was to pass, finally
returning to the siege and capture of Constantinople by Mehmet II
and the ruins of ancient Rome in the fourteenth century.[10] He
claims that he had seriously considered ending the work with the
'General observations', that is, with the fall of the western Empire.
What induced him to continue and when did he make the decision?
The motivating factor was less, perhaps, a clear view or overall
concept of 'fall' or 'decline' than it was a natural inclination, fed by
a return to reading Greek authors in the summer following the
publication of volumes II and III in 1781. The intention to continue
was announced in the preface to a new edition published in 1782,
and he now set to in earnest to read Procopius and Agathias and the
other sources for Justinian.[11] The overall structure of the *History*
was more the product, therefore, of an organic growth than of a
preconceived scheme, and some of its features are perhaps to be
explained more easily in relation to what materials were to hand
than to serious planning. Nevertheless, the arrangement of the
later parts as a series of portraits of 'nations' exterior to Byzantium,
rather than as a continuous chronological narrative, was deliberate
and considered. We can see something of this episodic and
sequential treatment also in the arrangement of the Justinianic
material.

Justinian's reign posed something of a difficulty for Gibbon,
coming as it did at a point in the narrative so soon after the

---

[9] For the difference of coverage, see Ghosh, 'Gibbon observed', p. 145.
[10] *Decline and fall*, ed. Bury, v, ch. 48; cf. *Memoirs*, ed. Hill, p. 151.
[11] *Memoirs*, ed. Hill, p. 214, though see Ghosh, 'Gibbon observed', p. 155 n. 167; the first aim
  of the work as a whole may have been focussed on Rome and the city of Rome itself rather
  than Constantinople and Byzantium.

'General observations'. He had already acknowledged that Justinian 'subverted' the Gothic and Vandal kingdoms of Italy and Africa, and that a long series of emperors was to continue on the Byzantine throne.[12] Yet the 'General observations' which follow refer disparagingly to the 'tardy, doubtful and ineffectual' aid given by the 'Oriental Romans' after the fall of the west, and place Justinian by implication in the list of 'Greek' emperors whose interest for the historian Gibbon only very grudgingly acknowledges. Moreover, immediately before the 'General observations' Gibbon had written of the 'total extinction' of the Roman Empire in the west.[13] He was already obliged therefore to see Justinian's reconquest as marking at best only a temporary recovery, worthy of some admiration but not in itself sufficient to stem the course of decline. This of course chimed in very well with what he had read in Procopius, whose account confirmed, and partly no doubt dictated, his own inclinations. In Procopius he found, as he did also in Tacitus and Ammianus, an historian congenial to his own ideas, and even a stylist like himself: Procopius' 'style', Gibbon writes, 'continually aspires, and often attains, to the merit of strength and elegance', 'His reflections . . . contain a rich fund of political knowledge'. So great was Gibbon's admiration that he was prepared to overlook the sycophancy which he elsewhere detected in Procopius' *Buildings*, or 'edifices', in order to emphasize his standing as a critic: 'the historian, excited by the generous ambition of pleasing and instructing posterity, appears to disdain the prejudices of the people and the flattery of courts.'[14] All three major historians followed by Gibbon in the *History* – Tacitus, Ammianus and Procopius – were in their different ways prototypes for himself, sly in their criticism, loud in their role as upholders of ancient morals, passionate in their attachment to the Roman tradition and good models for a philosophy of decline.

In approaching his account of the reign of Justinian, therefore, Gibbon had to fit this episode of military and imperial recovery into his general picture of decline, and was in so doing able to turn to a major contemporary writer whose strong opinions have dominated every account of the reign before and since Gibbon himself.[15] He

---

[12] *Decline and fall*, ed. Bury, IV, ch. 38, p. 159.   [13] *Ibid.*, p. 162.
[14] *Ibid.*, ch. 40, p. 210.
[15] See Averil Cameron, *Procopius and the sixth century* (London, 1985).

prefaces his account of Justinian directly with an introduction to Procopius. It suited him to see in the latter a senator and a prefect of the city of Constantinople (an identification which now seems unlikely), for he could then describe him as 'a soldier, a statesman and a traveller', and reinforce his high opinion of Procopius' *Wars* as being based on 'personal experience and free conversation'. The character of Belisarius, Justinian's general, is central to Gibbon's portrayal of the age.[16] Acceptance of Procopius' high opinion of his patron, Belisarius (in the early stages at least), enables Gibbon to glide smoothly over Procopius' *Buildings*, a eulogistic account of Justinian's fortifications and other imperial building, despite the fact that he recognized its flattery to be something of an embarrassment in view of his emphasis on the reliability of Procopius as a critical historian. He could thus explain the flattery to himself as a necessary bow to the emperor who was jealous of the praise given to Belisarius in Procopius' other work. In the case of Justinian, as often elsewhere, Gibbon attributes his own motives to the characters in *Decline and fall*. Later, in the same vein, he suggests that the retired general Belisarius would have viewed the success of his rival Narses with some chagrin: 'I desire to believe, but I cannot affirm, that Belisarius sincerely rejoiced in the triumph of Narses.' Both generals were in fact suspected by the jealous emperor, but as Gibbon points out, Narses, 'the favoured eunuch', held his confidence for longer than did Belisarius, and the story of the wars of Justinian culminated, for Gibbon, in 'the *simple* and *genuine* [my italics] narrative of the fall of Belisarius and the ingratitude of Justinian'.[17] Gibbon in fact frames his whole narrative of the wars with these suggestions as to the personal motives of Justinian; the history of Justinian is treated as a moral tale. At the beginning, in his introductory section on Procopius as an historian, he alleges that the jealousy of Justinian for Belisarius coloured the emperor's reception of the latter's *History of the wars*: 'although he [i.e. Procopius] respectfully laid them at the foot of the throne, the pride

[16] See also L. Gossman, *The empire unpossess'd. An essay on Gibbon's 'Decline and fall'* (Cambridge, 1981), pp. 61–3 (Justinian as the authoritarian father and Belisarius as the pious son); on the other hand, reading the *History* at the age of sixteen, Disraeli felt that Gibbon 'had not made the most of the character of Belisarius' (W. F. Monypenny and G. E. Buckle (eds.), *The life of Benjamin Disraeli, earl of Beaconsfield*, vol. I, p. 33 (1929 edn); I owe this reference to Roland Quinault.
[17] See *Decline and fall*, ed. Bury, IV, pp. 423–5, 429.

of Justinian must have been wounded by the praise of an hero [Belisarius] who perpetually eclipses the glory of his inactive sovereign'.[18] Gibbon has in effect allowed the categories and judgments laid down by Procopius to shape and colour his own account. The phrase 'inactive sovereign' looks like a comment of his own; in fact it echoes Procopius' explicit critique, just as the characterization of Belisarius accepts Procopius' own valuation in parts of the *History of the wars* while ignoring the more negative picture given by Procopius elsewhere.

The most notorious of Procopius' works was the *Secret history*, or in Gibbon's parlance the 'anecdotes', and despite its lack of fit with the *Wars*, Gibbon relished it greatly. It amused him that the circumstances of its late discovery in the Vatican Library cast some discredit on Cardinal Baronius, and he could not resist making it into a major source for his own work.[19] He allows (necessarily) that its sensationalism casts some doubt on the reliability of Procopius as an historian ('such base inconsistency must doubtless sully the reputation, and detract from the credit, of Procopius'), but defends the latter by claiming that the evidence of the *Secret history* is supported by internal evidence from the *Wars* and by other contemporary sources (which he does not cite). If we look more closely we will find that even though he sometimes acknowledges Procopius' exaggerations,[20] it is in fact the *Secret history* rather than the *Wars* which has provided his explanatory structure and general view of the reign.

It has also provided his characters. Gibbon constantly refers in his footnotes to the 1623 *editio princeps* of the work by Alemannus, which he possessed, and which was an important guide while he was writing this section, although it omitted the offending chapter about the early exploits of Theodora.[21] Of the strange account in the *Secret history* of Belisarius' wife Antonina and her passion for the young man Theodosius, Gibbon writes: 'the diligence of Alemannus could add but little to the four first and most curious chapters of the *Anecdotes*. Of these strange *Anecdotes*, a part may be true, because

---

[18] *Ibid.*, p. 210.
[19] *Ibid.*, p. 211 n. 17.
[20] Compare *ibid.*, p. 368 n. 72, 'we may reasonably shut our ears against the malevolent whisper of the *Anecdotes*'.
[21] In contrast there is no mention of a copy of the *Buildings* in the card copy of his Lausanne library: see G. Keynes, *The library of Edward Gibbon: a catalogue*, 2nd edn (London, 1980).

probable, and part true, because *im*probable. Procopius must have *known* the former, and the latter he could hardly *invent*.'[22] The reputation of Procopius is saved.

Gibbon obviously enjoyed the *Secret history*. He recounts the whole story of Belisarius' wife in some detail, while admitting that it detracts from Belisarius' reputation ('the hero deserved the appellation which may not drop from the pen of the decent historian'), and that it reveals Procopius in the role of the slave at an antique Roman triumph who reminds the victor that he has feet of clay.[23] David Womersley has shown how Gibbon has enhanced the already sensational narrative of Procopius with extra details of his own.[24] But more famously still, Gibbon accepts and enhances all that Procopius says about the empress Theodora and her exploits before her marriage. It is of Theodora that he makes the notorious statement that 'her murmurs, her pleasures and her arts must be veiled in the obscurity of a learned language', quoting the offending lines in Greek in his note, adding his own comments, and comparing her favourably with courtesans in Latin poetry – 'her charity was *universal*'. Four highly-wrought footnotes make sure that the reader has got the most out of this carefully written passage.[25] It is less often noted, however, that Gibbon has also deliberately chosen to begin his own account of Justinian's reign with a long section on Theodora (seven pages in Bury's edition), within which he gives pride of place to the description of her performances in the Hippodrome. 'The prostitute, who had polluted the theatre of Constantinople, was adored as a queen in the same city.'[26] Gibbon makes a show of looking for extenuating factors; these are, however, limited. Theodora is allowed the virtues of courage (in the Nika revolt) and mercy (to repentant prostitutes), and even chastity after her marriage (though based on the silence of the

---

[22] *Decline and fall*, ed. Bury, IV, p. 335 n. 128.   [23] *Ibid.*, pp. 335, 334.

[24] Womersley, *Transformation*, pp. 284–5.

[25] *Decline and fall*, ed. Bury, IV, p. 213. At n. 23 Gibbon makes it clear that he had consulted a number of other editions and gone to considerable trouble in order to make good Alemannus' omission of ch. 9 ('somewhat too naked'). Note 24 contains his famous remark that 'I have heard that a learned prelate, now deceased, was fond of quoting this passage in conversation'; it has been suggested that the learned prelate was Bishop Warburton (*Memoirs*, ed. Hill, p. 178 n. 1).

[26] *Decline and fall*, ed. Bury, IV, p. 215. For this Gibbon has earned some fair criticism, though for reasons different from mine, for example from J. C. Morison, *Gibbon* (London, 1902), pp. 159–61.

sources rather than on positive evidence); and even Gibbon can
allow some indulgence to her regrettable tendency towards
Monophysitism, though he did not have the benefit of the very
favourable picture of her given by eastern Monophysite sources.[27]
He did not see her as the protectress of persecuted clergy and
monks, but instead accepted with relish Procopius' version of her
vindictiveness: her spies were everywhere, 'her prisons, a labyrinth,
a Tartarus, were under the palace'.[28]

After such a beginning, in which modern readers may well detect
a high degree of gender prejudice,[29] any account of Justinian
himself will inevitably come as an anticlimax. Indeed, until we
come much later in the narrative to his legislation and his religious
policy, topics which Gibbon treats separately, Justinian is the
absent figure from the account of his reign, just as he is also in
the *Wars* of Procopius. Gibbon was aware of the problem himself: he
admits that his source, Procopius, 'represents only the vices of
Justinian, and those vices are darkened by his malevolent pencil',
but he points out that later historians such as Evagrius and Zonaras
were equally critical.[30] Not even Justinian's churches and fortifications are allowed to cast credit on him: 'cemented with the blood
and treasure of his people',[31] they are notable in Gibbon's view not
for any vision on the part of the emperor but chiefly for what they
show about the skills of contemporary architects. Gibbon's final
verdict on Justinian is negative. The military successes in the west
receive only half a sentence ('the design of the African and Italian
wars was boldly conceived and executed'), to be eclipsed by
criticism of an emperor who did not go to war himself.[32] Justinian's
equestrian statue, 'melted into cannon by the victorious Turks',
ironically ends the account.[33] It was bad enough that the emperor,

[27] Notably John of Ephesus (Syriac), *Lives of eastern saints*, for which see S. Ashbrook Harvey,
Asceticism and society in crisis: John of Ephesus and the 'Lives of the eastern saints' (Berkeley and
Los Angeles, 1990).
[28] *Decline and fall*, ed. Bury, IV, p. 216, n. 31.
[29] Gibbon was well aware that he was using Theodora as a female exemplar: see p. 216. She
is one of the 'unnatural women' who recur in the *History*, a theme that is associated with
the weak and 'feminine' qualities which he sees at work in Christianity and in the 'Greek'
emperors: see Gossman, *The Empire unpossess'd*, pp. 43–7.
[30] *Decline and fall*, ed. Bury, IV, p. 236 and n. 82.
[31] *Ibid.*, p. 242.   [32] *Ibid.*, pp. 431–2.
[33] For this statue and its fate see Cyril Mango, 'The columns of Justinian and his successors'
and 'Justinian's equestrian statue', in his *Studies on Constantinople* (Aldershot, 1993),
chs. x–xi.

who, like Philip II 'declines the dangers of the field', should be depicted as a warrior at all, and suitably ironic that the statue itself, which had been erected in the place occupied by the pillar of Theodosius and which weighed, according to Gibbon, 7,400 pounds of silver, had been ignominiously destroyed. In this concluding section, the reader's attention is mischievously directed away from the character or achievements of the emperor to the fate of his statue. The account begins and ends with carefully chosen sidelights with wholly negative implications. We have been told, in Gibbon's 'obituary' of Justinian, that he 'was neither beloved in his life nor regretted at his death'.[34] We have been reminded immediately before of the superior qualities of Belisarius and of the 'envy and ingratitude of his sovereign'.[35] Now we have still further traducing of Justinian. Compared to Philip II for unwarlikeness, his statue, which had displaced a silver column of extraordinary weight and size, to be erected in stone and brass, had been melted down by the conquerors of Byzantium, and even its earlier restoration by Andronikos I is ascribed merely to the 'indulgence of a future prince' to Justinian's memory.

Not surprisingly, Belisarius emerges as the hero of the narrative. Again, Gibbon is aware of defects, but chooses to excuse them in the interests of narrative construction. 'The name of Belisarius can never die'; Gibbon does not believe the slander that he was guilty of plotting against Justinian in his last days – 'his innocence was acknowledged', though he died not long after, his death perhaps 'hastened by resentment and grief'.[36] A long footnote denies credence to the medieval legends of his being reduced to blindness and beggary – a scene depicted as recently as 1781 by the French painter David. Earlier, Belisarius' ignominious recall by Justinian from the Gothic war has called forth an extended eulogy by Gibbon in which he accepts without question the enthusiasm of Procopius, and the general's inglorious performance in the second Italian expedition (about which Procopius is in fact highly critical) is excused by comments inserted by Gibbon himself.[37] Similarly, his disappointing campaign against the Persians in the early 540s is narrated in a way which covers the unimpressive reality with flat

---

[34] *Decline and fall*, ed. Bury, IV, p. 431.   [35] *Ibid.*, pp. 431–2.
[36] *Ibid.*, pp. 429–30, and see McKitterick below, p. 173 n. 33.
[37] *Decline and fall*, ed. Bury, IV, pp. 332–4, 406–7, and cf. p. 294.

assertions of the moral dignity of Belisarius the man. So sure is Gibbon of this that he can detect it even behind Procopius' rhetoric: of the letter allegedly sent by Belisarius to Justinian complaining of being kept short of troops and supplies, Gibbon notes that 'the soul of an hero is deeply impressed on the letter; nor can we confound such genuine and original acts with the elaborate and often empty speeches of the Byzantine historians'.[38] Procopius, it seems, is elevated by implication to 'Roman' status, and Belisarius stands for the fearless uprightness which Gibbon so much admired. Before Gibbon, Montesquieu had already found in Belisarius matter for admiration, but Gibbon had more difficulty in reconciling the man and his reputation.[39] However, he is unwilling to do more than register the counterarguments, and certainly unwilling to follow Procopius into complete disillusionment, preferring to find reasons of his own for his hero's lapses. Not surprisingly, he found the admiring portrayal by Agathias of the aging Belisarius, called from retirement to defeat the Cotrigurs, congenial, despite its 'imperfect representation' and 'prolix declamation'.[40]

In Belisarius, as presented by Gibbon, David Womersley has detected a character which the historian has found difficult to understand, 'opaque where others are transparent'.[41] Gibbon has chosen to defend Belisarius against himself, and inserts his own surmises as to Belisarius' state of mind in a clear attempt to show the latter's heroic nature at points where it seems to be endangered by Procopius' narrative. He has deliberately enhanced the contrast between Belisarius and Justinian that is inherent in the earlier parts of Procopius' work, while glossing over the very different picture which emerges in Procopius' later writing. This has allowed him consistency of characterization: Justinian remains the 'sluggish and inactive emperor', who was nevertheless also a capricious tyrant. It also better suits Gibbon's positioning of Justinian within the long Greek decline which in his view followed the fall of the Roman Empire in the west in AD 476, as represented in his 'General observations'; as elsewhere, Gibbon is ready at every moment to undercut the impression that Justinian may have been a successful emperor in order to preserve the integrity of his own conception of decline.

---

[38] *Ibid.*, p. 399 n. 23. [39] See Womersley, *Transformation*, p. 235.
[40] *Decline and fall*, ed. Bury, IV, pp. 425–6. [41] Womersley, *Transformation*, p. 235.

The very shape of Gibbon's narrative may therefore have been dictated, as he admits himself, by the works of Procopius. He describes his plan: to begin with Theodora, the Blues and Greens and Justinian's administration, then to describe the wars, and only later the 'jurisprudence and theology of the emperor'.[42] He has thus given most prominence to the very sections of the *Secret history* which have always been the most notorious, namely those on Theodora and on the Nika revolt, and has devoted the greater part of his narrative to military history. A clutch of modern novels about Justinian and Theodora do the same.[43] We must therefore inquire why, when he does describe Justinian's internal government, Gibbon begins with a statement about the prosperity of the east that is at first sight memorable, especially after his account of the fall of the west. Gibbon presents the sixth-century east as prospering from trade and industry: society was enriched by the division of labour and the facility of exchanges, and 'every Roman was lodged, clothed and subsisted by the industry of a thousand hands'.[44] What may appear to be a departure from his sources in this remarkable judgment is explained by the fact that Gibbon has found the essence of the account of the silk industry which follows in Procopius and other contemporary writers.[45] Characteristically, the idealized tone of the opening description gives way abruptly to a much blacker picture once he reaches the subject of Justinian himself;[46] again dictated by the *Secret history*, Gibbon's assessment of the emperor's administration, deliberately placed *before* the narrative of his military successes, is only marginally less hostile than Procopius' own.

Likewise, the account of Justinian's buildings follows closely on Procopius', even to the order in which they are mentioned.[47] But while his description of St Sophia in Constantinople occupies four pages in Bury's edition, it is undercut by Gibbon's own memorable concluding remarks:

---

[42] *Decline and fall*, ed. Bury, IV, p. 211.
[43] See Cameron, *Procopius*, p. 67 for examples.
[44] *Decline and fall*, ed. Bury, IV, p. 227. The tone, here as elsewhere in chapter 40, represents Gibbon's style at its most vigorous: 'his language . . . has a Miltonic splendour' (J. W. Burrow, *Gibbon* (Oxford, 1985), pp. 96–7).
[45] *Decline and fall*, ed. Bury, IV, pp. 233–4.
[46] The indictment begins at p. 234 and extends to p. 240, to be followed by a more detailed narrative, again with hostile intent.
[47] *Ibid.*, pp. 244–5.

a magnificent temple is a laudable monument to national taste and
religion, and the enthusiast who entered the dome of St Sophia might be
tempted to suppose that it was the residence, or even the workmanship, of
the Deity. Yet how dull is the artifice, how insignificant is the labour, if it
be compared with the formation of the vilest insect that crawls on the
surface of the temple![48]

Gibbon hints that he found the list of Justinian's building works
tedious to repeat and draws from them a lesson of weakness, not
strength.[49] Here his scepticism served him well. He was not taken
in by Procopius' claims as to size or strength of fortifications, or
reality of urban creations: 'the new foundations of Justinian
acquired, perhaps too hastily, the epithets of impregnable and
populous', and of the forts, 'it seems reasonable to believe that the
far greater part consisted only of a stone or brick tower . . . which
was surrounded by a wall or a ditch, and afforded in a moment of
danger some protection to the peasants and cattle of the neighbouring villages'.[50] Interestingly, while J. B. Bury interposed in his
edition a defence of Justinian's fortifications, Gibbon was more
right than he knew; he could not draw on modern archaeology,[51]
and he could add only limited details from other ancient sources,
but his interest was aroused and he was alert to geography and to
the geopolitics of empire. The section broadens out into a bridge
to the narrative of the Persian war. So much for Justinian's internal
policies, which have been described for the most part only in the
light of the extremely hostile *Secret history*, and even then not fully.
Constantinople itself has been described much earlier in the
History,[52] and Gibbon does not need to repeat the description here.
But with the sharp eye that we have already noted, he makes an
observation on the city's strategic vulnerability that again is
negative in tone: the rich gardens and villas of its territory, he

---

[48] *Ibid.*, p. 248; see further below. The exemplary quality of insects is a theme also used by
Hume; Gibbon alludes here to an existing comparison between a great church and a mere
fly drawn by Berkeley, and found after him in Thomson's *Seasons*; the moral he draws,
however, favours the fly and disparages the grandiosity of the building: see Womersley,
Transformation, pp. 272–3.

[49] *Decline and fall*, ed. Bury, IV, p. 250.

[50] *Ibid.*

[51] The claims made in Procopius' *Buildings*, a formal panegyric of the emperor, need to be
treated with caution, even if sometimes they are confirmed by a remarkable discovery, as
in the case of the Nea church in Jerusalem; see Cameron, *Procopius*, ch. 6, and cf. p. 95.

[52] In chapter 17, *Decline and fall*, ed. Bury, II, pp. 140–57.

says, attracted barbarian attacks, and the emperor Anastasius
was forced to erect a long wall, a 'last frontier', which in fact
'proclaimed the impotence of his arms' and which Justinian had to
supplement.[53]

The central, narrative, part of Gibbon's presentation of Justinian
therefore owes a great deal to his reading of Procopius; if anything,
he has enhanced its implications by his narrative technique, and
sharpened its judgments by downplaying the contradictory
elements. Just as Procopius does in his *History of the wars*, Gibbon
keeps religion for separate treatment. To find his account of
Justinian's Fifth Ecumenical Council, held in AD 553–4, we have to
turn ahead to chapter 47, where he begins with the warning that a
study of Justinian's religious policies will only add to the negative
picture already formed, while confirming the impression given
in Procopius' *Secret history*. Gibbon explicitly affirms his debt to
Procopius, defending him (against Alemannus) for his 'wise and
moderate sentiments' in judging dogmatic speculation to be folly,
and deeming it sufficient to 'know that power and benevolence are
the perfect attributes of the Deity'.[54] Predictably, Gibbon chooses
to follow the 'rational' critic and in so doing implicitly to reject
the earlier view of Justinian as model Catholic emperor and
legislator.[55] He shared Procopius' disapproval of Justinian as a
persecutor and a participant in religious controversy.[56] Like
Procopius, Gibbon pours scorn on the emperor's theological
pretensions,[57] and is delighted when in old age Justinian himself
lapses from orthodoxy: 'the Jacobites [the object of Gibbon's most
withering scorn] no less than the Catholics were scandalized'.[58] The
prospect of an ecclesiastical history to be written by Procopius, as is
hinted at in the *Secret history*, struck him with a mixture of curiosity
and anticipation.[59] Gibbon had much to say about eastern

---

[53] *Ibid.*, IV, p. 253. For the vulnerability of Constantinople in relation to resources and defence see the papers in C. Mango and G. Dagron (eds.), *Constantinople and its hinterland* (Aldershot, 1995).

[54] *Decline and fall*, ed. Bury, V, p. 133.

[55] A view which had led to an outraged reaction to the publication of the *Secret history* in 1623 by Alemannus and to attacks on its authenticity. For a recent discussion of Justinian's religious policies see C. Capizzi, *Giustiniano I tra politica e religione* (Messina, 1994), and for his 'catholicism', B. Biondi, *Giustiniano Primo, principe e legislatore cattolico* (Milan, 1936).

[56] Cf. *Decline and fall*, ed. Bury, V, p. 134: 'toleration was not the virtue of the times'.

[57] As he does on the 'cowardice' of Pope Vigilius, *ibid.*, p. 137.

[58] *Ibid.*, pp. 153–5 n. 139.

[59] 'It would have been curious and impartial', *ibid.*, p. 139, n. 139.

Christianity, despite his air of fastidious disdain, and owed a
great deal to the tenth-century Arabic *Annals* of the Alexandrian
patriarch Eutychius, which he had read in the Latin translation by
Pococke.[60] But so far as Justinian was concerned, he was content to
take the hostile Procopius at face value.

What of Justinian as legislator and codifier of Roman law? Again,
Gibbon separates the discussion from the historical narrative, and
puts it in the context of a discussion of Roman law since the
Republic. Here, too, while Justinian's contribution, in the Digest,
the Institutes and the Code, is recognized and defended, the
emperor meets with criticism. Gibbon goes about his task somewhat obliquely, by first setting up the expectation that one might
have hoped for a restoration of genuine ancient Roman law, the law
of the Republic and early Empire, the law, that is, of the days of
freedom and relative freedom, before autocracy set in.[61] By this
standard Justinian must fail. Gibbon affects to recognize that time
has moved on, nor can Justinian be fairly accused of deliberate
suppression. But this is faint praise: Justinian has restored, not the
genuine Roman law of ancient times, but the jurisprudence of
the middle Empire, an achievement, it is true, but only second-best.
In his own legislation the emperor has shown traits which Gibbon
deplores: Christian severity, harsh laws on divorce and homo-
sexuality, the latter, Gibbon notes with a degree of pleasure,
resulting in the punishment of two bishops.[62] Though there were
favourable as well as unfavourable portrayals of the emperor in the
sources he has read, Gibbon prefers to dwell on the negative. He
does not even do justice to the contradictory nature of the
contemporary sources themselves.[63] Here, Justinian the emperor is
all but lost in Gibbon's own musings on Roman law;[64] when he does
re-emerge, it is as the descendant of Constantine and the Christian
emperors, the mouthpiece of religious bigotry masquerading as
Roman restoration.

---

[60] *Ibid.*, p. 155 n. 136.
[61] *Ibid.*, IV, p. 466; compare Matthews, above, pp. 25–6.
[62] *Decline and fall*, ed. Bury, IV, p. 505; for an extremely hostile modern account of Justinian,
see Tony Honoré, *Tribonian* (London, 1978), ch. 1.
[63] For which see Cameron, *Procopius*, chs. 2 and 14.
[64] On Gibbon's views see further M. H. Hoeflich, 'Edward Gibbon, Roman lawyer', *The
American Journal of Comparative Law* 39 (1991), pp. 803–18, and see also McKitterick, below,
p. 170.

The crafting of this section is as deliberate as that of the historical narrative, and it ends on the expected negative note: over the many centuries of Roman legal history (he counts from the Twelve Tables), confusion and contradiction had set in, and were only partly removed by Justinian. The new codification could not be maintained intact: only six years later Justinian issued a new edition of the Code, and 'every year, or, according to Procopius, each day of his long reign was marked by some legal innovation'.[65] The emperor was only partly successful even in what he did achieve; and even then, he removed a confusion which had acted as a measure of protection to the ordinary population. In reality, Justinian was a capricious tyrant; the chapter concludes with the words: 'the Romans were oppressed at the same time by the multiplicity of their laws and the arbitrary will of their master'.[66] The chapter as a whole is artful to a degree: it defends Justinian only to condemn him, and to leave the reader with the picture of an emperor who, far from being the Catholic legislator and bringer of order, is the instigator of change for change's sake; who is, in other words, still the Justinian of Procopius' *Secret history* who is the bringer of disorder.[67] The portrayal is worth comparing with the extremely hostile presentation of Constantine in chapter 18 of the *History*. There, too, jealousy and suspicion are highlighted;[68] much space is given to the episodes in his family history which cast discredit on the emperor,[69] and while (despite Gibbon's remarks on his later degeneration) Constantine himself is praised for firmness of moral character, he is implicitly condemned for his inability to guide the moral development of his sons.[70] No credit is given in this section to Constantine the Christian emperor, any more than it is to Justinian; that topic is reserved for chapter 20, and while Gibbon grudgingly gives Constantine the benefit of the doubt in relation to

---

[65] See Gossman, *The Empire unpossess'd*, pp. 38–9, with pp. 34–40 on Gibbon's discussion generally.

[66] *Decline and fall*, ed. Bury, IV, p. 510.

[67] See Cameron, *Procopius*, pp. 59–60; A. Carile, 'Consenso e dissenso fra propaganda a fronda nelle fonti narrative dell'età Giustinianea' in G. G. Arch (ed.), *L'imperatore Giustiniano. Storia e mito*, Giornate di studio a Ravenna, 14–16 ottobre 1976 (Milan, 1978), pp. 37–93, especially pp. 48–61.

[68] *Decline and fall*, ed. Bury, II, pp. 204–12.

[69] Especially the mysterious death of his son Crispus, *ibid.*, II, pp. 206–12, firmly attributed by Gibbon to Constantine; Gibbon elaborately dismisses the attempts of the 'modern Greeks, who adore the memory of their founder', to excuse the emperor (p. 210).

[70] *Ibid.*, II, p. 213.

the sincerity or otherwise of his religious policy, he leaves many hints with the reader that an alternative explanation is possible. He embeds the judgment, furthermore, within the much longer and famously critical account of the development of the church from the time of Constantine onwards, in which Constantine's active involvement in religious matters is explicitly termed 'despotism'.[71] Positioning of individual sections within or in relation to the broader narrative is a technique used to great effect both here and in the Justinianic section.

Gibbon's use of visual evidence in the section on Justinian is also determined by his reading of Procopius. He repeats and enlarges on the latter's sly comparison of Justinian's appearance with that of Domitian, while admitting to Procopius' malice in including it.[72] As far as Theodora is concerned, he can supplement Procopius' description of the empress in the *Secret history* by referring to 'a mosaic at Ravenna', of which he had read in Alemannus' edition.[73] Justinian's equestrian statue gave him occasion for ironic comment. To St Sophia, as we have seen, he gives a long description, based in the first place on Procopius but also drawing on other contemporary or near-contemporary Byzantine sources (Paul the Silentiary, Agathias, Evagrius) as well as the travellers Gyllius and Grelot.[74] He can therefore comment in the face of Procopius' eulogy that in fact 'the spectator is disappointed by an irregular prospect of half domes and shelving roofs', and that 'the scale of dimensions has been much surpassed by several of the Latin cathedrals'.[75] Procopius' description of the palaces on the Bosphorus is adorned with further reference to Alemannus' edition.[76] In general, however, Gibbon has little visual material on which to draw for this part of the *History*. In contrast to his treatment of Arabia later,[77] he is not tempted into an account of Athens in his own day by the story of the closing of the Academy. Francis Haskell has written recently of Gibbon's reluctance to use visual evidence except when his

---

[71] *Ibid.*, II, ch. 21; see especially *ibid.*, II, p. 354.

[72] *Decline and fall*, ed. Bury, IV, p. 430 n. 109.

[73] *Ibid.*, IV, p. 212 n. 20. This is the well-known mosaic panel of Theodora and her retinue, matched by another of Justinian, in the church of San Vitale, Ravenna (AD 547).

[74] *Ibid.*, IV, pp. 244–8; Gibbon lists his sources at p. 245 n. 103, 'among the crowd of ancients and moderns who have celebrated the edifice'.

[75] *Ibid.*, IV, p. 246.

[76] *Ibid.*, IV, p. 249 n. 108.   [77] *Ibid.*, IV, ch. 50.

knowledge was derived from literary sources,[78] and his use of Procopius' *Buildings* and concentration on topography and construction rather than visual details bears that out.

All in all, then, Gibbon presents a dark view of Justinian and his age, and especially of the vaunted recovery of the west. Belisarius is praised as being 'above the heroes of the ancient republics'; 'under his command, the subjects of Justinian often deserved to be called Romans'.[79] But Belisarius' victories and those of Narses were none the less 'encompassed with the darkest shades of disgrace and calamity'.[80] The emperor undermined his generals; and even the Gothic victories, by denuding defences, allowed new barbarian invaders to cross the Danube. By a forced turn, the invasions of Gepids, Lombards and Slavs were made contingent on the victories over the Goths; moreover, they were followed by the immediate appearance of the Turks.

Gibbon found in Justinian's major historian, Procopius, a critical view which allowed him to preserve the closure laid down in his account of the fall of the western Empire, and to give a detailed narrative of Justinian's conquests without having to admit that they had significantly reversed the course of history. His references to the personal grievances of Procopius and to the bias of the *Secret history* look like objective criticism, and obscure the true extent of his own collusion with the general interpretation which he found there.

Something of the contradictions in Gibbon's account, as well as in that of his model, can be seen from his various attempts to position the reign of Justinian in the general context of Roman rule and Greek decline. He can write that by the end of the sixth century, Rome 'had reached the lowest point of her depression'.[81] Yet a further peak in the narrative is reached with the reign of Heraclius, 'of the characters conspicuous in history . . . one of the most extraordinary and inconsistent', and from whose reign 'Byzantine' history was to be reckoned, in eight hundred years from the reign of Heraclius to the Turkish conquest.[82] Gibbon's dilemma

---

[78] F. Haskell, *History and its images* (New Haven, 1993), p. 187.

[79] *Decline and fall*, ed. Bury, IV, pp. 340–1.

[80] *Ibid.*, IV, p. 342.   [81] *Ibid.*, V, p. 31.

[82] *Ibid.*, V, p. 169, but see p. 170, where he seems to count from the reign of Maurice.

is apparent. The implication is that Justinian was still to be regarded as 'Roman',[83] whereas his earlier narrative of Justinian's reign had implied, or even stated, the opposite. Justinian, he says there,[84] denied to Belisarius the chance to restore the Roman name, and confirmed the rule of 'the Greeks': 'the appellation of Greeks was imposed as a term of reproach by the haughty Goths'. In the same passage, Justinian's armies are assigned to the enervated and unwarlike climate of 'Asia', rather than the manly air of 'Europe'. A Janus-like figure in many accounts, not least that of Procopius, Gibbon's Justinian has not escaped the same fate.

Challenged to write an account of the sixth century, Gibbon found himself faced by problems both of organization and of interpretation. In his general picture, Justinian belonged within the rhythm of decline which he ascribed to the Christian emperors from Constantine onwards, and to the line of so-called 'Greeks' whose history Gibbon found so depressing. Yet there was also a sense in which the reconquest, like Justinian's codification of Roman law, interrupted Gibbon's narrative, and interposed a 'Roman', rather than a 'Greek', interpretation. The work of Procopius, in which such contradictions were resolved by reducing them to questions of personal moral character, provided Gibbon with a way out of the dilemma, which he thankfully adopted, the more so since many aspects of Procopius' historical approach – notably his religious detachment, his seeming rationalism and his distrust of autocracy – corresponded with his own. Having not only accepted but even accentuated Procopius' categories of analysis, Gibbon also accepted Procopius' limitations. He produced a Justinian who could only be explained in the cardboard terms of tyrannical autocrat and religious bigot. It is not to be wondered at, then, if he did not succeed in forging out of his narrative of this period a wholly convincing bridge between the view expressed in the 'General observations' and the long narrative of Greek decline expressed in the remaining part of the *Decline and fall*.

[83] 'The line of empire, which had been defined by the laws of Justinian and the arms of Belisarius, recedes on all sides from our view: the Roman name, the proper subject of our inquiries, is reduced to a narrow corner of Europe', *ibid.*, v, p. 169.

[84] *Ibid.*, IV, p. 341.

CHAPTER 3

Gibbon and the middle period of
the Byzantine Empire

J. D. Howard-Johnston

That small fraction of the *Decline and fall* which dealt with the Byzantine Empire in its early medieval heyday had a profound effect on subsequent scholarly explorations of the subject, especially in the English-speaking world. The rhetorical artifice with which Gibbon expounded his views worked best on those nurtured in his native language. For who, apart from those with an extreme aversion to the Latinate mode of English prose, could fail to respond to the rolling periods, the rich vocabulary, the grave and not-so-grave irony of Gibbon? His Byzantium was projected onto the collective mind of the educated classes – an oriental despotism presenting 'a dead uniformity of abject vices', in which the effects of civil or domestic slavery were compounded by 'the spiritual despotism, which shackles not only the actions but even the thoughts of the prostrate votary'.[1] His greatest anglophone successor, J. B. Bury, was happy to assume the role of scholiast to the *Decline and fall*, confining his own independent contributions to Byzantine studies mainly to articles and two important monographs on the ninth century.[2] The general trend, though, has been one of reaction. British, American and Australian Byzantinists have sought out the distinguishing features of Byzantium, sometimes approaching the position of Arnold Toynbee who made it the one thing it evidently was not, a free-standing civilization, distinct from its late Roman predecessor. They have rushed to the defence of Byzantine culture, even if their case has often rested more on the historical interest of texts and artefacts than their literary or artistic merit.

---

[1] *Decline and fall*, ed. Bury, v, p. 170.
[2] J. B. Bury, *The imperial administrative system in the ninth century* (London, 1911) and *A history of the eastern Roman Empire from the fall of Irene to the accession of Basil I (AD 802–867)* (London, 1912).

Gibbon gives relatively short shrift to the main middle period of the Byzantine Empire. Chapter 48 presents a potted history of court politics spanning five and a half centuries, from the definitive loss of Rome's rich Near Eastern provinces which had occurred by the time of the death of Heraclius in 641 to the capture of Constantinople by the forces of Latin Christendom in 1204. The opening part of chapter 49 outlines the history of icon-veneration and the first, early medieval, outbreak of iconoclasm. The activities of the learned partisans of Catholicism and Protestantism, busily amassing arsenals of arguments in favour of their opposed causes, like their distant Byzantine precursors, naturally drew Gibbon's attention both to the topic and to their own antics. But Gibbon's most important contribution is made in chapter 53. Here he delineates the main structural features of the Byzantine state in the tenth century, working up from its economic base through its institutional and military articulation to its cultural production. He concludes, in a memorable peroration, that the Byzantines

held in their lifeless hands the riches of their fathers, without inheriting the spirit which had created and improved that sacred patrimony: they read, they praised, they compiled, but their languid souls seemed alike incapable of thought and action. In the revolution of ten centuries, not a single discovery was made to exalt the dignity or promote the happiness of mankind. Not a single idea has been added to the speculative systems of antiquity, and a succession of patient disciples became in their turn the dogmatic teachers of the next servile generation.[3]

Of course, the case is overstated. The *rhetor* has overpowered the historian in Gibbon. But none but the most starry-eyed of Byzantinists can fail to be impressed by the thrust of Gibbon's argument which is aimed unerringly at the vital parts of the subject. Although no historian's style could be further removed from Gibbon's, Cyril Mango, the most distinguished holder of the Bywater and Sotheby Chair of Byzantine and Modern Greek Language and Literature at Gibbon's old university, has reached broadly similar conclusions. In his lapidary prose and with his own dry brand of wit, he has argued cogently that Byzantine writers belonged to a small, insulated, metropolitan world. They formed coteries, angled for the favour of the great and the good of the day,

---

[3] *Decline and fall*, ed. Bury, VI, p. 107.

operated ingeniously but contentedly largely within the confines of inherited late antique forms, and never succeeded in activating properly their imagination or in engaging fully with great issues.[4]

This brief analysis of Gibbon's domestic history begins from a fundamentally pro-Gibbonian position. There may also reasonably be a presumption of erudition, since Gibbon flagged his commitment to scholarship in his early *Essai sur l'étude de la littérature* and demonstrated its range and depth in the first four volumes of the *Decline and fall*. The analysis will take the form of a brief survey of the contents of each of the two chapters and part-chapter itemized above, interspersed with comments which take stock of current learned opinion. Some general conclusions will be offered at the end.

After outlining the ground which he will cover in his last two volumes, at the start of chapter 48, Gibbon justifies an acceleration in his pace by the nature of his subject. His line is that contraction of empire, decline of morals and ossification of thought render early medieval Byzantium unworthy of close probing by a historian: 'a prolix and slender thread would be spun through many a volume . . . the annals of each succeeding reign would impose a more ungrateful and melancholy task. These annals must continue to repeat a tedious and uniform tale of weakness and misery.'[5]

These withering remarks seem to bespeak a limited conception of history, suggesting as they do that the historian should attend to achievements, to what is uplifting and to progress rather than the nondescript, let alone decay and degradation. It is not an outlook which many of us share, nor indeed was it Gibbon's, since he was ready to plunge whole-heartedly into the depressing story of the final phase of Byzantine decline, after the Fourth Crusade, and brought the full armoury of his scholarship to bear on this last part of his project.[6] It appears rather to be a pose, assumed for a while, to explain or excuse the skimpiness of what is to follow on the middle period.

The main body of the chapter is narrowly focussed on the court and the character of individual rulers. Gibbon feeds on the fare, mostly rather thin gruel, provided by Byzantine chroniclers and

---

[4] Cyril Mango, *Byzantium. The Empire of new Rome* (London, 1980), chs. 6 and 13.
[5] *Decline and fall*, ed. Bury, v, p. 169.   [6] Bryer, below, pp. 101–16.

historians. He is eager to find entertaining anecdotes which he may serve up, but has to make do with a few scraps until he reaches the middle of the twelfth century and the long tale of extraordinary adventures, amorous and military, of Andronicus Comnenus. Throughout the chapter he strives to liven up his narrative, sometimes straying beyond what is warranted by a cool appraisal of the sources. He is writing an eighteenth-century version of the classicizing history favoured in late antiquity. His basic material, which may be categorized as the higher tabloid, is embellished with snatches of direct speech, moralizing interjections, occasional historical generalizations and numerous *bon môts*.

For the most part, he is pulled hither and thither by the bias in his sources. Emperors vilified by contemporary psogists (whose pamphlets have left indelible marks on later chronicles), such as Justinian II, Nicephorus I and Michael III, are Gibbon's targets too. 'Calumny', he believes, 'is more prone to exaggerate than to invent; and her licentious tongue is checked in some measure by the experience of the age and country to which she appeals.'[7] This is a charitable but almost certainly an ill-founded supposition, especially when it is applied to the culture of an autocracy in which the genre had a long pedigree and anonymity could shield an author from reprisals. There is plenty of fiction in the detritus of Byzantine psogs (lampoons) which has come down to us. Indeed skill in detecting and discarding psogical fancies is a *sine qua non* of Byzantine scholarship in the late twentieth century.[8]

The minority of emperors who were fortunate enough to get a good press or who are extolled in extant *encomia* rank on the whole high in Gibbon's estimation. His list is headed by John Comnenus. It also includes Basil I, the subject of a laudatory biography commissioned by his grandson Constantine Porphyrogenitus,

[7] *Decline and fall*, ed. Bury, v, p. 187.
[8] The importance of the genre was recognized over a century ago by H. F. Tozer, 'Byzantine satire', *Journal of Hellenic Studies* 2 (1881), pp. 233–70, but a systematic study of its development in the Byzantine period is still awaited. *Psogos* was one of the fourteen types of prose composition listed in the *Progymnasmata* of Aphthonius, an influential rhetorical textbook written at the end of the fourth century: G. L. Kustas, *Studies in Byzantine rhetoric* (Thessalonica, 1973), pp. 22–3. The most notable extant example is the *Secret history* of Procopius, ed. and trans. H. B. Dewing (London and Cambridge, Mass., 1935). Another choice specimen, which portrayed Photius as a precursor of Faust, is embedded in summary form in a text not known to Gibbon, the *Annales* of Ps.-Symeon Magister, ed. I. Bekker, *Corpus Scriptorum Historiae Byzantinae* (Bonn, 1838), pp. 668–74.

Basil II (who lacks an *encomium* but joins this company because of his undoubted military achievements), and two much-praised Comneni, Alexius and Manuel.

There are, however, occasions when Gibbon asserts his independence. He peels off the upper layer of iconophile prejudice in the early ninth-century chronicle of Theophanes, and thus rehabilitates the eighth-century emperors Leo III (briefly) and his son Constantine V (at greater length, noting his public works, his undeniable and undenied military achievements and his posthumous reputation). The generalization with which he introduces the reign of Theophilus (829–42) (which does not entirely square with the thrust of his opening sally about the history of Byzantium) leads the reader to think that Theophilus too will be re-assessed. 'The wisdom of a sovereign is comprised in the institution of laws and the choice of magistrates, and, while he seems without action, his civil government revolves round his centre with the silence and order of the planetary system.'[9] But instead of acting as the cue for a careful scrutiny of the emperor who defended Asia Minor against the last sustained Arab offensive and sponsored a revival of scholarship,[10] this observation is left hanging in the air, and Gibbon, taking his lead from the Continuators of Theophanes, portrays Theophilus as the very type of the oriental despot, arbitrarily dispensing justice.

An apologia for a chapter which races through time and is not buttressed by footnotes is introduced at the end:

In a composition of some days, in a perusal of some hours, six hundred years have rolled away, and the duration of a life or reign is contracted to a fleeting moment; the grave is ever beside the throne; the success of a criminal is almost instantly followed by the loss of his prize; and our immortal reason survives and disdains the sixty phantoms of kings, who have passed before our eyes and faintly dwell on our remembrance.[11]

In chapter 49 Gibbon deals with the iconoclast controversy as it unfolded in the east in the eighth century, before turning to its consequences in the west (and their effect on relations between the two halves of Christendom). Ecclesiastical history as usual brings

---

[9] *Decline and fall*, ed. Bury, v, p. 197.
[10] Warren Treadgold, *The Byzantine revival 780–842* (Stanford, 1988), ch. 5.
[11] *Decline and fall*, ed. Bury, v, pp. 242–3.

out the best of his scholarship and wit. The text is now underpinned by footnotes packed with learning and peppered with mordant remarks. The historian watches with a certain lofty and amused disdain the past exertions of Catholic and Protestant antiquarians and is confident that 'with this mutual aid, and opposite tendency, it is easy for *us* to poise the balance with philosophic indifference'.[12]

An excellent account is given of the growth of icon-veneration in the late antique Christian empire. It stole by insensible degrees into the church: the cult of the saints opened the way, an icon being a memorial 'more interesting than the skull or the sandals of a departed worthy';[13] gradually the use of icons became more public and was justified by their educative function; then 'the scruples of reason, or piety, were silenced by the strong evidence of visions and miracles';[14] and finally the mortal frame of Christ was portrayed, otherwise 'the spiritual worship of Christ might have been obliterated by the visible relics and representations of the saints'.[15] A firm date is established for the completion of this process by reference to the first securely attested public appearance of the Mandelion (the perfect impression of Christ's face on a linen towel) at Edessa. A powerful argument from silence leads Gibbon, as also latterly Averil Cameron, to place the manufacture of the image after the Persian siege of 540 (in fact 544), since Procopius breathes not a word of it in his full account of the episode.[16] It is a learned exposition, based mainly on material quarried from Basnage's *Histoire des églises réformées*.

Gibbon then notes, in passing, that eastern Christendom never proved receptive to statuary (for the obvious reason that it was too closely associated with idolatry), in the course of a side-swipe at the quality of early Christian painting – 'The Olympian Jove, created by the muse of Homer and the chisel of Phidias, might inspire a philosophic mind with momentary devotion; but these Catholic images were faintly and flatly delineated by monkish artists in the last degeneracy of taste and genius.' This then prompts him to pen one of his most entertaining footnotes – ' "Your scandalous figures stand quite out from the canvas: they are as bad a group of statues!"

12 *Ibid.*, v, p. 251 n. 18.   13 *Ibid.*, v, p. 245.
14 *Ibid.*, v, p. 246.   15 *Ibid.*, v, p. 246.
16 Averil Cameron, *Continuity and change in sixth-century Byzantium* (London, 1981), ch. v, 'The sceptic and the shroud'.

It was thus that the ignorance and bigotry of a Greek priest applauded the pictures of Titian, which he had ordered, and refused to accept.'[17]

Various reasons are suggested for the mood of revulsion against icons which swept over Byzantium in the eighth century. The absence of early documents sanctioning their use encouraged dissident voices among 'many simple or rational Christians'.[18] There was also continuing resistance in the remoter parts of Asia Minor from sections of its heterogeneous population. But the principal explanation, for Gibbon as for Peter Brown, was to be found in the intellectual and emotional reaction to the catastrophes of the seventh century.[19] The charge of idolatry was levelled with renewed force against eastern Christendom, by Jews and Mohametans. 'The servitude of the Jews might curb their zeal and depreciate their authority; but the triumphant Musulmans, who reigned at Damascus and threatened Constantinople, cast into the scale of reproach the accumulated weight of truth and victory.'[20] The accession of Leo III in 717 before long gave the opposition forces access to the powers of church and state. Gibbon charts the development of official iconoclasm step by step, up to the Council of Hieria in 754, at which he suspects that 'a large majority of the prelates sacrificed their secret conscience to the temptations of hope and fear'.[21] He then watches, with a certain confusion of the emotions, as Constantine V institutes a general persecution of monks, champions of icons and as such his chief adversaries. Avarice was a second important motive for his attack on these 'faithful slaves of the superstition to which they owed their riches and influence',[22] a suggestion of Gibbon's which foreshadows the materialistic explanations offered by some twentieth-century historians.

Gibbon's history of iconophilism and iconoclasm is in a different league from the political history presented in the previous chapter. It is learned and entertaining. The evidence, much sifted by his clerically programmed predecessors, is handled judiciously,

---

[17] *Decline and fall*, ed. Bury, v, p. 249 and n. 14.

[18] *Ibid.*, v, p. 250.

[19] Peter Brown, 'A dark age crisis: aspects of the iconoclastic controversy' in *Society and the holy in late antiquity* (London, 1982), pp. 251–301.

[20] *Decline and fall*, ed. Bury, v, p. 250.

[21] *Ibid.*, v, p. 253. [22] *Ibid.*, v, p. 254.

and sound conclusions, which stand the test of time, are reached. At the end, Gibbon turns away to follow the trail west to Italy, where the Papacy took the lead in opposing iconoclasm and sponsoring rebellion. This initially took the form of withholding revenue, including that raised by the recently introduced poll-tax, which, Gibbon notes in a happy aside, was denounced as most cruel by the zealous Maimbourg but 'most unluckily for the historian, it was imposed a few years afterwards in France by his patron Louis XIV'.[23] The dispute was soon to result in the loss of Ravenna to the Lombards and the Carolingian intervention in Mediterranean politics.

Gibbon begins chapter 53 with a survey and a not altogether flattering appreciation of the compilations of Constantine Porphyrogenitus and his father Leo VI. Between them these provide a unique assemblage of official and literary material on different aspects of the practical functioning of the state and society in Byzantium and its relations with the wider world.[24] Considerable erudition is displayed in the footnotes. Editions and locations of key manuscripts are specified, with the occasional barbed comment. Thus, after noting the wanderings of a splendid manuscript of the *De cerimoniis* on its way to Leipzig, Gibbon cites the *editio princeps* of Leich and Reiske of 1751–4, adding that it was published 'with such slavish praise as editors never fail to bestow on the worthy or worthless object of their toil'.[25] These imperially sponsored texts open a window onto the middle Byzantine state in the tenth century, and Gibbon, like his antiquarian predecessors (Du Cange is rightly singled out for praise) and his successors, peers through at what is revealed after the passage of three dark centuries. He supplements their information with material taken from Byzantine chronicles covering the period and the sharp-eyed observations of a disenchanted western ambassador, Liudprand of Cremona.

One category of source, though, comes in for severe criticism.

---

[23] *Ibid.*, v, p. 260 n. 38.
[24] Constantine has attracted more scholarly attention than his father: see, for example, Paul Lemerle, *Le premier humanisme byzantin* (Paris, 1971), ch. 10, and Ihor Ševčenko, 'Re-reading Constantine Porphyrogenitus' in Jonathan Shepard and Simon Franklin (eds.), *Byzantine diplomacy* (Aldershot, 1992), pp. 167–95.
[25] *Decline and fall*, ed. Bury, VI, p. 62, n. 2.

The lives of the saints, and in particular the new edition prepared in the late tenth century by Symeon the Metaphrast, are characterized as a 'dark fund of superstition . . . enriched by the fabulous and florid legends' of the editor. 'The merits and miracles of the whole calendar are of less account in the eyes of a sage than the toil of a single husbandman, who multiplies the gifts of the Creator and supplies the food of his brethren.'[26] Gibbon's disdain is directed mainly at the (unproductive) activity of saints, but is extended to embrace the texts which describe them. In neither respect can his attitude be justified. The holy man, who appeared in many guises and in a whole range of milieux, played a vital mediating role throughout Byzantine society, from the peasant villages at its base to the emperors and their great magnates at its apex.[27] No greater mistake could be made by a historian in search of information and understanding of Byzantium in its early medieval heyday than to disregard the rich stream of Byzantine hagiography. The authors attended far more to the realities of life and the specific characteristics and acts of their heroes than to the demands of the genre. Hence, as long as due allowance is made for the conceptual framework imposed by religious belief on the work of individual hagiographers (and their individual quirks), the lives of the Byzantine saints yield information of great value to historians, especially to historians concerned with economic and social institutions. In addition, the conceptual framework itself and its slow evolution over the centuries can be used as a means of direct entry into the ambient thought-world of hagiographers, their subjects, their readership and society at large. Gibbon, whose principal concern was with economic, social and intellectual history, immeasurably impoverishes his study of Byzantium in the tenth century, by cutting himself off from this vital source of information.

In the course of the chapter, Gibbon first examines the economic base of the Byzantine state. He then considers its constitution and performance in war, before concluding with a sketch of its intellectual and literary output. His stance on each of these subjects

---

[26] *Ibid.*, VI, p. 64–5.
[27] Peter Brown, 'The rise and function of the holy man in late antiquity' in his *Society and the holy in late antiquity*, pp. 103–52; Sergei Hackel (ed.), *The Byzantine saint* (London, 1981).

will be discussed in turn below. But it should be noted at the outset that there is a certain discordance if his conclusions are put together. For the spirit of individual and collective enterprise which he discerns in the economic sphere seems to be entirely confined to it. All political initiative has been squeezed out of society, even its highest echelons, by its inherited repressive regime. In war Byzantium's performance is feeble, for lack of martial qualities in its population; while in peace, in educated circles, inertia reigns and no writer is capable of introducing fresh insight or escaping from the tyranny of tradition which prizes complexity and obscurity much more than simplicity and clarity. In the end the reader is left without an explanation for the extraordinary endurance shown by Byzantium over eight centuries, except for the assertion that it could buy its way out of trouble with the wealth generated in the one sphere where initiative and energy were to the fore.

Since he recognizes the pervasive influence of the material environment on the social order and state structure in all historical epochs, Gibbon turns first to the economy of tenth-century Byzantium. Immediately he encounters a frustrating dearth of information about population, taxation and troop strengths. He is forced therefore to rely on the limited, anecdotal evidence supplied by chroniclers (and medieval travellers) and his own presumption about wider economic circumstances in the east Mediterranean in the early Middle Ages. The economic scene which he conjures up is remarkably cheerful and unGibbonian.

In spite of the pernicious effects of prayer and fasting on the capacity of individuals to work, in spite of the loss of labour to unproductive monasticism and the loss of working days to religious festivals, Gibbon characterizes the Byzantines as 'the more dexterous and diligent of nations' and gives their economy a glowing testimonial:

their country was blessed by nature with every advantage of soil, climate, and situation; and, in the support and restoration of the arts, their patient and peaceful temper was more useful than the warlike spirit and feudal anarchy of Europe. The provinces that still adhered to the empire were repeopled and enriched by the misfortunes of those which were irrecoverably lost. From the yoke of the caliphs, the Catholics of Syria, Egypt, and Africa, retired to the allegiance of their prince, to the society of their brethren: the movable wealth, which eludes the search of oppression, accompanied and alleviated their exile; and Constantinople received into her bosom the fugitive trade of Alexandria and Tyre.[28]

He quarries positive evidence that industry flourished in Greece from a variety of sources, and is ready to extrapolate from it. He envisages wealth streaming towards the centre in the form of plentiful cash revenues, and has some of it recycled to stimulate further wealth-creation. He approves of imperial building programmes, such as Basil I's, since they fed industry, however useless (in Gibbon's terms) some of the individual structures might be.

These conclusions of Gibbon, with the exception of his comments on the beneficial effects of state-spending, are diametrically opposed to modern perceptions of the early medieval economy and of Byzantium's role within it. For there can be no doubt that Islam, far from depressing economic activity in the vast tracts of the Near East and Mediterranean world which it conquered, promoted long-distance commercial exchange, urban growth and highly differentiated industrial production on an unprecedented scale. The evidence is to hand in the material remains of the cities which grew up then, and in texts of all sorts, most notably the geographies written in the tenth century for the information and delectation of a widely dispersed urban readership with an avowed interest in trade. The explanation for economic growth at this pace and on this scale is to be sought in an Arab ethos, which had long prized mercantile activity, and in the early establishment of an Islamic single market with no artificial impediments to trade.[29]

Far from there being a flight of capital and entrepreneurs from Islam to Byzantium, there was an increasing concentration of economic activity within the Caliphate and a steady eastward movement of its commercial centre of gravity, away from the shores of the Mediterranean and into the continental interior. Byzantium continued to play a part in long-distance trade, but from an increasingly marginal position. And there were many signs of relative impoverishment, chief among them the near-universal decline of provincial urban life. Cities dwindled in size, building standards fell, and their old elites vanished, leaving behind only a

---

[28] *Decline and fall*, ed. Bury, VI, p. 69.
[29] Xavier de Planhol, *Les fondements géographiques de l'histoire de l'Islam* (Paris, 1968); Maurice Lombard, *L'Islam dans sa première grandeur (VIIIe–XIe siècle)* (Paris, 1971).

rump of local government officials and episcopal staff.[30] Even in Constantinople, squalor was everywhere to be seen if a traveller looked behind the magnificent façades of the grand public buildings and private residences inherited from late antiquity.[31] So unobtrusive indeed was Byzantium's economic presence on the fringe of the Caliphate, that one distinguished Islamicist forgot about Byzantium's existence altogether when he wrote a masterly sketch of Islamic civilization in its early medieval heyday, and, later, assumed, unless there were specific indications to the contrary, that references to Rumi traders in the archives of the Cairo Geniza were to west Europeans, thereby diminishing Byzantium's involvement in the Egyptian market.[32]

Gibbon fares better, but only a little better, when he shifts his gaze to the constitution and social order. For a brief while, Byzantine autocracy wears eighteenth-century apparel:

The princes of Constantinople were far removed from the simplicity of nature; yet, with the revolving seasons, they were led by taste or fashion to withdraw to a purer air from the smoke and tumult of the capital. They enjoyed, or affected to enjoy, the rustic festival of the vintage; their leisure was amused by the exercise of the chase, and the calmer occupation of fishing; and in the summer heats they were shaded from the sun and refreshed by the cooling breezes from the sea. The coasts and islands of Asia and Europe were covered with their magnificent villas . . . [33]

But soon it resumes the aspect of oriental despotism. The authority of the emperor is absolute. He is the sole fountain of honour; titles and offices are bestowed and resumed at his arbitrary will; distinctions of noble and plebeian birth are levelled and all subjects abase themselves before him in what Gibbon calls a prostitution of 'the most humble postures, which devotion has applied to the Supreme Being'.[34] Consequently 'a lethargy of servitude' benumbs the minds of the Byzantines.[35]

The loss of almost all secular records leaves Gibbon, as it leaves

---

[30] Cyril Mango, *Byzantium*, ch. 3.
[31] Paul Magdalino, *The Empire of Manuel I Komnenos, 1143–1180* (Cambridge, 1993), pp. 109–23.
[32] S. D. Goitein, 'The intermediate civilization. The Hellenic heritage in Islam', *Studies in Islamic history and institutions* (Leiden, 1966), pp. 54–70, and *A Mediterranean society*, vol. 1 *Economic foundations* (Berkeley and Los Angeles, 1967), pp. 42–59.
[33] *Decline and fall*, ed. Bury, VI, p. 75.
[34] *Ibid.*, VI, p. 83.   [35] *Ibid.*, VI, p. 90.

his latter-day successors, with no choice but to attempt to reconstruct the governmental system from a hierarchically ordered list of ranks which chances to have survived. At this point, though, Gibbon flounders. He is unaware that the key such text, the *Cletorologium* of Philotheus, compiled on the orders of the emperor Leo VI in 899, is embedded in Leich and Reiske's edition of the *De cerimoniis* of Constantine Porphyrogenitus.[36] Instead he turns to a *fourteenth-century* list of ranks, that of Ps.-Codinus, and grafts information about court titles extracted from it onto the tenth-century material which he is using in this chapter.[37] Confusion results, which is much confounded by his preoccupation with autocracy and its immediate environment, the court and high-ranking courtiers.

His concern with titles leads Gibbon both to exaggerate the power of the emperor, and, more important, to ignore the bureaucratic armature of the state and the development of a powerful and far from cowed aristocracy. For emperors were much weaker than he supposes, except perhaps at moments of great crisis when all minds were focussed on the common struggle for survival against overmighty foes. A new aristocracy grew up in the eighth and ninth centuries, initially mainly within the military (and, to a lesser extent, the civilian) apparatus of government. Soon successful individuals began to consolidate their positions and entrench their families' status by acquiring landed property, land providing them and their descendants with useful bases outside the official world of government for the development of additional, local clientages. By the early tenth century, the various nexuses in which these families were allied formed powerful vested interests (they were collectively termed 'the powerful') and were viewed by the imperial authority as a dangerous threat to the traditional social order and the efficient functioning of the state.

Autocracy was far from absolute in Byzantium. Even titles were not entirely within the arbitrary gift of emperors, since they were traditionally correlated with grades of office. There was more constraint over the allocation of office, since rival nexuses of power

---

[36] *De cerimoniis*, ii, 52–4, eds. H. Leich and I. Reiske, vol. ii (Leipzig, 1754), pp. 406–61. The fullest commentary is Bury's *The imperial administrative system in the ninth century*; the most recent (including a revised edition of the text) is that of Nicholas Oikonomidès, *Les listes de préséance byzantines des IXe et Xe siècles* (Paris, 1972).

[37] Modern edition: Pseudo-Kodinos, *Traité des offices*, ed. Jean Verpeaux (Paris, 1966).

entertained expectations which an emperor would ignore at his peril. Appointments, like the whole process of government, at the centre and in the provinces, involved much delicate balancing of competing interests and much negotiation. Emperors needed a whole range of powers to master their great magnates – military force, overt and covert, legislation and exhortation which went hand in hand, wealth far exceeding that of any aristocratic family, and the whole panoply of court ceremonial, one of the principal functions of which was to entrench the imperial authority in the collective mind of court and governing apparatus. Many Byzantinists now go so far as to assert that the imperial authority steadily lost ground over the tenth and eleventh centuries, that all its powers were ultimately unable to halt the rise of the aristocracy, and that the aristocratic nexus of Comneni, Ducae and Bryennii which was victorious at the end of the eleventh century had to devise a new management system making use of aristocratic forms and connections in order to maintain its control.[38]

Why then did Gibbon go so far astray? Why did he envisage a universal servitude of Byzantine subjects to an autocracy which was absolute? Why did he suppose that servitude in turn engendered widespread attitudes of servility? He suffered from one grave disadvantage: he had no knowledge of the legislation of tenth-century emperors directed against 'the powerful';[39] hence he could not take the easy, direct route, followed by his successors, into a field central to his historical approach – the study of the social order and its evolution as it was articulated and revealed in law-codes and legislation. He was therefore hampered in identifying the prime moving social forces in Byzantine history, forces which might increase or decrease the material resources available to the state, which might promote or discourage the circulation and mutation of ideas. However, there were other more sinuous routes into the

---

[38] George Ostrogorsky, *History of the Byzantine state* (Oxford, 1968); Rosemary Morris, 'The powerful and the poor in tenth-century Byzantium: law and reality', *Past and Present* 73 (1976), pp. 3–27; Paul Lemerle, *The agrarian history of Byzantium from the origins to the twelfth century* (Galway, 1979); Michael Angold (ed.), *The Byzantine aristocracy IX to XII centuries* (Oxford, 1984) and *The Byzantine Empire 1025–1204* (London and New York, 1984); Jean-Claude Cheynet, *Pouvoir et contestations à Byzance (963–1210)* (Paris, 1990); Michel Kaplan, *Les hommes et la terre à Byzance du VIe au XIe siècle* (Paris, 1992).

[39] Ed. K. E. Zachariae von Lingenthal, *Jus graeco-romanum*, vol. III (Leipzig, 1857); modern edition, Nicolas Svoronos, *Les novelles des empereurs macédoniens concernant la terre et les stratiotes* (Athens, 1994).

subject, which he could have taken. There are numerous passages in the chronicles used by him (the Continuatus of Theophanes and Cedrenus) which refer to the growing confrontation between emperors and 'the powerful' in the tenth century, and Anna Comnena and Zonaras (both much cited by Gibbon) give full accounts of the manoeuvrings of magnate families and their affinities, both before and after the Comnenian *putsch*. An attentive reading of these available narrative sources should have alerted him to the existence, independent attitudes and growing importance of the Byzantine aristocracy. In the event, the texts only triggered a fleeting awareness of this aspect of Byzantine history: in an aside embedded in chapter 48, Gibbon notes the appearance of those tell-tale markers of aristocratic self-consciousness, namely surnames, *à propos* of the rise of Comneni in the mid-eleventh century.[40]

The military performance of Byzantium is the third principal topic covered in this chapter. There is a certain ambivalence in the discussion. Gibbon is well aware of Byzantine expertise in the arts of war, since he is familiar with the *Tactica* of the Emperor Leo VI which documents it.[41] Byzantine naval and military technology, he recognizes, was as advanced as that of the Arabs and well ahead of that of Latin Christendom; their equipment was satisfactory (though he notes that Leo urged more archery practice to improve that arm); and their order of battle, consisting as it normally did of two lines and a reserve, combined offensive capability with defensive security. They also had the wealth necessary to fund naval

---

[40] 'From this night of slavery, a ray of freedom, or at least of spirit, begins to emerge: the Greeks either preserved or revived the use of surnames, which perpetuate the fame of hereditary virtue; and we now discern the rise, succession, and alliances of the last dynasties of Constantinople and Trebizond' (*Decline and fall*, ed. Bury, v, p. 220). Cf. Evelyne Patlagean, 'Les débuts d'une aristocratie byzantine et le témoignage de l'historiographie: système des noms et liens de parenté au IXe–Xe siècles' in Michael Angold (ed.), *The Byzantine aristocracy*, pp. 23–43.

[41] Gibbon inclines to attribute the text to Constantine Porphyrogenitus, but is aware of the alternative (correct) attribution to his father. He notes that there are deficiencies in the edition of the learned John Lami (Florence, 1745) which he uses and suggests that it may be improved by recourse to material in the imperial library of Vienna. Lami's edition, which was reproduced in J.-P. Migne, ed., *Patrologia Graeca* (162 vols., Paris, 1857–66), vol. cvii (1863), cols. 669–1094, remains the only complete edition of the text. R. Vári's revised edition, *Leonis imperatoris Tactica*, vols i and ii, 1 (Budapest, 1917–22), which halts at xiv, 38, does not quite reach the half-way mark.

and military action on a large scale,[42] and the central political authority vital for the direction and coordination of operations. Gibbon therefore appreciates the importance of the naval and military component in Byzantine statecraft, which, of course, relied on other types of action (propaganda, diplomacy, client-management and covert operations) to defend or forward Byzantine interests.

None the less he disparages the navy and army which ensured Byzantium's survival against manifold external dangers through a dark age prolonged over two and a half centuries, and which then recovered broad swathes of lost territory under the Macedonian dynasty. The vital element of individual courage was missing, he insists, contrasting the ethos of the Byzantines with what Leo characterized as the mindless courage of the Franks.[43] He takes Byzantine insistence that war be approached in a scientific manner, with careful planning and calculation of benefits and risks, as evidence of trepidation in the face of battle. His concluding turn, including some digs at Constantine Porphyrogenitus, provides another example of rhetoric bowling over historical judgment:

But neither authority nor art could frame the most important machine, the soldier himself; and, if the *ceremonies* of Constantine always suppose the safe and triumphal return of the emperor, his *tactics* seldom soar above the means of escaping a defeat and procrastinating the war. Notwithstanding some transient success, the Greeks were sunk in their own esteem and that of their neighbours. A cold hand and a loquacious tongue was the vulgar description of the nation; the author of the Tactics was besieged in his capital; and the last of the barbarians, who trembled at the name of the Saracens or Franks, could proudly exhibit the medals of gold and silver which they had extorted from the feeble sovereign of Constantinople. What spirit their government and character denied, might have been inspired in some degree by the influence of religion; but the religion of the Greeks could only teach them to suffer and to yield.[44]

This piece of polemic is capped by two comparisons, neither favourable to Byzantium. The enemy of bigotry, who should have

---

[42] Gibbon cites what is still some of the best evidence of Byzantine naval and military capability, a set of documents detailing the forces sent by Leo against Crete in 911, together with information about their pay and equipment, which is included in *De cerimoniis*, ii, 44.

[43] Leo, *Tactica*, xviii, 80–98, ed. Migne, *Patrologia Graeca*, cvii, cols. 965–68, a section based on the late sixth-century *Strategicum* of Maurice.

[44] *Decline and fall*, ed. Bury, VI, p. 95.

deplored Islamic *jihad*, contrasts the 'base superstition' of the Greeks which imparted no impetus to their military endeavours with the 'high-spirited enthusiasm' of Islam. His 'philosophic eye' sees, with evident approval, that 'the vital though latent spark of fanaticism still glowed in the heart of their religion, and among the Saracens who dwelt on the Christian borders it was frequently rekindled to a lively and active flame'.[45] He then turns to the other great power centre in early medieval western Eurasia, the Carolingian Empire which, by the tenth century, had shattered into a multitude of warring lordships. It was a world in which 'every peasant was a soldier, and every village a fortification; each wood or valley was a scene of murder and rapine; and the lords of each castle were compelled to assume the character of princes and warriors'.[46] Although he does not deny the advantages enjoyed by his own generation when war has receded to the periphery of the great powers of Europe and the main body of a nation 'enjoys in the midst of war the tranquillity of peace, and is only made sensible of the change by the aggravation or decrease of the public taxes',[47] he has too much Germanic *amour propre* to refrain from taking pride in the effects of anarchy and discord in hardening the powers of mind and body, in promoting courage, self-reliance and loyalty to friends.

Gibbon's Byzantium is enfeebled, religiously and morally. There was, he implied, no higher cause than self-preservation backing the long, dour defensive struggle against the Arabs and other enemies, and much of the fighting was delegated to foreign mercenary forces. Gibbon has, however, made too much of the evidence which he cites. The Emperor Leo's expressed wish to replicate some of the institutions which underpinned *jihad* in the Arab marchlands, and Nicephorus Phocas' failed attempt to have soldiers slain in battle declared martyrs, should not be taken as evidence that Christianity did not inspire those fighting for Byzantium.[48] Nor should it be inferred from references to the presence of foreign units in Byzantine field armies that they formed anything more than a

---

[45] *Ibid.*, VI, p. 96.   [46] *Ibid.*, VI, p. 98.
[47] *Ibid.*, VI, p. 98.
[48] Gilbert Dagron, 'Byzance et le modèle islamique au Xe siècle. À propos des *Constitutions tactiques* de l'empereur Léon VI', *Comptes rendus de l'Académie des Inscriptions et Belles-Lettres* (1983), pp. 219–43.

small, though eye-catching, minority.[49] An attentive reading of tenth-century and earlier chronicles available to Gibbon reveals cumulatively compelling evidence both for Byzantine consciousness that theirs was a religious struggle (for which the obvious parallels were to be found in the Old Testament) and for a thorough militarization of Byzantium when the Arab (and, to a lesser extent, the Bulgar) threat was at its height. The patriotism which Gibbon took as the principal gauge of the health of the body politic was to be seen at every level of Byzantine society.[50]

Byzantium was immersed in war in the dark age (mid-seventh to mid-ninth century), and was steeled by war. Faced with a greatly superior adversary in the east, that war took on a pronounced guerrilla character. The old antagonisms between soldier and civilian faded away once what remained of the old eastern Empire became the prime target of Islamic *jihad* and all the emperor's subjects came under threat. Every advantage offered by geography and climate, above all the natural rampart guarding Byzantium's Anatolian heartland on the south-east, was exploited by regional defensive forces, pursuing the limited but attainable objective of minimizing the damage which invading armies might do. Civilians and their livestock were evacuated to the nearest natural or artificial stronghold, while highly mobile forces harassed enemy raiding and foraging forays, so as to diminish the swathe of destruction and hasten their departure. State and society were geared to war. The central departments of state were remodelled to channel all available resources into the war effort. Army commands embraced the whole territory of the state, and drew a large proportion of its citizenry into the defensive struggle. In the dark age there were some 150,000 men under arms, serving in the guards regiments, the navy and the main body of the provincial 'theme' armies.

If only Gibbon had been alert to the evidence lurking in the

---

[49] The general discussion of army organization in section iv of Leo's *Tactica* presupposes that the army is a national one, recruited from the emperor's subjects. The first clause makes this quite clear (ed. Vári, vol. I, pp. 48–50): the general is instructed to enlist men from the area under his command who are fit (physically and psychologically) for military service and who come from households capable of supporting themselves during their absence.

[50] Hélène Ahrweiler, *L'idéologie politique de l'Empire byzantin* (Paris, 1975), ch. 2; cf. Peter Brown, 'A dark age crisis', pp. 284–92.

narrative sources, chronicles and saints' lives, and above all in the *Tactica* of Leo VI, he would have realized that Byzantium in the middle period had reverted to the Roman republican model which he prized so highly. A large citizen army, its core composed of peasant villagers serving in the infantry and of rich peasants or small gentry supporting the heavier demands of cavalry service, gave Byzantium its extraordinary powers of endurance and resilience. Much of the old elite of senatorial and urban landowners had faded away, being replaced as the key elements in the social order, recognized as such by the imperial government, by the country and its peasant and small gentry population. Although changes were afoot by the tenth century (the war was now being carried into the Arab marchlands, recruitment tended to be concentrated in Byzantine frontier provinces, and a new, service-based aristocracy was emerging), the Byzantine army still retained its basic character as a citizen force and the state remained committed to war.[51]

Byzantium was as thoroughly militarized as any developed, pre-industrial sedentary society has ever been. The war effort, prolonged over so many generations, had a profound effect on its economy (bled dry by defence needs which an efficient apparatus of government strove to meet) and on its culture. It is Byzantine culture which Gibbon treats in the final, memorable section of chapter 53. He passes over its material manifestations, in architecture and architectural decoration, in mosaics and frescoes, in miniature art in a wide variety of media – perhaps because he had no direct personal knowledge of the monuments. His prime concern is with learning, science and literature. He has entered safer territory, where his instincts and his philosophic approach can work in harmony with each other and in accord with the evidence.

He outlines the course of Byzantium's intellectual re-awakening after the dark age, associating the first crucial stage with court sponsorship, itself triggered by emulation of the Caliphal court at Baghdad. Except for the dating of its inception (in the reign of Michael III (842–67) rather than that of Theophilus (829–42) where it is now placed), Gibbon's account is satisfactory, if impressionistic,

---

[51] J. D. Howard-Johnston, *Studies in the organization of the Byzantine army in the tenth and eleventh centuries* (D.Phil., Oxford, 1971).

and correctly highlights the personal contribution of Photius.[52] 'By the confession even of priestly hatred, no art or science, except poetry, was foreign to this universal scholar, who was deep in thought, indefatigable in reading, and eloquent in diction.' His *Bibliotheca* is praised: in this compendium reviewing a wide range of writers, Photius 'abridges their narrative or doctrine, appreciates their style and character, and judges even the fathers of the church with a discreet freedom, which often breaks through the superstition of the times'.[53]

The revival of learning and literature was sustained through the reigns of Leo VI and Constantine Porphyrogenitus. Gibbon touches again on their programme of harnessing learning to the practical needs of the state, mentioning the revised legal code (the *Basilica*), the military handbook (the *Tactica*) and the treatise on husbandry (the *Geoponica*) which they commissioned. It was a process which he sees reaching its culmination in the twelfth century, when scholars and writers were once again familiar with the whole range of classical Greek works which had survived the dark age. Since there was no linguistic barricade separating educated Byzantines from 'the sublime masters who had pleased or instructed the first of nations', Gibbon views them as the privileged heirs of antiquity and expects much of them – discoveries beneficial to mankind, new speculative ideas, compositions of history, philosophy or literature showing 'intrinsic beauties of style or sentiment, of original fancy'.[54] None of this can he find. But he reserves his most scathing remarks for the orators who sought to impress audiences with their artifice:

In every page our taste and reason are wounded by the choice of gigantic and obsolete words, a stiff and intricate phraseology, the discord of images, the childish play of false or unseasonable ornament, and the painful attempt to elevate themselves, to astonish the reader, and to involve a trivial meaning in the smoke of obscurity and exaggeration. Their prose is soaring to the vicious affectation of poetry; their poetry is sinking below the flatness and insipidity of prose.[55]

There is much truth in this, and the modern reader has good reason to be grateful to Paul Magdalino for conjuring up the world

---

[52] Paul Lemerle, *Le premier humanisme byzantin* (Paris, 1971), chs. 6 and 7; N. G. Wilson, *Scholars of Byzantium* (London, 1983), chs. 4 and 5.
[53] *Decline and fall*, ed. Bury, VI, pp. 104–5.
[54] *Ibid.*, VI, p. 107.   [55] *Ibid.*, VI, p. 107–8.

of *rhetors* and intellectuals in twelfth-century Constantinople, after spending years in their company as they competed for favour from some fifty to sixty aristocratic and *apparatchik* households in the great city.[56] But why was it that so little of real worth was written in Byzantium? Gibbon's answer is that Byzantium was too isolated from neighbouring cultures, that the vital stimulus of competition with foreign courts was missing and that this could not be made good by rivalry between domestic patrons within the diminished frame of the early medieval empire. There was, of course, as he acknowledges, some intercommunication, cultural as well as diplomatic, with foreign courts, both Arab and western. Intellectual fashions, literary themes, and artistic motifs and techniques were transmitted both to and from Byzantium. But Gibbon is surely right to stress Byzantium's relative imperviousness to foreign influences, which was a consequence of a rather defensive and introverted pride.[57]

Two further contributory factors may also be suggested, both connected with Byzantium's searing experience in the dark age. For two and a half centuries, learning and the creative imagination were constrained in a society which was directing all available resources, including those of the mind, into the war effort. Generations of disregard for autonomous thinking, generations of preoccupation with the practicalities of administration, diplomacy and combat were not without a long-term effect. Individual initiative took time to assert itself. Patrons were too inclined to await a lead from the court. Many generations were to pass before a self-sustaining intelligentsia of writers and scholars emerged (in the one great city of the Empire, Constantinople, in the twelfth century). Even then, whole areas of ancient learning, notably geography and much of science, remained neglected.[58] Conventions, imposed by slowly evolving tradition, determined artistic and literary form and content. The dark age struggle for survival thus brought about a permanent deformation of Byzantine culture. There was, however, no complete break with the past at that time, and this too had a depressing effect on subsequent cultural output.

---

[56] Magdalino, *The Empire of Manuel I Komnenos*, ch. 5.
[57] J. D. Howard-Johnston (ed.), *Byzantium and the West c. 850–c. 1200* (Amsterdam, 1988), introduction.
[58] N. G. Wilson, *Scholars of Byzantium*, ch. 12, documents a belated revival of interest in both fields, in the Palaeologan period.

The core of classical literature remained familiar to the educated elite, even in the grimmest times (the eighth century). When there was more leisure and imperial encouragement to explore their classical heritage, Byzantine scholars were able to extend knowledge into its peripheral areas, but they could not be expected to feel the same shock and thrill as was registered in the Renaissance at the rediscovery of the great masterpieces of Greek literature. Uninterrupted and easy access to classical texts probably inhibited rather than encouraged Byzantine writers in the age of revival.

Gibbon's portrait of Byzantium is entertaining from start to finish. It includes some penetrating sallies – the account of the background and course of the iconoclast controversy, the devastating indictment of Byzantine literature and intellectual life – but much of it is rather superficial. Gibbon's customary scholarship is in evidence, in the sense that he attends to what is said by the sources available to him. But in his haste, he has left gaps in his reading and may handle what he has read rather uncritically. He was also gravely handicapped by lack of first-hand knowledge of the terrain and monuments of Byzantium. Reading, however voracious, was no substitute for travel and personal observation. Only by visiting the east could Gibbon have gained a proper understanding of the articulation of the landscape in the core territories of Byzantium, of the scale and distribution of resources, of the ease or difficulty of communication between localities. Without such understanding, he could not bring geographical factors, important though they were in his eyes, fully to bear on history, especially economic history. He also deprived himself of direct knowledge of the physical remains of Byzantium, which would have greatly enriched (and probably re-oriented) his version of Byzantine history.

The political history, as Gibbon himself confesses, was a patchwork put together at high speed, and he does relatively little to assert his independence of judgment against the thrust of the narrative he uses.[59] The reconstruction of Byzantine institutions

---

[59] A. D. Momigliano, 'Gibbon's contribution to historical method' in his *Studies in historiography* (London, 1969), p. 40 notes that Gibbon shows only intermittent shrewdness in appraising his sources and that he did not exploit the advances made by contemporary German scholarship in searching out what lay behind the extant texts. In the case of the Byzantine chronicles he uses, Gibbon is liable to become the plaything of the sources of his sources, unaware of the extensive deposits left by psogs, encomia and romances.

rests on but a few piles which have been driven into the often yielding ground of Byzantine sources, and the whole structure seems all too precarious to a modern eye. For Gibbon's views on three of the four principal aspects of Byzantium which he isolates in chapter 53 are not only at variance with the collective careful reading of the sources, written and material, which his successors have undertaken, but they also do not explain Byzantium's most striking achievement, its survival against all the odds in the seventh, eighth and ninth centuries.

The evidence was to hand in the narrative sources known to him, but Gibbon failed to see what it was that he was looking at – a society which succeeded by near-superhuman collective effort in preserving its liberty against the greatly superior powers threatening it from without. Had he dipped into some of the saints' lives he disregarded, he would have come across individuals among the soldiers who can be seen in aggregate fighting generation after generation for Christian Romania across the pages of Byzantine chronicles. And if only he had seen them and appreciated their significance, he could have incorporated within his magisterial work the sort of history he had once contemplated writing about the Swiss, a *History of the liberty of the Byzantines*. As it is, only direct divine intervention in human affairs could explain the survival of Gibbon's enfeebled and servile Byzantium, unable to call on anything except cash and guile.

One crucial component of the Byzantine state, an apparatus of government capable of tapping its resources down to the level of the individual peasant household and of channelling them into the war effort, is not discussed at all. This omission leaves a gaping hole in the centre of his argument, as it would in any general analysis of early medieval Byzantium. For it was state action mediated by a ramified but centralized bureaucracy which, in a crisis extending over many generations, reshaped the economy (drawing off most of the surplus which had previously sustained provincial city life), the social order (first fostering peasantry and small gentry as the fiscal and military foundation of the state, later engendering an aristocracy of service) and the culture inherited from late antiquity. It follows that the historian must examine the structure and functioning of the different parts of the administrative system in order to achieve a proper understanding of Byzantium.

So severe a critique can only be applied to Gibbon's coverage of the middle period of Byzantine history. Haste, selective use of the sources and a willingness occasionally to resort to short cuts if they were available (for example, 'the neat and concise abstract' of Le Beau, *Histoire du bas empire*[60] instead of the original text of Theophanes Continuatus) are the main reasons for this sudden and temporary drop in historical standard. It is evident that Gibbon has not allowed himself the time to graze at leisure in the sources for this period, since he misses vital matter even in texts, such as the *De cerimoniis* of Constantine Porphyrogenitus and the *Tactica* of Leo VI, which he values highly. He also makes a revealing remark about the *Alexiad* of Anna Comnena – 'an elaborate affectation of rhetoric and science betrays, in every page, the vanity of a female author'.[61] This betrays his own superficial reading of an important text which is densely packed with detailed accounts of military operations and political machinations, such as might prompt a reader, unaware of the author's identity, to suppose that it was the work of a highly placed military man.

Gibbon was unfortunate in one important respect: he swept through the early medieval sector of his subject before the learned world became aware that a corpus of tenth-century imperial legislation on social issues was preserved in appendices added to the most popular Byzantine legal handbook of the period, the *Synopsis major* of the *Basilica*.[62] If ever he had chanced upon these texts, he would have fastened upon them, such was the value which he attached to legal sources, and would have appreciated both the overriding social importance of the peasant, as tax-payer and soldier, to the Byzantine state and the threat to the traditional order posed by the rising service-based aristocracy. A thorough and critical reading of his principal sources might have compensated for this lack; so too might a closer acquaintance with hagiography. But Gibbon had not the time for the former and wilfully turned away from the latter.

In general, Gibbon gives a distorted picture of the middle period of the Byzantine Empire. The erudition which normally restrained him from following in the tracks of Voltaire was missing, and he turned temporarily into the sort of flamboyant *philosophe*, sparkling with polemical rhetoric, of which he normally disapproved. He

---

[60] *Decline and fall*, ed. Bury, VI, p. 77 n. 35.   [61] *Ibid.*, V, p. 226.
[62] Nicolas Svoronos, *La Synopsis major des Basiliques et ses appendices* (Paris, 1964).

allowed the prejudices of his own time to colour too much of his thinking and to govern too much of what he wrote. Thereby he created a great gulf between himself and his subject, and, instead of striving to gain an understanding of an alien thought-world, preferred to gaze down upon it with a mixture of amusement and disdain.

CHAPTER 4

Byzantine soldiers, missionaries and diplomacy under Gibbon's eyes

Jonathan Shepard

To devote space to medieval Byzantium must evoke Gibbon's disdain. He professed reluctance to give up many pages of his *History* to it. The Byzantines laboured under a double despotism, the tyranny of their emperors and the 'spiritual despotism' which shackled thoughts as well as deeds: 'From these considerations, I should have abandoned without regret the Greek slaves and their servile historians, had I not reflected that the fate of the Byzantine monarchy is *passively* connected with the most splendid and important revolutions, which have changed the state of the world.'[1] It is in order to illuminate the rise of Islam and the Christian west that Gibbon deigns to cover the history of Byzantium: 'As, in his daily prayers, the Musulman of Fez or Delhi still turns his face towards the temple of Mecca, the historian's eye shall be always fixed on the city of Constantinople.'[2]

Constantinople thus offers a convenient compass bearing to Gibbon as he charts the development of more dynamic organizations and religious movements. Byzantine historical narratives and prescriptive works are tapped as sources about other peoples. What the Greeks have to say about their own warfare, in theory or practice, serves largely to heighten the contrast between them and the vigorous barbarians. Thus 'the love of freedom and of arms was felt, with conscious pride, by the Franks themselves, and is observed by the Greeks with some degree of amazement and terror. "The Franks", says the emperor Constantine, "are bold and valiant to the verge of temerity; and their dauntless spirit is supported by the contempt of danger and death."'[3] The Greeks, in contrast, are

---

[1] *Decline and fall*, ed. Milman, ch. 48, p. 398 (vol. IV of Milman's edition contains chs. 41–9; vol. V, chs. 50–9).
[2] *Ibid.*, ch. 48, p. 398.   [3] *Ibid.*, ch. 53, pp. 261–2.

under their monarch's thumb and their books on military strategy are 'destitute of original genius; they implicitly transcribe the rules and maxims which had been confirmed by victories' in the eras of Spartan or Macedonian hegemony or the Ages of Augustus or Trajan.[4] In so far as there is deviation from these maxims, it is a change for the worse, evincing a defensive outlook: the tactics prescribed in one emperor's manual 'seldom soar above the means of escaping a defeat, and procrastinating the war', and details of the troops' manoeuvres betray their timidity.[5] Gibbon discerns a revival in martial aptitude and ardour in the late eleventh and the twelfth centuries: 'It is under the Comnenian dynasty that a faint emulation of knowledge and military virtue was rekindled in the Byzantine empire.'[6] Yet credit here is partly due to the mingling of 'the nations of Europe and Asia . . . by the expeditions to the Holy Land', and Alexius I Comnenus is likened to 'the jackal, who is said to follow the footsteps, and to devour the leavings, of the lion', that is, the Crusaders.[7] As for the victories of the Byzantines in the century and a half before the First Crusade, they are attributable to the soldier emperors Nicephorus Phocas, John Tzimisces and Basil II and to their 'subjects and confederates'. The role of the confederates is stressed: 'The wealth of the Greeks enabled them to purchase the service of the poorer nations . . . A commerce of mutual benefit exchanged the gold of Constantinople for the blood of Sclavonians and Turks, the Bulgarians and Russians: their valour contributed to the victories of Nicephorus and Zimisces.'[8]

If Gibbon's Greeks are derivative for their theories and rather parasitic in the practice of war, they *do* have something to teach the barbarian occupiers of eastern Europe. A full chapter is given up to the migrations of the Slavs, Bulgars, Hungarians and Rus, and to the story of their respective conversions to Christianity. The contribution of Greek missionaries and bishops is acknowledged: 'The triumphs of apostolic zeal were repeated in the iron age of Christianity . . . A laudable ambition excited the monks both of Germany and Greece, to visit the tents and huts of the barbarians: poverty, hardships, and dangers were the lot of the first missionaries; their courage was active and patient; their motive pure and

---

[4] *Ibid.*, ch. 53, p. 231.
[5] *Ibid.*, ch. 53, p. 258. [6] *Ibid.*, ch. 53, p. 271.
[7] *Ibid.*, chs. 53, 59, pp. 271, 465. [8] *Ibid.*, ch. 53, p. 254.

meritorious.'[9] Nor was their impact wholly negative: 'The establishment of law and order was promoted by the influence of the clergy; and the rudiments of art and science were introduced into the savage countries of the globe. The liberal piety of the Russian princes engaged in their service the most skilful of the Greeks, to decorate the cities and instruct the inhabitants.'[10] Gibbon even considers the possibility of advantages to Russia 'from her peculiar connection with the church and state of Constantinople', whose learning was then so superior to that of the Latins. However, 'the Byzantine nation was servile, solitary, and verging to an hasty decline'.[11]

Gibbon's appraisal of the Byzantines' achievement is thus at its most positive on their mission work and most derogatory concerning their military record and capacity for independent thought or cultural innovation. About their diplomacy he has little explicit to say. The nearest to a characterization of Byzantine diplomacy comes after mention of Greek gold's ability to enlist foreigners into Byzantine service: 'if an hostile people pressed too closely on the frontier, they were recalled to the defence of their country, and the desire of peace, by the well managed attack of a more distant tribe'.[12] Gibbon notes that this policy is 'perpetually' recommended by the *De administrando imperio*, the handbook commissioned by Constantine VII in the mid-tenth century. If challenged over his neglect of diplomacy, he might have replied that these techniques of subsidies and manipulation had already been perfected by Justinian:[13] to recount in detail their perpetuation in the tenth century would have been otiose. At any rate, Byzantine diplomacy does not receive consideration from Gibbon as a discrete topic.

Two questions arise from this. Has fresh evidence come to light, such as to transform the factual basis upon which Gibbon's judgments rest? And, whether or not significant new evidence has surfaced, how well-founded are Gibbon's judgments, and how well-aimed his points of emphasis? It seems to me that his chapter on eastern Europe shows him at his most perceptive, although his access to the sources was minimal and the body of evidence has since been transformed. Greek and Slavic *Vitae* of the holy men,

[9] *Ibid.*, ch. 55, pp. 317–18.   [10] *Ibid.*, ch. 55, pp. 318–19.
[11] *Ibid.*, ch. 55, p. 319.   [12] *Ibid.*, ch. 53, p. 254.
[13] *Ibid.*, ch. 41, p. 7; ch. 42, pp. 71–4, 84–5; ch. 43, p. 139 and n. 31; ch. 45, p. 242.

recounting their missionary work, have been published, as have Slavonic liturgical works and translated extracts from the Church Fathers. Gibbon knows nothing of the mission to central Europe of Constantine-Cyril and Methodius, the two brothers sent to Moravia by Michael III in 863. Nor is he aware of the skilful Slavonic translations of the Gospels and liturgical texts or of the original compositions of prayers, hymns and homilies which the brothers and their pupils carried out.[14] Further, the first full edition of the twenty-five surviving letters addressed by the patriarch of Constantinople, Nicholas Mysticus, to Symeon of Bulgaria (893–927) was published only in the mid-nineteenth century.

Even so, Gibbon was perspicacious in emphasizing the role of footloose monks from the orthodox church in spreading the Gospels. As he observed, the heterodox, too, proved highly effective as proselytizers, whether from a positive urge to convert or simply through upholding rigorous observance in the border regions to which they fled or were consigned. At any rate, they made an impact on the local inhabitants. Communities of eastern-rite monks were strewn from the northern foothills of the Caucasus along the Crimean coast and across the Balkans as far west as Hungary: there was a Greek house near Visegrád, on the Danube. A holy man, St Nikon 'ho Metanoeite' ('the "Repent!"'), played an active part in trying to convert the Muslims of Crete after the Byzantine reconquest in 961, and he later founded a monastery near pagan Slavs in the Peloponnese.[15] A monk-priest from Mount Athos is recorded as travelling in Poland, tonsuring individuals there, in the 1020s. The monastery of 'the Holy Mount' (as Athos was known

---

14 F. Dvornik, *Byzantine missions among the Slavs* (New Brunswick, 1970), pp. 107–9, 117–18, 129–30, 174–83; D. Obolensky, *The Byzantine commonwealth* (London, 1971), pp. 140–6; C. Hannick, 'Die byzantinischen Missionen' in *Kirchengeschichte als Missionsgeschichte*, II.1, *Die Kirche des früheren Mittelalters*, ed. K. Schäferdiek (Munich, 1978), pp. 287–9, 294–9; V. Vavřínek and B. Zásterová, 'Byzantium's role in the formation of Great Moravian culture', *Byzantinoslavica* 43 (1982), pp. 172–8; I. Dujčev (ed.), *Kiril and Methodius: founders of Slavonic writing* (New York, 1985), pp. 145–50, 153–6; D. Obolensky, *Six Byzantine portraits* (Oxford, 1988), pp. 18–33; K. Nichoritis, 'Unknown stichera to St Demetrius by St Methodius' in *The legacy of Saints Cyril and Methodius to Kiev and Moscow*, ed. A.-E. N. Tachiaos (Thessaloniki, 1992), pp. 79–85.

15 *Life of Saint Nikon*, chs. 20, 21, 62, ed. and trans. D. F. Sullivan (Brookline, Mass., 1987), pp. 82–7, 206–13; Obolensky, *Byzantine commonwealth*, pp. 79–80, 159; M. Weithmann, *Die slavische Bevölkerung auf der griechischen Halbinsel* (Munich, 1978), p. 49. 'Pious monks called down from the mountains and out from the caves' were instrumental to missionary work in Bulgaria according to Theophanes Continuatus, *Chronographia*, v.96, ed. I. Bekker (Bonn, 1838), p. 342.

among the Slavs) at Vladimir-Volynsk near the upper reaches of the western Bug offers further testimony to Athos' encouragement of monasticism in distant parts in the eleventh century.[16] In fact, the monks of Athos could claim to have been the foremost disseminators of orthodoxy, allowing the Rus to occupy a house on the holy mountain within a generation of Prince Vladimir's adoption of Christianity *c.* 988 and, more strikingly, urging individual Rus to take back good monastic practice to their own people. A Rus-born novice on the Holy Mount was told by his *higoumene*: 'Go back to Rus, and the blessing of the Holy Mount be upon you, for from you there shall come to be many monks!'[17] This Rus, who had been named Anthony, obeyed and the cave which he scooped out of the earth near Kiev eventually developed into the Monastery of the Caves, the principal centre of monasticism and historical writing among the Rus. This monastery, in turn, became active in evangelizing the remoter areas. It is no accident that one of the very few recorded martyrs for the faith in pre-Mongol Rus was a monk from the Cave Monastery, one Kuksha: *c.* 1100 he was put to death by the Viatichi, a tribal grouping whom he had been trying to convert.[18]

Gibbon was ignorant of Kuksha, whose enterprise is celebrated in the *Paterikon* composed in the Cave Monastery, and he said virtually nothing about Mount Athos or other monasteries which had links with the missionary churches.[19] But in highlighting the initiatives of the monks and 'the dictates of vanity and interest' of barbarian chieftains,[20] Gibbon was implicitly playing down the role of the imperial Church 'Establishment'. Such a distinction has force and deserves fuller exegesis than can be given here. Byzantine emperors played a central, indispensable part in despatching those missions which made for foreign potentates' courts. But they were to a large extent responding to requests made, or visits paid, by

---

[16] *Das Paterikon des Kiever Höhlenklosters*, ed. D. Abramovich (Kiev, 1931), repr. with introduction by D. Tschiževskij (Munich, 1964), pp. 44, 146; *Paterik of the Kievan Caves Monastery*, trans. M. Heppell (Harvard, 1989), pp. 50–1; 166 and n. 534.

[17] *Povest' Vremennykh Let*, s.a. 1051, ed. V. P. Adrianova-Peretts and D. S. Likhachev (Moscow and Leningrad, 1950), vol. I, p. 105; *Russian primary chronicle*, trans. S. H. Cross and O. P. Sherbowitz-Wetzor (Cambridge, Mass., 1953), pp. 139–40.

[18] *Paterikon*, ed. Abramovich-Tschiżewskij, pp. 110–11; trans. Heppell, p. 128; see also S. Franklin and J. Shepard, *The emergence of Rus, 750–1200* (London, 1996) pp. 310–13.

[19] *Decline and fall*, ed. Milman, ch. 53, p. 234 n. 13; ch. 63, pp. 129–30.

[20] *Ibid.*, ch. 55, p. 318.

foreign potentates. And the missionary ground had often been prepared by wandering or eremitic monks.

To emphasize the pivotal role of local potentates in opting for conversion and systematically imposing Christian observance on their peoples may seem an obvious enough point, but it is not so evident from the Byzantine sources on which Gibbon had to rely. He made the most of such non-Byzantine materials as were available to him, applying his historical imagination. Thus he was able to note the interest of Rus princes in education: 'three hundred noble youths were invited or compelled' to study, at the behest of Prince Iaroslav.[21] Likewise he picked up from a passing remark by Liudprand of Cremona the keen interest of the Bulgarians in education. He observes that among the nobles receiving instruction in 'the schools and palace of Constantinople' was the future ruler of Bulgaria, Symeon.[22]

Had Gibbon enjoyed access to the South Slavs' writings or to the works of Theophylact of Ochrid, he would have been able to dilate on the political culture which Khan Boris of Bulgaria, Symeon and Symeon's son Peter fostered in Bulgaria. He would have found ample evidence to substantiate his generalizations about the progress of arts and sciences and the establishment of a Christian order. Schools as well as churches were instituted, and a Byzantine law-code which had most probably been translated in Moravia was copied in Bulgaria.[23] Byzantine styles of architecture, decoration and icon-painting were adopted by the Bulgarian ruling elite, most

---

[21] *Ibid.*, ch. 55, p. 319. Gibbon (drawing on P.-C. Levesque, *Histoire de Russie, tirée des chroniques originales, des pièces authentiques et des meilleurs historiens de la nation*, vol. 1 (Paris, 1782), p. 193) errs slightly. The students were sons of 'elders and priests' rather than of 'nobles': *Novgorod IV chronicle* s.a. 1030, *Polnoe Sobranie Russkikh Letopisei*, IV.1 (Petrograd, 1915), p. 113; *Sofia I chronicle* s.a. 1030, *Polnoe Sobranie Russkikh Letopisei*, V (Leningrad, 1925), p. 126.

[22] *Decline and fall*, ed. Milman, ch. 55, p. 293; cf. Liudprand, *Antapodosis*, III.29, in *Opera*, ed. J. Becker (Hannover and Leipzig, 1915), p. 87.

[23] A. Milev (ed.), *Gr'tskite zhitiia na Kliment Okhridski* (Sofia, 1966), pp. 125–33, 136–41; trans. Dujčev, *Kiril*, pp. 115–18, 120–2. I. Dujčev, 'Les rapports littéraires byzantino-slaves', reprinted in Dujčev's *Medioevo Bizantino-Slavo* vol. II (Rome, 1968), pp. 3–14, 17, 20, 26–7; B. Zásterová, 'Über zwei grossmährischen Rechtsdenkmäler byzantinischen Ursprungs', *Beiträge zur byzantinischen Geschichte im 9.–11. Jahrhundert*, ed. V. Vavřínek (Prague, 1978), pp. 376–9; Vavřínek and Zásterová, 'Great Moravian culture', pp. 185–8; Obolensky, *Byzantine portraits*, pp. 22, 24–6, 30–2, 62–4; I. G. Iliev, 'The manuscript tradition and the authorship of the Long Life of St Clement of Ohrid', *Byzantinoslavica* 53 (1993), pp. 68–73. The extent of the dissemination and enforcement of the law-code in Bulgaria remains unclear: P. Schreiner, 'Die Byzantinisierung der bulgarischen Kultur', *Abhandlungen der Akademie der Wissenschaften in Göttingen, philol.-historische Klasse, Dritte Folge* 177 (1989), p. 52.

spectacularly at Preslav, which Symeon made his royal residence.[24] Symeon's role as the educator of other members of the elite was glorified by an encomiast: Symeon has 'stuffed his palaces' with books and gathering 'like a labour-loving bee', 'from every flower of writing' he pours forth honey 'from his lips before his boiars'.[25] This was not empty rhetoric. Symeon was interested in both scholarship and the dissemination of edifying knowledge in digestible portions: he himself picked out passages in the copious sermons of St John Chrysostom for translation into Slavonic.[26] The Bulgarian leadership took more literally than is often supposed the concept of the ruler as paragon and educator propounded by leading Byzantine churchmen of the later ninth century. There survives a letter addressed by Photius to Khan Boris enjoining him, as a Christian prince, to govern ethically, set an example and propagate the faith among his subjects.[27]

Photius wrote the letter while Patriarch of Constantinople. Yet it is doubtful whether Gibbon would have felt obliged to concede a more dynamic role to the imperial Church Establishment in mission work, or to revise his verdict on the sterility of Byzantine culture, as evinced by the products of the capital. In fact, it is the silence of the Byzantine chronicles and imperially commissioned works which led Gibbon almost to overlook the scholarly activities of Symeon's court. Symeon features in the Byzantine chronicles as an aggressive and insolent barbarian, who was gullible enough to be tricked by Patriarch Nicholas Mysticus. Nicholas is alleged to have crowned him with part of his own headgear, rather than with a truly imperial crown (*stemma*).[28] Nicholas was himself well-aware of Symeon's erudition, as his letters to Symeon show, and he takes it for granted that Symeon is familiar with Byzantium's early history

---

[24] I. Božilov, 'Preslav et Constantinople: dépendance et indépendance culturelles', in *The 17th International Byzantine Congress. Major Papers* (New York, 1986), pp. 435–8; Cyril Mango, *Byzantine architecture* (London, 1986), pp. 172–5; M. Restle, '"Eklektizismus" und "Synkretismus" in der bulgarischen mittelalterlichen Kunst', *Abhandlungen der Akademie der Wissenschaften in Göttingen, philol.-historische Klasse, Dritte Folge* 177 (1989), pp. 63–6.

[25] K. Kuev, 'Pokhvala na tsar Simeon – rekonstruktsiia i razbor', *Palaeobulgarica* 10 (2) (1986), pp. 4–5, 9, 11, 13; trans. Dujčev, *Kirill*, p. 152.

[26] F. J. Thomson, 'Chrysostomica Palaeoslavica', *Cyrillomethodianum* 6 (1982), pp. 22, 45–8.

[27] Photius, *Epistulae et Amphilochia*, ed. B. Laourdas and L. G. Westerink, vol. I (Leipzig, 1983), pp. 17, 22, 26–7, 29–30, 39.

[28] Theophanes Continuatus, VI.5, p. 385.

and ideology, and with 'the Divine Words.'[29] But there is no acknowledgment in his letters of Symeon's efforts to enlighten his people through the vigorous sponsorship of translation work. Only occasionally does Byzantine propaganda or historiography fully recognize the fact that the Bulgarians were, by the tenth century, a Christian people of impeccable Orthodoxy or treat them as fellow-members of the same body. This concept is propounded in a speech composed for the celebration of the peace made between Byzantium and Bulgaria in 927. The two parties to the treaty are likened to Jerusalem and Samaria, which are now 'allies, and all are in community of brotherly love and concord'.[30] Yet even here, Symeon is ridiculed for the quality of his Greek, which was fluent but spoken 'with a barbarian accent'. And it cannot be said that this statement of the shared values of Byzantium and its convert peoples had many sequels in imperial court literature.[31]

Gibbon's response to the Slavic *Vitae* of SS Cyril and Methodius can only be surmised, but he might well have found in them further grounds for his emphasis on the initiatives of local rulers and individual holy men.[32] He would have had more revising to do in his presentation of the Byzantines at war. Here, too, many primary sources have been published since Gibbon's death, and Byzantium's army and warfare is receiving intensive scholarly attention. Gibbon questioned the utility and significance of the tactical manuals known to him: 'the discipline of a soldier is formed by exercise rather than by study'; 'the battles won by lessons of tactics may be numbered with the epic poems created from the rules of criticism'.[33] In fact, the Byzantines were capable of putting pen to paper about contemporary warfare, and there are a number of works based on empirical experience of the tenth century, notably that dubbed *Skirmishing* or *Le traité sur la guérilla* by its respective

---

[29] Nicholas I, Patriarch, *Letters*, ed. and trans. R. J. H. Jenkins and L. G. Westerink (Washington, D.C., 1973), pp. 110–11; cf. pp. 30–5, 134–7, 164–5; J. Shepard, 'Symeon of Bulgaria – Peacemaker', *Godishnik na Sofiiskiia Universitet 'Sv. Kliment Okhridski'. Nauchen tsent'r za slaviano-vizantiiski prouchvaniia 'Ivan Duichev'* 83 (3) (1989, appeared 1991), p. 15.

[30] I. Dujčev, 'On the treaty of 927 with the Bulgarians', *Dumbarton Oaks Papers* 32 (1978), pp. 278–9.

[31] G. Prinzing, 'Die Illusion vom orthodoxen "Commonwealth"', *Bericht über die 37. Versammlung deutscher Historiker in Bamberg 12. bis 16. Oktober 1988* (Stuttgart, 1988), p. 150.

[32] *Vita Constantini*, ch. 14; *Vita Methodii*, ch. 5; in *Kliment Okhridski. S'brani s'chineniia*, ed. B. S. Angelov and K. Kodov, vol. III (Sofia, 1973), pp. 104, 188.

[33] *Decline and fall*, ed. Milman, ch. 53, p. 231.

recent editors. This sets out the tactics which have been tried and tested in repulsing the Muslim raiders in south-east Asia minor. The preface expressly states that they were obsolete now that the Saracens' power had waned; however, some record needed to be kept, in case of a resurgence of Muslim power.[34] The author, himself a veteran of border warfare, provides for a war of movement, requiring of a commander split-second decisions and intimate knowledge of the local terrain. He lays down a methodology, specifying the various possible types of attack, from a raiding party to a full-blown expedition.[35] One of the first tasks of a commander is to try and discover which type he is facing: he may, for example, examine the hoof-marks and other tracks left by the enemy, or reconnoitre from the heights.[36] The manual presupposes self-reliance; the commander cannot assume that relief will arrive in time from other units or the central government, and he must be quick to size up a situation and to improvise. This recalls Gibbon's own prescription: 'the talents of a commander are appropriated to those calm, though rapid, minds which nature produces to decide the fate of armies and nations'.[37]

Guerrilla warfare tactics gave way in the mid-tenth century to a more direct form of combat, in which soldiers were trained to charge the enemy and fight in formation.[38] A chronicler observed Nicephorus Phocas' penchant for drilling his troops even while at Constantinople, and Nicephorus himself wrote a treatise on the deployment and tactics of large armies in battle, assigning a central role to heavily-armed cavalrymen (*kataphraktoi*).[39] Other phases of Byzantium's expansion are registered by the work known as *Campaign organization* and by the *Tactica* of Nicephorus Ouranos.

---

[34] *Skirmishing*, in *Three Byzantine military treatises*, ed. and trans. G. Dennis (Washington, D.C., 1985), pp. 146–7.

[35] *Skirmishing*, pp. 160–3, 174–5, 188–91, 204–7, 214–15, 222–7; *Le traité sur la guérilla*, ed. G. Dagron and H. Mihăescu (Paris, 1986), pp. 178–80.

[36] *Skirmishing*, pp. 150–1, 160–1, 164–7, 184–5, 192–3.

[37] *Decline and fall*, ed. Milman, ch. 53, p. 231

[38] Theophanes Continuatus, VI.41, pp. 459–60.

[39] John Scylitzes, *Synopsis Historion*, ed. I. Thurn (Berlin and New York, 1973), p. 278. Nicephorus' treatise: I. A. Kulakovsky, 'Strategika imperatora Nikifora', *Zapiski imperatorskoi Akademii po Istoriko-Filologicheskomu Otdeleniu*, vol. VIII (9) (1908), pp. 10–12. E. McGeer showed that the successive manuals of the second half of the tenth century provide for 'the shifting balance between infantry and cavalry on the battlefield': 'Infantry versus cavalry: the Byzantine response', *Revue des Etudes Byzantines* 46 (1988), p. 144; cf. H.-J. Kühn, *Die byzantinische Armee im 10. und 11. Jahrhundert* (Vienna, 1991), pp. 125–7.

Part of Ouranos' manual draws on that of Phocas, but it has been shown that chapters 63–5 draw on Ouranos' own experience as military governor of Antioch at the beginning of the eleventh century. He gives advice on raiding and laying waste to Muslim territories, and on reducing troublesome enemy fortresses.[40]

Gibbon might retort that this array of sources published since his *History* modifies rather than overturns his observations and in some ways even confirms them. Firstly, the contents of *Skirmishing* bear out Gibbon's remarks about the defensive stance of Byzantine tactics and they indicate more clearly than Leo VI's *Tactica* the extent to which the Byzantines tended to avoid frontal engagement with the Muslim marauders. They preferred to make their border-lands as inhospitable as possible, shadowing the raiding bands, foreseeing the direction in which they would go and picking off the smaller bands. One of *Skirmishing*'s underlying assumptions was that the raiders would more often than not enjoy numerical superiority, and the imbalance of resources and manpower seems to have escaped Gibbon's notice. Indeed, he writes of the 'arts and riches' of the Greeks as being 'at least equal to the Saracens'[41] and much of his lambasting of the indolence and languor of the Greeks rests on the assumption that they had the means to be a match for neighbouring peoples, but lacked the fighting spirit of the barbarians and Muslim 'enthusiasts'. Gibbon can hardly be blamed for this error. In fact, he complains at the lack of information available on the revenues and resources of the Empire and notes the weak light shed on the Byzantine provinces. It was only in the later twentieth century that the very modest proportions of medieval Byzantium's population-centres, commercial enterprises and monetary economy in comparison with those of classical antiquity became clear.[42]

---

[40] J.-A. de Foucault, 'Douze chapitres inédits de la *Tactique* de Nicéphore Ouranos', *Travaux et Mémoires* 5 (1973), pp. 286–303; E. McGeer, 'Tradition and reality in the *Taktika* of Nikephoros Ouranos', *Dumbarton Oaks Papers* 45 (1991), pp. 132–3.

[41] *Decline and fall*, ed. Milman, ch. 53, p. 254.

[42] See A. P. Kazhdan, *Derevniia i gorod v Vizantii IX-Xvv.* (Moscow, 1960), pp. 207–12, 247–8, 263–70, 288–9, 299; C. Foss, 'Archaeology and the "Twenty cities" of Byzantine Asia', *American Journal of Archaeology* 81 (1977), pp. 469–86; Cyril Mango, *Byzantium. The Empire of new Rome* (London, 1980), pp. 48–50, 69–82; J. Lefort, 'Population et peuplement en Macédoine Orientale, IX–XV siècles', *Hommes et richesses dans l'empire byzantin*, vol. ii, *VIII–XV siècle*, ed. V. Kravari, J. Lefort and C. Morrisson (Paris, 1991), pp. 63–9, 82; C. Morrisson, 'Monnaie et finances dans l'empire byzantin, X–XIV siècles', *ibid.*, pp. 294–8.

Secondly, Gibbon would have had to acknowledge that the shift to an offensive stance is fully registered in the prescriptive manuals. In fact, the new battle formations and their careful deployment in action were being prescribed in Phocas' treatise not long after he had introduced them.[43] But Gibbon would not have been wholly bereft of ammunition. He had, after all, never denied the significance of the victories won by Phocas and Tzimisces, and he would recognize that by the late tenth century the Byzantine army was a formidable fighting force; fast-moving expeditionary forces comprising 16,000 fighting men are regarded as routine in the treatise *Campaign organization*, which provides for the contemporary problem of invading Bulgaria through its 'rugged, wooded mountain passes'.[44] He would, however, also have pointed out the abiding regard for the prescriptions and precedents provided by the writings of the ancients: Byzantine writers repeatedly affirmed that much of use could be learnt from them. It has been shown that chapters 63–5 of Ouranos' *Tactica* draw on his experience on the Syrian frontier, while chapters 56–62 are based on Phocas' treatise and also take account of a change in infantry tactics which presumably occurred in the generation following Phocas' death.[45] The fact remains that the overwhelming mass of Ouranos' treatise is derivative – from the *Tactica* of Leo VI, which are themselves a collation of earlier works; or, in the case of chapters 75–8, from collections of classical writings on military matters.[46] When Ouranos does give empirical advice, there is an air of apology, as there is in Leo VI's discussion of naval warfare. Leo states that he has relied mainly on 'the limited experience' of what his commanders have told him, in default of much coverage of naval tactics in 'the ancient manuals'. Ouranos writes: 'Many and varied are the means which the ancients thought up for conducting siege warfare,

---

[43] Kulakovsky, 'Strategika', pp. 12–17; McGeer, 'Infantry versus cavalry', p. 138; Kühn, *Die byzantinische Armee*, p. 125. The change in strategy was accompanied by thorough-going reorganization and expansion of the army's size: Kühn, *Die byzantinische Armee*, pp. 123–4, 126–31, 140–7, 158–64. On the government's various attempts to ensure recruitment and regular resourcing of its field armies, see J. Haldon, 'Military service, military lands and the status of soldiers: current problems and interpretations', *Dumbarton Oaks Papers* 47 (1993), pp. 27–9, 35–41, 49–51, 65–6.

[44] *Campaign organization*, in *Three treatises*, ed. Dennis, pp. 246–7, 288–9 (as in n. 34).

[45] McGeer, 'Tradition', p. 132.

[46] Ouranos' *Tactica* has yet to be published in full: a list of partial editions is in A. Dain, 'Les stratégistes byzantins', *Travaux et Mémoires* 2 (1967), p. 371; McGeer, 'Tradition', pp. 129 n. 2; 131–2.

but I have set down only the methods that our generation is actually using.'[47]

This can, of course, be interpreted positively, as an indication that the Byzantines tried out the ancients' siege devices and made up their own minds in the light of current conditions. And none of it would matter much if military commanders went about their business regardless of the archaic nostrums and war-games played out on the pages of military treatises. But it could be argued that the large-scale expeditions of the later tenth and earlier eleventh centuries were of limited effectiveness in relation to the resources devoted to them. Gibbon himself noted that even the victories of Phocas and Tzimisces resulted to a large extent from protracted sieges and blockades, rather than glorious cavalry charges of the sort which Phocas' treatise envisages.[48] Siege warfare was virtually the only topic on which Ouranos allowed himself to depart radically from the examples of the ancients. But lack of expertise or inattention to siege warfare seems to have rendered Basil II's repeated raids into Bulgaria rather ineffectual. John Scylitzes noted as a mark of Bulgarian collapse that they barred the mountain passes to Basil's armies.[49] But these tactics, together with refuges for ordinary people in hilltop strongholds, blunted the impact of Basil's offensives for many years. As late as 1014, the inhabitants of a district could still withdraw into the fortress of Melnik 'and did not worry much about the Romans'.[50] Gibbon might have cited this as evidence of the misplaced strategic priorities of seasoned campaigners and armchair strategists alike. And he could have collated Byzantine expressions of frustration with the verdicts of two foreign writers on Basil II's Bulgarian campaigns: that the eventual conquest was accomplished 'not by pitched battle' but through the death of Tsar Samuel and the opening up of divisions within the Bulgarian royal family.[51]

---

[47] Leo VI, *Tactica*, xix.1, Migne, *Patrologia Graeca* cvii, col. 989; de Foucault, 'Douze chapitres', pp. 302–3; McGeer, 'Tradition', p. 138.
[48] Leo the Deacon, *Historia*, ed. C. B. Hase (Bonn, 1828), pp. 51–4, 55–61, 71–4, 81–2; Scylitzes, *Synopsis historion*, pp. 268–73; *Decline and fall*, ed. Milman, ch. 52, p. 225.
[49] Scylitzes, *Synopsis historion*, p. 348.
[50] *Ibid.*, p. 351.
[51] Adémar of Chabannes, *Chronique*, iii.32, ed. J. Chavanon (Paris, 1897), p. 155; Aristakes of Lastivert, *Récit des malheurs de la nation arménienne*, trans. H. Berberian and M. Canard (Brussels, 1973), p. 7; J. Shepard, 'Bulgaria: the rival Balkan empire', *New Cambridge Medieval History: c. 900–c. 1024* (vol. iii), ed. T. Reuter (Cambridge, 1997).

There remains a field of Byzantine activity which Gibbon did not discuss at length: diplomacy. This is a singular omission. Gibbon recounts the Byzantines' dealings with the barbarians at many stages in his narrative and he notes the requests for an imperial marriage-tie on the part of various barbarian rulers, including Charlemagne, Otto of Saxony and Vladimir of Kiev.[52] Yet he does not ponder what these overtures might reveal about Byzantium's standing among other ruling elites. Nor does he explore the possible connections between diplomacy and Byzantine missions, even though one of the self-proclaimed aims of the emperor was to propagate the faith. Gibbon's omission is noteworthy, seeing that he was aware that barbarian requests for a marriage-alliance were common, as he was also aware of the role of local rulers in requesting religious missions.[53]

One hesitates to charge Gibbon with wilful neglect of Byzantine diplomacy. Since its history has yet to be written, that would be to condemn him for failure to be two hundred years ahead of his time. Moreover, Gibbon's professed concern was with 'the important revolutions, which have changed the state of the world'. But his own narrative makes clear that the Byzantines played a key role in such developments as the establishment of Norman fortune-seekers in southern Italy, the triggering off of the First Crusade and the establishment of the Turkish sultan in Anatolia in the later eleventh century. In Gibbon's own words, the sultan's 'arms were introduced by the Greeks, who aspired to reign on the ruins of their country'.[54] Moreover, Gibbon made extensive use of the handbook on foreign affairs which Constantine VII commissioned and partly wrote for the guidance of his son and heir. Gibbon exempts it from his blanket condemnation of Byzantine treatises as confused and derivative. It is 'discriminated by peculiar merit: the antiquities of the nations may be doubtful or fabulous; but the geography and manners of the barbaric world are delineated with curious accuracy'.[55] Yet he does not examine how or why the De

---

[52] Decline and fall, ed. Milman, ch. 49, p. 509 and n. 121; ch. 53, p. 252.
[53] Constantine VII, De administrando imperio, ch. 13, ed. G. Moravcsik and R. J. H. Jenkins (Washington, D.C., 1967) (hereafter cited as DAI), pp. 70–5; Decline and fall, ed. Milman, ch. 53, p. 249; above, pp. 82–3.
[54] Decline and fall, ed. Milman, ch. 57, p. 395. Cf. ch. 56, pp. 328–9 (Normans); ch. 58, pp. 408, 431–2 (Crusade).
[55] Ibid., ch. 53, p. 232.

administrando differs from the other treatises, or what this suggests about the importance of diplomacy to Byzantium or about Byzantium's distinguishing characteristics.

It seems to me that Gibbon failed to do justice not only to the singularity of the *De administrando* but also to what might be termed its 'originality'. One must stress that there was no ready-made classical model upon which Constantine VII and his assistants could base their work or from which they could draw information. This was for two reasons. Firstly, there was no classical tradition of writings on the theory and practice of conducting foreign relations analogous to those on strategy and warfare. 'Diplomacy' did not, in the ancient world, enjoy the same social or cultural cachet as did the practice or understanding of war, and expertise in diplomacy – however defined – does not seem to have been regarded as a particularly desirable or salient imperial attribute. Secondly, one of the main purposes of the *De administrando* was to show how the world had *changed* since classical antiquity, outlining the territories lost to invaders and recounting how, more recently, the Empire's position had been improved by Constantine's father and grandfather, Leo VI and Basil I. So there could be no question of Constantine merely regurgitating maxims or data taken from classical historians and geographers. Of necessity, a Byzantine emperor wishing to issue precepts on diplomacy had to 'do it himself'.[56]

Constantine was able to draw on earlier historical writings to make up the collection of extracts known as *De legationibus*, 'On embassies'. Altogether fifty-three collections were commissioned by Constantine and 'Virtues and vices', 'Victory' and 'Plots against emperors' feature among the titles. The aim of the project is set out in the standard preface of each collection: to cull beneficial materials from the listed writers and 'unbegrudgingly' to 'put [them] forward publicly'.[57] So far as the collection *De legationibus* is concerned, we need not suppose that its contents fell far short of the stated goal. The work is conveniently divided into two sections, 'Roman embassies to the foreigners' and 'Foreign embassies to the Romans'. Much attention is paid to negotiations of truces

---

[56] Cf. F. Millar, 'Emperors, frontiers and foreign relations, 31 BC to AD 378', *Britannia* 13 (1982), p. 21.
[57] Constantine VII, *Excerpta de legationibus*, ed. C. de Boor (Berlin, 1903), pp. 1–2; H. Hunger, *Die hochsprachliche profane Literatur der Byzantiner*, vol. 1 (Munich, 1978), pp. 361–2.

interspersed with campaigning, and to treaty-making. The second section contains lengthy extracts from Priscus' eyewitness account of a mission to Attila's camp.[58] There may well be some correlation between the areas upon which these extracts focus and those which concerned Constantine VII most keenly in the mid-tenth century. Thus it is probably no accident of scholarship that extensive passages dealing with Theodosiopolis and elsewhere in western Armenia were extracted from Menander.[59] Theodosiopolis (modern Erzerum) was the target of repeated Byzantine assaults during the first half of the tenth century, and it was finally captured and held in 949, around the time when *De legationibus* was being compiled.[60] And we may note that the extensive coverage of dealings with the Huns, Avars, Turks and other nomadic peoples accords with the attention to steppe diplomacy enjoined by the opening chapters of Constantine's *De administrando*.[61] To assemble earlier instances of dealings with foreign peoples against a geopolitical background comparable to one's own does not necessarily denote poverty of invention.

None the less, it is the contrasts between the collection of extracts in *De legationibus* and the *De administrando* that are most telling. The former is arranged by author rather than geographically or chronologically, whereas the latter is designed to give a *tour d'horizon* of the post-classical world, starting to the north of the Black Sea, descending to the Middle East and then following the line of Arab conquests round to Spain and the western Christian powers, before shifting towards the Balkans and partially repeating the cycle, taking in the Black Sea and Caucasia. The works excerpted for *De legationibus* nearly all belong to classical or late antiquity, whereas the *De administrando* draws on writings of the ninth and tenth centuries, with the exception of a sixth-century geographical dictionary.[62] The *De legationibus* is, like the other

---

[58] *De legationibus*, ed. de Boor, pp. 122–48; *Fragmentary classicising historians of the later Roman empire*, vol. II, ed. and trans. R. C. Blockley (Liverpool, 1983), pp. 246–79, 282–7, 288–95.

[59] *De legationibus*, ed. de Boor, pp. 200–3, 470–1, 211–18; Menander, *History*, ed. and trans. R. C. Blockley (Liverpool, 1985), pp. 164–71, 202–15, 228–31. I owe this point to William Kennedy, Research Fellow at Dumbarton Oaks Research Center in 1984–5.

[60] A. A. Vasiliev, *Byzance et les Arabes*, vol. II.1 (Brussels, 1968), pp. 318–19.

[61] *DAI*, chs. 1–8, pp. 48–57.

[62] B. Beaud, 'Le savoir et le monarque: le traité sur les nations de l'empereur byzantin Constantin VII Porphyrogénète', *Annales* (1990), no. 3, p. 554.

collections, to be accessible to 'the many',[63] and it serves to demon-strate and substantiate the emperor's role as keeper and gracious dispenser of knowledge to his subjects.[64] The *De administrando*, in contrast, is strictly confidential, drawn up by a father anxious to instruct his son on means of retaining hegemony, Solomon-like, on the throne. In fact, as the preface implies, this is knowledge to be *denied* to others, for it holds the key to overawing foreign peoples and maintaining legitimate pre-eminence over all mankind.[65]

The *De administrando* also offers clues as to the special relation-ship between emperors and diplomacy in Byzantium, a relationship which prompted Constantine to essay an original composition devoted to the changes in foreign affairs over the past three hundred years. He regarded mastery of this field (rather than of, say, changes in Byzantium's administrative structure) as the 'wisdom' necessary for enduring rule. Constantine had his reasons: the conduct of diplomacy could to a large extent be the personal affair of the emperor, carried out under his direct supervision and drawing on his expertise, without reliance on expensive armies and potentially rebellious generals. Moreover, this centrality of the emperor to the workings of diplomacy could regularly be given impressive visual form by the ceremonies of court receptions and the entertainment of ambassadors and visiting potentates. Here, symbol, gesture and deed merged into one. The emperor in his palace was master of a controlled environment and playing to his strengths.[66] This was a more coherent stance than was the periodic staging of triumphs designed to project a civilian emperor as the source of military victories.[67] And it was correspondingly

---

[63] *De legationibus*, ed. de Boor, p. 1.

[64] P. Lemerle, *Le premier humanisme byzantin* (Paris, 1971), pp. 280–2, 288; E. Patlagean, 'La civilisation en la personne du souverain', *Le temps de la réflexion*, vol. IV (Paris, 1983), pp. 189–90, 193.

[65] *DAI, prooimion*, pp. 46–7; cf. Patlagean, 'La civilisation en la personne du souverain', pp. 193–4; Beaud, 'Le savoir et le monarque', pp. 561–2.

[66] Averil Cameron, 'The construction of court ritual: the Byzantine *Book of Ceremonies*' in *Rituals of Royalty. Power and ceremonial in traditional societies*, ed. D. Cannadine and S. Price (Cambridge, 1987), pp. 117–23, 129, 136; J. Shepard, 'Byzantine diplomacy c. 800–1204: means and ends' in *Byzantine diplomacy*, ed. J. Shepard and S. Franklin (Aldershot, 1992), pp. 48–53, 61–3; F. Tinnefeld, 'Ceremonies for foreign ambassadors at the court of Byzantium and their political background', *Byzantinische Forschungen* 19 (1993), pp. 198–206, 208–9.

[67] On the efforts of ninth- and tenth-century emperors to gain an aura of military success: M. McCormick, *Eternal victory: triumphal rulership in late antiquity, Byzantium, and the early medieval West* (Cambridge, 1986), pp. 131–2, 152–66.

more convincing in the eyes of foreigners and the emperor's own subjects alike.

If Gibbon could now be brought to acknowledge his cursory treatment of Byzantine diplomacy as a fault, he might still maintain that Byzantine emperors' formal espousal of the role of gift-giver and gracious host vindicated his own fulminations against the treachery and sordidness of Byzantine political history. Reliance on diplomacy was partly a reflection upon the emperor's perennial dread of military coups, and the emperor's special relationship with barbarian warlords was one of his means of keeping outlying provinces or ambitious commanders in check. Gibbon could supplement his 'Vindication' with the findings and judgments of more recent scholars. These confirm his reservations about the text upon which my claim for the singularity of Byzantine diplomacy has turned, the *De administrando*. For example, Karl Leyser (who would have had so much to offer this volume) contrasted the 'freshness and novelty' of Liudprand's *Legatio* with the 'somewhat out of date' treatment of Italy and the Lombards in Leo VI's *Tactica* and the *De administrando*.[68] B. Beaud pointed out the discrepancy between certain of the stated aims of the *De administrando* and its contents: the preface's aspiration to relate 'the position and climate' and dimensions of each land echoes the approach of classical geographers, but the *De administrando* fails to give a systematic description of the whole inhabited world, latitude by latitude.[69] That Constantine's grasp on learning was slight was demonstrated by I. Ševčenko in a devastating appraisal, couched as confession. The emperor emerges as a bumbling autodidact, incapable of polished Attic Greek, muddle-headed and heavily reliant on teams of ghost-writers. Ševčenko cites with approval Gibbon's verdict on the scholarship of Constantine, and he stresses the paucity of sources used for the *De administrando*.[70] Thus Gibbon's warning that its version of 'the antiquities of the nations may be doubtful or fabulous' has received ringing endorsement from modern *Quellenkritik*.

[68] K. Leyser, 'The tenth century in Byzantine–Western relationships' in *Relations between East and West in the Middle Ages*, ed. D. Baker (Edinburgh, 1973), p. 48.
[69] *DAI, prooimion*, pp. 46–7; Beaud, 'Le savoir et le monarque', p. 557.
[70] I. Ševčenko, 'Re-reading Constantine Porphyrogenitus' in *Byzantine diplomacy*, ed. J. Shepard and S. Franklin (Aldershot, 1992), pp. 172 n. 11, 178–81, 186–7, 190–3.

The *De administrando* may now seem to be the exception proving the rule about Byzantine scholarship's slipshod and derivative nature, as diagnosed by Gibbon: when obliged to venture beyond the bounds of classical learning and to collate and shape a body of relatively recent information, the Byzantines were inconsistent and uncritical, using a narrow range of sources of dubious quality. But there is more to be said. Neither Gibbon nor more recent historians have done justice to the uses of the past which the *De administrando* makes and which also coloured Byzantium's actual dealings with particular peoples at specific times. Byzantine statesmen were well aware of the unique advantage accruing to them from the antiquity and continuity of their polity. It was older than any other existing power and had once encompassed the territory of most contemporary rulers of significance. The Byzantines could produce records purporting to demonstrate this fact, but in order to convey their message of 'gold-standard' legitimacy and ultimate ascendancy, they did not really need to concoct records or forge 'documents'. Their professed name of 'Romans' said it all, and it is no accident that one of the few firm sticking-points of Byzantine diplomacy was the denial of the name 'Roman' to any other potentate.[71] Gibbon noted that the Byzantines 'alleged a lineal and unbroken succession from Augustus and Constantine; and, in the lowest period of degeneracy and decay, the name of Romans adhered to the last fragments of the empire'.[72] Gibbon and his successors have tended to interpret this as a mark of the static, absurdly unrealistic ideology of the Byzantines. This is to ignore the possible uses to diplomacy of 'Roman' as a kind of claim to hegemony, warranty, or title-deed to lands. It is no accident that one of the most 'pragmatic' chapters of the *De administrando* invokes the name 'Romans' and represents latter-day emperors as abiding by the sacred norms instituted by Constantine the Great. Northern barbarians are to be told that Constantine had forbidden the marriage of a Roman emperor to any foreign house save a Frankish one. Bans on various

---

[71] F. Dölger, *Byzantinische Diplomatik* (Ettal, 1956), pp. 114, 141–3, 146–8; G. Rösch, *Onoma basileias* (Vienna, 1978), pp. 37–8, 111–16. The title 'emperor of the Romans' first appeared on the silver coins of Michael I about the time of his recognition of Charlemagne as an 'emperor' in 812: P. Grierson, *Catalogue of the Byzantine coins in the Dumbarton Oaks Collection: Leo III to Nicephorus III, 717–1081*, vol. II.1 (Washington, D.C., 1973), pp. 64, 178, 364.

[72] *Decline and fall*, ed. Milman, ch. 53, p. 265.

other kinds of gift or concession to foreigners are also attributed to him.[73]

The sense of invoking Rome's name, with its widely known connotations of legitimate hegemony, may seem obvious enough. What is less obvious is the fact that Constantine VII is offering his son *supplementary* grounds for asserting Byzantine hegemony over certain areas which were of keenest concern. He supplies stories which relate in one way or another to the restoration of 'Roman' overlordship or moral authority *after* the areas had been overrun by the barbarians. Undoubtedly the range of written sources was very narrow, and the data – some of it word-of-mouth – was clumsily collated by Constantine and his assistants. But there is a principle of selectivity running through the work. Constantine merely outlines the rise of Mahomet and the loss of the Middle Eastern provinces to the Arabs, followed by North Africa and Spain. There was no question of any Roman recovery of these lands· over the intervening years and, at the time of writing (*c.* 950), there was every prospect of Byzantium remaining on a war footing and on the defensive. The *De administrando* shows awareness that the Abbasid caliphate was fragmenting, and Constantine registers appropriate protocols and ceremonial for diplomatic exchanges with the various new formations in another work.[74] But there remained little scope for *démarches* beyond the arranging of truces and prisoner-exchanges. Things were different in the central Mediterranean and the Balkans. There, Byzantium possessed bases and enclaves scattered along the south Italian and Dalmatian coasts and was interested in the potentates and tribes of their hinterlands and in more distant but potentially troublesome or useful powers such as the Franks or the Hungarians. The *De administrando* recalls that Italy had formed part of the Roman Empire and recounts the loss of most of the Italian peninsula to the Lombards; the arrival of the Slavs in the Balkans is also recounted.[75] The stories are tendentious and largely inaccurate, but Constantine was not merely indulging

---

[73] *DAI*, ch. 13, pp. 66–73; P. A. Yannopoulos, 'Histoire et légende chez Constantin VII', *Byzantion* 57 (1987), pp. 159–61.

[74] *DAI*, ch. 25, pp. 108–9; Constantine VII, *De cerimoniis aulae byzantinae*, II.1, 15, 47, 48, ed. J. J. Reiske, 1 (Bonn, 1829), pp. 522, 570–94, 682–6, 689–90; J. Shepard, 'Messages, ordres et ambassades: diplomatie centrale et frontalière à Byzance' in *Voyages et voyageurs à Byzance et en Occident*, ed. A. Dierkens and J.-M. Sansterre (Liège, 1997).

[75] *DAI*, ch. 27, pp. 112–17; ch. 30, pp. 138–41; ch. 31, pp. 146–9; ch. 32, pp. 152–3.

in antiquarian fantasy or enunciating the principle of imperial primacy for its own sake. He was also trying to base claims to Byzantine hegemony over these regions on relatively recent history. Thus he recounts at length the feats of Basil I in liberating the Dalmatian towns and southern Italy from the Arabs and feels able to claim that 'the men of Capua and the men of Benevento have been under the authority of the Romans in complete servitude and subjection, for that great benefit which was done to them'.[76] Byzantine claims to overlordship over the Serbs and Croats are given a different basis – that they were settled in their lands by the emperor Heraclius and received protection from him against the Avars. Heraclius was, above all, responsible for their baptism, teaching the Serbs 'fairly to perform the works of piety and expound[ing] to them the faith of the Christians'.[77] Roman emperors thus have strong moral authority over them, as they do over the southern Italians.

This was not necessarily to be used to justify annexation or direct intervention. But it supplemented and reinforced the general claim to hegemony which the name 'Roman' implied. As the 'benefactor' of Italians and Slavs the emperor now had all the more right to bestow titles on, and harbour exiles or pretenders from among, the ruling families of these peoples, posing as their ultimate arbiter.[78] And tales of liberation and baptism could serve to deny the right of *other* interested parties to exercise authority in these areas. Thus the underlying theme of an extensive chapter about southern Italy is that it was not the disorganized Franks but the 'Romans' who were chiefly responsible for the expulsion of the Moslems.[79] The emperor's concerns about the Balkans are spelled out unmistakably. It is said both of the Serbs and of the Croats, in different chapters but identical words, that their rulers have 'never been subjected to the prince of Bulgaria'.[80] The De administrando's lumbering narratives about the Balkans are partly intended to

---

[76] DAI, ch. 29, pp. 134–5.
[77] DAI, ch. 32, pp. 154–5.
[78] The DAI (ch. 32, pp. 156–61) gives a detailed account of the emperor's exercise of this right over Serbian princes in the earlier tenth century. See also Shepard, 'Byzantine diplomacy', pp. 60–1; T. S. Brown, 'Ethnic independence and cultural deference: the attitude of the Lombard principalities to Byzantium c. 876–1077', Byzantinoslavica 54 (1993), pp. 8–9.
[79] DAI, ch. 29, pp. 128–35.
[80] DAI, ch. 31, pp. 150–1; ch. 32, pp. 160–1.

provide counterarguments to Bulgarian hegemony over the Serbs, Croats and other Slavs, while the tale of the liberation of southern Italy serves to counter any future Frankish claims in that area.[81] Thus there is method, or at least some rationale, in the *De administrando*'s seemingly random and tendentious antiquarianism. 'History', in the sense of a written version of meritorious imperial deeds, could be invoked to justify current spheres of influence and to denounce the intrusions of others. It is in such insistent use – and recasting – of the past that one of the distinctive qualities of Byzantine diplomacy resides.[82]

One may, then, categorize Constantine's *De administrando* as amounting to a collection of briefing-materials for negotiations, altercations and other dealings with foreign potentates. The data is very heterogeneous and ill-matched, but there is a certain design. It is no accident that the *De administrando* eschews a 'historical' approach to areas where Byzantium had few territorial ambitions and where appeals to history, religion and imperial Roman *gloire* would cut little ice. This was the case in the steppes to the north of the Black Sea. There roamed the nomadic Pechenegs, branded as 'the devil's brats' even by the Hungarians.[83] Byzantium could only claim past dominion over the Crimea and some stretches of the Sea of Azov's coasts. Moreover, as the *De administrando* clearly states, the Pechenegs were quite recent arrivals in the Black Sea steppes: had been there 'for fifty-five years up to the present day'.[84] They were therefore the least likely of peoples to be responsive to claims and arguments drawn from Byzantine versions of history, whether classical or 'modern'. Yet they were the dominant force in the steppes and, with skilful handling, could be manipulated against other potentially menacing peoples. Constantine expressly says as much.[85]

The only language which the Pechenegs understood was that

---

[81] In 968 Liudprand invoked Louis II's achievement in expelling the Muslims from southern Italy. One of his subsequent interlocutors was Basil the Parakoimomenos, who was probably involved in, or at least provided documents for, the composition of the *De administrando*: *Legatio*, chs. 7, 15–18, in *Opera*, ed. Becker, pp. 179, 183–5; Ševčenko, 'Re-reading Constantine Porphyrogenitus', p. 191.

[82] On occasion the Bulgarians themselves were reminded that they occupied former Roman territory; see Theodore Daphnopates, *Correspondance*, ed. J. Darrouzès and L. G. Westerink (Paris, 1978), pp. 64–5.

[83] *DAI*, ch. 8, pp. 56–7.

[84] *DAI*, ch. 37, pp. 166–7.   [85] *DAI*, chs. 4, 5, pp. 50–3.

of gift-giving, entertainment and hostage-taking. So the *De administrando* concentrates on these techniques and on practical means of dealing with them.[86] Constantine does not spin yarns purporting to give the emperor moral authority over them. It is not that bribery, hostages and low cunning were absent from Byzantium's dealings with potentates in the Balkans, the Latin west and Armenia. There too, divide-and-rule formed part of the emperor's stock-in-trade. But for these regions, he had other devices, attuned to their superior cultures – and needed 'historical' stories to counter any which foreign potentates might present in vindication of their claims. Moreover, the Scandinavian Rus, the Khazars and even, by *c.* 950, the Hungarians were believed to have gained enough glimmerings about Byzantium's culture and past to be treated to tales involving Constantine the Great. The Pechenegs, in contrast, were so 'greedy' and treacherous that visiting agents were not even to leave the walls of Cherson or their boats before taking hostages. So it seemed worthwhile for detailed stipulations about this to be entered into Constantine's manual for his son.[87]

Through such measures as this – the recording, as well as practice, of careful handling techniques – the Byzantines achieved some success in employing poor yet martial peoples to distract or overawe their more sedentary neighbours. These instruments of policy were a practical supplement or alternative to other devices, such as the invocation of rights and moral authority based on 'historical' anecdotes. Gibbon remarks on 'the political management of the Greeks' and on their 'perpetual and useful correspondence' with 'neighbouring tribes'. But the former phrase lurks in a footnote, while the latter is never fully expounded.[88] To do so would require Gibbon to temper his indictment of the indolence and imitativeness of the Greeks and, perhaps, to acknowledge a certain rationale in their efforts to refashion history in the service of diplomacy.

Gibbon can, then, be faulted for his reluctance to collate or explain the evidence before him of the singular qualities of Byzantine diplomacy. Fuller recognition of its initiatives might have helped construct a more cohesive narrative. Gibbon would

[86] *DAI*, chs. 4–8, pp. 50–7.   [87] *DAI*, chs. 7, 8, pp. 54–5.
[88] *Decline and fall*, ed. Milman, ch. 55, p. 315 and n. 71; cf. ch. 53, p. 254 n. 70.

have had ample opportunities for highlighting other reverses and unforeseen side-effects of the diplomacy besides Alexius' precipitation of the First Crusade. In fact, the study of Byzantine diplomacy could be regarded as revealing the Byzantines' limited cultural range and sketchy background knowledge of the world around them. Gibbon would not have been so facile as to ascribe the failures of Byzantine arms solely to the classicizing tendencies of those in court circles who wrote on military matters. *Skirmishing* would have opened his eyes to the battle-seasoned 'horse-sense' of commanders. Yet he might have had something negative to say about the Byzantines' tendency, once the tide turned in their favour in the tenth century, to look back to the Roman past for both inspiration and concrete examples. He would have had greatest cause for self-congratulation over his treatment of Byzantine missionary work. The Constantinopolitan sources were of little avail in tracing the deeds of monks and holy men, and the latter made tempting targets for darts of irony. But the historian's eye discerned a link between them, the conversion of barbarian rulers and the cultural advance of those rulers and their peoples. Gibbon's insight and judgment on this theme bears out his claim to be a 'philosophical' historian.

CHAPTER 5

Gibbon and the later Byzantine Empires

Anthony Bryer

In memory of my parents, 1994

I take the sixth and last quarto volume.[1] It is also the least regarded, maybe because editors from Guizot to Bury were flagging, if not out of their depth, when they came to it. But it is perhaps the most remarkable. In time and place it covers more ground than any other: in time from the First Crusade to the last fall of Constantinople in 1453; in place from Cublai's canal to Pekin to Poggio's vision of Rome in 1430. It was written faster than any other volume: thirteen months from 18 May 1786 to between the hours of eleven and twelve on 27 June 1787.[2] Since 15 October 1764 Gibbon had had a *rendez-vous* to keep with the barefooted friars in Rome. Did he then really know where and when it was to be? By starting in Rome on Christmas Day 800, Bryce actually planned to end his history of the Holy Roman Empire in Vienna in 1806.[3] After the reception of his first three volumes, Gibbon evidently knew where he was going to end up, though perhaps not even then how to arrange his grand and still lively themes, such as the confrontation of Rome by nomadic societies. But he claims a constancy in volume VI, chapter 64, which introduces the Mongols and Ottomans thus: 'The reader is invited to review the chapters of the second and third volumes; the manners of pastoral nations, the conquests of Attila

---

[1] E. Gibbon, *The history of the decline and fall of the Roman Empire*, vol. VI (London, 1788), to which all further reference. I do not know whether having only the first edition to hand is a help or a hindrance. My copy has neat manuscript post-proof corrections, not noticed in Norton, *Bibliography*, pp. 57–63, but all, so far as I can see, adopted in the edition of D. Womersley (Harmondsworth, 1994), which has different pagination.

[2] E. Gibbon, *Memoirs of my life and writings*, ed. A. O. J. Cockshut and S. Constantine (Keele, 1994), p. 205, n. 72.

[3] J. Bryce, *The Holy Roman Empire* (Oxford, 1864).

and the Huns, which were composed at a time when I entertained the wish, rather than the hope, of concluding my history.'[4]

I look for signs of haste. Stylistically there are none. In these choppy seas the rhythm which Gibbon set up from volume II – waves of words with a breaker around every fourth sentence – shipwrecks whole nations at the same steady pace. For variety we read it today from the footnotes up. Sometimes obscure skirmishes run along the footnotes, as they do along the bottom of the Bayeux tapestry; in volume VI the skirmishes are not just with our familiar sparring-partner, Voltaire, but introduce new and outlandish historians such as Barletius and Cantemir. It may only be an impression that Gibbon is more reckless in judgment on this last stretch. His prose is not given to quotation: there is too much to remember. But although, or because, it is not in the *Oxford Book of Quotations*, volume VI surely has the most reckless and commonly misquoted passage of all. It refers to the Council of Constance:

Of the three popes, John the twenty-third was the first victim: he fled and was brought back a prisoner: the most scandalous charges were suppressed; the vicar of Christ was only accused of piracy, murder, rape, sodomy, and incest; and after subscribing his own condemnation, he expiated in prison the imprudence of trusting his person to a free city beyond the Alps.[5]

In this sequence of statements, Gibbon grades degrees of scandal, but the shock wave breaks silently with the last. That Constance (Konstanz), an imperial free city from 1192–1547, had been so prevailed upon by a German emperor to imprison the then penitent and former anti-Pope John XXIII was scandal enough in 1415–18. But in 1786–7, when Gibbon wrote those words in Lausanne, he and his library lay in tax and thrall to another Transalpine free city. Protestant Bern ruled Francophone Lausanne from 1536–1789. Was this not the greatest scandal of all?[6] Such contemporary concerns should not surprise: after all, in the next century it was the subsequent fate of the cantons of Switzerland that inspired George Grote to write a twelve-volume *History of Greece* (London, 1846–56).

In fact Gibbon had for volume VI almost as much chronicle evidence as for the other five put together. For Byzantium alone, as

---

[4] *Decline and fall*, VI, p. 288 n. 1.   [5] *Ibid.*, VI, p. 605.
[6] Gibbon, *Memoirs*, ed. Cockshut and Constantine, p. 215.

Gibbon makes touching tribute, there was an overlapping relay from Anna Comnena in the twelfth century to George Sphrantzes in the fifteenth, in the Paris *Corpus* from 1648 and in the Venice *Corpus* from 1729.[7] He read and comments on each author individually. In the west there was Muratori and the work of the Maurists – but if anyone has evidence that Gibbon touched a Bollandist, I should like to hear of it. Yet volume vi is not a work of compression, or even synthesis, but of extraction. The clue comes in a note in one of his memoirs: 'I have followed the judicious precept of the Abbé de Mably . . . who advises the historian not to dwell too minutely on the decay of the eastern empire; but to consider the barbarian conquerors as a more worthy subject of his narrative, "Fas est ab hoste doceri".'[8]

Thus great illustrative themes are taken at slow measure: the caging of Bajazet, or the conquest of Constantinople, where after fifty pages the remaining thirty-year reign of Mehmed II is dealt with in a sentence or four. But the great themes are the barbarian conquerors, now Turks and Tatars, against which the better documented Byzantium is a backdrop.

I have called this paper 'The later Byzantine Empires', but in fact Gibbon recognizes only one out of those of Nicaea, Epirus, Constantinople and Trebizond. Trebizond, the last Byzantine Empire, survived in the Pontus until 1461, but gets only two mentions in Gibbon, for the good reason that the library of its greatest son, Cardinal Bessarion (?1399–1472), was only effectively opened in Venice after 1806.[9] The Marcian Library preserves the chronicle of Panaretos, a remorseless account of the political history of the Empire of Trebizond. The despotate of Epirus gets similar short notice. Yet, acting on the precepts of the abbé de Mably, I doubt if Gibbon would have allotted them more space had he been able. A much more serious omission, indeed throughout the work, is an understanding of the Slav presence in the Balkans, most notably Stefan IV Dushan's Serbian kingdom (1331–45) and empire (1345–55). Even without Slav sources Gibbon should have sensed the pressure of Serbia in the works of John VI Kantakouzenos. But

---

[7] *Decline and fall*, vi, p. 517 n. 97.

[8] Gibbon, *Memoirs*, ed. Cockshut and Constantine, p. 204 n. 71; G. Keynes (ed.), *The Library of Edward Gibbon. A catalogue* (London, 1990; 2nd edn, London, 1980), pp. 185, 203–4.

[9] *Decline and fall*, vi, pp. 182–3, 512; cf. J. Gill, *Personalities of the Council of Florence and other essays* (Oxford, 1964), p. 54.

Gibbon is the first to sense the nature of this Byzantine emperor-monk's apology for his life. As emperor, John (1341–54), he had been a sort of Byzantine de Gaulle: only he could have introduced the Turks under Orhan (1324–60), son of Osman, the original Ottoman, across the Straits into Europe. But Gibbon complains that as a monk with the monastic name Joasaph (1354–83), Kantakouzenos' reading of the Koran had not rid him of the vulgar partiality of his new profession. Here we must draw the line of prejudice some-where, perhaps between 1354 and 1786. As a critic Gibbon was wary enough in interpreting the motives of his principal source. But he was recklessly tough on Kantakouzenos for seeking enlightenment not from some prospective loom over the Swiss Alps, but in the still stunning light of Mount Tabor. Dammit! Kantakouzenos had done his best for Gibbon by marrying his own daughter, Theodora, to Orhan (whereby hang even greater prejudices), but such calibration was still outshone by the example of Saladin. Along with Kantakouzenos, Gibbon also complains of the 'long and barren pages of the Byzantine annals'.[10] Yet he did not find them such. He found of the fifteenth-century Chalkokondyles that his 'proper subject is drowned in a sea of episode',[11] but, my! how he uses them – including spotting the equivocal attitude of Niketas Choniates to the Latins, and the light that Pachymeres sheds on the Mongols. He uses Akropolites largely for an episode, the anecdote that John Vatatzes' crown, called 'eggy', was bought from the proceeds of an imperial poultry farm, and hence to commend the self-sufficiency of the economy of the empire of Nicaea.[12]

Gibbon lacked the documentary, let alone archaeological, evidence, that has only recently transformed the study of the later Byzantine Empires, but which still fit some of his incipient concerns. Documents include charters, in Byzantium particularly

---

[10] *Decline and fall*, VI, pp. 221, 259–61, 277 n. 36, 278 n. 38. 'A pernicious tenet has been imputed to the Mahometans, the duty of *extirpating* all other religions by the sword. This charge of ignorance and bigotry is refuted by the Koran, by the history of the Musulman con-querors, and by their public and legal tolerance of the Christian worship': VI, p. 9. On Kantakouzenos's own tolerance, see A. Bryer, 'Greek historians on the Turks: the case of the first Byzantine–Ottoman marriage' in R. H. C. Davis, J. M. Wallace-Hadrill, R. J. A. I. Catto and M. H. Keen (eds.), *The writing of history in the Middle Ages, essays presented to Richard William Southern* (Oxford, 1981), pp. 471–93.
[11] *Decline and fall* VI, p. 327 n. 66.
[12] *Ibid.*, VI, pp. 128 n. 13, 130 n. 18, 159 nn. 72–3, 160 n. 74, 168 n. 90, 170 nn. 92–4, 172 nn. 97–8, 173 nn. 99, 222, 228 n. 14.

those from Mount Athos and in Turkey of the *defter* registers, along with the Venetian commercial archives, let alone Bessarion's library. But the instincts are there. He takes the *Assizes of Jerusalem* at face value, but at least he takes them.[13] I am not making Gibbon out to be a proto-*Annales* man, but his concern for material culture would have allowed him to take snuff with, say, Lefebvre des Noëttes. It ran to weights and measures in Constantinople and coinage and exchange in Caffa.[14] On windmills, gunpowder and other Greek technological failings, except their fire, I fear that he would have fallen not for K. D. White, but Lynn White Jr.[15] He was concerned with numbers, rather than people, making great demographic leaps with fresh reports of travellers: Chandler, Pococke, Smith, Tournefort, Spon and Wheler, Peysonnel and de Tott.[16] But the travellers gave him a genuinely vivid sense of geography.

Why did Gibbon add only two maps to his book? His sense of time and place was critical. He may almost have forgiven 'M. de Voltaire . . . [who] unsupported by either fact or probability, has generously bestowed the Canary Islands on the Roman Empire', for in pursuit of higher truth that *philosophe* had also found Paris on the banks of the Bosphorus.[17] But there was no mercy for cartographers. The final footnote to Gibbon's first chapter, referring to Thomas Templeman's *A new survey of the globe* (London, 1729), ends with a

---

[13] *Ibid.*, VI, pp. 66–7.

[14] *Ibid.* VI, pp. 251 n. 49, 281–3, 370 n. 81, 396 n. 34, 475 n. 24, 484 n. 36; cf. R. Lefebvre des Noëttes, *L'Attelage et le cheval de selle à travers les âges* (Paris, 1931); E. Schilbach, *Byzantinische metrologie* (Munich, 1970).

[15] *Decline and fall*, VI, p. 208, 350 n. 43, 375–7; for such material determinism, cf. L. White, Jr, *Medieval technology and social change* (Oxford, 1962), but also, for example, K. D. White, *Roman farming* (London, 1970).

[16] For example, *Decline and fall*, VI, pp. 49 n. 94, 58 n. 106, 250 n. 48, 255 n. 56, 314 n. 48, 348 nn. 37–9, 349 n. 40, 396 n. 34, 488 n. 44, 512 n. 88, 513 n. 89; it is worth noting that Gibbon owned a history of the discovery and conquest of the Canary Islands (London, 1764), cf. Keynes, *Library*, pp. 43, 92, 218, 226, 256, 269. Gibbon is quite as critical of travellers to countries he never visited as he is of geographers, for example of the engaging and Munchausenish Baron F. de Tott, whose castles of 1773 still adorn the Bosphoros, to 'the consternation of the Turks. But that adventurous traveller does not possess the art of gaining our confidence.' *Decline and fall*, VI, p. 477 n. 26.

[17] *Decline and fall*, I, p. 26 n. 87; G. Murray, *Voltaire's 'Candide': the Protean gardener, 1755–1762*, Studies on Voltaire and the Eighteenth Century, vol. LXIX (Geneva, 1970), pp. 349–85. The folding maps in front of Gibbon's original vols. II and III include the Canary Islands and not Tikrit, while Isauria is singled out in Black Letter, although it just escaped the Goths. But they are otherwise exemplary and T. Kitchin's cartography bears distinctive marks of Gibbon's editorship.

Parthian snap: 'I distrust both the doctor's learning and his maps.'[18]
In our volume VI he complains that: 'We want a good map of
Epirus.'[19] Indeed, we still do. But he had them in his head. Whence
came his view of pasture and steppe? It can be done. Josef Markwart
was to write the definitive historical geography of southern
Armenia and the sources of the Tigris without leaving the
Mekhitarist monastery in Vienna. In this volume Gibbon describes
and places the elegant palace of Nymphaion (where Vatatzes died
and where Michael VIII Palaiologos made treaty with the Genoese
and in 1261 heard that Constantinople had fallen to him) simply
from Akropolites and other evidence.[20] It was, and still is, there,
just as he said it would be. It is a pity that the *Dilettanti* never
commissioned Gibbon to pinpoint the site of Troy, which took
Englishmen so much trouble, even when an Englishman found he
already owned it.[21]

Volume VI is, however, still about barbarians, and how barbarous
they were not. 'The Turks of Asia were less barbarous perhaps than
the shepherds of Bulgaria and Servia.'[22] Chapter 58, on the first
four crusades, was a more delicate matter. Brutish Crusaders, even
pusillanimous Greeks, long delayed the progress of society and the
maturity of Europe, until in Gibbon's day light broke from Scotland
with David Hume (1711–77), William Robertson (1721–93) and Adam
Smith (1723–90). We are left with two flawed figures, with whom
one could at least reason: Saladin of Tikrit (1138–93) and Voltaire
of Ferney (1694–1778). Note the geography. Ferney was a safe haven
just over the Lausanne border. But the 1966 *Guide Bleu* simply
signals Tikrit ('3,000–4,000 inhab.') as a railway station on the

---

[18] *Decline and fall*, I, p. 28 n. 89.

[19] *Ibid.*, VI, p. 457 n. 40: N. Hammond, *Epirus* (Oxford, 1967), would be the first to agree.
Gibbon did not animadvert (well, not much) on Byzantine geographical errors, such as
those of Chalkokondyles: 'Had these modern Greeks never read Strabo, or any of their
lesser geographers?': *Decline and fall*, VI, p. 391 n. 23 (the answer is, well, sometimes): see
Angeliki E. Laiou, 'On political geography: the Black Sea of Pachymeres' in R. Beaton and
Charlotte Roueché (eds.), *The making of Byzantine history. Studies dedicated to Donald M. Nicol*
(London, 1993), pp. 95, 99, 110. But, without clapping eyes on the evidence, Gibbon was
even harder on the great botanical traveller J. Pitton de Tournefort (1656–1708): 'I must
regret the map or plan which Tournefort sent to the French minister of the marine',
Decline and fall, VI, p. 469 n. 12.

[20] *Ibid.*, VI, pp. 226 n. 9, 231 n. 18; cf. J. Markwart, *Südarmenien und die Tigrisquellen* (Vienna,
1930) (no map).

[21] Marcelle Robinson, 'Pioneer, scholar, and victim: an appreciation of Frank Calvert
(1828–1908)', *Anatolian Studies* 44 (1994), pp. 153–67.

[22] *Decline and fall*, VI, p. 272.

Baghdad–Mosul line. Yet, by linking the historical geography of J. B. B. d'Anville (1697–1782) with Sharaf al-Din's *Zafar-nama* of Timur (1336–1405), Gibbon spotted the strategic importance of the place as early as chapter 19, or AD 360. This in 1916 did not escape an Australian prisoner of war there either: 'The Arabs of Ticret were of a more warlike type than any I had seen elsewhere. Gibbon records that for a long time during Persian dominion in Mesopotamia they retained their independence.'[23] Given such intelligence, no one should have been surprised that it is Saddam Hussein of Tikrit and other natives of that place who rule Iraq today. But Gibbon is more subtle: while he twitted Voltaire of Ferney for his preference for Turks, he explained that Saladin of Tikrit was a Kurd.[24] Anyway, both were more rational than any crusader.

I am not, however, concerned with *Lettres Persanes*, Turkish Spies, or how Islam was perceived or used during the Enlightenment. More important is that Gibbon understood that the Seljuk were not the Ottoman Turks, and that Tamburlaine was no real relation of Ghengis Khan, however spelled.

Most important is Gibbon's examination of the 'Origins of the Ottomans, AD 1240, &c.', written in 1786, which since 1934 has burgeoned into a small industry, already recognized as perhaps more interesting to connoisseurs of ideological or national historiography than anything that it adds to Gibbon. Like Gibbon in late eighteenth-century Lausanne, his late twentieth-century Ottomanist *epigoni* may plead complications of context too – such as writing under the shadow of the Ottoman Empire in Republican Turkey, or under that of Paul Wittek in the School of Oriental and African Studies in London from 1949–61.[25] But none that I can find

---

[23] T. W. White, *Guests of the unspeakable: the odyssey of an Australian airman – being a record of captivity and escape in Turkey* (Sydney, 1928), p. 69, apparently referring to E. Gibbon, *The history of the decline and fall of the Roman Empire*, II (London, 1781), p. 158 n. 61. Otherwise, VI, p. 210 n. 69; and on the strategic geography of Ferney: Gibbon, *Memoirs*, p. 151 and Murray, *Voltaire*, pp. 301–48.

[24] *Decline and fall*, VI, pp. 92, 510 n. 84.

[25] *Ibid.*, VI, pp. 310–12. Cf. C. Heywood, 'Between historical myth and "mythistory": the limits of Ottoman history', *Byzantine and Modern Greek Studies* 12 (1988), pp. 315–45; and H. Berktay, 'The "other" feudalism. A critique of 20th-century Turkish historiography and its particularisation of Ottoman society' (Ph.D. thesis, Birmingham University 1990). The index of *New approaches to state and peasant in Ottoman history*, ed. H. Berktay and Suraiya Faroqhi, *Library of Peasant Studies* X (London, 1992), refers to the *hoca* K. (H.) Marx (d. 1883) and the *gazi* Osman (d. 1324) in a ratio of 28:1. By just as startling a contrast,

thought to refer to Gibbon, who in two quarto pages and three footnotes defined the whole debate 150 years before it was resumed. I am not capricious in saying that the jury is still out on the succinct instructions with which he first sent it, and have yet to be bettered.

Gibbon begins by giving the Ottoman state a precise birthday: 'It was on the twenty-seventh of July, in the year twelve hundred and ninety-nine of the Christian aera, that Othman first invaded the territory of Nicomedia.'[26] His sources are contemporary but Byzantine. His problem is that 'I am ignorant whether the Turks have any writers older than Mahomet II.'[27] Strictly speaking, that is still true: they did, but we remain ignorant of them.[28] So we must return to Gibbon's analysis of the (not invariably hostile) Greek witness of whom or what Osman (1281/99–1324), the eponymous founder of the Ottoman Empire, represented:

if we describe that pastoral chief as a shepherd and a robber, we must separate from those characters all idea of ignominy and baseness. Othman possessed, and perhaps surpassed, the ordinary virtues of a soldier; and the circumstances of time and place were propitious to his independence and success . . . He was situate on the verge of the Greek empire: the Koran sanctified his *gazi*, or holy war, against the infidels; and their political errors unlocked the passes of mount Olympus, and invited him to descend into the plains of Bithynia.[29]

There we have it in three: was he the rude shepherd of later romance (shepherds are rarely rude); was he a Turkish Robin Hood, running a protection racket from Söğüt along the trade routes of the Sangarios (historians like describing trade routes in lieu of economy); or was he a *gazi*, wielder of the holy scimitar of Islam, who by 27 July 1299 was blessed with the only infidel border in sight which happened to promise winter grazing? I refer to a sample of works which do not refer to Gibbon, but which since 1934

C. Imber, *The Ottoman Empire, 1300–1481* (Istanbul, 1990 (where the index score is Marx 0: Osman 3)), begins his book by quoting A. Conan Doyle, *The adventures of Sherlock Holmes*: 'It is a capital mistake to theorise before one has data. Insensibly one begins to twist the facts to suit theories, instead of theories to suit facts.' Gibbon had something to say about all this, but none thought to consult him.

[26] *Decline and fall*, VI, p. 311.

[27] *Ibid.*, VI, p. 312 n. 41.

[28] V. L. Ménage, 'The beginnings of Ottoman historiography' in B. Lewis and P. M. Holt (eds.), *Historians of the Middle East, Historical writing on the peoples of Asia*, vol. IV (London, 1962), pp. 168–79.

[29] *Decline and fall*, VI, p. 311.

have expanded such themes in pursuit of what Marc Bloch called the fallacy of origin.[30]

Gibbon knew that the Ottoman states of 1299 and 1453 were not the same. But he now had a secondary source, described on its title page: Demetrius Cantemir, late prince of Moldavia, *The history of the growth and decay of the Othman Empire*, translated by N. Tindal, M.A., vicar of Great Waltham in Essex (London, 1734). In a remarkable example of how history can fail to imitate art, Dimitrie Cantemir (1673–1723), last native prince of Moldavia (1710–11) (although his son Antioh told Voltaire that they were descended from Timur), persuaded himself that the Ottoman Empire, of which he was tributary, really was in decay. So he threw in his lot with Peter the Great, who was promptly defeated by the Ottomans, and therefore awarded Cantemir's throne to more pliant Phanariot Greek *hospodars* from 1712–1821. Lord Dacre has described how Antioh Cantemir laboured to promote his father's work in England, where the supposed father of Romanian historiography was almost entirely ignored until taken up by Gibbon in volume vi.[31] Gibbon was in fact not uncritical of Dimitrie Cantemir: 'The author is guilty of strange blunders in Oriental history; but he was conversant with the language, the annals, and institutions of the Turks.'[32] But Gibbon belatedly brought Cantemir into the blood-

---

30 M. Fuad Köprülü's Sorbonne lectures of 1934 are now ed. and trans. by G. Leiser, *The origins of the Ottoman Empire* (New York, 1992). P. Wittek's London lectures of 1937 on *The rise of the Ottoman Empire*, Royal Asiatic Society Monograph xxiii (London, 1938), have been reprinted several times. For a pastoral thesis of origins, see R. P. Lindner, *Nomads and Ottomans in medieval Anatolia*, Indiana University Uralic and Altaic Series cxliv (Bloomington, 1983). C. Foss promises what may be termed the 'Robin Hood' view, ever hopeful in the face of the conclusion of C. Imber, 'The legend of Osman Gazi' in Elizabeth Zachariadou (ed.), *The Ottoman Emirate (1300–1389)*, Halcyon Days in Crete i (Rethymnon, 1993), p. 75: 'The best thing that a modern historian can do is to admit frankly that the earliest history of the Ottomans is a black hole. Any attempt to fill this hole will result simply in the creation of more fables.'

31 H. Trevor-Roper, 'Dimitrie Cantemir's *Ottoman History* and its reception in England', *Revue Roumaine d'Histoire* 24 (1985), pp. 51–66. I am struck by Cantemir's inside information, by comparison not only with what was generally available in England in many editions of works by Richard Knolles (1550–1610) and Sir Paul Rycaut (1629–1700), but, say on the origins of the Ottomans with: P. A. [Poulet], *Nouvelles relations dv Levant . . .* (1667), pp. 306–7 (whose primitive maps escaped Gibbon's stricture); or [Mme. de Gomez], *Anecdotes, ou histoire secrette de la Maison Ottomane*, vol. i (Amsterdam, 1722), pp. 9–13. Doubtless someone is doing a Ph.D. thesis on the subject. But I am more impressed by how Gibbon found an inside source in Cantemir.

32 *Decline and fall*, vi, p. 312 n. 41. But Gibbon's judgment was not so prudent. He knew that Cantemir had access to more Oriental sources and languages than he. The two historians shared Greek, though of very different kinds. Yet Gibbon swallowed

stream of English historiography, along with a Persian distich
which still haunts, in one form or another, every subsequent
account of the fall of Constantinople. For the record, Cantemir's
(or rather Tindal's) own version of what the conquering Sultan
Mehmed II said when surveying the scene from St Sophia on 29 May
1453 is:

The Spider has wove her Web in the Imperial Palace,
the Owl has sung her watch Song upon the Towers of *Efrasiyab*.[33]

Cantemir's etymology for *Tekfur*, a Turkish term for a non-Muslim ruler, as a derivation
of the Greek genitive *tou kyriou* (VI, p. 357 n. 60; *Satyres de Prince Cantemir traduit de Russe en
François*, l'Abbé Count O. de Guasco (London, 1750), p. 51). As an alternative term I do not
think that Gibbon made the genuine Greek connection between Turkish *efendi* and
English *authentic*. But it does make one wonder about Gibbon's Greek and his sense of
sound. German was his blind spot, but may be a clue to why he wondered about the name
of *Werdan*, Heraclius's general who rode on a white mule decorated with gold chains to
face the naked warriors of Islam in 633–4 (V, p. 303 n. 57), for it had 'little of a Greek
aspect or sound. If the Byzantine sources have mangled the Oriental names, the Arabs,
in this instance, likewise have taken ample revenge on their enemies. In transposing the
Greek character from right to left, might they not produce, from the familiar appellation
of *Andrew*, something like the anagram *Werdan?*' Well, yes, except that, even before such
crossword puzzles, the Greek for *Andrew* was *Andreas* and 'W' a letter and sound (other
than soft 'B' or 'V') unknown to Theophanes. But some have since found 'W' quite useful
in transliterating from Armenian, which seems to be at the bottom of both cases – as
in *T'agawor*, or *Wardan*. Cf. G. M. Young, *Gibbon* (London, 1948), p. 21; J. F. Haldon,
Byzantium in the seventh century (Cambridge, 1990), p. 50; A. Bryer, 'The Grand Komnenos
and the Great Khan at Karakorum in 1246' in *Itineraires d'Orient. Hommages à Claude Cahen*,
ed. R. Curiel and R. Gyselen, Res Orientales VI (Bures-sur-Yvette, 1994), p. 259.

33 *Cantemir*, p. 102 n. 16 also gives a transliteration from Persian: *Perdè dari mikuined ber kysr
Caisar ankebut Bumi nueubet mizènedber kiumbeti Efrasiyab*. This appears to come direct from
a witness, Tursun Beg, who calls it one of the 'sugar-diffusing pronouncements' of his
sovereign. But Tursun Beg's account was not published until ed. M. Arif, *Tarih Ebu'-Fat'h*
(Istanbul, AH 1330/1914 AD), p. 57. Cantemir writes that the Conqueror 'is reported to say
an extempore Distich in the *Persian* Language'. Gibbon, who admits Cantemir as his
only authority, alters (a) Tindal's English wording of his translation of Cantemir; and
(b) writes that Mehmed II 'repeated an elegant distich of Persian poetry' (*Decline and fall*,
VI, p. 507 and n. 77). The first does not matter too much: I could fill a page of Western
versions of these famous lines and improvements upon them, slipped in by scholars
who should know better. What matters is (b): whether the Conqueror extemporized
(Cantemir, Tursun) or repeated (Gibbon, *alios*) the elegiac distich. This would tell us
something about the young Turkish Sultan's upbringing, which also included copy-book
Greek. To me the obvious Persian reference is to Rustam's night attack on Afrasiyab's
palace in Ferdowsi's *Shah-Nama* (X, 18 in most editions and translations). But the key-
word of *ankebut*, the spider, does not appear in the concordance of F. Wolff, *Glossar zu
Firdosis Schaname* (Berlin, 1935). Could it be that, when with the last Sasanid happening in
653 Ferdowsi laid down his pen in 1010, his tale still had some mileage? His text could be
recited. But its 'matter' (as Milton calls other such matters), was still malleable, even
live, open to courtly extemporization. Perhaps most remarkable is that Gibbon spun the
Persian distich on from Mehmed, by an authentic voice picked up by Cantemir from
Tursun, to reach us under various echoes today. I thank Feridun Ala, Lord Dacre and
Rhoads Murphey for discussion and refer for a start to a bibliographical web to J. Raby,

For the authentic transmission of such ejaculatory poetry we must be grateful. But why was Gibbon so indifferent to the long monkhood of Emperor Kantakouzenos, yet intrigued by a brief Ottoman parallel? Cantemir aroused the imagination of both Voltaire and Gibbon with his description of the abdication of Sultan Murad (Amurath) II (1421–51) in favour of the young and future conqueror, twice to escape to a sort of Sufi *ashram* not far from Nymphaion, in the period 1444–6: 'Resigning the sceptre to his son, he retired to the pleasant residence of Magnesia; but he retired to the society of saints and hermits. It was not until the fourth century of the Hegira, that the religion of Mahomet had been corrupted by an institution so adverse to his genius; but in the age of the Crusades, the various orders of Dervishes were multiplied by the example of the Christian, and even the Latin, monks.'[34] Today it is Russian scholars who have again taken up the waspish connection which Gibbon first made between the *fraticelli* and dancing dervishes, but the answer may be that Gibbon was piqued that Voltaire had read Cantemir first and had been attracted to Amurath's strange example: 'Voltaire ... admires *le Philosophe Turc*; would he have bestowed the same fame on a Christian prince for retiring to a monastery? In his way, Voltaire was a bigot, an intolerable bigot.'[35] *Touché!*

This Amurath's grandfather was Bajazet the Thunderbolt, great-grandson of the original Othman, who was (as every schoolboy knows, who knows the *dramatis personae* by these names) taken by Tamburlaine on the windy battlefield of Angora (now somewhere around Esenboğa airport, Ankara) on 28 July 1402 and died in captivity on 8 (Gibbon says 9) March 1403. Of this momentous event, Gibbon rightly seizes upon the iron cage in which Timur supposedly imprisoned Bayezid I, not as a moral, but as an historiographical lesson. His side-headings to five quarto pages are a running commentary on his method: 'The story of the iron cage / disproved by the Persian historian of Timour; / attested, 1. by the French; / 2. by the Italians; / 3. by the Arabs; / 4. by the Greeks; /

'El gran Turco. Mehmed the Conqueror as patron of the arts of Christendom' (D.Phil. thesis) (Oxford University, 1980), p. 210, and Olga M. Davidson, *Poet and hero in the Persian Book of Kings* (Ithaca, New York, 1994). Maybe someone can find the spider.

[34] *Decline and fall*, VI, pp. 442–3; *Cantemir*, pp. 88–9, 91.

[35] *Ibid.*, VI, p. 442 n. 13; K. A. Zhukov in XVIIIth International Congress of Byzantine Studies, *Summaries of communications*, vol. II (Moscow, 1991), pp. 1277–8.

5. by the Turks. / Probable conclusion.' Gibbon's likely conclusion is now probably more accessible than subsequent discussion of the same evidence to the same effect, for example published in Bucharest in 1942 or Weimar in 1981, all without reference to him, so I refer modern readers to Gibbon first.[36]

Timur does not come out of Ankara too badly, but must be admitted to have had problems of Public Relations with western historiography. By comparison Saladin was a chic client to take over from Voltaire for the then politically enlightened, to whom he was certainly more easily sold than Attila the Hun. But Timur presented Gibbon with a challenge perhaps unparalleled until Robert Maxwell (1923–92) undertook the promotion of Cantemir's successor, Nicolae Ceauşescu (1918–89). Arabshah's testimony was difficult to gloss over and it is a pity that Gibbon had only word of a manuscript which was to turn out to be Clavijo's eyewitness account of the dying Timur's last *qurultay* at Samarkand in 1404, for he would surely have responded to the openness of that Castilian envoy's report.[37] Instead our apologist was faced with pyramids of skulls, which litter Timur's conquests, and need some explaining – if only with the resort of any mass murderer: 'it was a small baby'. Gibbon cared for numbers. He was able to reduce a statistically dodgy headcount of 330,000 in volume III to a revised estimate ('Timour's amiable moderation') of 'near 300,000' skulls in volume VI.[38] But he made the most of the rule of natural law and traditional Mongol tolerance. Gibbon proposed that 'A singular conformity may be found between the religious laws of Zingis Khan and of Mr. Locke ("Constitutions of Carolina", in his works, vol. IV, p. 535. 4to edition, 1772).'[39] In turn he presented Timur as a Lawgiver, a Tatar Locke, citing the liberal *Institutions* then ascribed to him. But I cannot refer to them so precisely, for they are today regarded as nothing to do with Timur, if not spurious.[40] How sad.

---

[36] *Ibid.*, VI, pp. 352–6; M. M. Alexandrescu-Dersca, *La campagne de Timur en Anatolie (1402)* (Bucharest, 1942; reprinted London, 1977), pp. 120–2; K.-P. Matschke, *Die Schlacht bei Ankara und das Schicksal von Byzanz* (Weimar, 1981).

[37] *Ibid.*, VI, p. 359 n. 64.

[38] *Ibid.*, III, pp. 368 n. 25; VI, p. 363 n. 69.

[39] *Ibid.*, VI, p. 291 n. 6; cf. P. M. Kitromilides, 'John Locke and the Greek intellectual tradition: an episode in Locke's reception in south-east Europe' in G. A. J. Rogers (ed.), *Locke's philosophy* (Oxford, 1994), pp. 217–35.

[40] *Decline and fall*, VI, pp. 331 n. 1, 332 n. 2, 363–4; Hilda Hookham, *Tamburlaine the Conqueror* (London, 1962), p. 321.

In the Balkans, Gibbon may be credited with placing Albania (or Epirus) on the western historical map too, for although within sight of Italy, it was already in his day less known than the interior of America. Yet it was the perpetual seminary of the Turkish army – he rather approved of *devshirme*, which the Greeks call *paidomazoma*, the 'harvest of children' (and worse); Gibbon had been called up for military service too.[41] Under such terms George Kastrioti, a Geggish princeling called Skanderbeg (1405–68), had been brought up at the civil court of Murad II, the *Philosophe Turc*. His fate was to become the national hero of Albania, which has made him as irretrievable as King Arthur. By an historiographical fluke, Skanderbeg is probably still better known in the interior of China than of America, although Albanians are said to be strong in the Bronx.[42] But I doubt if he is now much known anywhere as the 'Champion of Christendom', the title bestowed upon him by Pope Nicholas V (1447–55) – we can do without some Public Relations Officers. Gibbon seized upon the problem from the start: 'I could wish for some simple, authentic memoirs of a friend of Scanderbeg, which would introduce me to the man, the time, and the place. In the old and national history of Marinus Barletius, a priest of Scodra ... [1537] ..., his gawdy and cumbersome robes are stuck with many false jewels.'[43] Quite so.

In Byzantium one would expect Gibbon to misbehave most over the 'Dispute concerning the light of mount Thabor, AD 1341–1351' and its associated civil war.[44] I have spoken above of Gibbon on the *Memoirs* of the Emperor John/monk Joasaph Kantakouzenos. Did the distempered fancies of the Cantacuzene, cloistered on Mount Athos, match the dervish dances of Amurath in Magnesia? Every Byzantinist must fear for Gibbon at this point. We know his interest in the Greeks and the Irrational, and how informed it can be. But this time he had for the prosecution only the second-hand witness of the Calabrian monk Barlaam (1290–1348); and for the defence not a word then in print from the spiritual works of Gregory

---

[41] *Ibid.*, VI, pp. 373–4.
[42] *Ibid.*, VI, pp. 454–9; A. Bryer, 'Skanderbeg: national hero of Albania', *History Today* 12 (1962), pp. 426–34, 444–5; the *Toronto Sun*, 29 June 1986, reported a population of 30,000 Albanians in the Bronx, many of them armed.
[43] *Decline and fall*, VI, p. 454 n. 36.
[44] *Ibid.*, VI, pp. 278–80.

Palamas (1296–1359), archbishop of Salonica and last sainted Father of the Orthodox Church. The issue was *hesychasm*, which he does not traduce (beyond one quotation which is forgivable because irresistible); indeed Gibbon gives Hesychasts their most useful name in English: Quietists.[45] But, like the then Serbian threat, he ignores their political arm in Salonica: the Zealots. To be critical: Gibbon would not be a safe pair of hands with other fourteenth-century Peasants' Revolts. Yet Byzantine and Ottoman Peasants' Revolts were ignored by British historians who analysed such matters a generation ago. Even today's historians of the Balkans in the 1940s have not thought to put the inspirational EAM/ELAS movement in the context of the Hesychast/Zealot relationship of the 1340s. It is worth trying out. Salonica is re-inhabited, but there are constants, such as the Serbs and Mount Athos.

With Councils, Schisms and suchlike, Gibbon was on home ground. But he knows that the Orthodox were not on home ground at the Council of Florence in 1438–9, and that Quietism and Scholasticism do not mix. He nowhere puts it like that but, by using the 1660 edition of Silvester Syropoulos critically for the first time, he described with unfeigned sympathy how the homesick Greeks were made to dance to a tune in alien mode.[46] Who says that Gibbon was impatient with Greek theology, if not an outright mishellene? His measured account of the fall of Constantinople in 1453 used the essential testimony of Leonard of Chios and has set a stately example ever since. But the conqueror's Persian distich does not conclude the work – not by 140 quarto pages. Gibbon was perhaps the first seriously to ask about what the Greeks call '*Ta meta ten Alosin*' – 'those Things after the fall'. He is good on Greek dissemination of letters – Manuel Chrysoloras (1353–1415), or Aldus Manutius (1449–1515) whose paperbacks he owned, but best on Bessarion of Trebizond, who had got his priorities right – and, like all good heroes, could snap too. In 1447 Bessarion's 'election to the chair of St Peter floated for a moment on the uncertain breath of a conclave'. 'The cardinals knocked at his door, but his conclavist refused to interrupt the studies of Bessarion; "Nicholas," said he, "thy respect has cost thee an hat, and me the

---

[45] *Ibid.*, VI, p. 279; cf. J. Meyendorff, *A study of Gregory Palamas* (London, 1964).
[46] *Decline and fall*, VI, pp. 403 nn. 50–1, 406.

tiara."[47] So they elected Nicholas V, the patron of Skanderbeg, instead.

When I am introduced at wine and cheese parties as a Byzantinist, people still ask me whether we have yet overcome the bad press given by Gibbon, before turning on their heel. I do not know why or when this myth started, but wish that volume VI especially had been written late enough to be treated as history rather than literature, for it would have saved us much time and trouble. Not surprisingly Gibbon is reflected by Adamantios Korais (1748–1833), a morning star of Neo-Hellenism.[48] But until J. B. Bury's edition of the *Decline and fall* of 1896–1914, the truth is that (despite notable exceptions), Gibbon's sixth volume was not so much abused (as he feared), but ignored (which was worse).[49] Charles Lebeau's plodding *Bas Empire* of 1757–86 was historiographically far more influential. So was the Ritter Joseph von Hammer-Purgstall's *Histoire de l'Empire Ottoman*, which was mainly known through its eighteen-volume French translation of 1835–43, and eventually found its way into Turkish in 1908 – which Gibbon has never done; nor I think has he been properly published into Greek. So where are his *epigoni?* Gibbon's view of his own teachers in Oxford is notorious, and in volume VI he has a final crack: 'The Oxford professor is a laborious scholar, but the librarian of Modena enjoys the superiority of a modern and national historian.'[50] Like Charles Ducange (1610–88), Edward Gibbon (1737–94) was an academic celibate, so left no legitimate offspring. Yet we may establish a respectable genealogy through F. P. G. Guizot (1787–1874), who edited Gibbon before 1812 and (among many other things) taught N. D. Fustel de Coulanges (1830–89). In turn de Coulanges taught Ferdinand Lot (1866–1952) in 1886, who in 1932 taught Sir Richard Southern (1912–), an Oxford professor through

---

[47] *Ibid.*, VI, p. 425 and n. 103; but Gill, *Personalities*, p. 51, suggests that it was at the 1455 conclave that Bessarion escaped election.

[48] Cf. S. Fassoulakis, 'Gibbon's influence on Koraes', in *Nicol Studies*, pp. 169–73.

[49] Cf. Byron (who had a good memory) quoting Gibbon, or perhaps extemporizing (for I can no more track it down than Mehmed's spider), in 'In the wind's eye', ed. L. A. Marchand, *Byron's Letters and Journals*, vol. IX (London, 1979), p. 117 (letter of 1 March 1822). But Gibbon was not ignored in one historiographical sequence. T. Hodgkin, *Italy and her invaders*, vol. I (Oxford, 1880), p. 3, regarded Gibbon's work as 'unsurpassable'. In turn Hodgkin's history is called 'unsuperseded' by C. Wickham, *Early medieval Italy* (London, 1981), p. 195.

[50] *Decline and fall*, VI, p. 418 n. 85.

whom generations yet unborn may claim descent – unless, like Iggy Pop, you prefer to start at the beginning again: 'The grandeur of the subject appealed to me, as did the cameo illustration of Edward Gibbon, the author, on the front cover. He looked like a heavy dude.'[51]

51 I. Pop, 'Caesar lives', *Classics Ireland* 2 (1995), p. 94.

CHAPTER 6

Gibbon and the Merovingians

Ian Wood

Gibbon's account of the Merovingian kingdom occupies an interesting position in the *Decline and fall*. The chapter in question, chapter 38, is placed immediately before the 'General observations on the fall of the Roman Empire in the west', even though those observations might as reasonably have followed Gibbon's account of Odoacer, of Visigothic Spain or of Theodoric the Ostrogoth, in chapters 36, 37 and 39 respectively. Nor can it be chance that the author chose to structure his work in this way. In the opening paragraph of chapter 37, the chapter which concludes with a discussion of Vandal and Visigothic Arianism, Gibbon explains that 'I have purposely delayed the consideration of two religious events, interesting in the study of human nature, and important in the decline and fall of the Roman empire. I. The institution of the monastic life; and, II. The conversion of the Northern barbarians.'[1] Since the positioning of these two discussions was deliberate, it is reasonable to assume the same for the ordering of the accounts of the creation of the successor states and their early history. It follows, therefore, that Gibbon saw chapter 38 of the *Decline and fall*, and consequently the history of the Franks, with their pendants, the Visigoths and the Anglo-Saxons, as a culmination in the history of the western Empire. Yet while the Merovingian kingdom held a special interest for Gibbon, that interest was not expressed in narrative form. Only half of what Gibbon has to say about the Franks in chapter 38 is covered by a narration of events – and most of that is devoted to the reign of Clovis (481–511) – the rest is contained in what is, for the *Decline and fall*, an unusually long

---

[1] *Decline and fall*, ed. Milman, III, p. 341. I should like to thank Dr Rosamond McKitterick for comments on matters early medieval, and Professors Alan Forrest and Norman Hampson and, most especially, Dr Mike Broers for their advice on the eighteenth century.

discussion of political and legal structures. In this respect, Gibbon's account of the Merovingian kingdom is different in kind from his accounts of the kingdoms of the Vandals, Visigoths, Ostrogoths and Lombards, to say nothing of the Anglo-Saxons. An exploration of Gibbon's account of the early Merovingians may explain its peculiarities, and highlight its virtues and its weaknesses.[2]

It is easy to offer one conjecture as to why the kingdom of the Franks should have interested Gibbon. While the original idea for the *Decline and fall* was conceived on the steps of the Frari on 15 October 1764,[3] the next four years seem to have been dedicated to an unrealized project on 'the Swiss revolutions'.[4] This subject had doubtless been inspired by his long early sojourn in the town of Lausanne. Not surprisingly the regions of the Lac Leman and the upper Rhône valley feature in the Roman *History*: Gibbon describes the country between the lake and the Jura as 'That fortunate district', and discusses the non-relationship of the name Leman with the tribal name of the Alamanni.[5] Soon after he pauses on 'the monastery of Agaunum, or St Maurice, in Vallais'.[6] Gibbon's treatment of France is much like that of Switzerland, and for similar reasons. He visited Paris on his return from Rome in 1765,[7] and would do so again later. The landscape of France, moreover, is the subject of plaudits similar to those given to Switzerland.[8] Gibbon knew and admired much of what had once been Frankish territory.

If the geographical setting of Merovingian history was congenial to Gibbon, so too were some of the themes, which coincided neatly with issues which excited him in earlier chapters of the *Decline and fall*. Indeed he first seems to have juxtaposed the notions of decline and fall in a short work which was concerned largely with Frankish history, the essay 'Du gouvernement féodal, surtout en France'.[9]

---

[2] The significance of the chapter is discussed by P. B. Craddock, *Edward Gibbon, luminous historian, 1772–1794* (Baltimore, 1989), pp. 152–3, 156–9, but without any consideration of its position in the historiography of the early Middle Ages.

[3] *Memoirs*, ed. Bonnard, p. 136.

[4] *Ibid.*, pp. 140–2, 146. He was already considering this project in 1762, *ibid.*, p. 122.

[5] *Decline and fall*, ed. Milman, III, p. 385.

[6] *Ibid.*, III, p. 393 and n. 44.

[7] *Memoirs*, ed. Bonnard, p. 137.

[8] *Decline and fall*, ed. Milman, III, p. 82.

[9] *Miscellaneous Works*, 3, pp. 183–202. On the significance of the work for the development of Gibbon's thought, P. B. Craddock, *Young Edward Gibbon: gentleman of letters* (Baltimore, 1982), p. 245.

Moreover, Clovis was 'a new Constantine', even in the sources.[10] Further, the Frankish Church was as subject to superstition as was the Gallo-Roman Church, which had preceded it. Indeed, according to Gibbon, the Gallo-Romans compensated for their loss of power and riches through their predominance in the early Merovingian Church, and hence their control of superstition.[11] Modern historians might be happier with a reformulation of this in terms of a combination of *Bischofsherrschaft* and episcopal control of the cult of the saints:[12] although Gibbon's notion of superstition is scarcely compatible with modern interpretations of early medieval religion, influenced as they are by social anthropology, here it is more in his language than in his reading of the evidence that the eighteenth-century historian differs from his twentieth-century counterpart. Yet Gibbon did not lampoon the Christian Franks or their religion with the vehemence which his comments on Constantine and the fourth-century Empire might have led his readers to expect. The Franks themselves he treated more harshly in his earlier work 'Du gouvernement féodal': 'Dans l'intervalle du quinzième[13] siècle au huitième, les barbares (je parle surtout des François) étoient dévenus plus corrompus sans être plus civilisés.'[14] This is not quite the picture in the *Decline and fall*, where Clovis' conversion is seen as beneficial: Christianity was a moderating force on the Frankish king,[15] even though the Merovingian was 'susceptible of transient fervour'. This was a point which Gibbon, with his love of reported speech,[16] illustrated with a 'rash expression', 'prudently concealed' by Gregory of Tours, but 'celebrated' by Fredegar – that is Clovis's exclamation that had he been at the crucifixion he would have avenged Christ's injuries.[17] Certainly in the *Decline and fall* Gibbon

[10] Gregory of Tours, *Decem libri historiarum*, ii.31, ed. B. Krusch and W. Levison, *Monumenta Germaniae Historica, Scriptures Rerum Merovingicarum* i, i (Hannover, 1951): *Decline and fall*, Milman, iii, p. 387.
[11] *Ibid.*, iii, pp. 389, 418.
[12] See especially, Martin Heinzelmann, *Bischofsherrschaft in Gallien* (Munich, 1976) and Peter Brown, *The cult of saints* (Chicago, 1981), pp. 69–127, and his *Relics and social status*, The Stenton Lecture 1976 (Reading, 1977), reprinted in his *Society and the holy in late antiquity* (London, 1982), pp. 222–50.
[13] Sic. Surely a mistake for *cinquième*.
[14] Gibbon, 'Du gouvernement féodal, surtout en France', p. 190. He does, however, see the clergy as attempting to tame the French in the tenth century, *ibid.*, p. 198.
[15] *Decline and fall*, ed. Milman, iii, p. 383.   [16] *Ibid.*, iii, pp. 268–9, n. 43.
[17] *Ibid.*, iii, p. 388 and n. 31: Fredegar, iii.21, ed. B. Krusch, *Monumenta Germaniae Historica, Scriptores rerum Merovingicarum* ii (Hannover, 1888).

had reservations about the Merovingian's Christianity: he saw
Clovis as 'being incapable of feeling the mild influence of the
Gospel, which persuades and purifies the heart of a genuine
convert'.[18] Despite this, he could write that 'On the memorable day,
when Clovis ascended from the baptismal font, he alone, in the
Christian world, deserved the name and prerogatives of a Catholic
king.'[19] More surprising still, Gibbon allowed that Christianity
could have been a factor in Clovis's victory over the Alamanni[20] –
the role of religion is something that he does not even consider in
his account of Constantine's victory at the Milvian Bridge,[21] and
when he does consider the evidence for Constantine's dream before
the battle it is with considerable scepticism.[22] If anything Gibbon
was too inclined to believe Gregory of Tours' account of the
conversion of Clovis: since the late nineteenth century, debate
about the reliability and veracity of this section of the bishop's
narrative has raged in earnest.[23]

Naturally Gibbon did not follow Gregory in ascribing Clovis'
success south of the Loire in 507 to divine backing for his
Catholicism.[24] Instead, like many after him, he fell into the trap
of rationalizing Gregory's account, substituting the Catholic
aristocracy for God, and thus turning the Gallo-Roman nobility into
a fifth column working for the Franks against the Visigoths.[25] In
this interpretation Gibbon depended on a forged letter of Pope
Anastasius, and on the erroneous conflation of two fragmentary
letters of Avitus of Vienne.[26] This bogus evidence goes some way
towards excusing the eighteenth-century historian for advocating
a case for which there is no evidence whatsoever.[27] With less

---

[18] *Decline and fall*, ed. Milman, III, p. 388.

[19] *Ibid.*, III, p. 388.

[20] *Ibid.*, III, p. 386. Like most historians Gibbon placed the battle wrongly at Tolbiac, *Decline and fall*, ed. Milman, III, p. 388. See I. N. Wood, *The Merovingian kingdoms 450–751* (London, 1993), pp. 45–6.

[21] *Decline and fall*, ed. Milman, I, pp. 430–2.

[22] *Ibid.*, II, pp. 153–9.

[23] On the historiography of the debate see R. Weiss, *Chlodwigs Taufe* (Bern, 1971), and M. Spencer, 'Dating the baptism of Clovis', *Early Medieval Europe* 3 (1994), pp. 97–116.

[24] Gregory of Tours, *Decem libri historiarum*, III praefatio: *Decline and fall*, ed. Milman, III, pp. 386–8.

[25] *Decline and fall*, ed. Milman, III, p. 394.

[26] *Ibid.*, III, p. 389 n. 34. Avitus of Vienne, ed. R. Peiper, *Monumenta Germaniae Historica, Auctores Antiquissimi* VI 2 (Berlin, 1882), epp. 46, 46a. J. Havet, 'Questions mérovingiennes II: Les découverts de Jerome Vignier', *Bibliothèque de l'Ecole des Chartes* 46 (1885), pp. 258–9.

[27] Wood, *The Merovingian kingdoms*, p. 47.

justification, however, Gibbon misread Gregory of Tours' account of the Catholic aristocracy of Aquitaine, killing off Apollinaris at the battle of *Vogliacum*, despite the fact that he lived for another ten years, even becoming, as Gregory himself relates, bishop of Clermont.[28]

While Gibbon is less critical of Clovis' Catholicism than might have been expected, he is also more tolerant of accounts of the miraculous. Certainly he dismisses Gregory of Tours' *De virtutibus sancti Juliani* as being concerned with 'about fifty foolish miracles performed by his [Julian's] relics'.[29] Equally the white hart that led Clovis and his army across the river Vienne is denounced as a 'fraud or fiction', covering the betrayal of an unguarded ford by 'affectionate peasants',[30] while the collapse of the walls of Angoulême is interpreted not as a miracle echoing that at Jericho, but as the result of 'clerical engineers' undermining the foundations.[31] Unfortunately these 'clerical engineers' belong to the fantasy world which contains the Catholic fifth columnists. Yet, alongside such scepticism, Gibbon was prepared to record, with no apparent irony, miracles performed at the shrine of St Martin, and to state that 'earth, as well as heaven, rejoiced in the conversion of the Franks'.[32]

In his reading of Gregory, Gibbon, in fact, shows a strange mixture of credulity and condescension. Commenting on the *Histories* he remarked that

His style is equally devoid of elegance and simplicity. In a conspicuous station, he still remains a stranger to his own age and country; and in a prolix work (the five last books contain ten years) he has omitted almost every thing that posterity desires to learn. I have tediously acquired, by a painful perusal, the right of pronouncing this unfavourable sentence.[33]

---

[28] *Decline and fall*, ed. Milman, III, p. 396. Gregory of Tours, *Decem libri historiarum*, II.37; III.2. On the Catholic aristocracy of Aquitaine, I. N. Wood, 'Gregory of Tours and Clovis', *Revue Belge de Philologie et d'Histoire* 63 (1985), pp. 256–8.

[29] *Decline and fall*, ed. Milman, III, p. 299 n. 29. For modern consideration of these same miracles, R. Van Dam, *Saints and their miracles in late antique Gaul* (Princeton, 1993).

[30] *Decline and fall*, ed. Milman, III, p. 396.

[31] *Ibid.*, III, p. 397. J. Clive, 'Gibbon's humor' in G. W. Bowersock *et al.* (eds.), *Edward Gibbon and the decline and fall of the Roman Empire. Daedalus. Journal of the American Academy of Arts and Sciences* 105 (Cambridge, Mass., 1976), p. 189, takes this, wrongly, to my mind, as being typical of Gibbon's view of the miraculous in this period.

[32] *Decline and fall*, ed. Milman, III, p. 388.

[33] *Ibid.*, III, p. 416 n. 111.

That Gibbon really had perused Gregory with care is clear enough
from a discussion of the bishop's use of the word *infra*.[34] Recognition
of the virtues of vulgar Latin, however, was not something which
would have come naturally to an eighteenth-century scholar – the
discovery of Gregory's mastery of a highly effective narrative style
had to wait until Erich Auerbach's study of *Mimesis* in 1946.[35] The
complaint about an absence of information in Gregory is more
peculiar – though Gibbon later compared the narratives in
Gregory's *Histories*, Bede's *Historia Ecclesiastica* and Paul the Deacon's
Historia Langobardorum favourably with the historical writings of
Isidore of Seville and John of Biclaro – and in so doing radically
over-estimated the quality of evidence provided by Bede and others
for the history of Britain in the fifth and sixth centuries.[36] Gibbon
expected his sources to be reliable quarries for facts, not histories
interpreting the past with their own purposes in mind.[37] Yet the
Englishman used Gregory extensively. As a result, despite his
tendency to rationalize the miraculous where possible, he followed
the bishop blindly, without recognizing that the prolixity which
he criticized might have had a purpose.[38] Arguably in following
Gregory as directly as he did Gibbon wrote more credulously about
the Franks than about any other barbarian people.

Nevertheless it was not only in his treatment of the Christianity
of the Merovingian kingdom that Gibbon showed leniency. He was
inclined to believe the account of miracles at Tipasa in Vandal
Africa, because of the quality of the supposedly eyewitness
evidence, recorded first by Victor of Vita in his *History of the African
persecution*.[39] Moreover, other monarchs survive the gaze of the
eighteenth-century historian better even than does Clovis, despite
their Arianism, not least because they could at times be portrayed
as rational and moderate. The religious perspicacity of Alaric I

[34] *Ibid.*, III, p. 414 n. 105.
[35] E. Auerbach, *Mimesis* (Bern, 1946), pp. 81–97.
[36] *Decline and fall*, ed. Milman, III, p. 420 n. 122.
[37] Compare W. Goffart, *The narrators of barbarian history* (Princeton, 1988).
[38] See I. N. Wood, 'Gregory of Tours and Clovis', pp. 249–72. Also I. N. Wood, 'The secret
histories of Gregory of Tours', *Revue Belge de Philologie et d'Histoire* 71 (1993), pp. 253–70.
Goffart, *The narrators of barbarian history*, pp. 112–234.
[39] *Decline and fall*, ed. Milman, III, pp. 373–4; Victor Vitensis, *Historia persecutionis Africanae
provinciae*, sections 29–30, ed. K. Halm, *Monumenta Germaniae historica, Auctores Antiquissimi*
III, 1 (Berlin, 1879): trans. J. Moorhead, *Victor of Vita: history of the Vandal persecution*
(Liverpool, 1992), p. 76, with n. 15.

(395–410) is defended against the picture presented by the sixth-century Byzantine historian Zosimus, of a king prone to superstition,[40] while some truth is detected in Orosius' 'devout assertion, that the wrath of heaven supplied the imperfections of hostile rage' during the sack of Rome in 410.[41] Gibbon remarks that 'the devotion which reigned in the camp of Alaric . . . might edify, or disgrace, the palaces of Rome and Constantinople'.[42] For him the Visigothic king Theodoric I (418–51) 'exhibited in his distress the edifying contrast of Christian piety and moderation' before fighting against Litorius.[43] Equally positive is the eighteenth-century scholar's comment that the Arianism of the Ostrogoth Theodoric the Great (493–526) 'was not infected by zeal'.[44] On the whole Gibbon notes and approves in the barbarian leaders of the fourth, fifth and sixth centuries an absence of religious enthusiasm. This even holds true for the Huns, who 'respected the ministers of every religion'.[45] Yet those barbarians who did have a reputation as persecutors in this period also receive surprisingly cautious treatment. The Visigothic king Euric (466–84), whose reputation was only finally salvaged by K. F. Strohecker in 1937,[46] is already seen by Gibbon not as a persecutor, as he appears in one notorious letter of Sidonius Apollinaris,[47] but as he appears in another, 'a tribute of just, but reluctant praise'.[48] With much less reason Gibbon even finds a way of exonerating the Vandals: 'the wanton outrages against the churches and the clergy, of which the Vandals are accused, may be fairly imputed to the fanaticism of their allies.'[49] It is a position which is sustained by a somewhat lame appeal to the weakness of the sources,[50] and later by a more forceful accusation of fraud on the part of the Catholics,[51] but it

---

[40] E.g. Zosimus, *Historia nova*, v.6, ed. F. Paschoud, *Zosime Histoire nouvelle* (Paris, 1971–89): *Decline and fall*, ed. Milman, III, p. 57.
[41] *Decline and fall*, ed. Milman, III, p. 137. Gibbon's date is 411.
[42] *Ibid.*, III, p. 360.   [43] *Ibid.*, III, p. 258.
[44] *Ibid.*, III, p. 369: on Arianism and Catholicism in Italy, see J. Moorhead, *Theoderic in Italy* (Oxford, 1992), esp. pp. 89–97.
[45] *Decline and fall*, ed. Milman, III, p. 235.
[46] K. F. Strohecker, *Eurich, König der Westgoten* (Stuttgart, 1937). Compare *Decline and fall*, ed. Milman, III, p. 365, with n. 89.
[47] Sidonius Apollinaris, ep. VII.6, ed. A. Loyen, *Sidoine Apollinaire* (Paris, 1960–70): Gregory of Tours, *Decem libri historiarum*, II.25.
[48] Sidonius, ep. VIII.9. *Decline and fall*, ed. Milman, III, p. 381.
[49] *Decline and fall*, ed. Milman, III, p. 212.
[50] *Ibid.*, III, p. 214 n. 25.   [51] *Ibid.*, III, pp. 371–2.

is largely undermined by Gibbon's own narrative account of persecutions in Africa. It is, however, only with the persecution of the Jews in Spain that he finally abandons his view of the tolerant barbarian.[52]

Gibbon's slightly, but not wholly, exaggerated view of barbarian tolerance is part of his wider interpretation of the varying impact of Christianity, which is explored in the strangely fragmented chapter 37. Here the excesses of the ascetics are contrasted with the second glorious and decisive victory of Christianity, 'over the warlike Barbarians of Scythia and Germany, who subverted the empire, and embraced the religion, of the Romans'.[53] Comparison with the Christianization of the Empire is implicit. Of course Gibbon conceded that the Christianization of the barbarians involved the spread of superstition – and of course his understanding of superstition is at odds with modern work on the supernatural in the early Middle Ages. Despite his views on superstition, Gibbon argued that Christianity had much to offer those peoples who had crossed the Danube and the Rhine. Ulfilas, the Goth who translated the Bible into his native language, suppressed the Books of Kings from his translation of the Bible, wisely, in Gibbon's eyes, 'as they might tend to irritate the fierce and sanguinary spirit of the Barbarians': indeed he taught 'doctrines of truth and virtue'.[54] In general the barbarians 'imperceptibly imbibed the spirit of genuine Christianity'.[55] More in accord with modern scholarship, they 'received, at the same time, the use of letters', which allowed the transmission of ancient texts.[56] Gibbon also remarked on the geographical expansion of Christianity, beyond the Rhine, 'to the nations of the Elbe, the Vistula and the Baltic', and he noted that it was a subject which would 'afford materials for an ecclesiastical, and even philosophical history' – high praise indeed.[57] For Gibbon the impact of Christianity on the barbarians, by comparison with the effect that it had on the

---

[52] Ibid., III, pp. 378–9.
[53] Ibid., III, p. 358.
[54] Ibid., III, p. 359. On Ulfilas and his Bible, see P. Heather and J. Matthews, The Goths in the fourth century (Liverpool, 1991), pp. 133–97.
[55] Decline and fall, ed. Milman, III, p. 365.
[56] Ibid., III, p. 362. Compare, for example, J. Goody, The domestication of the savage mind (Cambridge, 1977).
[57] Decline and fall, ed. Milman, III, p. 361, with n. 79.

Romans, was largely positive. To the latter the clergy preached 'patience and pusillanimity':[58] by contrast 'In the most corrupt state of Christianity, the Barbarians might learn justice from the *law*, and mercy from the *gospel*':[59] and more optimistically, 'the pure and genuine influence of Christianity may be traced in its beneficial, though imperfect, effects on the Barbarian proselytes of the North'.[60]

Thus, for Gibbon, the Christianization of the barbarians was beneficial. Although the spread of Arianism was a misfortune, it was not a disaster: Arian kings showed more toleration than Catholic emperors. In this context Clovis and the Franks look rather less significant than they do to those historians who have followed Gregory of Tours in his emphasis on the significance of a conversion to Catholicism rather than Arianism.[61] In fact even Gibbon may overplay the significance of Catholicism, as opposed to Arianism, in the success of Clovis and his Frankish followers. Yet it is certainly not for this reason that the Franks have a particular significance in the *Decline and fall*. Having provided a narrative of Frankish history up to the cession of Provence to the Franks by the Ostrogoths in 537,[62] Gibbon pauses to analyse the political and legal structures of the Merovingian kingdom. He opens his discussion with the statement that 'The Franks, or French, are the only people of Europe who can deduce a perpetual succession from the conquerors of the Western Empire.'[63] This signals a temporary engagement in an historical debate which raged in France in the decades before the French Revolution.

Gibbon himself was well acquainted with French scholarship. He was also fortunate. As he remarks, the first eleven volumes of the *Recueil des historiens des Gaules et de la France* had appeared by 1767.[64] This provided the majority of the sources necessary for an understanding of the Merovingian period. His own skill as a Latinist, and

---

[58] *Ibid.*, III, p. 440.

[59] *Ibid.*, III, p. 363.

[60] *Ibid.*, III, p. 441. This optimism contrasts with Gibbon's position in 'Du gouvernement féodal, surtout en France', p. 190.

[61] On this issue see Wood, 'Gregory of Tours and Clovis', pp. 249–72. Wood, *The Merovingian kingdoms*, pp. 43–9.

[62] *Decline and fall*, ed. Milman, III, p. 399. Gibbon dates the event to 536. I have followed H. Wolfram, *History of the Goths* (Berkeley, 1988), p. 315.

[63] *Decline and fall*, ed. Milman, III, p. 400.

[64] *Ibid.*, III, p. 380 n. 1.

his awareness of manuscript studies, made him a reasonable critic of the editions in front of him.[65] He also had a formidable knowledge of the secondary material which had lately been published in French. Of these he singled out the work of 'the free spirit of the count de Boulainvilliers', 'the learned ingenuity of the Abbé Dubos', 'the comprehensive genius of the president de Montesquieu', 'and the good sense and diligence of the Abbé de Mably'.[66] These descriptions contrast ironically with Gibbon's comment that 'the intemperate disputants have accused each other of conspiring against the prerogative of the crown, the dignity of the nobles, or the freedom of the people'.[67] Essentially, early Frankish history had become an ideological battleground for those concerned with the position of the French monarchy and the *parlements*.[68] This is scarcely surprising, given the argument that the Merovingians had to a large extent created France; that they had provided it with its first monarchs; and that under them the French nobility had originated.[69] As a result, Merovingian history effectively became an aspect of political debate in France.[70] Gibbon himself made no attempt in the *Decline and fall* to become involved in the politics of that debate, although his own political views were at odds with those of Mably:[71] rather he was aggravated by the disputants' exploitation of historical evidence. In discussing the division of

[65] *Memoirs*, ed. Bonnard, p. 131.
[66] *Decline and fall*, ed. Milman, III, pp. 400–1 n. 64.
[67] *Ibid.*, III, p. 400.
[68] See K. M. Baker, *Inventing the French Revolution: essays on French political culture in the eighteenth century* (Cambridge, 1990), pp. 31–58 on the uses of history in this period, and pp. 86–106 on Mably in particular: see also K. M. Baker, 'Representation' in K. M. Baker (ed.), *The French Revolution and the creation of modern political culture* (Oxford, 1987), pp. 472–7.
[69] For example, G. Bonnot de Mably, *Observations sur l'histoire de France* in *Collection complète des œuvres de l'Abbé de Mably*, vol. 1 (Paris, 1794–5), p. 177. *Decline and fall*, ed. Milman, III, p. 404 n. 74. On the origins of French medievalism, see D. R. Kelley, *Foundations of modern historical scholarship* (New York, 1970), pp. 271–300, esp. 293–7: on the eighteenth century, see Baker, *Inventing the French Revolution*, pp. 31–58.
[70] H. H. Milman commented on the end of this debate in his note to *Decline and fall*, ed. Milman, III, p. 408: 'It is curious to observe the recoil from the national vanity of the French historians of the last century.'
[71] *Memoirs*, ed. Bonnard, pp. 169–70. On Mably in general see Baker, *Inventing the French Revolution*, pp. 86–106: on his use of history for political purposes, see also Baker, 'Representation', p. 476: 'a principal purpose' of Mably's *Observations sur l'histoire de la France* 'was to reassert the claims for the Estates General as the representative body of the nation, as opposed to those of the *parlements* he so profoundly distrusted'. For an alternative, *parlementaire*, view, see L. A. Le Paige, *Lettres historiques sur les fonctions essentielles de Parlement: sur le droit des pairs et sur les loix fondamentales du royaume* (Amsterdam, 1753–4): Baker, *Inventing the French Revolution*, pp. 41–4.

France into two classes, which he termed 'noble and slave', he remarked:

This arbitrary and recent division has been transformed by pride and prejudice into a *national* distinction, universally established by the arms and the laws of the Merovingians. The nobles, who claimed their genuine, or fabulous, descent from the independent and victorious Franks, have asserted, and abused, the indefeasible right of conquest, over a prostrate crowd of slaves and plebeians, to whom they imputed the imaginary disgrace of a Gallic, or Roman, extraction.[72]

At the end of his discussion of the relative status of Romans and Franks Gibbon could conclude that 'We are now qualified to despise the opposite, and perhaps artful, misrepresentations, which have softened, or exaggerated, the oppression of the Romans of Gaul under the reign of the Merovingians.'[73] One may regard as too stark his conclusion that 'a degenerate people ... had been exposed to the arms and laws of the ferocious barbarians'. Nevertheless, it is clear that Gibbon's discussion of Merovingian history is a deliberate attempt to reclaim it from its political exploitation in pre-Revolutionary France.

By venturing into Merovingian history in chapter 38 of the *Decline and fall* Gibbon was engaging in a debate with French historians.[74] In so far as his concern was to reclaim that history from its political exploitation, he was not successful. When he met the Abbé de Mably at the house of the Comtesse de Froulay they argued over the English constitution.[75] They met again at the table of M. de Foncemange, when they do seem to have discussed the *Decline and fall*, but, according to Gibbon, Mably's 'jealous, irascible, spirit revenged itself on a work, which he was incapable of reading in the original'.[76] Nevertheless, the Englishman had some respect for his opponent: he praised 'the first part of the *Observations sur l'histoire*

---

[72] *Decline and fall*, ed. Milman, III, p. 412. On the question of Gallic descent, M. Ozouf, 'Les Gaulois à Clermont-Ferrand' in his *L'école de la France* (Paris, 1984), pp. 339–50, and more generally, L. Poliakov, *The Aryan myth: a history of racist and nationalist ideas in Europe* (London, 1971), pp. 17–36.

[73] *Decline and fall*, ed. Milman, III, p. 417. For this debate, Baker, *Inventing the French Revolution*, p. 53.

[74] On Gibbon and the *philosophes* see M. Baridon, *Edward Gibbon et le mythe de Rome* (Paris, 1977), pp. 288–94.

[75] Gibbon, *Memoirs*, ed. Bonnard, p. 169.

[76] *Ibid.*, p. 158. On this and other meetings see also Craddock, *Edward Gibbon, luminous historian*, pp. 90, 95–6.

de France', while noting that 'kings, Magistrates, Nobles and successful writers were the objects of his [Mably's] contempt'.[77] As a successful writer, and as a monarchist, who had commented that the Franks 'wisely established the right of hereditary succession in the noble family of the Merovingians',[78] Gibbon was an inevitable recipient of the scorn of the *philosophe*.

Mably's *Observations sur l'histoire de France* does, however, seem to have had a particularly profound, and sometimes deleterious, effect on chapter 38 of the *Decline and fall*. The first books of the *Observations* were published in Geneva in 1765. Gibbon effectively reviewed them for himself in his essay 'Du gouvernement féodal' shortly after their appearance – although the essay itself was only to appear in print in 1814.[79] In the essay Gibbon was content to follow Mably over most issues. When he came to write chapter 38 of the *Decline and fall*, however, he saw things rather differently. The structure of the chapter apparently follows that of book I of the *Observations*, which is largely devoted to Merovingian history. This similarity has the effect of highlighting Gibbon's stated differences of opinion and his silences.

Mably begins with the *Germani* of Tacitus and an allusion to the *Germania*,[80] whereas Gibbon begins with the same author's *Histories*:[81] the choice is indicative of a considerable divergence of approach. What then interests the *philosophe*, but not the Englishman, is the evidence for Germanic democracy.[82] Thereafter Mably recounts the early history of the Franks, or rather *Français* to use his own loaded word, as related by Gregory of Tours. His picture of Clovis is, not surprisingly, more stridently Catholic than is Gibbon's.[83] It is also more Roman, for although the Frenchman

[77] *Memoirs*, ed. Bonnard, p. 170.
[78] *Decline and fall*, ed. Milman, III, p. 260.
[79] On the problem of the date of the essay, Craddock, *Young Edward Gibbon: gentleman of letters*, pp. 245–6, arguing for 1765–70, and probably pre-1767.
[80] Mably, *Observations sur l'histoire de France*, pp. 129–34.
[81] *Decline and fall*, ed. Milman, III, pp. 380–1.
[82] Mably, *Observations sur l'histoire de France*, pp. 133–4. See F. Furet, 'Civilization and barbarism in Gibbon's History' in Bowersock (ed.), *Edward Gibbon*, p. 164: 'When he [Gibbon] comes to the famous theme of the Germanic freedoms, so important in the historiography of the period, especially in Montesquieu and Mably whom Gibbon had read attentively, the description of the system of assemblies and the independence of the soldiers do not arouse any "democratic" sympathy in him.' See also Baker, *Inventing the French Revolution*, p. 48.
[83] Mably, *Observations sur l'histoire de France*, p. 142.

dismisses the idea put forward by his compatriot, the Abbé du Bos, that Clovis was no more than 'un officier de l'Empire, un maître de la milice, qui tenoit son pouvoir de Zénon et d'Anastase',[84] he noted that 'ce prince, supérieur à sa nation et à ses contemporains avoit des lumières, des talens, et même des vertus, qui auroient honoré le trône des Empereurs Romains'.[85] Gibbon followed neither du Bos nor Mably in such considerations, but stuck rather closer to the portrait offered by Gregory. In so doing he ignored a whole avenue of approach, dismissing even the consulship of Clovis as 'a name, a shadow, an empty pageant'.[86] The significance for the Franks of Rome's authority and institutions was, sadly, not a major issue for Gibbon, and he underestimated the significance of Roman titles, and indeed of the survival of Roman institutions, for the barbarian world; topics which were already, and have continued to be, the subjects of fruitful debate.[87]

Having provided a narrative of the reign of Clovis, Mably then turned to questions of government, of the seizure of land by the barbarians, and the take-over of public authority, all of which not only degraded the *Gaulois*, in his republican eyes, but also destroyed the popular governmental traditions of Germany.[88] Gibbon had his doubts about the oppression of the *Gaulois* even when he wrote his essay 'Du gouvernement féodal'.[89] In the *Decline and fall*, while prudently avoiding some of the issues raised by Mably, Gibbon did offer a critical response on the question of the seizure of land by the barbarians.[90] Having noted that the Visigoths and the Burgundians

---

[84] *Ibid.*, p. 141.
[85] *Ibid.*, p. 139.
[86] *Decline and fall*, ed. Milman, III, p. 398. Compare the recent assessment of M. McCormick, 'Clovis at Tours, Byzantine public ritual and the origins of medieval ruler symbolism' in E. K. Chrysos and A. Schwarcz (eds.), *Das Reich und die Barbaren* (Vienna, 1989), pp. 155–80.
[87] Furet, 'Civilization and barbarism in Gibbon's History', p. 164; Baridon, *Edward Gibbon et le mythe de Rome*, p. 293. For recent work see especially H. Wolfram. *Intitulatio I: Lateinische Königs- und Fürstentitel bis zum Ende des 8. Jahrhunderts* (Vienna, 1967): P. Classen, 'Fortleben und Wandel spätrömischen Urkundenwesens im frühen Mittelalter' in P. Classen (ed.), *Recht und Schrift im Mittelalter* (Sigmaringen, 1977), pp. 13–54: P. Classen, 'Kaiserreskript und Königsurkunde. Diplomatische Studien zur römisch-germanisch Kontinuitätsproblem', *Archiv für Diplomatik* 2 (1956), pp. 1–115; revised edition, *Kaiserreskript und Königsurkunde. Diplomatische Studien zum Problem der Kontinuität zwischen Altertum und Mittelalter*, Byzantine Texts and Studies 15 (Thessalonica, 1977).
[88] Mably, *Observations sur l'histoire de France*, pp. 143–52.
[89] Gibbon, 'Du gouvernement féodal, surtout en France', pp. 199–200.
[90] *Decline and fall*, ed. Milman, III, pp. 407–8 and n. 87.

took over '*two thirds* of the subject lands',[91] he commented that 'The silence of ancient and authentic testimony has encouraged an opinion, that the rapine of the Franks was not moderated, or disguised, by the forms of a legal division.'[92] In refusing to follow Montesquieu and Mably in their unfounded theories, he postulated that the Merovingians had access to 'the Imperial patrimony, vacant lands, and Gothic usurpations'. This interpretation can itself claim little evidential support, but there are enough hints of Frankish royal control of what had been imperial sites to make at least the first part of Gibbon's hypothesis likely.[93]

Mably's third chapter begins with a discussion of the Germanic laws and their limitations.[94] In his corresponding discussion Gibbon is, as usual, more factual and more specific, with regard both to Germanic and later to Roman law, rightly observing that the Theodosian Code provided the law of the clergy.[95] In Mably's *Observations* the supposed weakness of the laws leads directly into a discussion, which is continued through the two following chapters, of the nature of the aristocracy, beginning with the *leudes* who served the sons of Clovis, before their successors evolved a desire for hereditary land, and consequently emasculated royal power.[96] Gibbon rightly ignored Mably's discussion of the development of the *leudes*, though he did follow him on the history of the benefice.[97] Here both historians were in a world of pure guesswork. Mably, like many after him, radically overestimated the importance of Chlothar II's edict of Paris, issued in 614.[98] In his essay 'Du

---

[91] Gibbon's position is based on a direct reading of the sources. W. Goffart, *Barbarians and Romans: Techniques of accommodation, AD 418–584* (Princeton, 1980), has argued that the texts refer to income from land and not land itself, but his case has not received universal agreement.

[92] *Decline and fall*, ed. Milman, III, p. 408.

[93] K. F. Werner, 'Conquête franque de la Gaule ou changement de régime' in his *Vom Frankenreich zur Entfaltung Deutschlands und Frankreichs* (Sigmaringen, 1984), p. 11.

[94] Mably, *Observations sur l'histoire de France*, pp. 153–4.

[95] *Decline and fall*, ed. Milman, III, pp. 401–7, 417–18. On the Theodosian Code and the clergy, see I. N. Wood, 'The Code in Merovingian Gaul', in J. Harries and I. N. Wood (eds.), *The Theodosian Code* (London, 1993), p. 167.

[96] Mably, *Observations sur l'histoire de France*, pp. 155–80.

[97] *Decline and fall*, ed. Milman, III, pp. 409–10, with n. 90. In 'Du gouvernement féodal, surtout en France', p. 186, he seems more impressed. In the same work, pp. 188–9, he has some very lucid comments on the relationship between armies and land.

[98] Mably, *Observations sur l'histoire de France*, p. 177. Mably's date for the council and edict is 615. See J. M. Wallace-Hadrill, *The long-haired kings* (London, 1962), pp. 214–16: A. C. Murray, 'Immunity, nobility and the *Edict of Paris*', *Speculum* 69 (1994), pp. 18–39: also Wood, *The Merovingian kingdoms*, pp. 142–3.

gouvernement féodal' Gibbon appears to have accepted Mably's emphasis, but the edict finds no place in the *Decline and fall*.[99] Not only did the Frenchman give the edict a constitutional significance which it never had, but he also made it central to his interpretation of benefices. Unfortunately the surviving evidence makes it difficult to reconstruct the history of benefices before the eighth century.[100] In his discussion of Charles Martel, Mably, in fact, offers a much more accurate reading of the late Merovingian benefice.[101] By that time his work had stretched far beyond the chronological horizon of Gibbon's thirty-eighth chapter, even though, for his evidence, the Englishman had drawn on Carolingian and later sources, not all of which were as useful as he assumed.[102] For the sixth and seventh centuries, however, while Gibbon's Merovingian history is not that of the French Abbé, it is deeply influenced by it, and it is structured in the same way.

Mably's *Observations sur l'histoire de France* clarify the purpose of chapter 38 of the *Decline and fall*. They may also help to explain its very prominent position, immediately before the 'General observations'. At the time of his visit to Rome in 1764 Gibbon was deeply concerned with the question of 'gouvernement féodal'.[103] The next year the first volumes of Mably's work appeared. Shortly after, Gibbon wrote his essay 'Du gouvernement féodal'. With regard to feudalism he commented: 'Enfin j'apperçois l'aurore de la nouvelle institution, j'en fixe la date, je marque ses progrès. Je la vois sortir de la terre, cette plante foible et tardive. L'arbre s'élève. Il couvre l'Europe entière de son ombre.'[104] In the same work, however, he saw the barbarians, and most particularly the Franks, as the destroyers of the empire.[105] Mably, the Franks, feudal government

---

[99] Gibbon, 'Du gouvernement féodale, surtout en France', p. 187.

[100] H. Wolfram, 'Karl Martell und das fränkische Lehenswesen' in J. Jarnut, U. Nonn and M. Richter (eds.), *Karl Martell in seiner Zeit* (Sigmaringen, 1994), pp. 61–78: I. N. Wood, 'Teutsind, Witlaic and the history of Merovingian *precaria*' in W. Davies and P. Fouracre (eds.), *Property and power in the early Middle Ages* (Cambridge, 1995), pp. 31–52.

[101] Mably, *Observations sur l'histoire de France*, p. 204. Gibbon follows him in 'Du gouvernement féodal, surtout en France', pp. 190–1, 201.

[102] Cf. his use of Aimoin of Fleury and of Agobard of Lyons, *Decline and fall*, ed. Milman, III, pp. 387 n. 26 and 407 n. 83.

[103] G. Giarrizzo, 'Gibbon's other historical interests' in Bowersock (ed.), *Edward Gibbon*, p. 244.

[104] Gibbon, 'Du gouvernement féodal, surtout en France', p. 190.

[105] *Ibid.*, pp. 185–6, 190, 194, 199. See also Craddock, *Young Edward Gibbon: gentleman of letters*, p. 245.

and the decline and fall of the western Empire came to the centre of Gibbon's attention at the same time. It is no wonder then that the chapter which immediately precedes the 'General observations on the fall of the Roman Empire in the west' should be devoted to the Merovingians. In Gibbon's eyes the ensuing development of feudalism lay with them. If their history is followed by a brief coda on the Anglo-Saxons, what could be more appropriate for an English historian?

The constitutional history of the Merovingians was bound to fall beyond the grasp of eighteenth-century scholarship. The laws of the Franks, their recensions and their dates had yet to be unravelled, and they remain problematic.[106] So too most aspects of Frankish social history, especially the question of the origin of the Merovingian aristocracy, are still matters for debate.[107] Gibbon had at times been lured out of his depth, away from history to the realms of the political theory of the *philosophes*. Such issues, which were certainly among those that led him to treat the Merovingian kingdom differently from the other successor states, are now of historiographical rather than historical interest.

Yet, if much of chapter 38 of the *Decline and fall* is of no more than historiographical interest, there are a number of observations which retain their value, even though they may in their own way be rooted in the circumstances of the late eighteenth century. For instance, Gibbon's comments on the importance of the territory to the east of the Rhine point to one aspect of Merovingian history which is easily forgotten because of the comparative weakness of documentation. These comments are not, of course, confined to a single chapter: to a large extent they may be seen as the natural continuation of an ancient historian's concern with the world of peoples hostile to the Empire. Nevertheless they add to an understanding of the contribution of the Franks to European history.

In the late Roman period the lands beyond the Rhine had seen a continuing process of formation and reformation among the barbarian peoples. The fluidity of such groups was well understood by Gibbon, who already saw this when he considered the early

---

[106] For a recent survey, Wood, *The Merovingian kingdoms*, pp. 108–17, and Rosamond McKitterick, *The Carolingians and the written word* (Cambridge, 1989), pp. 37–60.
[107] See now R. Kaiser, *Das römische Erbe und das Merowingerreich* (Munich, 1993), pp. 96–100.

history of the Franks in his essay 'Du gouvernement féodal',[108] and who has some fine pages in the *Decline and fall* on the creation of the Anglo-Saxons; pages which recognize, as many did not until recently, the importance of Bede's second list of the peoples who made up the invaders of England.[109] He also observed that it was success in war that created a 'national confederacy'.[110] The supra-national confederacy of Attila provided Gibbon with further insights into the peoples east of the Rhine[111] – and into the future hostilities that such confederacies could prepare. Among them is the hypothesis, still eminently worthy of consideration, that it was during Attila's retreat from the Catalaunian Plains that the Thuringians ravaged the lands of the Franks, and in so doing earned the vengeance of Clovis' sons 'fourscore years afterwards'.[112]

The late fifth and early sixth centuries saw a new set of develop-ments in the relations between free Germany and the world to the west of the Rhine and the south of the Danube. The Ostrogothic king Theodoric used all his diplomatic skills to exert influence as far north as the Baltic. Gibbon pushes his evidence to the extreme in talking of Æstians or Livonians travelling fifteen hundred miles to lay 'their offerings of native amber at the feet of a prince', of frequent correspondence between Theodoric and the northern homelands of the Goths, or Italians 'wearing the rich sables of Sweden', and of the retirement to Ravenna of the Gautic king Roduulf.[113] Nevertheless the notion of frequent correspondence apart, the points were firmly based on the official letters of the Italian senator Cassiodorus and on the sixth-century historical writings of Procopius and Jordanes.[114]

All this was shattered by the Franks: first by Clovis' destruction of the Alamannic kingdom, expanding as it was into northern Switzerland and into Alsace,[115] and subsequently by the Frankish conquest of Thuringia.[116] The kingdoms of both the Alamanni and

---

[108] Gibbon, 'Du gouvernement féodal, surtout en France', p. 186.
[109] *Decline and fall*, ed. Milman, pp. 424–6. Bede, *Historia Ecclesiastica*, ed. C. Plummer (Oxford, 1896), v.9. See now J. Campbell (ed.), *The Anglo-Saxons* (Oxford, 1982), pp. 29–31.
[110] *Decline and fall*, ed. Milman, III, p. 383.
[111] *Ibid.*, III, pp. 223–52.
[112] *Ibid.*, III, pp. 273, and n. 47.   [113] *Ibid.*, III, p. 460.
[114] For a modern summary of the same material, Wolfram, *History of the Goths*, p. 317.
[115] *Decline and fall*, ed. Milman, III, pp. 385–6. Gregory of Tours, *Decem libri historiarum*, II.30.
[116] *Decline and fall*, ed. Milman, III, pp. 399–400. Gregory of Tours, *Decem libri historiarum*, II.4, 7–8.

the Thuringians had been part of the diplomatic world of Theodoric
the Ostrogoth.[117] The importance of Clovis' victory over the first of
these peoples has perhaps been obscured in the last fifty years by a
debate about chronology: the date has become more important
than the event.[118] Gibbon was arguably fortunate in not having to
decide whether Clovis' victory took place in 497 or 506. The fall of
Thuringia has also received less attention than it perhaps deserves,
for these eastern territories were a great resource for the
Merovingians. Even for the Roman Empire the Alamanni seem to
have been a source of troops,[119] and they continued to be so for the
east Frankish kings, as Gibbon noted.[120]

Having already covered the history of the Roman Empire Gibbon
saw with exemplary clarity the significance of Merovingian
dominance east of the Rhine when he came to deal with the
successor states in the West. 'After the conquest of the Western
provinces, the Franks alone maintained their ancient habitations
beyond the Rhine. They gradually subdued, and civilized, the
exhausted countries, as far as the Elbe, and the mountains of
Bohemia; and the peace of Europe was secured by the obedience
of Germany.'[121] This was an achievement that had always eluded
the Romans, yet it is an achievement which few have observed
as sharply as did Gibbon – even allowing for the fact that his
description of Frankish dominance is a little too clear-cut and
perhaps a little too optimistic. Before the fifth century the Rhine
was a frontier;[122] afterwards, despite some periods in which
the Merovingians were unable to exercise much influence over the
peoples east of the Rhine, it was not. The result was a massive
change in political geography. It is a change that has been obscured
by the shadow of Pirenne, which has caused debate over the
transformation of the Roman world to concentrate on the survival

---

[117] For example, Cassiodorus, *Variae*, II.41, III.3, IV.1, ed. T. Mommsen, *Monumenta Germaniae Historica, Auctores Antiquissimi* XII (Berlin, 1894).

[118] This has continued to be true, despite the argument of Wood, 'Gregory of Tours and Clovis': cf. Spencer, 'Dating the baptism of Clovis, 1886–1993'.

[119] For example, *Decline and fall*, ed. Milman, III, p. 63. Cf. Paulus Diaconus, *Historia Romana*, X.170, ed. H. Droysen, *Monumenta Germaniae historica, Auctores Antiquissimi* II (Berlin, 1879) – the passage is often, wrongly, attributed to the fourth-century historian Eutropius.

[120] *Decline and fall*, ed. Milman, III, p. 414. See also Wood, *The Merovingian kingdoms*, p. 161.

[121] *Decline and fall*, ed. Milman, III, p. 386.

[122] On the extent to which the frontier acted as a barrier, see C. R. Whittaker, *Frontiers of the Roman Empire: a social and economic study* (Baltimore, 1994), esp. chs. 3 and 4.

of the Mediterranean. Yet, as Gibbon observed, the Merovingian hegemony in the east altered the political shape of Europe. It also helped effect a change in religious horizons – which, in time, saw the Christianization of Frisia, Saxony and ultimately Scandinavia and Prussia.

Gibbon's understanding of Merovingian expansion to the east should perhaps be seen in the light of his view of eastern Europe in his own day: Germany with its 'two thousand three hundred walled towns', 'the Christian kingdoms of Denmark, Sweden and Poland', and 'the powerful and civilized empire of Russia', all of which he portrays as the bulwarks of Europe, ready in case of an upsurge of 'Barbarism'.[123] 'If a savage conqueror should issue from the deserts of Tartary, he must repeatedly vanquish the robust peasants of Russia, the numerous armies of Germany, the gallant nobles of France, and the intrepid freemen of Britain.'[124] This vision of Europe under Tartar threat may not have seemed as unlikely in the eighteenth century as it does now,[125] and it may have given Gibbon his peculiar sensitivity to barbarian Europe east of the Rhine.

It may also be possible to infer another, rather more homely, influence on Gibbon's sensitivities. Among his earliest friends in Lausanne was Jacques-Georges Deyverdun, who was subsequently to become his close companion. Deyverdun may well have drawn Gibbon's attention to Germany and beyond. In 1761 he was appointed tutor to 'the grandson of the Margrave of Schwedt for the Royal family of Prussia', which meant leaving Lausanne for the banks of the Oder. As it so happened Deyverdun had to leave Germany on account of 'An unhappy though honourable passion', and spent much of the next four summers with Gibbon.[126] Subsequently, in 1772, he accompanied the young Philip Stanhope (1755–1815) to the University of Leipzig.[127] Three years later he went with Alexander Hume to Göttingen.[128] Gibbon and Deyverdun discussed the historian's plans in great detail. They worked together on *Mémoires littéraires*.[129] Deyverdun translated various

---

[123] *Decline and fall*, ed. Milman, III, pp. 442–3.

[124] *Ibid.*, III, pp. 443–4.

[125] For the international context, see J. M. Black, *Eighteenth-century Europe, 1700–1789* (London, 1990), pp. 294–302.

[126] *Memoirs*, ed. Bonnard, p. 138.   [127] *Letters*, letter 186, vol. I, pp. 320–1.

[128] *Ibid.*, letters 303, 311, vol. II, pp. 68–9, 76–7.

[129] *Ibid.*, letters 77, 78, vol. I, pp. 216–17, 219–21.

books of relevance to Gibbon's planned history of 'the Swiss revolutions'.[130] He read at least parts of the *Decline and fall* in draft,[131] and was also supposed to translate it into French.[132] Perhaps, in their discussions of Roman history, and by his own travels, Deyverdun had drawn Gibbon's attention to the importance of Germany east of the Rhine. If so, he may have prompted some of the more enduring observations on the Merovingians to be found in *The decline and fall of the Roman Empire*.

Gibbon's interest in the Merovingian kingdom was, therefore, fired in part by his concern with the end of the Roman Empire in the West – a concern which gave him a special perspective on the barbarian kingdoms. It was also aroused, however, by his interest in feudal government, and was subsequently stimulated by his desire to reclaim the sixth-century Franks from the debates of the *philosophes*, who had sought to hijack them for political ends. Yet some, at least, of the Englishman's perceptions seem to stem from his days in Lausanne, and the friendships he made there.[133]

---

[130] *Memoirs*, ed. Bonnard, pp. 140–2. On Gibbon's lack of German see also *Letters*, letter 341, vol. II, pp. 202–6. Also Craddock, *Edward Gibbon, luminous historian*, p. 301.
[131] *Letters*, letter 316, vol. II, pp. 81–2.
[132] *Letters*, letters 341, 345, 355, 357, vol. II, pp. 104–8, 112–13, 119–20, 121–4.
[133] For Gibbon's view of Lausanne and Deyverdun, e.g. *Letters*, letters 571, 574, 652, vol. II, pp. 326–30, 332–9, vol. III, p. 71.

CHAPTER 7

Gibbon, Hodgkin and the invaders of Italy

T. S. Brown

In a lecture given to the British Academy in 1919 G. M. Trevelyan spoke of the 'passionate and many-sided devotion' of the English 'to the literature, language, art, history and civilization of ancient, of mediaeval and of modern Italy; the English had always displayed a particular love for Italy'.[1] It is undoubtedly true that English scholars have made a distinguished contribution to the study of all periods of Italian history. As Trevelyan remarked, Gibbon is a note-worthy example: *Decline and fall* grew out of a plan to write a history of the city of Rome itself.[2] Following his instinct as a classicist, he saw Italy as representative of the western aspect of Mediterranean civilization, and lamented that the government and army of Rome had fallen into the hands of non-Romans and non-Italians. The effects of Gibbon's grand tour of the peninsula, and especially his visit to Rome, are well-known, and Italy figures prominently throughout *Decline and fall*. Since his treatment of the peninsula in the fifth century and beyond was undoubtedly influential, it is worthwhile to examine the strengths and weaknesses of his approach and the respects in which his interpretations have been confirmed or disproved by more recent research. In particular, does his view of a steady weakening of the Roman element in Italy require modification? To what extent did Gibbon's antipathy to the undoubtedly increased role of Christianity distort his view of key developments? Further insights can be gained into these questions by comparing Gibbon's views with those of another English writer, who stands half-way in terms of chronology and methodology between Gibbon's time and our own, and who adopted a more

---

[1] G. M. Trevelyan, 'Englishmen and Italians: some aspects of their relations, past and present' in his *Clio, a muse and other essays* (new edn, London, 1930), pp. 104–5.
[2] *Ibid.*, p. 108.

nuanced and sympathetic attitude to the changes which Italy experienced from the fifth century to the ninth, the Quaker banker and historian Thomas Hodgkin (1831–1913).[3]

Traditionally discussion of Gibbon's analysis of the reasons for Rome's decline and fall has concentrated on Christianity – but we should not forget the second element which triumphed according to his great theme – barbarism.[4] Here it is salutary to recall the considerable space devoted to invasions in his section on 'General observations on the fall of the Roman Empire in the west' – and also of course to the possibility of an attack on the Europe of his own day by contemporary barbarians.[5] The barbarism/civilization dichotomy is the most recurrent and fundamental of the polarities which run through his work. Gibbon's fascination with barbarians is most marked in the final section of the *Decline and fall*, volumes IV, V and VI, published in 1788, in which marvellous events and massive movements loom large at the expense of gradual change and sociological and philosophical analysis. Following the schema of the Scottish historians, the barbarians are seen to epitomize one of the stages of human progress – that of pastoralism or nomadism. Hence the numerous passages in which Gibbon describes the Germans (wrongly) as pastoral nomads and naturally inclined to war.[6]

However, the barbarians have a more positive role as well. The feudal society developed in the barbarian successor states of western Europe is seen as possessing the vigour and liberty lacking in the late Empire and being more propitious to the growth of commerce and a 'constitutional' balance of powers.[7]

In essence Gibbon deals with four phases of barbarian activity in

---

[3] On Hodgkin's life, see the sympathetic entry of H. W. C. Davis in *Dictionary of National Biography. Twentieth century, 1912–1921* (Oxford, 1927), pp. 250–1.

[4] Historians of ideas have paid more attention to Gibbon's views on barbarism and barbarians than historians of late antiquity and the early Middle Ages. J. W. Burrow's excellent introduction, *Gibbon* (Oxford, 1985) is one of many works that devotes a chapter to the theme.

[5] *Decline and fall*, ed. Bury, IV, p. 166.

[6] For example, *Decline and fall*, ed. Bury, I, pp. 213–36; III, pp. 69–132. Cf. Burrow, *Gibbon*, pp. 71–6, 80–1.

[7] E.g. *Decline and fall*, ed. Bury, I, p. 58: '[The Germans] restored a manly spirit of freedom; . . . freedom became the happy parent of taste and science.' Cf. D. Womersley, *The Transformation of 'The decline and fall of the Roman Empire'*, Cambridge Studies in Eighteenth-Century English Literature and Thought 1 (Cambridge, 1988), pp. 82–4, drawing a subtle comparison with the views of Rousseau and Hume.

Italy. The first is the fifth century up to 489 – when the peninsula was subjected to the invasions of Alaric, Attila and Genseric and then ruled by Ricimer and Odoacer. These were all Germanic commanders leading bands of German mercenaries. Thereafter the period of the Ostrogothic regime up to its final defeat by Justinian's forces in 554 was led by Theodoric and his successors. Thirdly, the Lombards, who invaded the peninsula in 568 and became the most durable and assimilated of the invaders, established a kingdom covering most of the peninsula which lasted until 774. Lastly, Italy was associated with Germanic kingdoms to the north, which followed the Frankish take-over of 774, and led to the imperial coronation of Charlemagne in 800. The conquest of the Ottonians, culminating in Otto I in 962, is seen as an extension of this.

The first phase will only briefly be considered here, even though Gibbon devoted a lot of space to it and included purple passages on the figures involved.[8] The events involved could not help but appeal to Gibbon's sense of irony and drama. Alaric's sack is described in the following terms: 'Eleven hundred and sixty-three years after the foundation of Rome the imperial city, which had subdued and civilized so considerable a part of mankind, was delivered to the licentious fury of the tribes of Germany and Scythia.'[9] Great emphasis is placed on this as the first stage in the physical decay of the city, a subject which so moved him on his visit of 1764 and which remained a preoccupation following his reading in Lausanne of the work of Pier Angeli di Barga, *De privatorum publicorumque Aedificiorum Urbis Romae eversoribus Epistola*, published in Florence in 1589.[10] Similarly, in his discussion of Attila the Hun's invasion of Italy in 452, great play is made of Rome's salvation, not by the Empire or the senate, but by Pope Leo the Great.[11] Unfortunately Gibbon's treatment of this period is marked by major exaggerations. For example, most scholars would now play down the slaughter and physical destruction carried out by Alaric's followers in 410 –

---

[8] On Gibbon's treatment of the events leading to the sack of Rome (410), see F. Paschoud, 'Gibbon et les sources historiographiques pour la période de 363 à 410' in P. Ducrey (ed.), *Gibbon et Rome à la lumière de l'historiographie moderne* (Geneva, 1977), pp. 219–45.

[9] *Decline and fall*, ed. Bury, III, pp. 321–2.

[10] *Le journal de Gibbon à Lausanne*, ed. G. A. Bonnard (London, 1945), pp. 82–3. Cf. G. Giarrizzo, *Edward Gibbon e la cultura europea del settecento* (Naples, 1954), pp. 185–6.

[11] *Decline and fall*, ed. Bury, III, p. 472 (an unusually generous tribute to a pope).

although great emphasis is placed on the psychological impact and the unleashing of an intense debate between Christian and pagan apologists.[12] Similarly Gibbon wrongly associated the foundation of Venice with Attila's invasion – as a result of Venetian myth-making which was widely accepted in the eighteenth century – thus Napoleon in 1797 styled himself 'the Attila of the Venetian people'.[13]

The sack of Rome by the Vandal king Genseric in 455 is described in equally colourful terms – 'Rome and its inhabitants were delivered to the licentiousness of the Vandals and Moors, whose blind passions revenged the injuries of Carthage.'[14] It has to be admitted that Gibbon does reject the traditional, crude image of these barbarians as wantonly destructive. Self-interest and a measure of Christianity moderated their ferocity; 'the Goths evacuated Rome on the sixth, the Vandals on the fifteenth day; and though it be far more difficult to build than to destroy, their hasty assault would have made a slight impression on the solid piles of antiquity . . . both Alaric and Genseric affected to spare the buildings of the city.'[15]

Most important of all, Gibbon failed to appreciate the degree to which Roman institutions, including city life and even the Roman senate, remained intact in this period, and that the major effect of the barbarian pressure on Italy was ironically felt outside the peninsula: the imperial government's resources and attention could no longer extend to other provinces. His characterization of the reign of Odoacer as exhibiting 'the sad prospect of misery and desolation' with Italy 'exhausted by the irretrievable losses of war, famine and pestilence', has in recent decades been disproved by a mass of epigraphic, archaeological and documentary evidence.[16] Here, as elsewhere, it is ironic that Gibbon took at face value the

---

[12] P. Heather, *Goths and Romans, 332–489* (Oxford, 1991), pp. 216–18; H. Wolfram, *History of the Goths* (Berkeley, 1987), pp. 158–9. Roman reactions: J. Matthews, *Western aristocracies and imperial court* (Oxford, 1975), pp. 300–2.

[13] *Decline and fall*, ed. Bury, III, pp. 469–71; cf. T. S. Brown, 'History as myth: medieval perceptions of Venice's Roman and Byzantine past' in R. Beaton and C. Roueché (eds.), *The making of Byzantine history. Studies dedicated to Donald M. Nicol* (Aldershot, 1993), pp. 145–57.

[14] *Decline and fall*, ed. Bury, IV, p. 5.

[15] *Ibid.*, VII, p. 309.

[16] *Ibid.*, IV, p. 55. Cf. A. Chastagnol, *Le Sénat romain sous le règne d'Odoacre* (Bonn, 1966) and J. Moorhead, *Theoderic in Italy* (Oxford, 1992), pp. 7–11.

querulous moralizing of Christian writers. But it has to be said that Gibbon did anticipate the views of later scholars by making comparatively little of what he called 'the extinction of the Roman empire in the West' in 476: this 'non-event', as Averil Cameron has recently called it,[17] is seen as the culmination of a long process of decline marked by 'military licence, capricious despotism, and elaborate oppression', during which the barbarians had gradually risen to become 'the masters of the Romans'.[18]

Likewise the fourth phase need not detain us for long. Gibbon's treatment of the Carolingians and Ottonians is rushed and over-simplified. In fact the significance of the Frankish conquest was played down; 'in the possession of their national laws the Lombards became the brethren, rather than the subjects, of the Franks'.[19] Gibbon says little about the effects of Carolingian rule, although he does highlight the Franks' alliance with the papacy and remark that 'the successors of Charlemagne neglected to assert . . . local jurisdiction'.[20] Otto I is seen very much as continuing the work of Charles and as initially a 'deliverer'.[21] However, following the line of his main secondary authority, the Italian antiquarian Muratori, he soon turns to a denunciation of the alien and ineffective rule of the Germans. Gibbon writes of 'the German caesars, who were ambitious to enslave the kingdom of Italy . . . [but] the effects of their intemperance were often imputed to the treachery and malice of the Italians, who rejoiced at least in the calamities of the barbarians. This irregular tyranny might contend on equal terms with the petty tyrants of Italy.'[22] The period of nearly four centuries from Otto III to Charles IV is covered in six pages.[23]

More profit can be gained from studying the second and third phases, where Gibbon's treatment is fuller and more sensitive.

Gibbon's treatment of the Ostrogothic period is not unnaturally dominated by Theodoric. Earlier writers such as Machiavelli,

---

[17] A. Cameron, *The Mediterranean world in late antiquity* (London, 1993), p. 33, and cf. B. Croke, 'AD 476: The manufacture of a turning point', *Chiron* 13 (1983), pp. 81–119.

[18] *Decline and fall*, ed. Bury, IV, pp. 51, 53–4.

[19] *Ibid.*, V, p. 268. Gibbon's shallow and cursory treatment of this period has often been condemned: 'Hardly anybody suffers a more unjust treatment than Charlemagne, whose main characteristics according to Gibbon must have been cruelty, lewdness and superstition' (P. Fuglum, *Edward Gibbon. His view of life and conception of history* (Oslo, 1953), p. 152).

[20] *Decline and fall*, ed. Bury, V, p. 299.   [21] *Ibid.*, V, p. 300.

[22] *Ibid.*, V, p. 322.   [23] *Ibid.*, V, pp. 301–7.

Muratori and Voltaire had exalted this figure as an ideal ruler, and one might expect him to be one of Gibbon's favourites.[24] Certainly he took issue with his condemnation by the aristocratic Italian writer Scipione Maffei for injustice,[25] and described him in fulsome terms as a 'rare and meritorious example of a Barbarian, who sheathed his sword in the pride of victory and the vigour of his age'[26] comparable with 'the best and bravest of the ancient Romans'.[27] 'The reputation of Theodoric may repose with more confidence on the visible peace and prosperity of a reign of thirty-three years, the unanimous esteem of his own times, and the memory of his wisdom and courage, his justice and humanity, which was deeply impressed on the minds of the Goths and the Italians.'[28]

Theodoric certainly had an important structural role, introducing as he does the final 'medieval' instalment of the work[29] (just as he was the introductory figure in Machiavelli's *Istorie fiorentine*) and serving as a dramatic contrast to the oriental and autocratic Justinian. Very striking is the detailed treatment of his personality and career, even his childhood, and the emphasis on his tolerance and encouragement of 'commerce'. 'A firm though gentle discipline imposed the habits of modesty, obedience and temperance; and the Goths were instructed to spare the people, to reverence the laws, and to disclaim the barbarous licence of judicial combat and private revenge.'[30] Theodoric had 'penetration to discern, and firmness to pursue, his own and the public interest. Theodoric loved the virtues which he possessed, and the talents of which he was destitute.' The 'beneficial traffic [of merchants] was encouraged and protected by the liberal spirit of Theodoric'.[31]

There are, however, flaws in this idyll, and Gibbon's picture is in some respects curiously half-hearted. Why is this?

One factor has to be the unsatisfactory nature of the sources – Gibbon himself pointed out the lack of historians leaving 'any just representation of the events which displayed . . . the virtues of

---

[24] On the Renaissance and Enlightenment myth of Theodoric, see Giarrizzo, *Edward Gibbon e la cultura europea del settecento*, pp. 448–51. A. Pizzi, 'Teoderico nella grande storiografia europea', *Romanobarbarica* 13 (1994–5), pp. 259–82, esp. pp. 274–7 on Gibbon.
[25] *Decline and fall*, ed. Bury, IV, p. 181 n. 34.
[26] *Ibid.*, IV, p. 185. [27] *Ibid.*, IV, p. 170. [28] *Ibid.*, IV, p. 181.
[29] Volumes IV, V and VI of the original edition, published in 1788.
[30] *Decline and fall*, ed. Bury, IV, pp. 182–3.
[31] *Ibid.*, IV, pp. 189, 193.

Theodoric', as opposed to the audacious praise of 'sacred and profane orators'.[32] Gibbon found the panegyrical quality of Cassiodorus and Ennodius not to his taste. To compensate he made extensive use of Jordanes and the *Anonymus Valesianus* to give a Gothic and Roman perspective respectively, but these remain among the most puzzling and problematic of early medieval sources to this day.[33]

Another undoubted explanation is a deep-seated antagonism to barbarians – Goths are unlettered and uncivilized. Gibbon accepted that the king was illiterate (as recorded in the *Anonymus*), a fact now questioned by most historians.[34] This is expressed with humorous irony when he describes how 'the Goths imperiously demanded that the grandson of Theodoric be rescued from the dastardly discipline of women and pedants and educated like a valiant Goth, in the society of his equals and the glorious ignorance of his ancestors'.[35] Gibbon said conspicuously little about the undoubted learning of notably literate Goths such as Theodoric's daughter Amalasuintha and Theodahad, her cousin and murderer.[36]

All in all Gibbon saw Theodoric's reign as a failure – or at least a missed opportunity:

---

[32] *Ibid.*, IV, p. 180. Among the latter Gibbon had Cassiodorus and Ennodius primarily in mind.

[33] On Jordanes (referred to by Gibbon as Jornandes and used in Grotius' edition of 1655: G. Keynes (ed.), *The library of Edward Gibbon. A catalogue* (London, 1940), p. 140), see B. Croke, 'Cassiodorus and the *Getica* of Jordanes', *Classical Philology* 82 (1983), pp. 117–34; W. Goffart, *The narrators of barbarian history (AD 500–800)* (Princeton, 1988), pp. 20–111; P. Heather, 'The historical culture of Ostrogothic Italy', in *Teoderico il Grande e i Goti d'Italia. Atti del XIII Congresso Internazionale di Studi sull' also medioevo* (Spoleto, 1993), pp. 317–33. On the *pars posterior* of the *Anonymus*, J. N. Adams, *The text and language of a Vulgar Latin chronicle (Anonymus Valesianus II)* (London, 1976); S. J. B. Barnish, 'The Anonymous Valesianus as a source for the last years of Theoderic', *Latomus* 42 (1983), pp. 572–96. J. Moorhead, *Theoderic in Italy*, pp. 261–3; G. Zecchini, 'L'Anonimo Valesiano II: genere storiografico e contesto politico' in *Teoderico il Grande*, pp. 809–18. Gibbon was able to read the *Anonymus* as an appendix to his copies of Ammianus Marcellinus (he possessed both the Leiden edition of 1693 and the Leipzig one of 1773: Keynes, *Library*, p. 49).

[34] *Decline and fall*, ed. Bury, IV, p. 171. On the passages in the *Anonymus* (cc. 61, 79), see Moorhead, *Theoderic in Italy*, pp. 104–5. In my view the passage about him having to use a stencil to sign his name is a popular misunderstanding of the use of stencils made by rulers and officials to write the large LEGI at the end of documents: cf. J.-O. Tjäder, '*Et ad latus*. Il posto della datazione e della indicazione del luogo negli scritti della cancelleria imperiale e nelle largizioni di enfiteusi degli arcivescovi ravennati', *Studi Romagnoli* 24 (1973), pp. 91–124.

[35] *Decline and fall*, ed. Bury, IV, p. 302.

[36] Briefly mentioned in *ibid.*, IV, pp. 302, 305.

The union of the Goths and Romans might have fixed for ages the transient happiness of Italy; and the first of nations, a new people of free subjects and enlightened soldiers, might have gradually risen from the mutual emulation of their respective virtues. But the sublime merit of guiding or seconding such a revolution was not reserved for the reign of Theodoric: he wanted either the genius or the opportunities of a legislator; and while he indulged the Goths in the enjoyment of rude liberty, he servilely copied the institutions, and even the abuses, of the political system which had been framed by Constantine and his successors.[37]

Gibbon also accepted the tyranny of his last years. 'The wisdom of Theodoric might be deceived, his power might be resisted, and the declining age of the monarch was sullied with popular hatred and patrician blood' – especially of course the murder of Boethius, 'the last of the Romans' and a more authentic hero in Gibbon's eyes.[38] Admittedly some excuse is given for the king's behaviour; 'a difference of religion is always pernicious and often fateful to the harmony of the prince and people' and 'by the bigotry of his subjects and enemies the most tolerant of princes was driven to the brink of persecution, and the life of Theodoric was too long, since he lived to condemn the virtue of Boethius and Symmachus'.[39] Old age and illness played their part. 'After a life of virtue and glory, Theodoric was now descending with shame and guilt into the grave: his mind was humbled by the contrast of the past, and justly alarmed by the invisible terrors of futurity.'[40]

Two other elements colour Gibbon's assessment. One is the king's failure to promote liberty or at least the Polybian ideal of equilibrium of power, both of which he regarded as central to Rome's early success.[41] The second stems from reservations concerning the pragmatic religious policy of this 'Christianized barbarian'. 'Satisfied with the private toleration of his Arian sectaries, he justly conceived himself to be the guardian of the public worship, and his external reverence for a superstition which

---

[37] *Ibid.*, IV, p. 187.
[38] *Ibid.*, IV, pp. 195, 197–202.
[39] *Ibid.*, IV, pp. 193, 197.
[40] *Ibid.*, IV, p. 203.
[41] *Ibid.*, IV, p. 187, quoted above. Cf. M. Baridon, *Edward Gibbon et le mythe de Rome. Histoire de idéologie au siècle des lumières* (Paris, 1977), pp. 619–22. Gibbon repeatedly emphasizes *conquest* and *heredity* as key bases of Theoderic's rule.

he despised may have nourished in his mind the salutary indifference of a statesman or philosopher.' But Theodoric's tolerant balancing act could not cope with the bigotry of his subjects, which found expression in the bitter papal schism between Laurentius and Symmachus (498–507) and anti-semitic outbursts in Rome and Ravenna in the later part of his reign.[42]

The failure of Theodoric's experiment was of course brought home by the bitter wars initiated by Justinian's attempt to reconquer Italy, nominally to avenge Amalasuintha, Theodoric's romanizing daughter, who was murdered by her cousin Theodahad in 535.[43] Gibbon gives a full account of the Gothic wars and interesting sketches of each of the succeeding Ostrogothic kings. Ironically Gibbon seems more at ease with Totila, the leader of the Gothic resistance to the Byzantines in the 540s. 'Totila was chaste and temperate; and none were deceived, either friends or enemies, who depended on his faith or his clemency.'[44] 'The virtues of Totila are equally laudable, whether they proceeded from true policy, religious principle, or the instinct of humanity.'[45] Totila is a clear-cut nationalist and a 'noble savage', who even receives approval on the important criterion of his attitude towards the monuments of Rome: 'We may remember that both Alaric and Genseric affected to spare the buildings of the city; that they subsisted in strength under the auspicious government of Theodoric; and that the momentary resentment of Totila was disarmed by his own temper and the advice of his friends and enemies.'[46]

When we turn to the third phase of invasions, Gibbon's treatment of the Lombards is short and unsatisfactory.[47] There are a

---

[42] *Decline and fall*, ed. Bury, v, p. 193. On religious problems in Theoderic's reign, see Moorhead, *Theoderic in Italy*, pp. 97–100 and 114–39; T. S. Brown, 'Everyday life in Ravenna under Theoderic: an example of his "tolerance" and "prosperity"?', in *Teoderico il Grande*, pp. 77–99.

[43] H. Wolfram, *History of the Goths* (Berkeley and Los Angeles, 1988), pp. 334–9. Theodahad placed himself at the head of a Gothic 'nationalist' party and became king.

[44] *Decline and fall*, ed. Bury, iv, p. 397.   [45] *Ibid.*, iv, p. 398.

[46] Ch. 72. Gibbon derived his charitable view of Alaric and Genseric from Orosius and Prosper of Aquitaine respectively (*Decline and fall*, ed. Bury, iii, p. 322 nn. 102, 103; iv, p. 5 n. 8).

[47] Less than half of ch. 45 is devoted to them, to which has to be added a paragraph on their Arian faith in ch. 37 and a handful of pages in ch. 49. Their crucial history in the seventh century is hardly mentioned except for Rothari (praised for the wisdom of his laws in *Decline and fall*, ed. Bury, v, pp. 29–30).

number of reasons for this, including his dependence on a limited number of secondary authorities. Notable among these was the contemporary Italian historian, L. A. Muratori (1672–1750), who published a vast collection of texts,[48] and also a wealth of material about medieval Italian culture in his *Antiquitates italicae medii aevi*.[49] Great as his admiration was for Muratori's erudition, Gibbon was even more influenced by the anti-clerical Neapolitan Pietro Giannone, whose *Istoria civile del regno di Napoli*[50] led to his persecution and death. Gibbon wrote in his *Memoirs* that this was one of 'three particular books' which 'may have remotely contributed to form the historian of the Roman Empire', and that in Giannone's work he 'observed with a critical eye the progress and abuse of sacerdotal power'.[51] The line Gibbon takes, following his sources, is generally one of admiration for the Lombards' wise moderation. 'The succession of their kings is marked with virtue and ability; the troubled series of their annals is adorned with fair intervals of peace, order and domestic happiness; and the Italians enjoyed a milder and more equitable government than any of the other kingdoms which had been founded on the ruins of the Western empire.'[52]

A particular weakness is his very romantic treatment, especially of the early kings Alboin and Authari. 'I should not be apprehensive of deviating from my subject if it were in my power to delineate the private life of the conquerors of Italy, and I shall relate with pleasure the adventurous gallantry of Autharis, which breathes the true spirit of chivalry and romance.'[53] In part this romanticism stems from his fondness for anecdotes from Paul the Deacon. Hence the tales of the Lombards' feud with the Gepids, the Gepid princess Rosamunda's marriage to Alboin and her being compelled to drink from her father's skull, followed by her adulterous affair

---

[48] *Rerum italicarum scriptores ab anno D ad annum MD* (2 vols., Milan, 1723–50). Gibbon certainly made use of this series: see, for example, his reference to Agnellus of Ravenna, *Decline and fall*, ed. Bury, v, p. 10. However Keynes, *Library*, pp. 203–4 lists the *Annali*, *Antiquitates* and *Novus thesaurus veterum insciptionum* of Muratori but not the *Scriptores*.

[49] 6 vols. (Milan 1738–43): Keynes, *Library*, p. 203. On Muratori's intellectual background see S. Bertelli, *Erudizione e storia in Ludovico Antonio Muratori* (Naples, 1960); A. Andreoli, *Nel mondo di Lodovico Antonio Muratori* (Bologna, 1972).

[50] (Venice, 1766). The book and the author's subsequent defence of his work are listed in Gibbon's library catalogue: Keynes, *Library*, p. 137.

[51] *Memoirs of my life*, ed. G. A. Bonnard (London, 1966), p. 79.

[52] *Decline and fall*, ed. Bury, v, p. 30. [53] *Ibid.*, v, p. 28.

with a Lombard noble, their murder of Alboin and flight to the
Byzantine capital of Ravenna – all told with uncritical relish.[54]

On a more profound level Gibbon also admired the Lombards for
certain qualities which he attributed to their society.[55] First, he
stressed the consultative element in their institutions: 'one of their
noblest chiefs . . . by the free suffrage of the nation in the assembly
of Pavia, Clepho . . . was elected as the successor of Alboin', and 'it
is certain that the Lombards possessed freedom to elect their
sovereign . . . in peace a judge, in war a leader, [the king] never
usurped the powers of a sole and unique legislator. The king of Italy
convened the national assemblies in the palace, or more probably
the fields of Pavia.'[56]

Secondly, drawing on his proud experience of the Hampshire
militia, he admired Lombard military arrangements: 'A Lombard
was born the soldier of his king and his duke; and the civil
assemblies of the nation displayed the banners, and assumed the
appelation of a regular army.'[57]

Thirdly he had nothing but praise for the Lombards' supposed
independence of clerical, and especially papal, influence. Following
Muratori, he took issue with the condemnation of their supposed
barbarity by pro-papal writers such as Baronius.[58] '[Their laws] are
the genuine fruit of the reason of the barbarians, who never
admitted the bishops of Italy to a seat in their legislative councils.'[59]
Here Gibbon was following a line dear to his own heart espoused by
the anti-clerical Giannone.[60] Gibbon in fact put his finger on an
interesting point – the Lombards had in some respects what Chris
Wickham has recently called 'a resolutely secular political
system',[61] but he failed to explain or develop this fully.

This is not the only weakness in Gibbon's treatment. He offers no
satisfactory explanation of the most remarkable feature of the

[54] *Ibid.*, v, pp. 4–8, 12–24.
[55] 'This strange apparel and horrid aspect often concealed a gentle and generous disposition; and . . . the captives and subjects were sometimes surprised by the humanity of the victor', *ibid.*, v, pp. 27–8.
[56] *Ibid.*, v, pp. 14, 29.
[57] *Ibid.*, v, p. 26.
[58] *Ibid.*, v, p. 30 n. 66, p. 31 n. 67, and cf. Giarrizzo, *Edward Gibbon e la cultura europea del settecento*, pp. 463–4.
[59] *Ibid.*, v, p. 30.
[60] Cf. Giarrizzo, *Edward Gibbon e la cultura europea del settecento*, pp. 465–6.
[61] C. Wickham, *Early medieval Italy* (London, 1981), p. 36.

Lombards – their transformation from ferocious barbarians to cultivated city-dwellers.[62] Their decline in the years before the Frankish conquest is also dealt with very cursorily: 'the love of arms and rapine was congenial to the Lombards', but they 'languished about twenty years in a state of languor and decay'. Scorn is reserved for the Spoletans, who sought refuge from the dissolution of the Lombard kingdom by declaring themselves the servants and subjects of St Peter.[63]

Following the take-over of 774 Gibbon rushed quickly on to the rise of later merchant cities: 'in the eleventh and twelfth centuries the Lombards rekindled the flame of industry and freedom . . . under the protection of equal law the labours of agriculture and law were gradually revived; but the martial spirit of the Lombards was nourished by the presence of danger'.[64] In this there were a number of features which Gibbon failed to appreciate or discuss – the role of the majority Roman population in these developments, the strong regional differences in Lombard Italy, or the dynamic strengths of localism. The one exception to this neglect is a glowing cameo portrait of Venice between AD 697 and 1200, in which the city received not unexpected praise for its commercial and political success, its prudent ambition, and its freedom from 'servile obedience to the Roman pontiff' and from 'the fever of super-stition'.[65]

Before attempting any conclusions regarding Gibbon's treat-ment of Italy and her invaders it is worthwhile to bring in a comparison with the work of another English scholar who dealt with the theme just over a century later. Thomas Hodgkin's eight-volume *Italy and her invaders* first appeared between 1880 and 1889 and constitutes the only substantial English contribution to the history of early medieval Italy until recent times.[66]

---

[62] Gibbon does admit that 'so rapid was the influence of climate and example that the Lombards of the fourth generation surveyed with curiosity and affright the portraits of their savage forefathers' (*Decline and fall*, ed. Bury, v, p. 27).
[63] *Ibid.*, v, pp. 265, 267, 272–3.
[64] *Ibid.*, v, pp. 302–3.   [65] *Ibid.*, vi, pp. 380–2.
[66] Hodgkin's work has received nothing like the attention it deserves. A notable exception is the brief study by D. Bullough, *Italy and her invaders* (Inaugural Lecture, University of Nottingham, 1968), to which the following discussion owes a great deal. Bullough also wrote the entry on Hodgkin in J. Cannon (ed.), *The Blackwell Dictionary of Historians* (Oxford, 1988), p. 195.

Hodgkin was, like Gibbon, an amateur scholar and there are a number of marked similarities in their approaches. Both authors, for example, include detailed physical and personality sketches. Although Hodgkin's Quaker belief precluded the sceptical approach towards Christianity found in Gibbon, he did at times denounce what he saw as the obscurantist effects of the Catholic church in Italy: in a letter written in Catania in 1882 he remarked that 'travelling in Italy makes me now, as it always does, a bitter Protestant; I feel what a frightfully degrading influence this kind of Christianity has exercised on the nation'.[67] Not surprisingly, however, the similarities are outweighed by the differences. Like many of his English contemporaries, Hodgkin was deeply impressed by achievement of Italian unity in the 1860s and first visited the peninsula in 1868. He displayed a strong interest in topography and, unlike Gibbon, a marked aesthetic appreciation of the art and monuments of the late antique and early medieval periods, especially those of Ravenna.[68]

It is clear from Hodgkin's letters that he was aware that his work would be unfavourably compared with Gibbon's, and in certain respects he marks a reaction against the earlier work.[69] Three aspects stand out. Hodgkin found Gibbon's view of 'the decline of Roman empire' unduly negative.[70] Closely related to this was his opinion that Gibbon's view of religion was too narrow and unsympathetic.[71] Finally, Hodgkin was much more positive about the Germanic contribution – naturally, perhaps for a long-time resident of Bede's Northumbria. Here it is less a question of the nationalist and racialist theories prevalent in the late nineteenth century than genuine admiration for recent scholars of *Germanentum*

---

[67] L. Creighton, *Life and letters of Thomas Hodgkin* (London, 1917), p. 125.

[68] Bullough, *Italy and her invaders*, pp. 11, 14. Particularly noteworthy is Hodgkin's use of a plate depicting the interior of the so-called 'Mausoleum of Galla Placidia' as a frontispiece to volume I. Gibbon never visited Ravenna, travelling straight from Bologna to Florence during his tour of Italy in 1764; G. A. Bonnard (ed.), *Gibbon's journey from Geneva to Rome: his journal from 20 April to 2 October 1764* (London, 1961), p. 118.

[69] For example, Creighton, *Life and letters of Thomas Hodgkin*, pp. 106, 144.

[70] In a letter of April 1912 he argued that the Empire experienced an 'upward tendency' with the accession of Diocletian: Creighton, *Life and letters of Thomas Hodgkin*, p. 388.

[71] See especially his discussion of the effects of Christianity on the Roman Empire: *Italy and her invaders*, vol. II, pp. 542–56. Cf. a letter of March 1912, 'I distrust Gibbon . . . whenever he gets on the question of Christianity v. paganism' (Creighton, *Life and letters of Thomas Hodgkin*, p. 387).

and *Stammeskunde* and a strong belief that Gibbon had not done justice to men like Theodoric.[72]

Hodgkin became much more of a specialist and his enthusiasm for early medieval Italy also found expression in other works, such as a partial translation of the key source for Ostrogothic Italy, the *Variae* of Cassiodorus in 1886, and a volume on Theodoric in 'The heroes of the nations' series published in 1891.[73] Writing when he did, Hodgkin possessed obvious advantages compared with Gibbon. His whole approach reflected the rehabilitation of the Middle Ages characteristic of the nineteenth century, evident first in the Romantics' discovery of medieval art and literature and later the great strides made in the scientific study of medieval history both on the Continent and in Britain.[74] He possessed considerable language skills – extending to Gothic as well as Latin and Greek.[75] He drew enormous benefit from the great explosion of historical writing in Germany and elsewhere, especially critical editions of sources such as the German *Monumenta* series and some revolutionary monographs of scholars such as Theodor Mommsen, Ludo Moritz Hartmann and Charles Diehl.[76] Some of these specialists, such as Felix Dahn, received fulsome and generous tribute as

---

[72] Bullough, *Italy and her invaders*, p. 13. In 1882 Hodgkin wrote to Edward Fry: 'Theoderic is going on as fast as I could reasonably expect . . . I cannot understand why Gibbon has slurred over this part of his history so hastily' (Creighton, *Life and letters of Thomas Hodgkin*, p. 144).

[73] *The letters of Cassiodorus* (London, 1886). *Theodoric the Goth: the barbarian champion of civilization* (London and New York, 1891). A second edition appeared in 1923. He had earlier published lectures on the important early fifth-century author Claudian, *Claudian, the last of the Roman poets* (Newcastle-upon-Tyne, 1875) and he later completed a study of a figure, whose treatment by Gibbon was particularly inadequate, Charlemagne: *Charles the Great* (London, 1897).

[74] C. Dellheim, *The face of the past: the preservation of the medieval inheritance in Victorian England* (Cambridge, 1982), and J. W. Burrow, *A Liberal descent: Victorian historians and the English past* (Cambridge, 1981). The popularizing and controversial study by N. F. Cantor, *Inventing Middle Ages. The lives, works and ideas of the great medievalists of the twentieth century* (New York, 1991), discusses briefly the rise of medieval scholarship in the nineteenth century (pp. 28–9), but does not mention Hodgkin.

[75] Bullough, *Italy and her invaders*, pp. 12, 15.

[76] Mommsen edited numerous texts in the *Auctores Antiquissimi* series of the MGH; Hodgkin also made extensive use of his editions of inscriptions and monographs such as his *Römische Geschichte* (5 vols., translated into English from 1862 onwards). The Austrian scholar L. M. Hartmann published his *Untersuchungen zur Geschichte der Byzantinische Verwaltung in Italien (540–750)* in Leipzig in 1889 and edited two volumes of the *Register* of Gregory the Great in 1887 and 1899. Diehl's *Etudes sur l'administration byzantine dans l'exarchat de Ravenne (568–751)* (Paris, 1888) is extensively quoted in Hodgkin's *Italy and her invaders*, vols. v and vi.

Hodgkin's main authorities,[77] while others became helpful correspondents.[78] Of particular value was the availability of critical editions of documents in Italy.[79]

Hodgkin travelled much more widely in Italy than Gibbon. A good example of the insights which this afforded is his sympathetic and incisive treatment of Ravenna, its rulers and people, throughout his work, culminating in a commendable twenty-page description of the city in volume I.[80] His fascination with the city, also displayed by his frequent choice of it as a topic for lectures, contrasts sharply with the lack of interest evinced by Gibbon, who failed to make the detour from Bologna to the ancient capital of caesars and exarchs during his Italian visit of 1764.[81] Apart from a brief description of its advantages as a refuge for the emperors in the fifth century, Gibbon says little in detail about the city which had succeeded his beloved Rome as capital of Italy, and even delights in associating it with the oppression of the exarchs.[82]

Italy and her invaders was sufficiently successful for a second edition of volumes I to VI to appear between 1892 and 1916, and a reissue of all eight volumes to be published in 1928.[83] However, Hodgkin's work suffered from being rapidly overtaken by new studies. The first volume of Ludo Moritz Hartmann's *Geschichte Italiens in Mittelalter*, for example, appeared in 1897.[84] It was Hartmann who

---

[77] Dahn's work, especially his *Die Könige der Germanen*, 12 vols. in 16 (Munich, 1861–1909) is quoted throughout Hodgkin's *Italy and her invaders*, but particular gratitude is expressed in the introduction to vol. III, pp. ix–x.

[78] Such as the Italian scholars Pasquale Villari and Ugo Balzani: Hodgkin, *Italy and her invaders*, v, p. iii.

[79] Such as G. Marini, *I papiri diplomatici* (Rome, 1805), and C. Troya, *Codice Diplomatico Longobardo* (5 vols., Naples, 1852–5).

[80] Hodgkin, *Italy and her invaders*, vol. I, pp. 851–71.

[81] Hodgkin lectured on Ravenna in cities as varied as Manchester and Sydney: Creighton, *Life and letters of Thomas Hodgkin*, pp. 198, 254, 311. Gibbon: *supra*, n. 68.

[82] *Decline and fall*, ed. Bury, III, pp. 259–60; v, pp. 23–4: 'Rome was oppressed with the iron sceptre of the exarchs and a Greek, perhaps a eunuch, insulted with impunity the ruins of the Capitol.'

[83] For fuller details, based on a study of the files of the Clarendon Press in Oxford, see Bullough, *Italy and her invaders*, p. 27 n. 21, who notes 'the publishing history of [Hodgkin's] *Italy and her invaders* is surprisingly complicated'. The second edition of vols. I and II appeared in 1892, that of vols. III and IV in 1896 and that of vols. v and vI in 1916. The total printing of the first two editions was 2,500 copies of vols. I–IV, and 2,250 of vols. v–vI. No second edition was prepared of vols. vII and vIII, 2,000 copies of which had been printed in the first edition. 500 sets of sheets were printed for the eight-volume reissue of 1928.

[84] The four-volume work, published in Gotha between 1897 and 1915, covered the period 476–1015.

wrote chapters on early medieval Italy in the *Cambridge Medieval History*.[85] In Italy Hodgkin's work had virtually no impact, partly because of the widespread inability of Italian writers to read long English works, and also because of their greater methodological and philosophical rapport with German and Austrian scholars such as Hartmann. But even in Britain *Italy and her invaders* became less fashionable in the twentieth century for a number of reasons. One is the gap which steadily grew between professional and amateur historians.[86] Other factors were the increase in chronological specialization, and especially a polarization between Roman and medieval history.[87] Even more significant was a change of emphasis in history courses at the universities, where the prestige of Stubbs, Maitland and Tout resulted in a shift from European history to English 'constitutional' history and the study of records, particularly central ones, as opposed to the more literary and topographical approach of Hodgkin. Even among the few English historians of Italy there was a shift of interest away from the early Middle Ages in favour of the city-states of the Renaissance.[88] Nevertheless scholars have continued to value Hodgkin's work for its critical approach to sources and emphasis on human qualities, and in his concern with *mentalités* and *l'espace*, and even with *histoire événementielle*, he appears more up-to-date to a historical world

---

[85] H. M. Gwatkin, J. P. Whitney (eds.), *The Cambridge Medieval History* II. *The rise of the Saracens and the foundation of the western Empire* (Cambridge, 1913), ch. 7, 'Italy under the Lombards', pp. 194–221, and 8a, 'Imperial Italy and Africa; administration', pp. 222–35.

[86] See Bullough, *Italy and her invaders*, pp. 15–18, who condemns Thomas Tout's reservations about Hodgkin in his obituary notice for the British Academy and rightly stresses the breadth and precision of Hodgkin's scholarship. The perceptions and prejudices of a professional elite could lead to the exaggerated emphasis on certain narrow approaches, such as constitutional history, and a less empathetic view of the past than that offered by 'amateurs' such as Hodgkin.

[87] Bullough, *Italy and her invaders*, pp. 17–18, who emphasizes the foundation of the consciously 'pre-medieval' *Journal of Roman Studies* in 1911, and points out that the ancient historian J. B. Bury was one of the few early twentieth-century scholars to display his admiration for Hodgkin.

[88] The perspective of works such as W. F. Butler, *The Lombard communes: a history of the republics of North Italy* (London, 1906) and of M. V. Clarke, *The medieval city state* (London, 1926) was directed towards later developments. Other scholars shared German historians' preoccupation with the involvement of the Holy Roman Empire in Italy. One of the few early twentieth-century scholars to appreciate medieval Italy on its own terms was C. W. Previté-Orton (1877–1947): see, for example, his *The early history of the House of Savoy (1000–1233)* (Cambridge, 1912) and 'Italy in the tenth century', ch. 7 of H. W. Gwatkin, J. P. Whitney, J. R. Tanner and C. W. Previté-Orton (eds.), *The Cambridge Medieval History* III. *Germany and the western Empire* (Cambridge, 1922), pp. 148–87.

heavily influenced by the *Annales* school than most of his late nineteenth- and early twentieth-century contemporaries.[89]

The difference in outlook and technique between Gibbon and Hodgkin can best be assessed by comparing their treatment of the key figure of Theodoric. Hodgkin's personal enthusiasm for the Ostrogothic king was less reserved than Gibbon's. Gooch wrote *apropos* the former that 'few volumes in English literature are more fascinating which describe the Gothic kingdom of Theodoric and its destruction at the hands of the armies of Justinian'.[90] In his preface to *Theodoric the Ostrogoth*, Hodgkin alludes to a conversation as a boy with a friend about the prospects of unification of Italy held soon after the counter-revolutions of 1848. Hodgkin, in a desperate attempt to salvage hope for the future, 'was driven back through the centuries, till at length I took refuge in the reign of Theodoric. Surely, under the Ostrogothic king, Italy had been united, strong and prosperous.'[91]

For all his admiration, Hodgkin's view of the king is in general more perceptive and subtle than that of Gibbon. The former's treatment of the sources is much more critical, and a more nuanced picture is presented of the king's status as a Germanic ruler sensitive to practical considerations and Roman constitutional niceties. Theodoric is described as 'no longer a king of the old Germanic pattern, bound to consult and persuade his people at every turn'; rather he was 'an uncontrolled, unthwarted ruler'.[92] Although Hodgkin, like Gibbon, had a Whiggish obsession in searching for consultative institutions, he admitted that there was no trace of anything like a single meeting of the 'Folc-mote'.[93] Also like his predecessor, he devoted considerable attention to Theodoric's difficulties, especially at the end of his reign. In contrast with Gibbon's picture, however, the stress is less on a tragic hero undermined by his own fatal flaws, and more on the very real political and religious problems which the king faced. Hodgkin

---

[89] Among numerous studies of the *Annales* school, P. Burke (ed.), *New perspectives on historical writing* (Cambridge, 1992), *passim*; and L. Stone, '"The revival of narrative": Reflections on a new old history', *Past and Present* 85 (1979), pp. 3–24.

[90] G. P. Gooch, *History and historians in the nineteenth century* (2nd edn, London, 1952: first published 1913), p. 375. Gooch was full of praise for the 'narrative power' of the whole work.

[91] Hodgkin, *Theodoric the Goth*, p. vi.

[92] Hodgkin, *Italy and her invaders*, vol. III, pp. 242–3.   [93] *Ibid.*, p. 243.

stuck to a generally up-beat conclusion that Theodoric's rule represented 'a time of great and generally diffused happiness for the Italian population'.[94] Here he, like Gibbon, relied strongly on the *Anonymus Valesianus*.[95]

I shall conclude by offering some brief comments on the view taken by historians today on the issues dealt with by Gibbon and Hodgkin.

The labelling of the invaders as 'barbarians' is not one which most early medieval historians would find helpful – even though anthropological and literary studies of 'barbarian' culture and of 'civilized' society's perception of it still proliferate.[96]

There has also been a strong reaction against older historians' preoccupation with the nature and consequences of invasions. This counterattack has been led by linguists and archaeologists, who argue that it fails to give due weight to peaceful processes of settlement and cultural diffusion.[97] This view has some validity, and historians themselves now place more emphasis on the peaceful and gradual aspects of the Germanic 'migrations'. A number of recent scholars have pointed to a large degree of continuity of the Mediterranean world in the archaeological, environmental and anthropological spheres from the early Empire until as late as the eleventh century.[98] I would still argue that the stress on invasions is justified in the case of Italy; there was a measure of violent conquest, new elites were established, the collapse of Roman state institutions had a knock-on effect on the closely associated elements of a sophisticated cultural and social system, and lasting

---

[94] *Ibid.*, p. 259.
[95] *Ibid.*, pp. 260–70. On the problems of this text cf. n. 33.
[96] E.g. B. Bronson, 'The role of barbarians in the fall of states' in N. Yoffee and G. L. Cowgill (eds.), *The collapse of ancient states and civilizations* (Tucson, Arizona, 1988), pp. 196–218; Y. A. Dauge, *Le barbare: recherches sur la conception romaine de la barbarie et de la civilisation* (Brussels, 1981); C. H. Berndt and Ronald M. Berndt, *The barbarians: anthropological view* (Harmondsworth, 1973); E. Hall, *Inventing the barbarian: Greek self-definition through tragedy* (Oxford, 1988).
[97] Such gradualist views, advanced, for example, by Colin Renfrew, *Archaeology and language: the puzzle of Indo-European origins* (London, 1987), have become widespread among historians as well: see, for example, C. Wickham, 'The other transition: from the ancient world to feudalism', *Past and Present* 112 (1984), pp. 3–36, reprinted in his *Land and power. Studies in Italian and European social history, 400–1200* (London, 1994), pp. 7–42.
[98] Cameron, *The Mediterranean world in late antiquity*, especially chs. 4 and 7; K. Randsborg, *The first millennium AD in Europe and the Mediterranean: an archaeological essay* (Cambridge, 1990); P. Hordern and N. Purcell, *The Mediterranean world* (Oxford, 1992).

geopolitical divisions were introduced which impeded the unification of Italy for 1300 years.[99]

In the case of the Ostrogoths, Gibbon's views have held up surprisingly well, although some aspects, such as the allocation of lands or revenue to Germanic *hospites*, have undergone the process of major reassessment.[100] The most recent study in English, John Moorhead's *Theoderic in Italy*, gives an interpretation of the great man's importance and achievement which differs remarkably little from that of either Gibbon or Hodgkin (even though he never quotes the former and places more stress on the romanizing element in his policies).[101] The handful of lines which Gibbon devoted to St Benedict finds an echo in the treatment accorded by Chris Wickham's standard history of early medieval Italy, where there is no mention of him whatsoever![102]

Recent studies have, overall, reflected a distinct change of emphasis; the Roman element is seen as dominant, providing the personnel, expertise, and cultural and ideological aspirations, while the Ostrogothic element was still fluid and unformed.[103] A related

[99] G. Tabacco, *The struggle for power in medieval Italy*, trans. R. Brown Jensen (Cambridge, 1989). These points are also dealt with in my forthcoming work *Italy from the invasions to the communes, 500–1200*. In contrast with the centralizing 'nationalist' historians of the nineteenth century, many exponents of the 'small is beautiful' school of history would now argue that this localization was no bad thing.

[100] W. Goffart initiated a major reassessment of this question in his *Barbarians and Romans AD 418–584* (Princeton, 1984). The debate is still unresolved. Recent contributions include S. Barnish, 'Taxation, land and barbarian settlement in the western empire', *Papers of the British School at Rome* 54 (1986), pp. 170–95, the papers by H. Wolfram, D. Claude, Jean Durliat and Goffart himself in H. Wolfram and A. Schwarcz (eds.), *Anerkennung und Integration. Zu den wirtschaftlichen Grundlagen der Völkerwanderungszeit 400–600* (Vienna, 1988), and C. Wickham, 'La chute de Rome n'aura pas lieu', *Le moyen age* 99 (1993), pp. 107–26.

[101] See especially the chapter in Moorhead, *Theoderic in Italy*, 'Goths and Romans', pp. 66–113. For a modern view of the Gothic element in Theoderic's position, see P. Heather, 'Theoderic as a Gothic Leader', *Early Medieval Europe* 4 (2) (1995). Two major conferences were held on Theoderic in 1992, in Ravenna and Milan. Neither produced much in terms of an overall reassessment of the reign, although the cultural achievements of Theoderic's reign were highlighted at the Milan gathering: e.g. P. Heather, 'The historical culture of Ostrogothic Italy', *Teoderico il Grande e i Goti d'Italia. Atti del XII Congresso Internazionale di Studi sull 'alto medievo* (Spoleto, 1993), pp. 324–32.

[102] *Decline and fall*, ed. Bury, v, pp. 66, 68, referring to him, not by name but as 'the father' or 'the founder' of the Benedictines. Wickham, *Early medieval Italy*, mentions Montecassino, pp. 12, 45, etc., but not its founder.

[103] The bibliography in this growth area of early medieval scholarship is now enormous: see, for example, P. Amory, 'The meaning and purpose of ethnic terminology in the Burgundian laws', *Early Medieval Europe* 2 (1993), pp. 1–28.

change of tack involves historians' preoccupation with problems of ethnicity. Neither the Goths nor the Lombards are now regarded as a single homogeneous people, and the notion of unity and ethnic identity stretching back centuries is recognized as the achievement of later propagandists and historians.[104] Theodoric's followers are now seen as a fluid amalgam of groups. The emphasis on the king's Amal descent, which Gibbon and Hodgkin took for granted, is acknowledged as fact manufactured for propaganda purposes, and, what is more, largely by *Roman* apologists to make Theodoric and his family more acceptable to their Roman subjects.[105] The king's relations with his Germanic subjects are now no longer understood in the Whig 'constitutional' terms beloved of both Gibbon and Hodgkin, with their emphasis on formal consultative processes. Leadership is seen as primarily achieved by success in war and rewarding of followers with land and offices – what the Germans call *Königsnähe*.[106]

In the sphere of Lombard studies, the amount of documentary material is considerably greater, and new fields have been opened to exciting and critical new examination. Again, one important example is ethnic identity. Even to label the Lombard invaders in 568 as a clearly identifiable people is no longer considered appropriate.[107]

The initial process of Lombard settlement has attracted a great deal of scholarly investigation, most of it, alas, still inconclusive.

---

[104] Important studies following the seminal work of R. Wenskus, *Stammesbildung und Verfassung* (Cologne and Graz, 1961) include W. Pohl and H. Wolfram (eds.), *Typen der Ethnogenese unter besonderer Berücksichtigung der Bayern: Berichte des Symposions der Kommission für Frühmittelalterforschung, 27. bis 30. Oktober, 1986. Stift Zwettl, Niederösterreich* (Vienna, 1990) and P. Geary, 'Ethnic identity as a situational construct in the early Middle Ages', *Mitteilungen der anthropologischen Gesellschaft in Wien* 113 (1983), pp. 15–26; and the brief but useful survey in W. Pohl, 'Conceptions of ethnicity in early medieval studies', *Archaeologia Polonia* 29 (1991), pp. 39–49.

[105] H. Wolfram, 'Gothic history and historical ethnography', *Journal of Medieval History* 7 (1981), pp. 309–19, and his *History of the Goths*, pp. 324–7 and *passim*; Heather, 'Theoderic as a Gothic leader'.

[106] See the work focussing on the Carolingians by Schmidt, Tellenbach, Werner *et al.*, conveniently assembled by T. Reuter, *The medieval nobility* (Amsterdam, 1979), and more recently, J. L. Nelson, 'Kingship and royal government' in R. McKitterick (ed.), *The New Cambridge Medieval History, vol. II, c. 700–c. 900* (Cambridge, 1995), pp. 385–430, and S. Airlie, 'The aristocracy', *ibid.*, pp. 431–50.

[107] See most recently D. Harrison, 'Dark age migrations and subjective ethnicity: the example of the Lombards', *Scandia* 57 (1991), pp. 19–36. N. J. Christie, *The Lombards* (Oxford, 1995).

This particularly applies to the initial division of lands and the treatment of the Roman population.[108] On the related question of Lombard military arrangements, so dear to the hearts of both our writers, the new work has attracted more of a consensus, thanks especially to the studies of Giovanni Tabacco.[109]

Economic history has made especially great strides – in particular the study of agriculture. Here the illuminating studies of Vito Fumagalli and his pupils in Bologna have combined illuminating techniques of economic history with best Italian traditions of the careful study of local documents.[110] Likewise, in the sphere of social history, anthropological approaches to the study of law and family relations have produced a much more complex and nuanced picture than that prevailing in the eighteenth and nineteenth centuries.[111]

A radical reassessment has also been made of the role of the Byzantines and the Exarchate – a theme fully covered by Hodgkin but, with the exception of Venice, regarded with some disdain by Gibbon. The imperial territories are now seen, not as decadent eastern colonial outposts, but as vigorous survivals of late Roman society, which adjusted well to the new political and military conditions and ultimately produced such dynamic and autonomous

---

[108] The best treatment is now P. Delogu, 'Longobardi e Romani' in P. Cammarosano and S. Gasparri (eds.), *Langobardia* (Udine, 1990), pp. 111–67. Good recent discussions of the Lombard kingdom include Delogu, 'Il regno Longobardo' in Delogu, A. Guillou and G. Ortalli, *Longobardi e Romani* (Turin, 1980), pp. 3–126, J. Jarnut, *Geschichte der Langobarden* (Stuttgart, 1982), G. C. Menis (ed.), *I Longobardi* (Milan, 1990) and P. Delogu, 'Lombard and Carolingian Italy' in McKitterick (ed.), *New Cambridge Medieval History*, vol. II, pp. 290–319.

[109] G. Tabacco, 'Dai possessori dell'età carolingia agli esercitali dell'età longobarda', *Studi Medievali* 10 (1969), pp. 221–68, and his *I liberi del re nell'Italia carolingia e postcarolingia* (Spoleto, 1966).

[110] Fumagalli has complemented these studies with an incisive 'Le Goffian' study of the attitudes of medieval Italian town-dwellers: *Landscapes of fear* (Cambridge, 1994), a translation of three Italian studies published between 1987 and 1990.

[111] Among numerous studies on law, C. Wickham, 'Land disputes and their social framework in Lombard-Carolingian Italy' in W. Davies and P. Fouracre (eds.), *The settlement of disputes in early medieval Europe* (Cambridge, 1986), pp. 104–24, revised in his *Land and power*, pp. 229–56; L. F. Bruyning, 'Lawcourt proceedings in the Lombard kingdom before and after the Frankish conquest', *Journal of Medieval History* 11 (1985), pp. 193–214; P. Bonacini, 'Giustizia pubblica e società nell'Italia carolingia', *Quaderni Medievali* 31–2 (1991), pp. 6–36; R. Balzaretti, 'Dispute settlement and the monastery of S. Ambrogio in early medieval Milan', *Early Medieval Europe* 3 (1994), pp. 1–18; *La Giustizia nell'alto medioevo (secolo V–VIII)*, Settimane di Studio del Centro italiano di studi sull'alto medioevo 42 (Spoleto, 1995).

trading centres as Naples and Venice.[112] Of particular relevance here is their beneficial effect on the Lombard kingdom both as political rivals and sources of administrative and cultural influence. The 'Byzantine', or as many would prefer, 'Roman' areas of Italy served as a catalyst promoting the increased political and cultural sophistication of the Lombard kingdom. To take a parallel which would have appealed to Hodgkin (author of a volume on English history before 1066)[113] the existence of an economically and militarily dynamic rival in eastern England, the Scandinavian-dominated Danelaw, accelerated the emergence of a strong and united English kingdom in the tenth century.[114]

Considerable attention has been paid to the study of insignia, titles, ideology – and here the systematic work of art historians has made a dramatic contribution. These are areas in which Gibbon, but not Hodgkin, showed little interest because of his eighteenth-century predilection for classical standards in art and architecture.[115]

[112] The most important studies are A. Guillou, *Régionalisme et indépendance dans l'empire byzantin au VIIe siècle: l'exemple de l'Exarchat et de la Pentapole d'Italie* (Rome, 1969); and his 'L'Italia bizantina dall'invasione Longobarda alla caduta di Ravenna' in Delogu, Guillou and Ortalli, *Longobardi e Romani*, pp. 219–338; V. von. Falkenhausen, *Untersuchungen über die byzantinische Herrschaft in Suditalien vom 9. bis ins 11. Jahrhundert* (Wiesbaden, 1967); and her *I Bizantini in Italia* (Milan, 1982), pp. 3–136; T. S. Brown, *Gentlemen and officers: Imperial administration and aristocratic power in Byzantine Italy, AD 554–800* (London, 1984), and his 'The interplay between Roman and Byzantine traditions in the Exarchate of Ravenna', in *Bisanzio, Roma e l'Italia nell'alto medioevo*, Settimane di Studio del Centro italiano di studi sull' alto medioevo 34 (Spoleto, 1988), pp. 128–67; also his 'Byzantine Italy, c. 680–c. 976', in McKitterick (ed.), *New Cambridge Medieval History* vol. II, pp. 320–48.
[113] T. Hodgkin, *The history of England from the earliest times to the Norman conquest* (London, 1906).
[114] Patrick Wormald, 'The making of England', *History Today* 45 9 (2) (February 1995), pp. 26–32. This analogy cannot be pressed too far, but it is interesting that in both cases the threat to the dominant kingdom from its neighbours contributed to its takeover by an external invader, the Franks in the case of the Lombard kingdom and the Normans in the case of England.
[115] For example, M. McCormick, *Eternal victory: triumphal rulership in late antiquity, Byzantium and the early medieval west* (2nd edn, Cambridge, 1990); H. Frohlich, *Studien zur langobardischen Thronfolge von den Anfängen bis zur Eroberung des italienischen Reiches durch Karl den Grossen (774)*, 2 vols. (Tübingen, 1980); A. Pertusi, 'Quaedam regalia insignia', *Studi veneziani*, vol. VIII (1965), pp. 3–123; H. Wolfram, *Intitulatio: Lateinische Königs- und Fürstentitel bis zum Ende des 8. Jahrhunderts* (Vienna, 1967); *Le sacre des rois. Colloque internationale d'histoire sur les sacres et couronnements royaux* (Paris, 1985). On early medieval Italian art see especially the work of H. Belting, for example his 'Probleme der Kunstgeschichte Italiens im Frühmittelalter', *Frühmittelalterliche Studien* 1 (1967), pp. 94–143. The discovery of the frescoes of Castelseprio in 1944 and the excavation of the monastery of S. Vincenzo al Volturno in 1980–6 are two cases which have revolutionized views of the artistic level and contacts of early medieval Italy: see respectively C. Bertelli, 'Castelseprio e Milano' in *Bisanzio, Roma e l'Italia*, Settimane di Studio 34, pp. 869–914

Perhaps the most important magnet for scholarly attention, however, has been the survival of urban life, since it is acknowledged that the Lombards, and the Goths before them, were unusual in adopting Roman cities as centres of administration and residence. Here a vigorous debate is in progress about the extent of and reasons for urban survival, and the most likely prospect of resolution comes from the astonishing advances made in the sphere of early medieval archaeology in Italy.[116]

A much more varied and complex picture of economic and political life has emerged than the simple picture offered by Gibbon: 'In the Italian cities a municipal government had never been totally abolished; and their first privileges were granted by the favour and policy of the emperors, who were desirous of erecting a plebeian barrier against the independence of the nobles.'[117] This is true as far as it goes, but Gibbon does not go very far.

There are in fact two important fields of enquiry whose importance Gibbon alluded to, but which still leave enormous scope for investigation.

One is the 'secularity' of Lombard Italy. This requires to be approached with some caution. The studies of Gian-Piero Bognetti and others have shown how close, and at times cordial, relations could be with Catholic bishops (although not usually the pope himself), and how pro-Catholic elements competed with Arian and quasi-pagan elements in the late sixth and early seventh centuries.[118] After the lasting conversion of the kings to Catholicism

---

and R. Hodges, *San Vincenzo al Volturno*, vols. I and II (London, 1993 and 1995; vols. III and IV in preparation).

[116] Among numerous studies G.-P. Brogiolo, 'Brescia. Building transformation in a Lombard city' in K. Randsborg (ed.), *The birth of Europe. Archaeology and social development in the first millennium ad* (Rome, 1989), pp. 155–65; C. La Rocca Hudson, '"Dark Ages" a Verona. Edilizia privata, aree aperte e strutture pubbliche in una città dell' Italia settentrionale', *Archeologia Medievale* 13 (1986), pp. 31–78; B. Ward-Perkins, 'The towns of northern Italy: rebirth or renewal?' in R. Hodges, and B. Hobley (eds.), *The rebirth of towns in the West AD 700–AD 1050* (London, 1988), pp. 16–17, and most recently L. Parioli and P. Delogu (eds.), *La storia economica di Roma nell'alto medioevo alla luce dei ricenti scavi archeologici* (Florence, 1993) and the studies by La Rocca, Brogiolo and others in R. Francovich and G. Noyé (eds.), *La storia dell' alto medioevo italiano (VI–X secolo) alla luce dell' archeologia* (Florence, 1994), pp. 545–739. For fuller biographies, see P. Skinner, 'Urban communities in Naples, 900–1050', *Papers of the British School at Rome* 62 (1994), p. 279 n. 4 and Wickham, *Land and power*, p. 117 n. 28.

[117] *Decline and fall*, ed. Bury, v, p. 302.

[118] G.-P. Bognetti, 'Santa Maria foras portas di Castelseprio e la storia religiosa dei Longobarda' in his *L'Età longobarda*, vol. II (Milan, 1966), pp. 13–673, as well as several other of his studies in that four-volume collection.

in the late seventh century there was a marked rapprochement with
the Romans within and outside the kingdom's boundaries in the
political and cultural as well as the religious spheres. This transformation is most evident perhaps in the remarkable artistic
production of the late Lombard period (whether or not the remarkable frescoes of Castelseprio (north-west of Milan), discovered
in 1944, can be dated to this period).[119] And, of course, by King
Liutprand's time the kings were adopting a quite aggressive policy
of pious patronage in a bid for wider support among Roman
elements inside and outside their kingdom.[120] Nevertheless, there
is a secular quality to Lombard society and government, at least in
comparison with Frankish Gaul, Visigothic Spain or Anglo-Saxon
England. This tendency to keep the Church at arm's length
deserves fuller discussion. Possible explanations include a greater
survival of late Roman secular institutions, the relatively low social
status of bishops compared with, for example, fifth- and sixth-
century Gaul, and, perhaps most convincingly, the continued
identification of the Catholic Church with a bitter political
opponent, the Empire, and the relatively late official acceptance
of Catholicism by the Lombard kings.[121]

Another very open question is the transformation of the
primitive Lombard kingdom into a sophisticated and relatively
prosperous regime. As we have seen, Gibbon remarked on this, but
failed to explain it satisfactorily. No doubt the current work on
urban life will throw new light on this process. But there is another
factor. The Roman element was much more resilient than Gibbon
imagined – whether we are talking of powerful senators in
Theodoric's time, the cities which survived and prospered in much

119 Bognetti's dating of the Castelseprio frescoes to the period soon after the conversion of
   the Lombards to Catholicism in the late seventh century for long attracted considerable
   support. More recently Bertelli, in 'Castelseprio e Milano', has adduced strong arguments in favour of an early ninth-century dating.
120 Delogu, 'Lombard and Carolingian Italy', pp. 294–8 and cf. P. Llewellyn, 'The popes and
   the constitution in the eighth century', *English Historical Review* 101 (1986), pp. 42–67.
121 Recent studies have rightly played down the traditional emphasis on the militant
   Arianism of the Lombards: for example, S. Fanning, 'Lombard arianism reconsidered',
   Speculum 56 (1981), pp. 241–58 and D. Harrison, *The early state and the towns: forms of
   integration in Lombard Italy, AD 568–774* (Lund, 1993). It is, however, important not to lose
   sight of the extent to which the Lombards kept at arms' length from the official Catholic
   hierarchy – an attitude unparalleled elsewhere in the early medieval west. The extreme
   position of Wickham on the question of Lombard 'secularity' (above, n. 61) strikes me as
   in need of refinement.

(but not all) of the Lombard kingdom, the Roman clerics, bureaucrats and landowners who flourished in Rome, Ravenna and the other autonomous Roman polities of the Exarchate, and even the creative flow of influences from Byzantium itself. But a key aspect which was not properly addressed by either Gibbon or Hodgkin and still requires fuller treatment from modern historians is the survival of Roman elements *within* the Lombard kingdom itself. Town-dwellers, peasants and clergy remained overwhelmingly Roman, professing Roman law. Thus the clergy of such cities as Verona and Milan, although playing a limited *political* role in the kingdom, were active in maintaining the *local* traditions, not just of their sees, but of the whole urban community.[122]

The conclusion that emerges, therefore, is an ironic one. Hodgkin, the urbane Christian, was more adept at identifying the key processes at work in early medieval Italy than Gibbon the sceptic. What happened was less a triumph of Christianity and barbarism than a more gradual victory of a particularly urban brand of Christianity and an adaptable, resilient *Romanitas*.

---

[122] On the role of clerical intellectuals see G. Fasoli, 'La coscienza civica nelle *'Laudes civitatum'* in *La coscienza civica nei communi Italiani* (Todi, 1972), pp. 9–44 reprinted in her *Scritti di storia medievale* (Bologna, 1974), pp. 293–318; and D. Bullough, 'Le scuole cattedrali e la cultura dell' Italia settentrionale prima dei Comuni' in *Vescovi e diocesi in Italia nel Medioevo (sec. IX–XIII)* (Padua, 1964), pp. 11–43. For the particular case of Ravenna: T. S. Brown, '*Romanitas* and *Campanilismo*: Agnellus of Ravenna's view of the past' in C. Holdsworth and P. Wiseman (eds.), *The inheritance of historiography* (Exeter, 1986), pp. 107–14.

CHAPTER 8

Edward Gibbon and the early Middle Ages
in eighteenth-century Europe

Rosamond McKitterick

A consideration of Gibbon and early medieval history in the context of eighteenth-century European knowledge of the period might be thought to be worth no more than a passing observation in proportion to the amount of attention Gibbon himself accorded it. Gibbon discusses western medieval Europe in chapter 49 of his history; it occupies sixty-six pages and embraces 600 years of western European history from the eighth to the fourteenth century from a relatively limited perspective. Instead, one might simply wish to refer to the fuller and more authoritative accounts in the wealth of early French, German and Italian scholarship on the period, of which Gibbon himself gives only some inkling, were it not for the enormous influence Gibbon has enjoyed in England, especially since the later nineteenth century. The *Decline and fall*, for example, was recommended at Oxford in 1884 as a text for European history 1272–1519. The old *Cambridge Medieval History*, designed by Bury, editor of Gibbon, and old-fashioned, especially volumes II and III, even as it appeared, was manifestly within the Gibbonian political narrative tradition and conceptual framework, with its preoccupation with empire and adoption of similar chronological and thematic emphases.[1] Gibbon's assessment of the emergent barbarian successor states in the context of decline had an unfortunate effect on English scholarship on the European early Middle Ages, with the honourable exceptions of Edward Freeman

---

[1] H. W. Gwatkin and J. P. Whitney (eds.), *The Cambridge Medieval History II. The rise of the Saracens and the foundation of the western Empire* (Cambridge, 1913) and H. M. Gwatkin, J. P. Whitney, J. R. Tanner, C. W. Previté-Orton (eds.), *The Cambridge Medieval History III. Germany and the western Empire* (Cambridge, 1922). On the genesis and production of the old *Cambridge Medieval History*, especially volume III, see Peter Linehan, 'The making of the *Cambridge Medieval History*', *Speculum* 57 (1982), pp. 463–94.

and Thomas Hodgkin,[2] until the middle of the twentieth century. Freeman commented in 1888, indeed, that he had been doing

a great deal on Pippin. The Germans do not understand the story, any of them, but Luden long ago, because they do not take in the position which the Emperors still kept in Italy and the world. The older scholars really understood that time much better than the later. They followed formulae a good deal, but they were authentic contemporary formulae, while people now follow modern formulae of their own making: 'effete Byzantine Empire', 'Greek of the lower Empire' and what not; phrases which have some meaning in the fourteenth and fifteenth century but which have none whatever when applied to the sole Roman emperors of the eighth. Gibbon has a good deal to answer for. You can find nearly every fact in him, but he began by making the subject ridiculous, by trotting out some absurd, and if possible, indecent anecdote, as if it were a summary of the whole reign. It is that chapter which gives the impression, and those which follow it never take it away.[3]

There are yet lingering traces of this impression concerning the 'dark ages' and the political development of medieval Europe as an unfortunate aftermath of the Roman Empire as a whole.[4] Mostly, however, the Germanic kingdoms of western Europe, and particularly the Carolingian and Ottonian realms, are being assessed on their own terms, in which the legacy of Rome has its distinctive place, but in which we witness new and different beginnings.[5]

Gibbon's treatment of the Middle Ages, therefore, cannot cavalierly be dismissed as of little value to either contemporaries or modern historians. We need to consider first the wider cultural understanding of early medieval Europe in the eighteenth century in order to determine the degree to which Gibbon's selection of themes and heroes may have had reference, not only to earlier historical scholarship but also to the expectations of Gibbon's public. To what extent, in short, was Gibbon able to offer his interpretation, albeit highly idiosyncratic, on a period that was in

---

[2] Thomas Hodgkin, *Italy and her invaders* (8 vols., Oxford, 1892–9); see also Brown, above, pp. 137–61.
[3] From the reference to Pippin, I presume that Freeman is referring to chapter 49, but it could also be a reference to chapter 48 discussed by Howard-Johnston, above, pp. 53–77. W. R. W. Stephens, *The life and letters of Edward A. Freeman* (2 vols., London, 1895), vol. II, p. 380; Freeman to Goldwin Smith, 25 April 1888. I am grateful to Roland Quinault for this reference.
[4] See Introduction above, pp. 6–7.
[5] See, for example, the new series *The Cambridge Medieval History*, of which *Vol. II c. 700–c. 900* (ed. R. McKitterick) has appeared (Cambridge, 1995).

fact familiar to his readers? Answers to this question are both specific, in relation to chapter 49, and more general, in relation to the wider context of Gibbon's audience. I consider each in turn.

Gibbon's object in chapter 49 was not to write a history of western Europe in this period, even if this is how these few pages have tended to be read subsequently. Their central theme is precisely defined by Gibbon himself as the 'objects of *ecclesiastical history* by which the decline and fall of the Roman empire were materially affected, the propagation of Christianity, the constitution of the Catholic church, the ruin of paganism, and the sects that arose from the mysterious controversies concerning the Trinity and incarnation'.[6] Much of the account in this chapter centres on the question of images and the discussion of iconoclasm in Rome and Francia. Gibbon's discussion of the image question is of considerable interest for he had devoted concentrated thought and attention to it; his much vaunted scholarship is in evidence in chapter 49 in these paragraphs at least. Images were of central importance to Gibbon's understanding of the significance of the developments of the Middle Ages, as he avers: 'since a question of popular superstition produced the revolt of Italy, the temporal power of the Popes *and the restoration of the Roman empire in the west*'.[7] The political events, therefore, are incidental and subsumed beneath the ecclesiastical and theological theme; they are briefly told and their significance is laconically indicated. Chapter 49, in short, is of a piece with the intentions of the later volumes as a whole referred to by Averil Cameron above, in which the later chapters of the history contained a series of portraits of nations 'exterior' to Byzantium rather than a continuous historical narrative.[8]

In historiographical and philosophical terms, Gibbon was joining the mainstream of European historical interpretation. He belonged to a period possessed of quite exceptional interest in the past, with a public that clearly read a great deal of history. The eighteenth century, after all, saw a remarkable expansion in the scholarly literature in books and periodicals. Of the more than 2,000 journals founded in the eighteenth century it has been estimated that 642 were historical and that 10 per cent of all books published in this

---

6 *Decline and fall*, ed. Bury, v, p. 244.
7 *Ibid.*, my emphasis.   8 Above, p. 37.

period in France and Germany were on historical topics.[9] Gibbon's treatment of the period from the sixth to the fifteenth centuries, despite his possession of a reasonably representative selection of the main French historians, is nevertheless superficial. Gibbon lacks the familiarity with the European Middle Ages, and the engagement and sympathy with the principal themes and questions of that history, so obvious in contemporary works of historical scholarship. He was clearly more attracted to the sweeping interpretative essays and to the Roman period, just as there was a strand even in French historiography and constitutional thought, exemplified in the work of Sièyes, which gives the impression of rejecting the Frankish past in favour of adulation of the Gallo-Roman period. Gibbon appears to have been overly influenced by concepts of decadence and decline and unable to take on board the positive celebration of the medieval past on the part of so many French scholars, let alone the Germans or Italians.[10] There is occasional grudging admiration for the rude barbarians in Gibbon's history, yet this is almost invariably for the wrong reasons insofar, for instance, as the roles of Charlemagne or Otto in relation to the creation of the Roman Empire are stressed. That is, these medieval rulers and the civilizations they represent are held against the yardstick of classical culture and found wanting.

Not the least of the problems is the language used in the surviving texts from the period. It is Latin, but little of it is

9 See Otto Dann, 'Das historische Interesse in der deutschen Gesellschaft des 18. Jahrhundert. Geschichte und historische Forschung in den zeitgenössischen Zeitschriften' in K. Hammer and J. Voss (eds.), *Historische Forschung im 18. Jahrhundert*, Pariser Historische Studien 13 (Paris, 1988), pp. 386–415, esp. p. 391; and Joachim Kirchner, *Bibliographie der Zeitschriften des deutschen Sprachgebiets von den Anfängen bis 1830* (Stuttgart, 1969). For the wider context of this, the importance of social interaction for the intellectual world and the development of a more professional academic society in the eighteenth century, see Anne Goldgar, *Impolite learning. Conduct and community in the Republic of Letters, 1680–1750* (New Haven and London, 1995).

10 Compare, for example, P. Giannone, *Opera* (14 vols., Milan, 1823–4), A. Muratori, *Annali d'Italia dal principio dell 'era volgare sino all'anno 1500* (Milan, 1974) and *Antiquitates Italicae medii aevi*, vols. i–vi (Milan, 1738–42) and especially G. Vico, *La Scienza Nuova seconda*, ed. F. Nicolini, Scrittore d'italia 112 and 113 (Bari, 1942) though Gibbon in fact refers the reader to this same scholarship: *Decline and fall*, ed. Bury, v, p. 289 n. 123. It is as if he wished to give himself the space simply to voice his opinions and fit his impressions into the structure and thesis of his work as a whole. See also A. Momigliano, 'Gibbon from an Italian point of view' and Peter Burke, 'Tradition and experience: the idea of decline from Bruni to Gibbon' in G. Bowersock et al. (eds.), *Edward Gibbon and the decline and fall of the Roman Empire, Daedalus. Journal of the American Academy of Sciences* 105 (Cambridge, Mass., 1976), pp. 125–52.

the Latin of the Augustan Age. Many French historians before Gibbon had foundered on the Latin of the early Middle Ages, and introduced notions of decadence in relation to a judgment of their language as measured against the Latin of Cicero. The emphasis of Gibbon in providing the Roman Empire as the political as well as the cultural context against which to assess the Middle Ages, and thus propagate entirely negative notions of decline and decadence, was, to say the least, unhelpful; we are still contending with the historiographical consequences. That this political emphasis was also out of tune with the purport and implications of much of French, German and Italian historical scholarship, if not its explicit arguments, is clear if Gibbon's work is compared with that of his contemporaries, both within and without Benedictine circles, so fully surveyed by Jürgen Voss, Otto Dann, Andreas Kraus and many others.[11] In these, some laudable attempts were made to understand medieval developments in their own terms.

Examination by such scholars as Arnaldo Momigliano, Peter Brown and David Jordan has made clear the extent to which Gibbon demonstrates in his *Decline and fall* a lack of sympathy with the early Middle Ages and random selectivity among the wealth of scholarship on the early medieval period available to him, both in principle and actually in his library. Certainly as far as the Middle Ages is concerned there is often an uncritical approach to the sources and scholarly treatises he did read, and an unwillingness to engage in the kind of detailed source criticism and scholarly analysis that was taken for granted in historical scholarship on the early Middle Ages on the Continent.[12] Gibbon's observation about the work of the great palaeographers and diplomatists Jean Mabillon and Montfaucon is particularly revealing in this respect:

---

[11] In Hammer and Voss, *Historische Forschung*. Compare also Wood, above pp. 125–31.

[12] In addition to the references cited in n. 9 above, see Jürgen Voss, *Das Mittelalter im historischen Denken Frankreichs. Untersuchung zur Geschichte des Mittelalterbegriffes und der Mittelalterbewertung von der zweiten Hälfte des 16. bis zur Mitte des 19. Jahrhunderts* (Munich, 1972), especially pp. 101–80; R. McKitterick, 'The study of Frankish history in France and Germany in the sixteenth and seventeenth centuries', *Francia* 8 (1981), pp. 556–72, reprinted in R. McKitterick, *The Frankish kings and culture in the early middle ages* (Aldershot, 1995), chapter 14; David P. Jordan, *Gibbon and his Roman Empire* (Urbana, Chicago and London, 1971); I. W. J. Machin, 'Gibbon's debt to contemporary scholarship', *Review of English Studies* 15 (1939), pp. 84–8 and Lionel Gossman, *Medievalism and the ideologies of the Enlightenment. The world and work of La Curne de Sainte-Palaye* (Baltimore, 1968).

the view of so many manuscripts of different ages and characters induced me to consult the two great Benedictine works, the *Diplomatica* of Mabillon and the *Palaeographia* of Montfaucon. I studied the theory without attaining the practice of the art; nor should I complain of the intricacy of Greek Abbreviations and Gothic alphabets since every day, in a familiar language, I am at a loss to decypher the Hieroglyphics of a female note.[13]

The basic lack of sympathy with the western Middle Ages so manifest in chapter 49 is particularly evident in Gibbon's treatment of Charlemagne and the Carolingian rulers. This requires further explanation. As noted above, it is within the contexts of ecclesiastical and theological dispute and the position of Rome and Italy that Gibbon introduces the history of the Franks under the Carolingian rulers. Perhaps predictably, in view of the famous events of 800, he concentrates on Charlemagne.[14] For this he acknowledges his debt to the *Histoire de Charlemagne* of G. Gaillard, published in Paris in 1782, and the fifth volume of Bouquet's *Recueil des historiens de France*. Comparison with both works would suggest that Gibbon took short cuts, skimming through Bouquet and concentrating on the narrative sources gathered together at the beginning of the volume, and that Gaillard in fact operated as a crib. A cursory reading of Bouquet is suggested, for example, by Gibbon's dismissal of Charlemagne's effectiveness as a ruler, most notably because of his lack of a system of law. Charlemagne's legislation is described as 'a series of occasional and minute edicts, for the correction of abuses, the reformation of manners, the economy of his farms, the care of his poultry and even the sale of his eggs'.[15] Gibbon's eye had clearly fallen on the *Capitulare de villis*, one of the few capitularies to be reproduced by Bouquet in its entirety. This judgment of Carolingian legislation is inadequate, not just from a modern vantage point but also in light of contemporary and seventeenth-century assessments.[16] Bouquet is admittedly highly selective in his reprinting of the capitularies, with sometimes only

---

[13] *Memoirs*, p. 131. See also Jordan, *Gibbon and his Roman Empire*, who comments further on Gibbon's attitudes towards the medieval period. Compare, however, the carefully nuanced analysis of David Womersley, *The transformation of 'The decline and fall of the Roman Empire'*, Cambridge Studies in Eighteenth-Century English Literature and Thought 1 (Cambridge, 1988).

[14] *Decline and fall*, ed. Bury, v, pp. 283–91.

[15] *Ibid.*, p. 285.

[16] On French legal scholarship see Donald R. Kelley, *Foundations of modern historical scholarship. Language, law and history in the French Renaissance* (New York and London, 1970).

the prefaces printed (notably that of the *Admonitio generalis* of 789).[17] Gibbon's library, moreover, seems to have lacked a copy of Etienne Baluze's edition of the Carolingian capitularies.[18] A close and unprejudiced reading of Bouquet might nevertheless have prompted Gibbon to modify his opinion; and the later legislation of the Carolingian rulers, notably that of Charles the Bald's 'Edict of Pîtrees', might, furthermore, have been of interest for its allusions to Roman law, quite apart from its reference to the legislation of Charles' predecessors, had Gibbon only known of it. But apparently he did not.

It is Gaillard's book, however, which may be responsible for the concentration on Charlemagne and the truncated account of his successors and of the subsequent medieval rulers of France and Germany. Chapter 49, read in the light of the *Histoire de Charlemagne*, becomes more a reaction to Gaillard and an attempt to enliven the latter's presentation of events, in Gibbon's inimitable way, than Gibbon's considered views built up on a close study of his sources, such as we have for other sections of the *Decline and fall*. Gaillard's *Histoire de Charlemagne* is certainly bland and dull, but it is Gaillard's themes which provide the topics on which Gibbon touches (such as his conquests, his coronation and whether Charlemagne could write). Gaillard's catalogue of west Frankish kings in short chapters at the end of his study, moreover, namely, 'Louis le Débonnaire', 'Charles le Chauve', 'Louis le Bègue', 'Louis et Carloman', 'Charles le Gros' and 'Charles le Simple', clearly precipitated Gibbon's contemptuous remark: 'The dregs of the Carlovingian race no longer exhibited any symptoms of virtue or power, and the ridiculous epithets of the *bald*, the *stammerer*, the *fat* and the *simple* distinguished the tame and uniform features of a crowd of kings alike deserving of oblivion.'[19]

This is not to say that Gibbon's account in chapter 49 is worthless. There are some very shrewd and interesting comments on many matters, not only on the issue of iconoclasm noted above, but also his remarking on the significance of the *Visio Wettini*, a ninth-century vision of Hell in which Charlemagne is suffering horribly,

---

[17] M. Bouquet, *Recueil des historiens des Gaules et de la France*. Nouvelle édition (Paris, 1869), vol. v, pp. 637–93. Gibbon worked from the 1738–86 edition.
[18] Geoffrey Keynes (ed.), *The library of Edward Gibbon: a catalogue* (2nd edn, London, 1980). E. Baluze, *Capitularia rerum francorum* (Paris, 1677) is not recorded in the catalogue.
[19] *Decline and fall*, ed. Bury, v, p. 292.

in assessing contemporary attitudes to Charlemagne's rule.[20] The latter in particular accords with some recent assessments.[21] The concentration on so narrow a range of issues, however, and the overall tone of disparagement for a long period of history with which one need not trouble oneself overmuch, is summed up in his judgment: '[Charlemagne's] real merit is doubtless enhanced by the barbarism of the nation and the times from which he emerged; but this apparent magnitude of an object is likewise enlarged by an unequal comparison; and the ruins of Palmyra derive a casual splendour from the nakedness of the surrounding desert.'[22] This contempt has had a lasting influence in the English-speaking world, even if Gibbon's reception on the Continent has been less adulatory.

Criticisms of Gibbon's methods and scholarship, quite apart from his views on Christianity, were already being voiced as early as 1788 in the *Göttingische Anzeigen von gelehrten Sachen*, but the reviews in that journal concentrate primarily on the presentation of the Roman period and rarely refer to the period after the sixth century. The exception is the now famous comment that once the secure base provided by Tillemont had gone, the blemishes abound.[23] Yet the praise of Gibbon, particularly in Germany, was primarily as a literary figure and a master of ironic wit and style rather than as a scholar. It has to be remembered that Gibbon was entering a crowded field with a copious scholarly literature and established themes and debates. The reaction to the *Decline and fall* on the Continent needs, moreover, to be set within the context of the reception of English books on the Continent in the eighteenth century, recently surveyed in masterly fashion for Germany by Bernhard Fabian.[24] The reception of English books, especially after the end of the Thirty Years War, has the appearance of the impact of an

---

[20] *Ibid.*, p. 284 n. 101, though it is Gaillard who is Gibbon's source of knowledge of the text.
[21] For modern commentary on the significance of this extraordinary vision see Paul Dutton, *The politics of dreaming in the Carolingian Empire* (Lincoln, Nebraska and London, 1994).
[22] *Decline and fall*, ed. Bury, v, pp. 283–4.
[23] *Göttingische Anzeigen von gelehrten Sachen* (17 May 1777), pp. 305–13 and *ibid.*, 25 December 1788, pp. 2049–56. See also Norton, *Bibliography*, pp. 76–7 for contemporary opinions of Gibbon's work.
[24] Bernhard Fabian, *The English book in eighteenth-century Germany*, The Panizzi Lectures 1991 (London, 1992) and Bernhard Fabian (ed.), *A catalogue of English books printed before 1801 in Göttingen University Library. Part II 1701–1800, compiled by Graham Jefcoate and Karen Kloth* (Hildesheim, 1987–8).

established culture on an emerging national culture within the conglomerate of territories comprising Germany. An astonishing variety of books of all qualities on biblical and classical scholarship, texts of devotion, poetry, whether admirable or indifferent, practical manuals and treatises on agriculture, medicine, horticulture, animal husbandry, cookery, history, science, geography, travel and fiction, plays and operas became available in German translation more or less immediately after publication, either from an intermediary French translation or directly from the English.[25] Thurneysen, an enterprising publisher, established his business in Basle by publishing reprints of books in English, and Gibbon's *Decline and fall* was among them.[26] That Gibbon's masterpiece was one of these, and thus part of a far larger phenomenon that had little necessarily to do with quality, is important to bear in mind when assessing the impact of the *Decline and fall*. On the Continent such impact was generally very limited, especially in Germany, though Gibbon had a number of staunch and influential admirers and emulators. Only chapter 44 on Roman law, translated into German by Hugo with a commentary,[27] was much admired because it presented an historical survey that had hitherto been lacking; it was widely used for the teaching of Roman law in German universities. Even American law schools in the nineteenth century used chapter 44 as a basic introduction to Roman law. It has also been argued that it was Gibbon's study of law in relation to society and the way in which law reflects both government and society in chapter 44 which played a major role in the revival of Roman law studies in the English-speaking world in the eighteenth century; Gibbon's writing on the subject became a standard source in the early nineteenth century.[28]

---

[25] For translations of Gibbon into French, German and Italian in the eighteenth and nineteenth centuries, and Swedish, Spanish and Russian translations made in the nineteenth century, see Norton, *Bibliography*, pp. 119–62.

[26] Fabian, *The English book*, p. 65 and fig. 21.

[27] Gustav Hugo, *Edward Gibbons historische Uebersicht des Römischen Rechts oder das 44ste Capitel der Geschichte des Verfalls des Römischen Reichs* (Göttingen, 1789). For further French and German translations of this chapter see Norton, *Bibliography*, pp. 172–3 nn. 114–16.

[28] M. H. Hoeflich, 'Edward Gibbon, Roman lawyer', *The American Journal of Comparative Law* 39 (1991), pp. 803–13. While the account may be inaccurate, Hoeflich considers that 'these factual inaccuracies pale into insignificance when viewed in terms of its greater achievement, that of providing a readable, thematically unified, comparatively based sketch of Roman law in Roman society' (p. 807). See also M. H. Hoeflich, 'Roman law in American legal culture', *Tulane Law Review* 66 (1992), pp. 1723–43.

In England the reception of the later volumes was deeply engaged with Gibbon's narrative. As was customary in reviews of the period, there are very full and lengthy summaries of the content and very little by way of critical commentary. The influence Gibbon's account exerted as far as attitudes to the periods he described are concerned can fairly be gauged from such comments as those in the *Critical Review* of 1788 and 1789 (which ran to nearly fifty pages of summary). On Mahomet and the divisions within the Christian church in the seventh century, the reviewer observes that 'these wanderings of the human mind are not pleasing . . . we shall hasten over a subject which even our historian's eloquence cannot adorn, and which his peculiar opinions often disfigure'. We are informed that Gibbon 'gives a short account as much as the history, if it can be called history, of the various periods affords, and points out how each prince contributed to or delayed the fall of the Roman Empire'. On the Franks and the Donation of Constantine, the forger 'now only excites a smile at the credulity of the darker ages'. The comments, meagre as they are, suggest someone already familiar with much that was in Gibbon's subject matter; it is read as an interpretation and warnings are given against errors in a general way (would that they had been specific!). Nevertheless the reviewer was clearly seduced by Gibbon's opinions in some respects: after what is described as 'nearly an unbroken abridgement of the volumes', readers are admonished with the observations that 'the faults in the text are numerous' and that readers 'must not be blind to the errors'.[29]

So far I have concentrated my comments on weighing Gibbon's treatment of the early Middle Ages in the balance with both modern and eighteenth-century scholarly accounts. If it has been found wanting, we also need to bear in mind that Gibbon's work was directed at a general public. Two further crucial questions, therefore, arise from Gibbon's brief treatment of the early Middle Ages in chapter 49 of *The decline and fall of the Roman Empire*. The first concerns the extent to which Gibbon's choice of topic and heroes is common to the selection in the histories of early medieval France, Germany, Spain and Italy available in the eighteenth century.

[29] *Critical Review* 66 (1788), pp. 335–44, 102–10, 257–67, 425–33; 67 (1789), pp. 95–105, 175–82. Quotations from 66, pp. 107, 108, 261–2 and 67, p. 178. Compare *Monthly Review* 78 (1788), pp. 468–72, 79 (1789), pp. 12–20, 121–33, 221–37.

Secondly, what image of, or general cultural attitude towards, late antiquity and the early Middle Ages was there in eighteenth-century Europe and how does Gibbon's accord with it? Many aspects of the former question have had a great deal written about them in the past twenty years.[30] They have also been touched on in other chapters in this volume. Reference has been made to Gibbon's great debt, not only to the historical collections and editions of sources for France, Germany and Italy but also to the enormous wealth of scholarly interpretation in French and Italian he could exploit in his own synthesis. It is clear that what Gibbon had read in the secondary literature and, guided by these, had read in selected sources, set the agenda for what he then chose to write about as far as the early Middle Ages was concerned, even if he can be shown to have been far more pioneering and innovative in some of his interpretations of other areas and periods than his contemporary fellow historians.[31] There were inevitably, however, contemporary presentations of the early Middle Ages outside Gibbon's competence, including, and perhaps especially, the greater bulk of German historical scholarship.

Yet it is not these that I wish to discuss further in the remainder of this chapter, but rather some of the implications of Gibbon's enterprise as a whole in the context of the wider cultural under-standing of early medieval Europe in the late seventeenth and the eighteenth centuries. This may in its turn throw light on the degree to which Gibbon's selection of heroes and themes may have had some reference to his public, whom he addresses so eloquently in the Preface to the *Decline and fall*.

A fruitful line of enquiry would be the public audiences for historical scholarship,[32] historical literature[33] and the genre of

---

[30] See the excellent collection of essays in Bowersock *et al.* (eds.), *Edward Gibbon and the decline and fall of the Roman Empire* (above, n. 10).

[31] As Bryer, for instance has demonstrated above, pp. 101–16.

[32] For a survey of the methodological and evidential hurdles for assessing the reading public for any category of publication, see the remarks by Robert Darnton, 'Reading, writing and publishing in eighteenth-century France: a case study in the Sociology of Literature', *Daedalus. Journal of the American Academy of Arts and Sciences* 100 (1971), pp. 214–56.

[33] I have in mind such plays and historical novels as Desfontaines, Rotrou, Chatonnières, or Marmontel's *Belisaire* (1767). The last named is referred to by Gibbon (chapter 43) where Marmontel's fictitious story of the blind Belisarius' begging for alms in his old age, rather than Procopius' account of Belisarius, was the inspiration behind the representation of Belisarius in paintings by such artists as Jacques-Louis David. See *Jacques-Louis David,*

history painting. In the last named case, the interest in paintings depicting scenes from the Roman Republic and Empire, the portrayal of contemporary military and political leaders in Roman dress[34] or in historical allegories, and subsequently in the evocation of incidents from a nation's medieval and early modern history appear to indicate the susceptibility and receptiveness of the public to the visual as well as literary representations of the past.[35] On the Continent, the paintings by such artists as Pietro Butoni and Jacques-Louis David are obvious examples. In England it was Joshua Reynolds, George III's protegé Benjamin West (many of whose English medieval paintings were based on Hume's *History of England*, though the Roman ones were on the same themes as were chosen by his Continental contemporaries)[36] and less well-known artists such as Robert Edge Pine, John Hamilton Mortimer, Samuel Wale, Andrea Casali, James Barry, Mauritius Lowe and Angelica Kaufmann in exhibitions at the newly established Society for the Encouragement of Arts, Manufactures and Commerce who catered to, or helped to cultivate, what was evidently a public taste for history paintings. Barry's six canvases, painted between 1777 and 1783, on 'The progress of human culture' from the Greeks to the eighteenth century, with its remarkable inclusion of portraits of the great and the influential in history (including the sixth-century Italian bureaucrat and writer Cassiodorus and King Alfred) are an

---

1748–1825. Musée du Louvre, Département des Peintures, Paris; Musée National du Château, Versailles, 29 octobre 1989–février 1990. (Paris, 1989), plate 47: 'Bélisaire demandant l'aumône' (Lille, Musée des Beaux-Arts (inv. P 436)), pp. 130–1; and compare Benjamin West's various portrayals of 'Belisarius and the Boy' (1802) in, for example, the Detroit Institute of Arts. See also Cameron above, p. 43, and Ghosh on the literature below, p. 308.

34　See, for example, Grinling Gibbons' statues of James II and Charles II on the north side of Trafalgar Square and at the Royal Hospital, Chelsea, respectively and David Green, *Grinling Gibbons. His work as carver and statuary, 1648–1721* (London, 1964), plates 57 and 58. Green, p. 57, suggests that Charles II 'caught' the Roman fashion from Louis XIV, whose equestrian statue in the Place Vendôme sports Roman dress and a periwig. See also J. M. Rysbrack's statue of George I (1736–39) and Joseph Wilton's representation of George II as Roman emperors clad in classical armour and toga, formerly in the Cockerell Building in Cambridge and now in the entrance hall of Cambridge University Library.

35　See Martin Postle, *Sir Joshua Reynolds. The subject pictures* (Cambridge, 1995) on the role of history painting in defining and locating social and political, as well as artistic hierarchies between 1770 and 1830.

36　Helmut von Erffa and Allen Staley, *The paintings of Benjamin West* (New Haven and London, 1986), especially pp. 33–54 and the catalogue of historical subjects, nos. 1–111.

eloquent expression of this.[37] The Society and its successor the Royal Academy of the Arts, indeed, sponsored an annual competition between 1759 and 1779 for 'the best original historical picture, the subject to be taken from the English [from 1761 this was changed to "British" and from 1763 to "British or Irish"] history'.[38] Lesser premiums were offered for paintings of scenes from Greek and Roman history.[39] It should be noted, moreover, that Edward Gibbon, with Samuel Johnson, was an early member of this Society.[40]

There is only space here, however, to explore one manifestation of early medieval history and its public in the eighteenth century, namely, the musical one. Let me begin therefore with a practical demonstration.[41]

> *Teofane ed Ottone*
> A' teneri affetti
> il cor s'abbandoni,
> al duolo perdoni
> chi gode così.
> Condisce i diletti
> memoria di pene;
> nè sa che sia bene
> chi mal non soffrì.
> . . .
> *Chorus*
> Faccia ritorno l'antica pace,
> l'altero orgoglio già si partì.

---

[37] Morris R. Brownell, *Samuel Johnson's attitude to the arts* (Oxford, 1989), pp. 69–78, William L. Pressly, *The life and art of James Barry* (New Haven and London, 1981) and James Barry, *An account of a series of pictures in the Great Room of the Society of Arts, Manufactures and Commerce, at the Adelphi* (London, 1763); see also John Sunderland, 'Samuel Johnson and history painting', and D. G. C. Allan, 'The chronology of James Barry's work for the Society's Great Room', both in D. G. C. Allan and John L. Abbot (eds.), *The virtuoso tribe of arts and sciences. Studies in the eighteenth-century work and membership of the London Society of Arts* (Athens, Georgia, 1992), pp. 183–93 and 336–58.

[38] Pine won first prize in 1763 for his painting of Canute rebuking his courtiers, and Mortimer the second prize for depicting Edward the Confessor stripping his mother of her effects.

[39] A list of the topics is in Robert Dossie, *Memoirs of agriculture and other oeconomical arts*, vol. III (1782), p. 422.

[40] Derek Hudson and Kenneth W. Luckhurst, *The Royal Society of Arts 1754–1954* (London, 1954), pp. 28–9.

[41] When this paper in its conference version was read, it was illustrated with the recording of this duet from *Ottone* by Hyperion (1993) CDA 66751/3 with the King's Consort, conducted by Robert King. James Bowman (countertenor) sings the role of Ottone and Claron McFadden (soprano) that of Teofane.

Arda e consumi d'amor la face,
la mente perfida che la tradì.

This duet between Otto II, emperor of Germany, and Theophanu, his Byzantine bride, with the final chorus, is the climax of Handel's opera *Ottone*, first performed in the King's Theatre, the Haymarket, on 12 January 1725. The title role was sung by the Italian castrato mezzo-soprano Senesino and that of Theophanu by the soprano Cuzzoni. The production ran for thirty-four performances; there was a run on tickets and they fetched as much as two or three guineas apiece.[42] *Ottone* was staged again in 1733 in celebration of the king's birthday, and the opening night was attended by Frederick, prince of Wales, and the entire court.[43] There were performances at Hamburg in the 1720s and in Paris in 1733. Performances continued intermittently in the London season throughout the eighteenth century.[44]

Handel's text had been adapted by Nicola Haym from Stefano Pallavicini's libretto for Lotti's opera *Teofane*, first performed in 1719 in Dresden to celebrate the marriage of Prince Frederick Augustus of Saxony and Archduchess Maria-Josepha of Austria. Handel himself, moreover, appears to have been in Dresden at the time. The appropriateness of the opera's subject – the immediate events leading up to the marriage in 972 between a German ruler and a foreign bride who was perceived as representing a great power – is clear on a superficial level. The historical context of the plot is imaginatively conflated with the revolt of Berengar of Friuli in the 950s and the accession of Basil II to the Byzantine throne, with Basil transformed into Theophanu's brother and disguised as a Muslim pirate! The Argument in the English translation of Pallavicino made by Haym in 1723, summarizes the plot and adds at the end

---

[42] Although they were ordinarily half a guinea, these prices make Covent Garden in the 1990s look quite cheap: a building labourer in Rochester in 1724 was paid 1s 8d per day, six days a week for his work according to Richard Neve (ed.), *The city and country purchaser, and builder's dictionary, or, The compleat builder's guide* (London, 1726), p. 54.

[43] Winton Dean, 'Handel's Ottone', *The Musical Times* no. 1544, vol. 112 (October 1971), pp. 955–8 and Christopher Hogwood, *Handel* (London, 1984), p. 83.

[44] At the King's Theatre in the Haymarket, at Covent Garden and at Drury Lane in 1734, 1745, 1748, 1752, 1770, 1771, 1789, 1790, 1791. See George Winchester Stone, *The London stage 1600–1800. A calendar of plays, entertainments and after pieces. Together with casts, box receipts and contemporary Comment, compiled from the playbills, newspapers, and theatrical diaries of the period* (Carbondale, Illinois, 1952), and Brent Ross Schneider, Jr, *Index to The London Stage 1660–1800* (Carbondale and Edwardsville, S. Illinois, 1979).

It is likewise supposed, that Adelberto, Son to Berengario, a Tyrant in Italy, by the instigation of his mother, here called Gismonda, should cause Rome to rebel against the Germans, who were not long e'er they retook it: This Action here attributed to the Second Otho, in History, is reckoned among those of Otho the Great. It is also a Fiction, that Theophane should fall in the Power of Adelberto, and that he should see her and fall in Love with her at the Time he was incognito in Constantinople. This occasions the greatest part of the Accidents which are seen in this Drama.[45]

The human passions of the mighty and honourable ruler Otto and his wisdom and skill in routing political challenges on the part of the ambitious schemers Adelberto, count of Rome and his mother Gismonda are susceptible of generalization. Yet one might have thought that any marriage, classical or mythological, would surely have served the purpose. Why then was the marriage of Otto II and Theophanu chosen in Dresden in 1719 and adopted thereafter by Handel?

It was in fact far from a matter of chance. Pallavicino and Lotti were alluding, in their own operatic medium, to the discovery in 1707 in the convent of Gandersheim and identification by Johann Georg Leuckfeld of the marriage charter of Otto and Theophanu, drawn up in 972. Leibniz, librarian of the Herzog August Bibliothek in Wolfenbüttel, subsequently visited Gandersheim, described the charter and reproduced it in his history of the house of Braunschweig-Lüneberg, a volume completed by 1715.[46] The charter is a resplendent document of purple-dyed parchment a yard and a half long, written and ornamented in gold. It attracted the interest not only of scholars but also of no less a person than George, elector of Hanover and king of England, who asked to see it and arranged for its loan to Hanover for seven months in 1716–17. The connections between Leibniz's historical work, Pallavicino, Handel and George I and the composition of *Ottone*, moreover, have been thoroughly established by the musicologist Fiona McLauchlan.[47]

---

[45] Fiona McLauchlan, 'Handel's Opera *Ottone* (1723): the composition and performance history during the composer's lifetime', unpublished University of Cambridge Ph.D. dissertation (1995), vol. ii, p. 249. I am grateful to Dr McLauchlan for permitting me to consult her thesis.

[46] G. Leibniz, *Annales imperii occidentis Brynsvicenses*, ed. G. H. Pertz, vol. iii (Hannover, 1846), pp. 292–3.

[47] McLauchlan, 'Handel's Opera *Ottone* (1723)', pp. 96–102. See also Charlotte Spitz, 'Die Opern "Ottone" von G. F. Handel (1722) und "Teofane" von A. Lotti (Dresden, 1722); ein Stilvergleich', in *Festschrift zum 50. Geburtstag Adolf Sandberger überreicht von seinen Schülern*

The charter was woven into the account of the historical fortunes of the house of Braunschweig-Lüneberg; and its relevance to the glorious Saxon past of the eighteenth-century German rulers, already elaborated in a number of works of seventeenth- and eighteenth-century German historical scholarship, was securely established. That such an important historical event should also be celebrated in musical and literary form in an opera reflect not only how much such a reference to the past could be taken for granted, but also what opera composers in the late seventeenth and eighteenth centuries could require of their audiences in terms of the recognition of allusion.[48]

Not all eighteenth-century operas have so apposite an historical theme, nor can they all be so precisely linked with an historical discovery and publication. Yet the incidence of historical topics from the fifth to the tenth centuries, and later in the Middle Ages, chosen by librettists and composers of the late seventeenth and eighteenth centuries needs some explanation other than the presumption that they fitted into a general contemporary cultural frame of reference.

It is also crucial to acknowledge the central place of music, and especially opera, in the culture of the eighteenth century[49] and how much its support depended on the many princely courts throughout Europe, not least those in Venice, London, Hanover and Hamburg, Dresden and Paris. In Hamburg, for example, the Oper am Gänsemarkt was established late in the seventeenth century as an explicit rival to the church music of the city.[50] It had its heyday

---

(Munich, 1918), pp. 265–71, who establishes the relationship between the libretti of Pallavicino and Haym.

[48] An example with reference to the Roman past is the commissioning (by the Bohemian Estates) and performance of Mozart's *La Clemenza di Tito* as part of Leopold II's coronation festivities in Prague in 1791. *La Clemenza di Tito* was originally a libretto by Pietro Metastasio commissioned by Queen Elizabeth Christine of Austria, with music by Antonio Caldara, in honour of the name day of the Hapsburg emperor Charles VI: see Peter R. Johnson, 'An Opera for "the German Titus": Mozart's *La Clemenza di Tito*', unpublished M.Phil. dissertation, Faculty of Classics, University of Cambridge, 1995, who examines the way in which the character and history of the emperor Titus was appropriated and used in the eighteenth century. Metastasio's libretto was set forty-five times by different composers.

[49] Thomas Bauman and Marita Petzoldt McClymonds, *Opera and the Enlightenment* (Cambridge, 1994).

[50] See Heinz Becker, 'Hamburg als Musikstadt', 40. *Deutsches Musikfest Hamburg* (Hamburg, 1965), pp. 169–202; also his 'Hamburg', *The New Grove Dictionary of Music and Musicians*, ed. Stanley Sadie (London, 1980), vol. VIII, pp. 63–8 and W. Schulz, *Die Quellen der Hamburger Oper 1678–1738* (Hamburg, 1936).

under Reinhard Keiser (with whom Handel served his apprentice-
ship between 1703–6). With the appointment of Telemann as
Director of the Opera all the music in the city was under the
direction of one man, for Telemann and his successor C. P. E.
Bach retained control of the annual civic ceremonies and the music of the
five parish churches. The great enthusiasm of the early eighteenth
century was for Italian opera; Keiser promoted it in Hamburg, and
Handel and Nicola Haym did so in London.

Let me give some examples of these operas, with the reminder,
by way of a preface, that the evidence is largely in the form of the
libretto, a distinctive literary form, published afresh for each new
production for purchase by the public and perusal during the
performance.[51] These libretti were often accompanied by prefatory
notes, description of sources and explanations of the chosen theme
by the authors. The librettist was in many cases, such as that of
Pietro Metastasio in Vienna, court poet to a particular ruling
house, and required to produce celebratory poetry and the text for
singing for all ceremonial occasions.[52] Maria Theresa, indeed, was
prepared to order a full-scale opera for many particularly important
family events. Metastasio was a librettist of consummate skill,
whose twenty-seven opera libretti were set over 800 times
altogether by different composers in the eighteenth and early

---

[51] An important collection of libretti is that in the Herzog August Bibliothek in
Wolfenbüttel: see E. Thiel and G. Rohr (eds.), *Kataloge der Herzog August Bibliothek
Wolfenbüttel xiv. Libretti. Verzeichnis der bis 1800 erschienenen Textbücher* (Frankfurt, 1970). See
also *The Venetian Opera libretti from the University of California, Los Angeles* (Cambridge
University Library microfilm) which includes in its 1286 libretti almost every opera
produced in Venice between 1637 and 1769; and Oscar T. Sonneck, *Catalogue of the librettos
written before 1800 in the Schatz collection of the Library of Congress* (Washington, 1914). Schatz's
collection contained 12,000 libretti, and the Library of Congress added many hundreds
more French and English opera libretti from before 1800. For a useful survey of operas,
albeit incomplete, see Alfred Loewenberg and E. J. Dent, *Annals of Opera, 1597–1940*
(3rd edn, London, 1978).

[52] Pietro Metastasio, *Opera drammatiche* (Venice, 1750) and ed. F. Nicolini, *Scrittori d'Italia 44,
46, 62* (Bari, 1912–14); Charles Burney, *Memoirs of the life and writings of the Abbate Metastasio*
(London, 1796) and J. Hoole, *Pietro Metastasio. Works, translated from the Italian* (London,
1767). The preface to *Artaxerxes*, with music composed by Thomas Arne, tells of the
reputation of Metastasio: 'too well established in the learned world to need any Apology
for giving the Public a translation of *Artaxerxes*, an Opera performed and admired all over
Europe' (*Artaxerxes. An English Opera as it is performed at The Royal Theatre in Covent Garden.*
The Music composed by Tho. Aug. Arne. Mus.Doc. London. Printed for J. and R. Tonson
in the Strand 1761). Not all librettists were of the literary standing of Metastasio or
Apostolo Zeno (see below), or of earlier writers such as Rinuccini, Busenello or Quinault
and later ones such as Goldoni and Da Ponte.

nineteenth centuries. Metastasio's predecessor, Apostolo Zeno (1668–1750) was a literary scholar and historian and court poet between 1718 and 1729. Zeno prided himself on his sources and usually listed them in the printed libretto together with a lengthy *argomento*, for he was a scholar in his own right, founder of the *Giornale dei litterati d'Italia* in 1710 and planner of a collection of Italian historical sources.[53] Haym was the official librettist of the Royal Academy of Music from 1722 to 1728 and supplied libretti for Handel, Ariosto and Bononcini.[54] Carlo and Stefano Pallavicino served at the court of Dresden (the latter also at Düsseldorf).[55]

The text of the libretto, therefore, was not the nonsense subservient to the music some twentieth-century audiences might assume, though not all courts scrutinized the libretto with quite the severity of the French.[56] Philippe Quinault (1635–88) (ancestor of my co-editor for this volume), the French playwright who collaborated with Lully, for example, had first to have his choice of subject approved by the king, the outline vetted by Lully, and the finished libretto had to be read out to and approved by a meeting of the Académie Française. The opera libretto was a literary creation conceived in the knowledge of both music and drama and with a lively sense of its audience. Themes developed in operas could make contemporary political allusions, either directly or by implication and historical analogy. In Bouvard, Bertin and LaGrange's opera *Cassandre* (1706) for example, Appollon declaims that Hector's son would live to found the French Empire. In the historical opera *Sabinus*, there is a tableau at the end of Act III where the allegorical Génie de la Gaule shows an amazed Sabinus the future glory of France: 'the back of the stage opens and one saw Charlemagne on his throne, surrounded by the peoples of his empire'.[57] Metastasio's happy endings, moreover, were produced in the conviction that

---

[53] *Rerum italicarum scriptores haetenus desiderati* (Vienna, 1718–29). See also Robert Freeman, 'Apostolo Zeno's reform of the libretto', *Journal of the American Musicological Society* 21 (1968), pp. 321–41.

[54] See Winton Dean, 'Haym, Nicolo Francesco', in *New Grove*, vol. VIII, pp. 415–16.

[55] I. Becker-Glauch, *Die Bedeutung der Musik für die Dresdener Hoffeste bis in die Zeit Augusts des Starken* (Kassel, 1951).

[56] See Herbert Schneider, *Die Rezeption der Opern Lullys im Frankreich der Ancien Régime*, Mainzer Studien zur Musikwissenschaft 16 (Tutzing, 1982), especially pp. 31–6; and A. R. Oliver, *The encyclopedists as critics of music* (New York, 1947). See also P. J. Smith, *The tenth muse: an historical study of the opera libretto* (New York, 1970).

[57] Smith, *The tenth muse*, p. 152 and see René Guiet, *L'évolution d'un genre: le livret d'opéra en France de Gluck à la Révolution (1774–1793)* (Paris, 1936), p. 47.

circumstances could be changed for the better by the force of reason, a reason that was in conflict with human desire and passion. Many of his plots are allegories of autocratic monarchy and demonstrate how reason can prevent passion from destroying social and political institutions such as the monarchy. Reference to real history made these points more effective, for they presented monarchy as an unalterable institution where the responses and fortunes of past kings were relevant to the careers of the present ones. Among others, he chose the Roman hero Attilius Regulus and a fifth-century Roman leader, Aetius. *Ezio* (Aetius) was set to music by Hasse, D. Scarlatti, Gluck, Handel, Galuppi, Jommelli and many more between 1728 and 1778.[58] *Attilio* in Hasse's setting was performed in Dresden in 1750 and in Rome in Jommelli's setting in 1753; it was restaged as a republican spectacle in Rome in 1799.[59]

For other opera composers and librettists, even though we usually do not know who was responsible for the choice of subject in the first place, the rulers of the Germanic kingdoms appear to have offered much inspiration, especially to those working for the rulers of the various German and Austrian courts. Polani, for example, devised an opera with libretto by Noris on *Berengario re d'Italia* (1710). Noris also wrote the libretti for Partenio's opera *Flavio Cuniberto* (1682)[60] and Legrenzi's opera *Totila*, the last Gothic ruler of Italy, for the Duke of Mantua in 1677.[61] Schürmann, active at the Braunschweig court, devised an opera based on Simonetti's text about the emperor Louis the Pious; it was performed in Braunschweig in 1726 and 1727 and revived in 1734.[62] With Mauro as librettist, Schürmann also composed the German opera *Heinrich der*

---

[58] Compare the account of Aetius' career in *Decline and fall*, ed. Bury, III, pp. 287, 398, 407, 447, 545 and see below, pp. 184–5.

[59] Attilius Regulus was a popular subject for history painting, in France as well as England, with, for example, paintings by both Benjamin West and Jacques-Louis David.

[60] The libretto for *Flavio Cuniberto* was adapted by Nicola Haym for Handel's opera *Flavio, re di Longobardi*.

[61] *Totila* was performed in Francesco Gasparino's setting as *Totila in Roma* in 1696. Compare the account of Totila in *Decline and fall*, ed. Bury, IV, pp. 395–416.

[62] *Ludovicus Pius oder Ludwig der Fromme. In einer Opera vorgestellt Auf dem grossen Braunschweigischen Theater in der Winter-Messe* 1726. Musik G. K. Schürmann. Einige Arien und Duette von K. H. Graun. Ballettmusik aus Opern von André Cardinal Destouches und André Canpra. Text Christian Ernst Simonetti (Wolfenbüttel, 1726); compare *Decline and fall*, ed. Bury, V, p. 292 (a passing reference only).

Löwe (Henry the Lion, married to an English princess), whose subject was a local hero buried in the cathedral at Braunschweig, in 1716 and five years later he took as his subject Henry the Fowler, father of the Emperor Otto I.[63] Steffani himself, who had worked in France and at the courts of Düsseldorf and Munich and who in 1727 was elected president of the Academy of Vocal Music in London, composed operas about Tassilo (*Il Tassilone*), the eighth-century duke of Bavaria deprived of his inheritance and duchy by his cousin Charlemagne, with text by Pallavicino, as well as about Henry the Lion (with text by Mauro, for the inauguration of Hanover's Italian opera house in 1689) and, with text by Silvani, about Alaric, the Gothic leader who had had the temerity to sack Rome in 410.[64] Vanschino took Odoacer, the Skirian *magister militum* of the Roman army who deposed Romulus Augustulus (the last Roman emperor in the west) in 476, and ruled as king of Italy, as his theme.[65] Roland, the vanquished hero of the defeat at Roncesvalles on Charlemagne's expedition to Spain in 778, perhaps predictably, was Lully's choice, with text by Philippe Quinault. The theme of Roland subsequently became much transformed with a magical setting as the opera *Orlando*, derived from Ariosto's *Orlando furioso* and set by many composers including Handel, Haydn and Schubert. Gasparini, who died in 1727, wrote the music for operas about Roderic (*Roderico*, first performed Livorno, 1686), the last Visigothic ruler of Spain, and Fredegund, the notorious Merovingian queen.[66] A subsequent version was performed in Braunschweig in 1720 and again in 1742 with Schürmann's music added to that of Gasparini.[67] Another version, *Fredegunda*, with music by Keiser and libretto derived from Silvani and first performed in Hamburg in 1715, was apparently one of Keiser's most popular operas.[68] Silvani, the librettist for *Fredegonda*, also wrote libretti for Biego's opera about

---

[63] *Heinrich der Vögler, Hertzog zu Braunschweig, nachmahls erwehlter Teustcher Kayser* (Hamburg, 1719), libretto by J. U. König; revived 1735; also performed in Stockholm 1734.

[64] *Alarico il Baltha cioè l'audace. Rè de Gothi*, libretto by O. Mauro (Munich, 1687) written for the birthday of the Bavarian electress Maria Antonia and based, according to the *Argomento*, on Orosius, Paul the Deacon, Jordanes, Augustine and Procopius.

[65] Compare *Decline and fall*, ed. Bury, IV, pp. 48–55.

[66] *Fredegonda*: first performed 1704, and in Braunschweig in 1712 and 1716.

[67] Roderic, see *Decline and fall*, ed. Bury, V, p. 474 n. 203 and p. 478 n. 211. Fredegund, see *Decline and fall*, ed. Bury, IV, p. 127 n. 84 and p. 139 n. 124.

[68] Libretto by J. U. König and see Loewenberg, *Annals of Opera*, col. 132.

Otto I (*Ottone il Grande*) and Charles the Bald (entitled *Carlo re d'Alemagna*).[69] As well as *Teofane*, Lotti contributed the opera *Irene augusta* with text by Silvani.[70] Telemann's opera about Genseric, the Vandal ruler, with libretto by Postel, was performed in Braunschweig in 1725.[71] Carlo Pallavicino wrote *Ricimero re di vandali* (this was in fact the Ricimer who was the power behind the imperial throne in the west in the early fifth century) for performance in Dresden, while Zeno and Pariati produced a libretto about the same man, called *Flavio Anicio Olibrio*, first set by Gasparini in 1707. Jommelli wrote an opera *Ricomero, Rè dei Goti*, with libretto by someone unknown, possibly adapted from the Zeno and Pariati version and performed in Rome on 16 January 1740.[72]

Many of these operas were performed in Braunschweig before the dukes of Braunschweig-Lüneberg in the late seventeenth and the eighteenth centuries. The tally of operas on historical subjects from other German opera houses is similar. Although much of the music from the attempts at Leipzig and Braunschweig between 1693 and 1720 to create a national opera is lost,[73] references to productions as well as surviving libretti reveal a steady stream of historical operas on classical and early medieval themes, especially in Braunschweig, such as *Giulio Cesare* (1694), *Agrippina* (1699), *Justino* (1700), *Athanagildo* (king of the Visigoths with music by Boxberg, 1701 and 1707), *Phocas* (1696, set in seventh-century Byzantium), *Ottone* (the tenth-century German ruler, 1702), *Pharamondo* (legendary ancestor of the Merovingian Frankish rulers, 1710).[74]

In Hamburg a particularly intense preoccupation with early medieval as well as Roman themes is apparent between 1702 and 1732. Schulze, drawing on libretti in collections in Berlin, Hamburg

---

[69] The libretto was originally for Vinnacesi's opera *L'innocenza guistificata* (1698) and afterwards set to new music with the title *Carlo re d'Alamagna* and then performed in German as *Judith, Gemahlin Kayser Ludwigs des Frommen oder die siegende Unschuld*, see below p. 183 and compare *Decline and fall*, ed. Bury, IV, pp. 293–4.

[70] Compare *Decline and fall*, ed. Bury, V, pp. 188–98, 294.

[71] Compare *ibid.*, IV, pp. 1–2.

[72] Marita Petzoldt McClymonds, 'Jommelli', in *New Grove*, vol. IX, pp. 689–95, and compare Gibbon's account of Ricimer, *Decline and fall*, ed. Bury, IV, pp. 13–16, 24, 28, 31, 42–5.

[73] Gustav Friedrich Schmidt, 'Die älteste deutsche Oper in Leipzig am Ende des 17. und Anfang des 18. Jahrhunderts. Neue Beiträge zur Literatur- und Formen geschichtlichen Betrachtung der altern Operntexte', in *Festschrift Adolf Sandberger*, pp. 209–54.

[74] H. Metschman, 'Das erste Jahrhundert der deutschen Oper', *Sammelband der internationale Musikgesellschaft* 3 (1901/2).

and Weimar, has been able to document productions of an extraordinary array of operas, with libretti, sometimes in German, by Besand, Hinsch, Ferind, König, Hoe, Wend and Glauche set to music by, among others, Keiser, Schürmann, Telemann and Mattheson. These include *Porsenna* (1702), *Claudio* (1703), *Almira* (1704), *Octavia* (1705), *Desiderius, König der Langobarden* (written to celebrate the birthday of the emperor Joseph I, 1709), *Boris Gudenow* (1710), *Kaiser Heraclius* (seventh-century Byzantine emperor, 1712), *Fredegunda* (Merovingian queen, 1715), *Trajano* (1717), *Genserico* (Vandal ruler, 1722),[75] *Nero* (1723), *Ottone* (tenth-century German emperor, 1726), *Flavio Bertarido* (Lombard king, 1729), *Emma und Eginhard* (Charlemagne's biographer of the ninth century and his wife, with music by Telemann, 1728) and *Judith, Gemahlin Kayser Ludwigs des Frommen* (ninth-century Frankish empress, also with music by Telemann, 1732).[76]

It is clear from the surviving libretti, moreover, that although the operas were sung in Italian, the audience was, more often than not, supplied with translations into French, German or English, as appropriate.[77] The words mattered. For one thing, the audience could be quick, on occasion, to catch topical and political allusions in seemingly innocent phrases, as in one of the instances cited by Johnson of performances of Piccini's *Didon* and Grétry's *Richard Coeur de Lion* in 1791, where royalists applauded lines that could be taken politically.[78] More generally, the themes of the operas as well as their texts had a wider resonance. The contexts of their composition and performance would repay investigation on the lines of that already undertaken, as indicated above, by Peter Johnson for *La Clemenza di Tito* and Fiona McLauchlan for Handel's *Ottone*. It is striking how many of the historical operas (quite apart from an enormous range of historical *plays*) continued to be performed in London throughout the eighteenth century. Although some operas, such as *Agrippina*, *Lotario* or *Giustino*, were not revived,

---

[75] *Der Grösse König der Africanischen Wenden Gensericus als Rom und Charthagens Überwinder.* Anno 1725. Originally by Conradi, performed in Hamburg as *Sieg der Schönheit* in 1722, this was a reworking by Telemann.

[76] Walter Schulze, *Die Quellen der hamburger Oper 1678–1738. Eine bibliographische-statitische Studie zur Geschichte der ersten stehenden deutschen Oper* (Hamburg, 1938), esp. pp. 80–102.

[77] See *Ezio*, for example, n. 83 below.

[78] James H. Johnson, *Listening in Paris. A cultural history* (Berkeley, Los Angeles and London, 1995), p. 110.

others, notably Handel's *Ottone* and *Rodelinda* and Hasse's *Ezio*, were restaged on a number of occasions.[79] Loftis' work demonstrates indeed that in Augustan England music drama was a favoured vehicle for the most overt political allegory.[80]

Further, Ruth Smith has established the essential contribution to the text in Handel's sacred oratorios in the light of the ubiquity and interdependence of religion and politics in eighteenth-century England, and that Handel's oratorios evoked moral and ideological issues which vitally concerned their audiences.[81] A similar conjunction might be proposed for the operas and their libretti and the extent to which they reflect and embody the ideas and moral and artistic criteria of their time.[82]

If we examine a sample or two of these libretti, in copies preserved by some eighteenth-century theatre-goers, we find the argument sets out the historical facts. That of Handel's *Ezio*, for example, performed in the King's Theatre in the Haymarket and supplied with an English translation to accompany the Italian, describes how

Aetius, an illustrious general of the imperial forces under Valentinian the Third returning from the famous victory of the Catalonian field, where he defeated and put to flight Attila, king of the Huns, was unjustly accused to the jealous emperor, and by him condemned to die. The author of this treachery against the innocent Aetius was Maximus, a Roman patrician, who being already incensed at Valentinian for attempting the chastity of his wife, endeavoured, tho' ineffectually, to engage the assistance of Aetius to murder the Emperor, at the same time artfully concealing his own desire for revenge; but Maximus knowing that the loyalty of Aetius was the greatest obstruction to his design, he fixed upon him the imputation of treason, and solicited his death; intending (as he afterwards did) to make the populace mutiny against Valentinian, by accusing him of the ingratitude and injustice, to which he himself had induced him. *All this*

---

[79] See Stone, *The London stage*, vol. IV (1747–1776) especially pp. clix–clxxiv.

[80] J. Loftis, *The politics of drama in Augustan England* (Oxford, 1963). Loftis has stressed how 'plays with settings all over the world and in all epochs of history resound with praise for the conception of constitutional monarchy that emerged from the [English] Revolution . . . all became locales for the declamation of Whig principles', p. 82; compare Robertson below, pp. 247–70.

[81] Ruth Smith, 'Intellectual contexts of Handel's English oratorios' in C. Hogwood and R. Luckett (eds.), *Music in eighteenth-century England. Essays in honour of Charles Cudworth* (Cambridge, 1982), pp. 115–33 and also her *Handel's oratorios and eighteenth-century thought* (Cambridge, 1995). See also C. MacDonald's review of Smith, *The Times Literary Supplement* 4826 (29 September 1995), p. 7.

[82] See Nicholas Till, *Mozart and the Enlightenment* (London, 1992), pp. 38–47.

[the librettist cheerfully concludes] *according to history, and the rest within the bounds of probability.* The scene is in Rome.[83]

Just as I have indicated in the notes above where the heroes and heroines of the particular operas cited also play a role in Gibbon's *History*, it is instructive to compare this version with the account of Aetius' career provided by Gibbon. Gibbon relates at length the illustrious achievements of Aetius (where he is quite as much concerned with the Hunnish Empire and the genius of Attila as he is with Aetius) before this final incident in Rome. There Gibbon has the events connected in a different way, for it is Valentinian out of jealousy who murders Aetius, and Maximus, revenging the rape of his wife by the emperor, who afterwards persuades two of Aetius' followers to murder Valentinian.[84] Both the libretto account and Gibbon's accounts are apparently based on the same Latin sources, though the librettist has conflated the two events to achieve greater dramatic confrontation.

In their reaction to the strength of Italian opera the English made their own contributions to the sense of national music with operas on English medieval themes, such as Addison's *Rosamond* set to music by Arne,[85] and Arne's setting of *Alfred*,[86] not to mention the performance of *King Arthur or The British Worthy* with text by Dryden and music by Henry Purcell.[87] Yet these also, as Loftis has made clear, had a contemporary political agenda. *Alfred* (1740), for example, embodied criticism of Walpole's foreign policy with its climax, 'Rule Britannia', representing 'the most famous lyric ever to be inspired by a commercial war'.[88] Handel himself, with his *Riccardo, re d'Inghilterra* (on Richard the Lion Heart; a French opera on the same topic was mounted in 1784), contributed in his own distinctive way to English interests.[89] With *Rodelinda, regina de' Langobardi*, one of his masterpieces, he was able to portray all that

[83] My emphasis. *Ezio. Drama per musica da rappresentarsi sopra il Teatro di S.M.B. Terza edizione. Ezio: an opera set to music. As it is represented at the King's Theatre in the Hay-Market. The third edition*. London. Printed for G. Woodfall, at Charing-Cross 1765 [Price One Shilling].

[84] *Decline and fall*, ed. Bury, III, pp. 447–79, especially 477–9.

[85] This is Rosamond Clifford, mistress of the English king Henry II, not Rosamond, queen of the Lombards and wife of Alboin.

[86] Compare *Decline and fall*, ed. Bury, IV, p. 202 and V, p. 151. Haydn in 1796 composed the incidental music for the play *Alfred, König der Angelsachsen, oder Der patriotische König* by J. W. Cowmeadow after A. Bicknell.

[87] *Decline and fall*, ed. Bury, IV, p. 150.   [88] Loftis, *Politics of drama*, p. 124.

[89] *Decline and fall*, ed. Bury, VI, pp. 347, 349–50, 353, 375, 378.

was noble in the Lombard traditions, in a magnificent celebration of political fidelity and conjugal love. The libretto was by Nicola Haym, based on an Italian model by Antonio Salvi (1710) in its turn derived from Corneille's play, *Pertharite, roi des Lombards*.[90] The composition was part of a magnificent twelve months from 20 February 1724 to 13 February 1725 in which *Giulio Cesare, Tamerlano*, and *Rodelinda* were completed and performed in London. Earlier, in Italy in 1707 he had composed *Rodrigo* (first performed in Florence), largely fictional but alluding to real events in the last years of Visigothic rule in Spain in the early eighth century, and *Lothario* (staged in London in December 1729) concerning the political changes of Italy in the middle of the tenth century with a libretto from the opera *Adelaide* (Lothar's wife) with music by Sartorio, first performed in Venice in 1672.[91]

Few of these operas afford much space to Christianity. This is easily accounted for, however, by the fact that opera was specifically secular, not sacred music, and the two were clearly distinguished in the eighteenth century.[92]

Some musicologists have been inclined to associate operas with medieval subjects together with those which adopt mythological and classical subjects as indicating personages sufficiently remote to play no proper part in the audiences' understanding of the plot or its characters. Walther Siegmund-Schultze has gone so far as to say, in relation to Handel's *Tamerlano*, for instance, that its portrayal of the fall of the Turkish ruler Bajazet (the subject of a different version in 1731) and its exemplification of powerful figures of oriental history in the fulness of their might, but also in their human passions and weaknesses, were set in a 'distant time and place' precisely because the 'audience was unlikely to ask questions'.[93] There is occasional support for this attitude among

---

[90] Graun, composer at the Prussian court 1741–56, also devised an opera *Rodelinda, regina de Longobardi*, with libretto by Bottarelli based on Salvi's libretto, performed in the Berlin Schloss in 1741; see E. E. Helm, *Music at the court of Frederick the Great* (Norman, Oklahoma, 1960), especially pp. 102–4.

[91] Also set by Rossini in 1817, and compare *Decline and fall*, ed. Bury, IV, p. 124.

[92] See Smith, *Handel's oratorios*.

[93] Preface to libretto, *Tamerlano* (CBS recording 1984, directed by Jean-Claude Malgoire), p. 2. The popularity and notoriety of the story of Bajazet (compare Bryer, above p. 111) is clear. The cover of the CBS recording depicts Bajazet from the painting by Andrea Celesti (1637–1712), *Der gefangene Sultan Bajazet vor Tamerlan in Potsdam*, Staatliche Schlösser und Gärten. On Bajazet see *Decline and fall*, ed. Bury, VII, pp. 33–64.

eighteenth-century librettists. Algarotti, for example, thought that vocal display was inappropriate to real personages and so set his scenes in South America, Egypt and China. On this assumption, figures from a remote past might be used to portray not only ideal kings and princes, but also how their power had been curtailed by the conflict between Enlightenment notions of a good or a bad ruler, and the influence on a ruler of his particular environment and relationships with women. Such settings are thought to have provided a neutral ground for the expression of love, fidelity, hate, betrayal, cunning, treason and honour, and the triumph of reason, without calling into question the supreme and ultimately impregnable power of the ruler.

Such a judgment is anachronistic, for in general terms it imposes modern ignorance of the historical contexts of the operas onto eighteenth-century audiences and neglects to explore the coherence and extraordinary degree of cross-referencing in eighteenth-century culture. What Lawrence Lipking has termed a common enterprise for histories and many other genres of writing and areas of scholarship of the eighteenth century, that is, no less than the 'ordering of the arts', provides a more plausible context for an appreciation of the reception and understanding of the early medieval forebears of eighteenth-century states.[94] Operas on historical subjects, which combined poetry, music and stage designs with history, might be understood as a practical manifestation of the conviction, not only of the central role of the arts in human history, which found its most persuasive apologists in Vico's *La Scienza nuova* and Herder's *Ideen zur Philosophie der Geschichte der Menschheit*, but also of the relevance of a particular segment of the past to eighteenth-century political understanding. Such use of drama for political purposes or for national glorification is, of course, perfectly familiar from Shakespeare's history plays and from the plays of Augustan England. Nicholas Rowe's play *Tamerlane* (1701), in particular, is a direct contradiction of Siegmund-Schultze's notion of the irrelevance of the medieval past and the story of Tamerlane and Bajazet to contemporary politics.[95]

Further, national identity found one of its expressions in music.

---

[94] Lawrence Lipking, *The ordering of the arts in eighteenth-century England* (Princeton, 1970) and Baumann and Petzoldt McClymonds, *Opera and the Enlightenment*.
[95] Compare Loftis, *Politics of drama*, pp. 23–34.

One protest against Jean-Jacques Rousseau's denigration of French music in *Lettre sur la musique française*, for example, from an academician of Bordeaux was couched in terms of the historical identity of the French, who therefore by definition and in relation to their glorious past had a national musical tradition of their own:

we French comprise the oldest and best preserved nation in Europe, as a result of the achievements of our kings, all of whom have been French, of our Salic laws and customs, which have always been Christian, both before and since Clovis, reaching back virtually to the times of the Apostles ... It would indeed be very surprising if we had no music of our own, given our perhaps excessively proprietary attitude to everything else we possess, even to the point of demanding that the rest of the world models itself on us. This is a fault that can be forgiven us, I think, bearing in mind the antiquity and permanence of what we possess – in the form of our territory, our arts, our customs, our laws, and even ourselves.[96]

The academician's reference to Clovis and the Salic law is enlightening, for it reflects the celebration, by librettists and composers (who had a large public reception for such celebration) of Germanic rulers, their power and their heroic fame. The operas proclaimed a conviction of the strength of a non-Roman past and accorded a distinctive character to a sense of national identity to which historians, philosophers, scholars and literary writers had also contributed. Such a positive portrayal of the Germanic rulers contrasts strongly with the superficial sneers of Gibbon.

While in many passages in his work, Gibbon nevertheless shares the opera composers' and librettists' admiration of the vigour of emerging nations of Europe, his tendency to belittle the early medieval states of western Europe in particular contradicted a more general sense of pride among the European nations of his own day and their sense of a past with which they were vitally concerned. It was perhaps fortunate for the success of his work in England, that although he was able to count on an audience relatively familiar with the topics he addressed, Gibbon had not seen fit to include the fortunes of the Anglo-Saxons or Normans as one of the 'new peoples to whom the torch was to pass'. The rulers of medieval England had their own English advocates with nationalist lines of interpretation and definition of the principal sources established by English

---

[96] *Letter from an academician of Bordeaux on the fundamental principles of music on the occasion of M. R[ousseau]'s attack on French music* (London, 1754).

scholars in the seventeenth and eighteenth centuries comparable with those by the French on the Franks and the Italians on the Lombards.[97] Had Gibbon worked the early medieval English kings into his narrative, a vital connection would have been made that might have altered the subsequent development of English historiography of this period, might have brought it further into the mainstream of European development, and yet set a rather different agenda than that of his contemporaries. That Gibbon was an Englishman is perhaps neither here nor there, yet there is a possible irony in the fact that the historian in whom the English appear to take the most pride was not an historian of his own national history. But Gibbon's public was not confined to England. It was a European public, to whom the main protagonists and events had long been a familiar part of their culture. The Gibbon whom we celebrate in this volume – famous, learned, influential, opinionated and contrary – was the interpreter of a common late antique and medieval past across Europe and the Mediterranean, both east and west.[98]

---

[97] David C. Douglas, *English scholars* (London, 1939) and J. G. A. Pocock, *The ancient constitution and the feudal law: a study of English historical thought in the seventeenth century. Reissue with retrospect* (Cambridge, 1987).

[98] I am very grateful to Andrew Jones, Roland Quinault and David McKitterick for their comments on this chapter.

CHAPTER 9

Gibbon and the 'Watchmen of the Holy City': revision and religion in the Decline and fall

David Womersley

We may be well assured, that a writer, conversant with the world, would never have ventured to expose the gods of his country to public ridicule, had they not already been the objects of secret contempt among the polished and enlightened orders of society.

> Edward Gibbon, *The decline and fall of the Roman Empire*,
> vol. I, ch. 2

We know, and what is better, we feel inwardly, that religion is the basis of civil society and the source of all good and all comfort. In England we are so convinced of this that there is no rust of superstition with which the accumulated absurdity of the human mind might have crusted it over in the course of all ages, that ninety nine in a hundred of the people in England would not prefer to impiety.

> Edmund Burke, *Reflections on the Revolution in France*

This essay is one of a series of interlocking studies, designed in the end to compose a monograph which will approach the last eighteen years of Gibbon's life by examining the complicated influence exerted by the historian's reputation over his writing. Gibbon was unabashed in acknowledging that the desire for fame was his prime motive as a writer. It is in the *Vindication* of 1779 that we find this most frankly stated: 'I have never affected, indeed I have never understood, the stoical apathy, the proud contempt of criticism, which some authors have publicly professed. Fame is the motive, it is the reward, of our labours . . . '[1] This sentiment was no affectation adopted for public effect. Similar comments occur in letters to Deyverdun and Suard: correspondents with whom Gibbon had no

---

[1] *English essays*, p. 232. He confessed to Suzanne Necker that he was indifferent to Parliament because there he would always be 'sans reputation' (*Letters*, vol. II, p. 264).

measures to keep, and therefore no reason for deception or dissimulation.[2]

The gods punish us by giving us what we crave. The success of the *Decline and fall* indeed furnished Gibbon with 'a name, a rank, a character, in the World' to which he would not otherwise have been entitled.[3] Some of this public reputation was acceptable to him, and nourished an innocent vanity. Some, however, he felt to be misleading. In particular, the response of the orthodox to Gibbon's treatment of Christianity, initially in chapters 15 and 16 of the *Decline and fall*, and subsequently in the rest of the history, in Gibbon's opinion misrepresented him as a late example of a tradition of anti-clerical free-thinking which had arisen first in England during the late seventeenth and early eighteenth centuries.[4] *The Gentleman's Magazine* was first to the assault: '. . . we see him [Gibbon], in short, attacking the Old and New Testaments, and their sacred Author, with as much virulence, though more disguised, and with the same weapons, however blunted, that have so often and so openly been used in the schools of Battersea and Ferney'.[5] It is arguable that Gibbon was on this point in the right. There were as many areas of divergence as of contact between his work and that of the earlier generation of freethinkers, such as Blount, Tindal, Toland and Bolingbroke, with whom his detractors in the 1770s and 1780s habitually associated him. The arguments of the *Decline and fall* were not focussed (as were those of the deists and freethinkers) on the sole and single aim of discrediting *sacerdotium*. Indeed, in the later volumes of the history Gibbon wrote appreciatively of the benefits to civil society which had flowed from the temporal government of the medieval papacy.[6] But to dismiss Gibbon's clerical adversaries as captious and misguided is to overlook much of the complexity of Gibbon's own position. As we shall

---

[2] To Deyverdun, *Letters*, vol. II, p. 106; to Suard, *Letters*, II, p. 122.

[3] *Autobiographies*, p. 346.

[4] For a recent and most interesting account of these writers, see J. A. I. Champion, *The pillars of priestcraft shaken: the Church of England and its enemies 1660–1730* (Cambridge, 1992). The standard survey is still that by Leslie Stephen, *English thought in the eighteenth century* (2 vols., London, 1876).

[5] *The Gentleman's Magazine* 46 (1776), p. 366. Ferney is an allusion to Voltaire, Battersea to Bolingbroke, whose family had long held land in that part of London.

[6] J. G. A. Pocock, 'Superstition and enthusiasm in Gibbon's History of Religion', *Eighteenth-Century Life* 8 (1981), pp. 83–94. See chapter 49 of the *Decline and fall* for Gibbon's sympathetic consideration of the medieval papacy.

see presently, Gibbon knew that he had, to a limited extent and through a failure of judgment, provoked this misreading of his work. It is also to render largely unintelligible the works of Gibbon's adversaries. If not as polished and intellectually searching as the *Decline and fall*, they were nevertheless neither so incoherent nor so crude as they have been made to appear by being considered apart from the polemical tradition within which they were composed, and within which they demand to be read.

Gibbon confronted the distorted and simplified image of himself which had been created in the controversy over the two last chapters of volume I of the *Decline and fall* directly (though also shrewdly) in his *Vindication* of 1779. But he equally struggled with it silently and implicitly in subsequent projects apparently and avowedly unconnected with his notoriety. Beginning with the revisions to the first volume of the *Decline and fall* (published in 1776), continuing with the lines of argument and exposition pursued in certain sections of the second and third instalments of the history (published in 1781 and 1788 respectively), and concluding with the literary projects of the last seven years of his life, such as the *Antiquities of the House of Brunswick*, and especially the six drafts of the *Memoirs of my life*, Gibbon wrestled with the caricature which his own desire for celebrity had helped to summon into being. By turns conciliatory, defiant, or sly in demeanour, and overt or concealed in method, during the years between the publication of the first volume of the *Decline and fall* and his death in 1794 Gibbon sought to regain control of his public character, and to shape it to his liking.

In his own lifetime, he failed. It proved impossible to destroy completely that plausible but false likeness of himself, which had been first modelled by Chelsum and Davis, and then polished by the hands of later adversaries. The alloy of insidiousness and irreligion in which it had been cast proved to be too durable. But to see Gibbon making the attempt is to gain an insight into late eighteenth-century conditions of authorship, and also to make visible for the first time an aspect of what we might call the historian's experience of himself. I say 'for the first time', because although Gibbon was unable to regain control of his reputation amongst his contemporaries, he has enjoyed greater success with later generations. For his *Memoirs* have ensured that his life has been retold with the plot, and in the terms, which he himself selected.[7] An important task for Gibbon scholars is to put the *Memoirs* to one side for the moment, and to understand the historian's life from a point of vantage not chosen by its subject. Once we have done so, there is much in the *Memoirs*, previously accepted as accurate, which we shall have to treat with caution. To be weighed against this loss, however, is the prize of a much deeper understanding of the multiplicity, and at times contradictoriness, of Gibbon's purposes as an author.

In this chapter, I shall examine the very beginnings of Gibbon's struggle to resume the direction of his public reputation: namely, the revisions he made in chapters 15 and 16 for the second edition of 1776, and the third edition of 1777.[8] These revisions show that these chapters underwent two distinct phases of revisal: the first, completed before any attacks on the supposed irreligion of the history had appeared, for the second edition published on 3 June 1776; and the second, completed in the knowledge of the first wave of attacks by Watson and Chelsum (but not Henry Davis), for the third edition published in May 1777. Moreover, the tendency of these two phases of revisal – their impact on the text of the history, and Gibbon's evident governing intention in making the revisions – is in each case coherent (that is to say, the individual corrections of the text when taken together indicate a single overall plan of revision). However, the ends at which Gibbon aimed in these two episodes of revision were directly opposed to each other. I shall begin by sketching how chapters 15 and 16 fit in to Gibbon's first volume, and how their subject connects with the broad theme of imperial decline. I shall go on to discuss, in terms unavoidably minute, the character of the revisions made in the second and third editions. I shall conclude by drawing out what I take to be the broader significance of these revisions for our understanding of what Gibbon was doing in chapters 15 and 16.

The first volume of the *Decline and fall* begins with three chapters

---

[7] This is particularly the case with Patricia Craddock's recent biography, which adds new information to our knowledge of the circumstances of Gibbon's life, but does not reconceptualize its subject.

[8] The revisions made for the fourth edition of 1781 are few in number, but bear significance in relation to the second instalment of 1781. Thereafter, in the editions of 1782 and 1789, Gibbon seems himself to have made no revisions to his text. The variants in these last two quarto editions are demonstrably printing house corrections, made by someone who, at certain points, did not understand Gibbon's prose.

surveying the political, military and social condition of the Roman Empire in the Age of the Antonines (AD 138–80). At the end of chapter 14, the narrative of the Empire's decline has been reduced to Constantine's final defeat of his rival Licinius, and to the reunification of the Empire under his sole monarchy (AD 324). Gibbon then concluded the first volume with the notorious two chapters on Christianity. Chapter 15 described the progress of the Christian religion from its origins as a minor sect to its installation as the established religion of the Empire, and explained that progress with reference to five secondary (that is to say, non-divine) causes: the zeal of the early Christians; the Christian doctrine of a future life; the miraculous powers ascribed to the primitive church; the pure morals of the first Christians; and the union and discipline of the Christian republic. Chapter 16 addressed itself to the subject of the persecutions suffered by the Christians, and suggested that the easy and tolerating temper of classical paganism would not have given rise to the number of martyrs which the Church had subsequently claimed.

When Hume wrote to congratulate Gibbon on the publication of volume I of the *Decline and fall*, he touched on the subject of chapters 15 and 16: 'When I heard of your undertaking (which was some time ago) I own that I was a little curious to see how you would extricate yourself from the subject of your two last chapters.'[9] The history of the decline of the Empire, then, necessarily implied some consideration of the rise of Christianity, and of the relation (if any) between religion and *imperium*. Historians prior to Gibbon had linked Christianity and empire within the framework of providence; but so roomy was that framework that it could accommodate a number of different, even contradictory, positions. A popular explanation held that God had delayed the birth of Christ in order that the universal pacification brought about by the empire would make easier the spread of the new religion. A second stated that it was necessary for the majority of mankind to have reached a degree of intellectual refinement before the Christian message could be properly received and recorded. A third (inverting our first explanation) insisted that Christianity had appeared in the world under the least propitious circumstances, and had recommended doctrines which were more likely to repel men than to allure them; no one could

---

[9] *Autobiographies*, p. 312.

doubt, therefore, that the success of Christianity was due to divine and miraculous intervention.[10] Common to all these various interpretations, however, was the contention that the timing and circumstances of the Christian revelation showed evidence of design. The unmistakable upshot of Gibbon's two last chapters – that the rise of Christianity could be fully explained by reference to human causes, and that the fledgling faith had not encountered opposition so extensive and determined that it could be vanquished by only the finger of God – was an affront to all these providential narratives.[11] Thomas Randolph put it concisely and accurately:

The speedy and wonderful Propagation of the Gospel, under the Circumstances in which it was first published, has been frequently urged by Christian Writers, as an irrefragable Proof of the Truth of the Christian Religion. But a late ingenious Historian has used his utmost Endeavours to invalidate the Force of this Proof, and attempted to account for the Success of the Gospel by natural Causes.[12]

The first volume of the *Decline and fall* was published on 17 February 1776.[13] Writing to his stepmother on 26 March, Gibbon conveyed two important pieces of information:

... my book has been very well received ... by every set of people except perhaps by the Clergy who seem (I know not why) to shew their teeth on

---

[10] Gibbon himself alluded, with mock reverence, to the first of these in the *Decline and fall* (*Decline and fall*, I, pp. 602–3). It had been most clearly put forward by William Robertson, in his sermon of 1755, *The situation of the World at the time of Christ's appearance* (Edinburgh, 1755). For the need for refinement, see East Apthorp, *Letters on the prevalence of Christianity* (London, 1778), p. vi. For the difficult doctrines of Christianity, see William Salisbury, *A history of the establishment of Christianity* (London, 1776), p. 109 and Joseph Milner, *Gibbon's account of Christianity considered* (York, 1781), p. 179. For the worldly disadvantages over which it triumphed, see John Leland, *Reflections on the late Lord Bolingbroke's letters on the study and use of history* (London, 1753), p. 96 and Joseph White, *Sermons preached before the University of Oxford* (Oxford, 1784), pp. 135–6.

[11] For an invocation of the finger of God, see White, *Sermons preached before the University of Oxford*, p. 105.

[12] Thomas Randolph, *The proof of the truth of the Christian religion* (Oxford, 1977), p. 1. Compare Milner, *Gibbon's account of Christianity considered*, p. 172: 'the whole energy of his [Gibbon's] fifteenth chapter is directed to establish positions, tending to account for its [Christianity's] progress by methods merely human. What consequences subversive of its divine authority would thence be deduced, its enemies will tell with pleasure.' Dalrymple countered Gibbon's analysis by maintaining that 'the things which Mr Gibbon considered as secondary or human causes, efficaciously promoting the Christian religion, either tended to retard its progress, or were the manifest operations of the wisdom and power of God' (Sir David Dalrymple, *An inquiry into the secondary causes which Mr. Gibbon has assigned for the rapid growth of Christianity* (Edinburgh, 1786), p. 210).

[13] Norton, *Bibliography*, p. 37.

the occasion. A thousand Copies are sold, and we are preparing a second Edition, which in so short a time is, for a book of that price a very uncommon event.[14]

This is the first indication that Gibbon knew he had provoked 'the Clergy', although for the time being he knew neither who would enter the lists against him, nor what they would write.[15] In the same breath, he reported that the second edition was in preparation. It is of the first importance to appreciate that the revisions Gibbon made for the second edition were planned and executed in this period of uncertainty and ignorance. On 24 May, once again to his stepmother, he returned to the subject of the second edition. 'My mornings have been very much taken up with preparing and correcting (though in a minute and almost imperceptible way) my new Edition which will be out the first of June.'[16] April and May 1776 were thus the months given over to revision. The second edition appeared on 3 June. The revisions it embodied, though minute, were far from imperceptible.[17] They demonstrate, moreover, that, despite his protestation to the contrary, Gibbon had a very good idea of where and how he had offended the orthodox.

Gibbon composed two accounts of his clash with 'the Clergy' over his handling of Christianity: the first, in the *Vindication* of 1779, the second in draft 'E' of the *Memoirs*, completed on 2 March 1791. The image he created of himself is in each case different. In the *Vindication*, Gibbon is a Lear of the world of historiography, more sinned against than sinning:

When I delivered to the world the First Volume of an important History, in which I had been obliged to connect the progress of Christianity with

---

[14] *Letters*, II, p. 100.
[15] Even as late as June 1776 Gibbon was unsure about the identities of those who were to oppose him. On 6 June he wrote to Holroyd that 'I now understand from pretty good authority that Dr Porteous the friend and chaplain of St Secker is actually sharpening his goosequill against the last two Chapters' (*Letters*, vol. II, p. 111). Porteous never published an attack on Gibbon, although Travis' *Letters* were dedicated to Porteous, and it may be that the hand of the Bishop of Chester guided the pen of his Archdeacon.
[16] *Letters*, vol. II, p. 110.
[17] Gibbon's revisions to the second, third and fourth editions of the *Decline and fall* produced several thousand variants. Many of these are very small, and in general Gibbon restricted his revisions so that in virtually all cases the pagination, and very often the lineation, of the text could be preserved. This was clearly convenient for the compositor setting up the new edition; it may be that Strahan and Cadell requested Gibbon so to restrict his revisions.

the civil state and revolutions of the Roman Empire, I could not be ignorant that the result of my inquiries might offend the interest of some and the opinions of others. If the whole work was favourably received by the Public, I had the more reason to expect that this obnoxious part would provoke the zeal of those who consider themselves as the Watchmen of the Holy City. These expectations were not disappointed . . . [18]

'I could not be ignorant': Gibbon admitted here what he would later deny, namely that he was aware that he ran the risk of offending those he mockingly called 'the Watchmen of the Holy City'. In the *Vindication* he professed to be unperturbed by the 'ordinary, and indeed obsolete charges of impious principles'.[19] He had been stung to reply only because Davis had attempted 'the ruin of my moral and literary character'.[20] Composing his *Memoirs* twelve years later, however, Gibbon retouched this self-portrait. The outcry of the orthodox was now entirely unforeseen by the innocent historian: 'I had likewise flattered myself that an age of light and liberty would receive, without scandal, an enquiry into the *human* causes of the progress and establishment of Christianity.' In addition, the pose of necessity struck in the *Vindication* ('I had been obliged to connect . . . ') was in the *Memoirs* moderated into an admission that the author had enjoyed scope for a certain discretion. The subject might have received a different and more emollient handling:

Had I believed that the majority of English readers were so fondly attached even to the name and shadow of Christianity, had I foreseen that the pious, the timid, and the prudent would feel, or affect to feel, with such exquisite sensibility, I might perhaps have softened the two invidious Chapters, which would create many enemies and conciliate few friends.[21]

Gone, too, was the proud and unshaken defiance of the *Vindication*. In the *Memoirs*, Gibbon explained the sequence of his emotions differently:

Let me frankly own that I was startled at the first vollies of this Ecclesiastical ordnance; but as soon as I found that this empty noise was

---

[18] *English essays*, p. 232. Cf. Apthorp, *Letters on the prevalence of Christianity*, p. vi: 'the Jewish and Christian revelations were *providentially* connected with the great revolutions in civil history' in order that their proofs should be written into the historical record without 'doubt, mistake, or ambiguity' (my emphasis).

[19] *English essays*, p. 233.

[20] *Ibid.*, p. 234.   [21] *Autobiographies*, pp. 311, 316.

mischievous only in the intention, my fear was converted to indignation, and every feeling of indignation or curiosity has long since subsided in pure and placid indifference.[22]

The findings of collation corroborate some of these assertions (although I will be very slow to believe that Gibbon composed his *Memoirs* in a mood of 'pure and placid indifference' to his reputation for irreligion). However, it is difficult to see how the heroic figure of the *Vindication* and the inadvertent figure of the *Memoirs* can both be true; indeed, Gibbon's revisions show them both to be in some measure false. The *Vindication* is misleading in its suggestion that Gibbon stoically endured the assaults of his detractors until his character as a gentleman was challenged: the revisions to the second and third editions show him anticipating, eluding and finally rebutting his adversaries on points of religious history. For their part, the *Memoirs* are less than candid in their suggestion that the unaware historian was overtaken by a controversy the possibility of which had not occurred to him: the revisions to the second edition, made before any attack had been published, show that Gibbon possessed a very accurate sense of which areas of his history would be offensive, and why.

As we have seen, Gibbon probably spent the months of April and May 1776 in revising the text of his first volume for its second edition.[23] The character of the changes he made in chapters 15 and 16 can be suggested if we look first at an amendment he made in the text of chapter 8, the chapter devoted to the Persians.[24] In the course of that chapter, Gibbon paid close attention to the refashioning of the religion of Zoroaster into a civil religion at the hands of Artaxerxes, the great founder of the dynasty of the Sassanides. The theology of the Magian religion was clarified on the basis of the intoxicated vision of 'Erdaviraph, a young but holy prelate'; its church government was remodelled into a regular hierarchy; and rival sects or religions were methodically

---

[22] *Ibid.*, p. 319. Cf. also: 'The freedom of my writings has, indeed, provoked an implacable tribe; but as I was safe from the stings, I was soon accustomed to the buzzing of the hornets' (*Autobiographies*, p. 346).

[23] *Letters*, II, p. 110. Norton suggested that the third edition of 1777 appeared to be more heavily revised than the second of 1776 (Norton, *Bibliography*, p. 43). Collation reveals that in fact the text of the *Decline and fall* was more substantially revised in 1776.

[24] This variant is not noted by Bury.

suppressed.[25] This persecution of heterodoxy was described as follows in the first edition:

The majesty of Ormusd [the embodiment of the principle of good in the Magian religion], who was jealous of a rival, was seconded by the despotism of Artaxerxes, who could not suffer a rebel; and with the assistance of what his prelates no doubt called wholesome severities, the schismatics within his vast empire were soon reduced to the inconsiderable number of eighty thousand.[26]

In the second edition, Gibbon made a small but significant deletion: 'The majesty of Ormusd, who was jealous of a rival, was seconded by the despotism of Artaxerxes, who could not suffer a rebel; and the schismatics within his vast empire were soon reduced to the inconsiderable number of eighty thousand.'[27] By removing the incidental blow aimed at the prelates of Zoroastrianism ('with the assistance of what his prelates no doubt called wholesome severities'), Gibbon muted the deistical character of the passage, reducing it almost to a mere statement of fact. It had been one of the principal tenets of the late seventeenth- and early eighteenth-century freethinkers that priestcraft might arise in any religion, and that, wherever it arose, it would align itself with political despotism, as it had done here in Persia. Such a sentiment lay behind the passage Gibbon deleted when preparing his second edition. Moreover, when the deleted phrase was taken together with the echo of the jealous God of the Old Testament in the statement that Ormusd was 'jealous of a rival', the Magian clergy appeared for a moment to be disturbingly close to the Christian priesthood. The intention which motivated the deletion of the phrase which detonated that injurious potential – an intention of removing language which suggested proximity to writers such as Collins, Toland and Tindal – was dominant also in Gibbon's revisions to chapters 15 and 16.

The substantive changes Gibbon introduced into these chapters

---

25 *Decline and fall*, I, p. 240. When given in this form, quotations from volume I of the *Decline and fall* cite the text of the third edition and refer to the pagination of the third and subsequent editions (with the notes at the foot of the page). The abbreviations *Decline and fall 1*, *Decline and fall 2* and *Decline and fall 3* are used to refer to the first, second and third editions respectively of volume I of the *Decline and fall*. References to later volumes of the history are in all cases to the first editions.

26 *Decline and fall 1*, p. 208.

27 *Decline and fall 2*, p. 208.

for the second edition were of three kinds: firstly, the adducing of fresh evidence in support of positions or contentions which, in the knowledge of imminent attack, appeared unguarded; secondly, the elimination of sceptical turns of phrase which were inessential to the central lines of argument; lastly, the excision of deistical language. Common to all these three kinds of revision, however, was the intention of confusing or obscuring the affiliations which existed between the topics, language and arguments of the *Decline and fall*, and those perceived to be typical of deism and freethought.

The first kind of revision can be most promptly dealt with. The branding of the Christian Jews with the 'contemptuous epithet of Ebionites' is supported in the footnotes of the first edition with nothing more than a scoff at a mistaken etymology: 'Some writers have been pleased to create an Ebion, the imaginary author of their sect and name. But we can more safely rely on the learned Eusebius than on the vehement Tertullian, or the credulous Epiphanius.'[28] In the second edition, the note was amplified by the addition of the following: 'According to Le Clerc, the Hebrew word *Ebjonim* may be translated into Latin by that of *Pauperes*. See Hist. Ecclesiast. p. 477.'[29] When Gibbon came to look again at this footnote in the spring of 1776, his allegation that 'Ebionite' was a term of contempt seemed to require some justification: without such justification, that passage and its note ran the risk of seeming an instance of that scorn for the Jews which freethinkers and deists such as Shaftesbury and Bolingbroke had been frequently reproached.

There were moments, then, when Gibbon brought forward corroborating authorities to prevent a point being read as simply his surrendering to a free-thinking and irreverent disposition. There were also moments, however, when Gibbon apparently realized that the wording he had used was pointlessly offensive. In these instances, he was prepared to re-phrase. In the first edition, when relating the views of the early Christians on chastity, he wrote that: 'It was their favourite opinion, that if Adam had preserved his obedience to the Creator, he would have lived and died in a state of virgin purity . . . '[30] In the second edition, 'lived and died' became 'lived for ever'.[31] The revision accommodated the *Decline and fall* to the orthodox Christian belief that man's disobedience had brought

---

[28] *Decline and fall 1*, p. lxvii n. 22.   [29] *Decline and fall 2*, pp. lxvi–lxvii n. 22.
[30] *Decline and fall 1*, p. 484.   [31] *Decline and fall 2*, p. 484.

death into the world. The implication in the text of the first edition that Adam would have died even had he remained in a state of innocence could have seemed a step towards the mortalist materialism with which freethinkers were routinely charged.[32]

The third kind of revision Gibbon made for the second edition involved the deletion of language drawn from the vocabulary of deism. Discussing the doctrine of the immortality of the soul in chapter 15, and remarking that it was more prevalent among barbarians than amongst the pagans of Greece and Rome, Gibbon noted that 'since we cannot attribute such a difference to the superior knowledge of the barbarians, we must ascribe it to the influence of an established priesthood, which employed the motives of virtue as the instrument of ambition'.[33] To this, in the first edition, he appended a note: 'The Druids borrowed sums of money on bonds made payable to the creditor in the other world. The success of such a trade is one of the strongest instances of sacerdotal art and popular credulity.'[34] The text, with its allusion to an established priesthood using virtue as the instrument of ambition, was already tinctured with deism. The footnote, however, strengthened that colouring into a virtual statement of allegiance: 'sacerdotal art' and 'popular credulity' were phrases redolent of writers such as Blount, Toland and Tindal, which announced a hostility towards the power exerted by priests in society. In the second edition, the footnote was completely rewritten:

If we confine ourselves to the Gauls, we may observe, that they entrusted, not only their lives, but even their money, to the security of another world. Vetus ille mos Gallorum occurrit (says Valerius Maximus, I. ii. c. 6. p. 10.), quos memoria proditur est, pecunias mutuas, quæ his apud inferos redderentur, dare solitos. The same custom is more darkly insinuated by Mela, I. iii. c. 2. It is almost needless to add, that the profits of trade hold a just proportion to the credit of the merchant, and that the Druids derived from their holy profession a character of responsibility, which could scarcely be claimed by any other order of men.[35]

---

[32] See, for instance, Richard Bentley, *Remarks upon a late discourse of free-thinking* (London, 1713), p. 14. Whitaker apparently accused Gibbon of favouring suicide: Patricia B. Craddock, *Edward Gibbon, luminous historian, 1772–1794* (Baltimore, 1989), p. 81.

[33] *Decline and fall*, I, p. 559.

[34] *Decline and fall* I, pp. lxviii–lxix n. 55. This detail was noted, and dismissed as 'but a silly story', by Henry Taylor, *Thoughts on the nature of the Grand Apostasy* (London, 1781), p. 43.

[35] *Decline and fall* 2, pp. lxviii–lxix n. 55.

The inclusion of references and quotation immediately tilted the balance of the note away from polemic and towards historical scholarship, while the greater elaborateness of the syntax, and the superior politeness of the language, in which Gibbon first related the institution of these loans, and then commented on them, occluded his allegiances. Whereas in the first edition a hint of deism in the text was corroborated and amplified in the note, in the second edition the note moved away from the language and polemical style of the deists, thereby neutralizing the deistical flavour of the text. The note in the second edition is, of course, 'ironic', and it would be no difficult task to unpick, for instance, the hostile implications of the comparison between the priest and the merchant. But here, as it also did at times elsewhere, Gibbon's irony arose as the defensive complication of a deistical impulse which had been at first more nakedly expressed.

There is, then, a striking degree of congruence which unifies the detailed changes Gibbon made to chapters 15 and 16 for the second edition. In the first edition Gibbon had in places employed vocabulary and forms of expression which could be read as signs of affiliation to the band of deists, freethinkers and esprits forts who had been attacked by the orthodox since the early years of the century as enemies to established and revealed religion. In the second edition, some of those signs were made ambiguous, or effaced. Let us be clear about the extent of these revisions. There was no profound re-modelling of these two chapters. By no means all the deistical or sceptical language was removed, and Gibbon's argument was not in the least affected. Moreover, if Gibbon's purpose in revising was that of conciliation, then he failed abjectly. For example, Henry Davis, Gibbon's most bitter antagonist, was prompted to enter the lists after reading this second, revised, edition.[36] But if Gibbon did not intend to remove the occasion of offence, why did he (who was by temperament so averse to the minutiae of correction and revisal) take trouble over these details of expression?[37] We know that Gibbon at one point entertained the

---

[36] In his A reply to Mr. Gibbon's Vindication (London, 1779), p. 14, Henry Davis informed his reader that 'my references answer to the second edition of Mr. Gibbon's History'. In his An examination of the fifteenth and sixteenth chapters of Mr. Gibbon's History ... (London, 1778), p. 142, however, he referred to the 'three several editions of Mr. G.'s history'.

[37] In the Vindication, Gibbon revealed that he did not correct his own proofs (English essays, p. 239).

radical notion of suppressing chapters 15 and 16 altogether, and was prevented from doing so only by Holroyd's firm advice neither to remove nor to alter.[38] If Gibbon nerved himself to let the chapters remain, collation shows that he was unable to follow Holroyd's advice in full and resist the temptation to draw back where on reflection he felt he had presented his enemies with too broad a target. In a letter to his stepmother of October 1776, when the attacks had just begun to be published, Gibbon wrote that he initially feared he would be 'hurt' by them. The revisions embodied in the second edition confirm and substantiate that fear of damage.[39]

The tone of Gibbon's comments on his opponents underwent a marked change once the attacks appeared in print, and Gibbon could assess the true gravity of the threat they posed. During the period of suspense, in which he revised for the second edition, he wrote of the coming replies with flaunted playfulness and ostentatious unconcern:

I now understand from pretty good authority that Dr Porteous the friend and chaplain of St Secker is actually sharpening his goosequill against the two last Chapters.

At present *nought* but expectation. The attack on me is begun, an anonymous eighteen penny pamphlet, which will get the author more Glory in *the next World than in* this. The Heavy troops, Watson and another are on their march.

With regard to another great object of hostilities [that is to say, in addition to the war with the American colonies], *myself*, the attack has been already begun by an anonymous Pamphleteer but the heavy artillery of Dr Watson and another adversary are not yet brought into the field.[40]

However, once Gibbon had read the attacks and judged their quality, his tone was inflected into hard accents. When he alluded to his opponents in a series of letters written in November 1776, after he had read the replies of Chelsum and Watson, he did so with a contempt unadorned by imagination or metaphor:

---

[38] MS note in interleaved copy of *Miscellaneous works*, Yale University, Beinecke Library, MS vault, section 10, drawer 3, section B, B 11i. The French translation of volume I of the *Decline and fall* appeared without chapters 15 and 16, and in his letters to Suard Gibbon made plain his willingness to make any cuts in this area of the work which Suard felt necessary in order to avoid offending the authorities (*Letters*, vol. II, pp. 122–3 and 132: Norton, *Bibliography*, pp. 123–6).

[39] *Letters*, vol. II, p. 118.

[40] *Ibid.*, vol. II, pp. 111, 117, 118.

An anonymous pamphlet and Dr Watson out against me: both (in my opinion) feeble; the former very illiberal, the latter uncommonly genteel.

By this time Mylady may see that I have not much reason to fear my antagonists.

Two answers (which you have perhaps seen) one from Mr Chelsham [sic] of Oxford the other from Dr Watson of Cambridge, are already born and I believe the former is choleric the latter civil, and both too dull to deserve your notice; three or four more are expected; but I believe none of them will divert me from the prosecution of the second Volume . . . [41]

When the play of fancy is succeeded by simple and unemotional disregard, it is tempting to read the earlier embellishment as a sign of agitation, and the posture of insouciance as the guise of anxiety.

The different character of the revisions Gibbon made to chapters 15 and 16 for the third edition confirms this reading of his letters. The third edition was in press in March 1777, and was published in May, although Cadell had envisaged the need for a third edition as far back as May 1776.[42] The second edition was still being advertised for sale in November 1776, and so was not by then exhausted.[43] Strahan and Cadell required a little over two months to reset, print and assemble a volume of this size.[44] If we assume that Gibbon did not settle down to the work of revision until he knew that the third edition was definitely required, we can therefore suppose that he was working on the emendations for the third edition between late November 1776 and February 1777 (he was of course at the same time working on the second volume of the history).[45] The revisions for the third edition were probably begun, then, at just the time when Gibbon's apprehension of his adversaries had petrified into scorn.

The different moods in which Gibbon emended for the second and third editions, and the different purposes these two phases of revisal served, are caught in the variants for a single footnote to chapter 16. Gibbon was in no doubt that the notorious passage in

---

[41] *Ibid.*, vol. II, pp. 120, 121, 129.
[42] Third edition in press: letter to Dorothea Gibbon of 29 March 1777 (*Letters*, vol. II, p. 141). Date of publication: Norton, *Bibliography*, p. 43. First envisaged: letter to Deyverdun of 7 May 1776 (*Letters*, vol. II, p. 105).
[43] Norton, *Bibliography*, p. 43.
[44] This was the time required for the second edition (Norton, *Bibliography*, p. 42). The third edition may conceivably have taken slightly longer because of the transferral of the notes from the end of the volume to the foot of the page.
[45] Norton, *Bibliography*, p. 43 n. 7.

Josephus which referred to Jesus was a later interpolation. In the first edition, he expressed his disbelief as follows:

The passage concerning Jesus Christ, which was inserted into the text of Josephus, between the time of Origen and that of Eusebius, may furnish an example of no vulgar forgery. The accomplishment of the prophecies, the virtues, miracles, and resurrection of Jesus, are fairly related. Josephus acknowledges that he was the Messiah, and hesitates whether he should call him a man.[46]

In the second edition, 'distinctly' was substituted for 'fairly'.[47] A personal judgment was deleted, and its place was taken by a more objective, and to that extent more impersonal, term. It is a revision entirely of a piece with that withdrawal from positions of exposure, which we have identified as the dominant characteristic of the second edition. Once again, Gibbon proved to have a shrewd eye for what his enemies would be unable to digest. Francis Eyre (reading Gibbon in the second edition) devoted fourteen pages of his *A few remarks on the 'History of the decline and fall'* to an elaborate defence of the authenticity of this passage of Josephus, designed to show 'how weak is the sophistry of the incredulous.'[48] William Salisbury, whose *A history of the establishment of Christianity* was published in 1776 and to whom Gibbon may therefore be responding in revisions made in this passage for the third edition, also championed the integrity of Josephus' text at length.[49] In that third edition Gibbon allowed the correction of 'fairly' to 'distinctly' to stand, but expanded the note to almost twice its size by adding more authorities in support of his position:

If any doubt can still remain concerning this celebrated passage, the reader may examine the pointed objections of Le Fevre (Havercamp. Joseph. tom. ii. p. 267–273.), the laboured answers of Daubuz (p. 187–232.), and the masterly reply (Bibliotheque Ancienne et Moderne, tom. vii. p. 237–288.) of an anonymous critic, whom I believe to have been the learned Abbè de Longuerue.[50]

---

[46] *Decline and fall 1*, p. lxxviii n. 35.
[47] *Decline and fall 2*, p. lxxviii n. 35.
[48] Francis Eyre, *A few remarks on the 'History of the Decline and Fall'* (London, 1778), pp. 48–61; quotation from p. 61.
[49] Salisbury, *A history of the establishment of Christianity*, pp. 217–29. There was apparently no copy of Salisbury's work in Gibbon's library.
[50] *Decline and fall 3*, p. 639 n. 36. Gibbon hardly ever revised on a second occasion a passage he had previously revised, or undid an earlier revision.

The tone of this addition is one of impatient contempt ('if any doubt can *still* remain'); and the parade of authorities is a rhetorically crushing blow which seems to admit of no reply (the reservation of the identity of the clerical author of the decisive and dismissive contribution to the debate is a particularly effective piece of timing, which confirms the conjecture of a recent scholar that the footnote in Enlightenment historiography was as much an instrument of polemic as of scholarship).[51] The defiance of criticism Gibbon showed in this revision was the ruling passion of the corrections he made for the third edition.[52]

In two instances, Gibbon silently acknowledged that his opponents had scored palpable, if not mortal, hits. In the first two editions, Gibbon had elaborated on the pagan disregard for the miracles of Christianity: 'The lame walked, the blind saw, the sick were healed, the dead were raised, dæmons were expelled, and the laws of Nature were perpetually suspended for the benefit of the church'.[53] Richard Watson, whose *An apology for Christianity* Gibbon censured as polite but feeble, had queried the adverb 'perpetually'.[54] Nothing of substance to Gibbon's argument depended on the point (although it does confirm what was also indicated by the revisions to the second edition, namely that Gibbon had been betrayed into exaggerated expression in this section of the history). In the third edition, therefore, Gibbon silently

---

[51] Champion, *The pillars of priestcraft shaken*, p. 30.

[52] The third edition allowed Gibbon in one respect greater scope for revisal. The surprisingly acceptable appearance made by putting the notes at the foot of the page, as had been done in the pirated Dublin edition, reconciled Gibbon to the same re-organization of the official editions (*Letters*, vol. II, p. 116). In his *Memoirs*, he said that he had often regretted his compliance (*Autobiographies*, p. 339 n. 64). But the complete repagination of the volume clearly meant that the work of the compositor would now, and now only, be not greatly increased by the introduction of new material. Gibbon nevertheless restricted his revisals of the text so as to permit the retention of most of the lineation of the first two editions, thereby relieving the compositor of one consideration. However, he did take advantage of the opportunity to introduce new footnotes; inserted at the moment of transition from endnotes to footnotes, they were invisible to the merely scanning eye. In his letters Gibbon seems always to have under-represented the extent of his revisions. In the *Memoirs*, as part of the fascinating myth of composition he there constructed, he contrived to suggest that, in careless facility, he eschewed revision altogether (*Autobiographies*, pp. 333, 334), while at other moments laying claim to laborious re-writing (*Autobiographies*, p. 308 (chapters 15 and 16) and pp. 315–16 (the Age of Constantine)).

[53] *Decline and fall 1* and *Decline and fall 2*, p. 518.

[54] Richard Watson, *An apology for Christianity, in a series of letters addressed to Edward Gibbon, Esq.* (Cambridge, 1776), pp. 147–8.

corrected 'perpetually suspended' to 'frequently suspended'.[55] A more substantial concession was made in connection with the gift of tongues, one of the miraculous powers claimed by the apostles and their first disciples. In the first two editions, Gibbon implicitly questioned the reality of this miracle, by noting that this power had not always been granted to those whose need of it was greatest: 'The knowledge of foreign languages was frequently communicated to the contemporaries of Irenæus, though Irenæus himself was left to struggle with the difficulties of a barbarous dialect whilst he preached the gospel to the natives of Gaul.'[56] This was a passage which Chelsum had attacked, on the grounds that Gibbon had lifted a point from Middleton's *Free enquiry*, and that the observation in any event was based on a misreading of Irenaeus: 'Our author's too fond attachment to Dr. Middleton, appears to have betrayed him into one very remarkable misrepresentation.'[57] In the third edition, Gibbon left the text untouched, but introduced a new footnote which materially complicated his own implicit position towards this alleged miracle, and which demands to be understood in relation to the accusation of being merely Middleton's pupil in religious scepticism: 'Irenæus adv. Hæres. Proem. p. 3. Dr. Middleton (Free Enquiry, p. 96, &c.) observes, that as this pretension of all others was the most difficult to support by art, it was the soonest given up. The observation suits his hypothesis.'[58] Gibbon was unmistakably putting distance between himself and Middleton; by reflecting critically on Middleton's hostile 'observation' about the gift of tongues, he implied that his own (unspoken) views were different. It is difficult to read this as anything but Gibbon responding to Chelsum's stricture by assuming a position which might be understood (and thus attacked) less easily. Was Gibbon already, in however private and tentative a fashion,

---

[55] *Decline and fall 3*, p. 618.
[56] *Decline and fall 1* and *Decline and fall 2*, p. 475.
[57] James Chelsum, *Remarks on the two last chapters of Mr. Gibbon's History* (London, 1776), p. 91 n. 1. Chelsum was followed by Smyth Loftus, *A reply to the reasonings of Mr. Gibbon* (Dublin, 1777), p. 116 (ref. to the second edition of 1778); Eyre, *A few remarks*, p. 19, and Davis, *An examination*, pp. 46–7. Middleton himself seems to have been following Shaftesbury; see John Brown, *Essays on the characteristics of the earl of Shaftesbury* (London, 1751), p. 297. The gift of tongues was plainly perceived by the 1770s to be one of the familiar topics of religious scepticism. The charge of being but an echo of Middleton is frequently made by Gibbon's enemies, and was in their eyes one of the clearest indications of his deistical sympathies.
[58] *Decline and fall 3*, p. 567 n. 74.

thinking about the *Vindication?*[59] If so, the insertion of this note marked a retreat to safer ground from which an attack might later be launched.

Elsewhere, the revisions to the third edition show Gibbon going onto the offensive. An instance of Gibbon's unleashing the full force of his scholarly armament only in the third edition can be seen in the textual history of another passage in which he touched upon one of the topics of deism, that of the character of the Jewish nation. The propensity of the Jews to idolatry during the age of miracles had been a favourite subject for the freethinkers, because the disparity between the behaviour of the Jews and their preternatural environment was a contradiction which called into question the historical accuracy of the Old Testament. In the first two editions, Gibbon had polished this familiar subject into an elegant form:

> The contemporaries of Moses and Joshua had beheld with careless indifference the most amazing miracles. Under the pressure of every calamity, the belief of those miracles has preserved the Jews of a later period from the universal contagion of idolatry; and in contradiction to every known principle of the human mind, that singular people seems to have yielded a stronger and more ready assent to the traditions of their remote ancestors, than to the evidence of their own senses.[60]

The text of this passage remained unchanged for the third edition and thereafter. It was sufficiently reminiscent of the deistical writing of the earlier part of the century for Joseph Milner (who read Gibbon's first volume in the second edition) to condemn it with mock uncertainty: 'whether it was copied from Lord Bolingbroke I must not presume to say'.[61] But for the third edition Gibbon added a note which honed the rusty weapon of the deists, blunted and ineffective from overuse, to a new edge: '"How long will this people provoke me? and how long will it be ere they *believe* me, for all the *signs* which I have shewn among them?" (*Numbers* xiv. 11). It would be easy, but it would be unbecoming, to justify the complaint of the Deity from the whole tenor of the Mosaic

---

[59] In a letter to Chelsum of 20 February 1778, Gibbon implied that he still had no intention of replying publicly to his critics: 'I must not suffer myself to be diverted from the prosecution of an important work, by the invidious task of controversy, and recrimination' (*Letters*, vol. II, p. 173).

[60] *Decline and fall 1* and *Decline and fall 2*, p. 452.

[61] Milner, *Gibbon's account of Christianity considered*, p. 5.

history.'[62] This is one of the few references to the text of the Bible in chapter 15; and it is one which, in this context, jeopardizes the reliability of the scriptures. Far from being copied out of 'that haughty infidel' Lord Bolingbroke, Gibbon could have retorted to Milner that the observation was nothing more than a deferential expansion of the words of God Himself.[63] It is this surprisingly respectable genealogy for the reflection of the freethinkers and deists which Gibbon plants, like a mine, at the foot of his page, and which makes the assumption of decorum and dignity in the refusal to engage in the 'unbecoming' business of dragging into the light all the support for this view of Jewish history contained in the 'Mosaic history' so much more deep than the play-acting it may at first seem to be.

Gibbon's footnotes in the third edition, then, were the vehicle of a new combativeness. However, for this edition he also revised the wording of his main text at a number of points, in a way which complemented, without duplicating, the more pugnacious pose he now struck at the foot of the page. As we have seen, for the second edition Gibbon had muted or removed language which, on reflection, seemed too plainly characteristic of deism or free-thinking. Those emendations were not undone for the third edition.[64] But we find him elsewhere refining and enhancing the style of passages pregnant with harm for Christianity. The hallmark of Gibbonian irony – a sustained pressure of insinuation poised on the threshold of perceptibility – seems in part to have been the product of this process of revision.[65]

An example occurs in the passage where Gibbon describes the variety, looseness and uncertainty of the religious sentiments of the polytheists. Having suggested that 'as long as their adoration was successively prostituted to a thousand deities, it was scarcely possible that their hearts could be susceptible of a very sincere or lively passion for any of them', Gibbon then turned to the

---

[62] *Decline and fall 3*, p. 539 n. 10.
[63] Milner, *Gibbon's account of Christianity considered*, p. 19.
[64] It is a striking feature of Gibbon's successive revisals of volume I that individual revisions, once made, are almost never subsequently altered. This suggests that Gibbon prepared the next edition from a copy of the previous edition. It may also suggest that he kept no separate record of revisions made for any particular edition.
[65] A happy confirmation of Gibbon's maxim on style, that 'the choice and command of language is the fruit of exercise' (*Autobiographies*, p. 308).

implications of this for the advent of Christianity and the appeal of the new religion to men.[66] In the first two editions, he implied that Christianity had filled the vacancy caused by the failure of polytheism: 'When Christianity appeared in the world, even these faint and imperfect impressions [the religious feelings inspired by polytheism] had been insensibly obliterated.'[67] In the third edition, Gibbon re-wrote the end of that sentence in such a way that a different relation between Christianity and paganism was implied: 'When Christianity appeared in the world, even these faint and imperfect impressions had lost much of their original power.'[68] In 1777, not only was paganism more durable (in that, instead of being 'obliterated' it still maintained a presence, albeit reduced, in the minds of men); Christianity too was set in a new light, in that the reinvigoration of men's religious lives which the new faith brought about now seemed, not so much a replacement for the exhausted and erased religious sentiments of paganism, but a refreshment of them. The revised wording of the third edition thus touched on the topic, made notorious earlier in the century by Middleton's *Letter from Rome* (1729), of the evident and scandalous continuities between paganism and Christianity. Gibbon would return to this subject openly in chapter 28, in which he recounted the simultaneous ruin of paganism, and introduction of the worship of saints and relics among the Christians. It is unlikely that he had reached this stage of the composition of the second instalment of 1781 when revising for the third edition of volume I: he had begun work on volumes II and III only five months or so earlier, in June 1776.[69] But it may be that he had planned that far ahead, and that the subject was for that reason in his mind.

This greater willingness to allow his hostility towards Christianity (considered as a sequence of historical institutions, if not as a creed) to make itself felt can also be seen in the way Gibbon re-wrote a sentence towards the end of chapter 16 in which he looked forward to one of the important topics of his second volume, the conversion of Constantine and the establishment of Christianity as the religion of the Empire. In the first and second editions, we read: 'The motives of his [Constantine's] conversion, as

[66] *Decline and fall*, I, p. 601.   [67] *Decline and fall 1* and *Decline and fall 2*, p. 503.
[68] *Decline and fall 3*, p. 601.
[69] Letter to Holroyd of 29 June 1776 (*Letters*, vol. II, p. 112).

they may variously be deduced from faith, from virtue, from policy, or from remorse, . . . will form a very interesting and important chapter in the second volume of this history.'[70] The various possible motives for Constantine's conversion which Gibbon listed here form a descending scale of integrity, stretching from the pure and best motive of religious faith; passing through its diminished (because secular) successor, virtue; moving on to that baser shadow of virtue which is policy (which yet might be partially redeemed if its concern is for the welfare of the empire's inhabitants as a whole, rather than merely the security or comfort of the emperor); and concluding in the moral basement of remorse, the craven and unworthy corruption of repentance. Gibbon clearly entertained a number of different explanations of Constantine's conduct, some of them compatible with the traditions of the Church, others at variance with those traditions. But to list the motives in this form of a moral spectrum put no pressure on the reader to choose one or other, or any combination of them, as the approved explanation; for the reason that this arrangement of possible motives seemed not to be the result of authorial choice, but rather to be determined by an internal principle of descending integrity. In the third edition, however, the motives were revised and re-ordered: 'The motives of his conversion, as they may variously be deduced from benevolence, from policy, from conviction, or from remorse; . . . will form a very interesting and important chapter in the second volume of this history.'[71] 'Faith' and 'virtue' have disappeared, to be replaced by an amiable but lesser moral strength, 'benevolence' (lesser, because an involuntary disposition rather than the result of conscious decision) and a neutral psychological motive, 'conviction' (which might be conviction to the good or to the bad). The top end of the range of possibility has thus been markedly diminished. But it is the revised arrangement of these four possibilities in the third edition which suggests to the reader that the less complimentary possibilities are the more likely. They now form not a continuous spectrum, but two doublets – benevolence/policy, conviction/remorse – in which the second is a base alternative to the first, and in which, furthermore, first and second seem to be related as reputation and reality. Gibbon was almost certainly composing and revising the chapters on Constantine when preparing the third

---

[70] *Decline and fall 1* and *Decline and fall 2*, p. 576.   [71] *Decline and fall 3*, pp. 691–2.

edition of volume I for the press.[72] This revision is entirely in keeping with the account of Constantine's conversion Gibbon would eventually publish in 1781.[73] The direction of influence, however, was conceivably from the revision to the first volume, to the work in progress on the second volume. It may be that the renewed confidence Gibbon felt in tackling subjects of religious controversy in late 1776 and early 1777, the first expressions of which were the intransigent revisions to the third edition of volume I, emboldened him to treat Constantine with the severity so evident in the first four chapters of the second volume.

The narrative of the process of revisal Gibbon undertook when preparing the second and third editions of the first volume of the *Decline and fall* is now clear. In the period of anticipation before any of the attacks on his supposed irreligion were published, Gibbon made in his second edition a number of small adjustments to his wording, all of which served to obscure or reduce the deistical character of his writing. Once the attacks had begun to appear, and Gibbon had found then unintimidating, the printing of the third edition became an opportunity for him to return to the conflict and press home his attack on the Christian Church by reinforcing a number of his footnotes, and by honing his style. The separate stages of revisal thus distinguished, and their opposed tendencies thus established, the further question arises of what our enhanced understanding of this process of revisal allows us to deduce more broadly about Gibbon's handling of religion in his first volume.

J. G. A. Pocock, meditating upon the *Decline and fall* within a series of overlapping contexts formed by the political, sociological and religious thought of the European Enlightenments, has formed the view that chapters 15 and 16 are unrepresentative of Gibbon's deepest concerns on the subject of religion: 'they are preliminary to Gibbon's main historical argument and . . . the controversy about them was in a sense premature'.[74] Gibbon's revisions to these chapters corroborate the speculations of the historian of ideas.

---

[72] These chapters cost him a great deal of trouble, if the *Memoirs* are to be believed (*Autobiographies*, pp. 315–16). Their composition and revision might therefore very probably have occupied Gibbon for the better part of a year after they were begun in June 1776 (*Letters*, vol. II, p. 112).

[73] See chapter 20 (*Decline and fall*, II, pp. 179–230).

[74] J. G. A. Pocock, 'Edward Gibbon in history: aspects of the text in his *The history of the decline and fall of the Roman Empire*', *The Tanner Lectures on Human Values* (Salt Lake City, 1990), p. 339.

We know that Gibbon felt these two chapters to be expendable. That is the clear indication of Holroyd's unpublished note to the *Memoirs*, stating that Gibbon retained them in the second and later editions of volume I only at his insistence. It is also implied by Gibbon's frequent assurances to his French translator, Suard, that he will make any cuts in these chapters Suard considers necessary to avoid giving offence; and also by the eventual appearance of the French translation of volume I minus the two last chapters.[75] Gibbon even suggested, in a letter to Suzanne Necker, that he had blundered with chapters 15 and 16: 'I myself have been misguided enough ["assez mal avisé"] to arouse the hatred of a powerful and numerous order of men, who have ever considered the forgiveness of injuries to be a point of doctrine rather than a principle of conduct.'[76] The suspicions of Henry Davis and East Apthorp, that the first fourteen chapters were nothing but the pretext for Gibbon's attack upon Christianity, and served but to introduce chapters 15 and 16 'with a better grace, and more decent appearance', can therefore safely be dismissed.[77]

But, at the same time, Gibbon also knew that the scandal these chapters had stimulated had, in some quarters, done him no harm. Calming his stepmother's fears that his reputation as an enemy to Christianity would cause him to be arrested when he visited France in 1777, Gibbon reassured her that 'the recent fame of my book is perhaps the circumstance which will introduce me [in Paris] with the most favour and eclat'.[78] And here we should touch once more upon our point of departure, the primacy of the desire for fame amongst Gibbon's motives as an historian. His subject he knew to be important, but he equally knew that success or failure depended more on the adroitness of the treatment than the intrinsic merits of the subject: 'the subject is curious and never yet treated as it deserves . . . Should the attempt fail, it must be by the fault of the execution.'[79] 'Execution' covers many aspects of the preparation

---

[75] Letters to Suard; *Letters*, vol. II, pp. 122–3, 132: publication of French translation, Norton, *Bibliography*, pp. 123–6.

[76] 'Moi-même j'ai été assez mal avisé pour encourir la haine d'un ordre puissant et nombreux qui a toujours considéré le pardon des injures comme un dogme plutôt qu'un précepte' (*Letters*, vol. II, p. 263).

[77] Davis, *An examination*, pp. i, 141; Apthorp, *Letters on the prevalence of Christianity*, p. 16.

[78] *Letters*, vol. II, p. 144.

[79] *Ibid.*, p. 75.

and composition of a work; scholarly foundations, of course, and lucidity of organization and style. It might equally comprise other attractions calculated to procure for the work favourable and plentiful notice. John Brown, that well-known analyst of mid-eighteenth-century mores, believed that 'no Allurements could engage the *fashionable* infidel World to travel through a large Quarto' – and the first volume of the *Decline and fall* is certainly that.[80]

My own conjecture runs as follows. When preparing volume I for first publication Gibbon's desire for literary celebrity led him to lace chapters 15 and 16 with some sophisticated, but inessential, irreligious and deistical language; by means of this allurement the fashionable infidel world might be persuaded to traverse his large quarto.[81] In the event, Gibbon underestimated the appeal of his subject in even those quarters apparently the most resistant to historical scholarship; his book sold like a sixpenny pamphlet on the news of the day.[82] Nor was that his only error. Far from being the attraction he intended, the deistical trimmings of the last two chapters had caused the only discordant notes in the paeans of admiration the *Decline and fall* aroused in the spring of 1776. Like many subsequent historians of the eighteenth century, Gibbon undervalued the strength, depth and prevalence of the religious sentiments of his time, and formed too light an opinion of the willingness of the late eighteenth-century Church of England to defend its ground.[83] For the second edition, therefore (as we have seen) some of the most egregiously misjudged instances of tone and language were removed or moderated. The controversy then broke, with the publication of the works by Chelsum and Watson. Gibbon,

---

[80] John Brown, *An estimate of the manners and principles of the times* (London, 1757), p. 57.

[81] Gibbon's exposure to deistical thought perhaps originated in his enforced residence with Mallet, the literary executor of Bolingbroke, after his conversion to Catholicism (*Autobiographies*, p. 130). Having failed to make him an infidel, his father then decided to try to make him a Protestant, and sent him to Lausanne. Gibbon's personal antipathy to religion has always been exaggerated; see Paul Turnbull, 'The supposed infidelity of Edward Gibbon', *The Historical Journal* 5 (1982), pp. 23–41.

[82] See the triumphant letter to Deyverdun of 7 May 1776 (*Letters*, vol. II, pp. 104–8), in which Gibbon says that the *Decline and fall* 's'est vendu, selon l'expression du libraire comme une brochure de six sous sur les affaires du temps' (*Letters*, vol. II, p. 106).

[83] This is a large subject, at present being transformed by a stream of exciting scholarship. Amongst recent studies, see in particular: J. C. D. Clark, *English society 1688–1832* (Cambridge, 1985), and J. Walsh, C. Haydon and S. Taylor (eds.), *The Church of England c. 1689–c. 1833* (Cambridge, 1993).

having discovered that the controversy did him little harm amongst those whose opinions he valued, and that his adversaries were not in themselves daunting, moved in precisely the opposite direction for the third edition. The, at times, broad deistical language which had been cut for the second edition was not restored, but other passages, latent with implication embarrassing for the church, were given a new astringency of style and reinforced with a greater power of documentation. One is suddenly put in mind of the extraordinary self-analysis in the journal entry for 8 May 1762 (Gibbon's twenty-fifth birthday): 'It appeared to me, upon this enquiry, that my Character was virtuous, incapable of a base action, and formed for generous ones; but that it was proud, violent, and disagreable in society.'[84] There was, in the event, to be little violence in Gibbon's life. But pride there may have been in the revisions for the third edition. Aspects of chapters 15 and 16 had been miscalculated. But once the dispute about those errors had become a public matter, and the indifferent weight and temper of his adversaries' weapons had been proven, then there could be no turning back.

This was the explanation for the irreligion of the two last chapters held by some of Gibbon's contemporaries. *The Gentleman's Magazine* linked Gibbon's attacks on Christianity with a desire to appeal to the world of fashion: 'Detesting its principles as much as we admire its style, we shall wave entering into farther particulars, or extracting the poison here diluted, satisfied with having warned our readers of the main design, and too fashionable principles of this too fashionable work, whose danger is enhanced by its ingenuity . . . '[85] And George Travis made the connection yet more explicitly:

The impartial public demand it [a clear statement of religious belief] from you; or the persuasion, already entertained by many, will soon become universal, that you conceived a decent *modicum* of infidelity (no matter how prepared) to be necessary to give *fashion* to a work, pompous, yet not substantial, – specious, yet not satisfactory, – labored, yet not accurate.[86]

Travis' literary judgment was manifestly weak; yet he may nevertheless have been an acute reader of the human heart. His suspicions about why Gibbon wrote as he did about Christianity are,

[84] *Gibbon's journal to January 28th, 1763*, ed. D. M. Low (London, 1929), p. 69.
[85] *The Gentleman's Magazine* 46 (1776), p. 367.
[86] George Travis, *Letters to Edward Gibbon Esq.* (Chester, 1784), p. 123.

at the least, not incompatible with the textual evidence.[87] It would be one last instance of the surprisingly accurate mutual understanding which seems, beneath the surface animosity, to have existed between Gibbon and his critics.

Gibbon himself scripted the encounter between the historian and his adversaries in two acts: dignified silence, followed by devastating rebuttal. But in reality, this was a drama with many more twists and reversals than Gibbon, reviewing his life in the 1790s, was prepared to admit. And just as he misrepresented the narrative of his brush with the 'Watchmen of the Holy City' when writing his *Memoirs*, so perhaps he also misconceived it. Most modern commentators have taken their cue from Gibbon, and have depicted the controversy as a reprise of *The Dunciad*: the hero of literature annoyed by critic insects.[88] Here, too, there is room for another treatment, in which the vocabulary and tactics of Gibbon's adversaries would be more sympathetically assessed by relocation in the polemical tradition of which they were a part. Once the attacks on Gibbon have been resituated in that context, we can propose a new explanation for the effectiveness of the *Vindication* as a reply to them. But that would be the subject of another paper.

---

[87] One popular explanation of these chapters – that Gibbon was taking revenge on Christianity for the sufferings he had endured after his conversion to Catholicism – I find quite discountenanced by the evidence of the revisions to the first three editions of volume I. This interpretation seems to have arisen with Porson, to have attracted Sainte-Beuve, and most recently to have ensnared Patricia Craddock, *Edward Gibbon, luminous historian*, pp. 62–3.

[88] For Gibbon's so conceiving the affair, see *Autobiographies*, pp. 316–19. For the persistence of this conception into the work of later scholars, see Patricia Craddock's headnote to *A vindication (English essays*, p. 570), and also her *Edward Gibbon, luminous historian*, pp. 120–31.

CHAPTER 10

Gibbon and international relations

Jeremy Black

Empire, Enlightenment, the classics: Thomas Ashe Lee, an officer in James Wolfe's regiment, had no sympathy with the Highland rebels in 1746. He wrote, after Culloden, of the British troops 'dispersed through the several parts of this heathenish country, converting them to Christianity, and propagating a new light among them. Some few of them bring in their arms, others skulk in the woods and mountains, but we take care to leave them no sustenance, unless they can browse like their goats.' Lee saw the Highlanders as barbarians, compared them unfavourably with the Gauls and sought an historical comparison with the campaign by reading Caesar.[1]

Such a locating of the present with reference to the classical past was commonplace in eighteenth-century Britain, a society whose reverence of and reference to the past was focussed on the classical world. In this context it is easier to understand why Gibbon's scholarship was so important to his contemporaries. A focus on the classical past was scarcely new. Aside from providing an acceptable pedigree and cultural context for civic virtues, the classical legacy was valuable in large part because it was so fluid and open to interpretation that did not fall foul of authority: a marked contrast to that of Christianity. Thus, Reed Browning has been able to suggest that political thought in the first half of the century was divided between Catonic and Ciceronian perspectives.[2] The pro-government *Whitehall Journal* of 6 November 1722, futilely criticized opposition writers, 'The state of the Roman Empire, under all its

---

[1] Earl of Ilchester (ed.), *Letters to Henry Fox* (Roxburghe Club, 1915), pp. 9, 13–14.
[2] R. Browning, *Political and constitutional ideas of the court Whigs* (Baton Rouge, 1982); J. M. Black, 'Ideology, history, xenophobia and the world of print in eighteenth-century England' in Black and J. Gregory (eds.), *Culture, politics and society in Britain 1660–1800* (Manchester, 1991), pp. 184–216.

varieties . . . they are all promiscuously made use of by these authors, to influence and illustrate politics . . . by no force of wit . . . can those words in any one Roman sense be applied to our English constitution.' Such references were more than suitable for a political culture whose self-image was that of high-minded and moral politics and that sought to debate current and recent differences with reference to constitutional questions that could be located in the classical past, more especially the late republic and early Empire. Thus, for example, the *Craftsman* could attack Walpole in the person of Tiberius' adviser Sejanus. What was absent from the discussion of foreign policy was not only the plundering of later imperial history for examples, let alone context, but, more generally, the use of the classics to provide more than occasional echoes. The rivalry between Rome and Carthage could of course be used to prefigure that of Britain and France, although Pitt the Elder, with his typical capacity to rethink a question that so infuriated many contemporaries, reversed the comparison in the debate on the address in 1755: 'we have been told indeed that Carthage, and that Spain in 88 were undone, notwithstanding their navies-true; but not till they betook themselves to land operations *and Carthage had besides a Hannibal who would pass the Alps*',[3] the last a reference to the Duke of Cumberland.

Nevertheless, in general, it was to the history of England over the last millennium that those seeking to make historical points about foreign policy and military strategy looked: to the Viking and Norman invasions, Anglo-French wars in the Middle Ages – both the Hundred Years War and earlier conflicts – to the Elizabethan war with Spain and the varied fortunes of seventeenth-century foreign policy and warfare. Much of this discussion has received surprisingly little attention and one of the more disappointing aspects of the Pocockian moment is that the great luminaries of political thought in this period, as indeed in most, have neglected foreign policy. That is why the recent contributions of Istvan Hont and John Robertson are so welcome.[4]

[3] Horace Walpole, *Memoirs of King George II*, ed. J. Brooke (3 vols., New Haven, 1985), vol. II, p. 70.
[4] I. Hont, 'The rhapsody of public debt: David Hume and voluntary state bankruptcy' and J. Robertson, 'Universal monarchy and the liberties of Europe: David Hume's critique of an English Whig doctrine' in N. Phillipson and Q. Skinner, *Political discourse in early modern Britain* (Cambridge, 1993), pp. 321–48 and pp. 349–73.

Needless to say, the neglect is not all one-sided. Scholars working on eighteenth-century foreign policy have been all too willing to focus on the details of diplomacy, at the expense of probing the political culture that framed expectations and responses. This could be linked with the clear lack of interest, if not distaste, in the need to consider the impact on foreign policy of domestic factors, particularly Parliament. There is an obvious preference for writing about what policy 'actually was', rather than assessing the contemporary debate about what it 'should have been',[5] even though the latter clearly affected the domestic situation, which should not be thought of in terms of a passive context. It is striking that an important recent detailed study of foreign policy in the period 1756–83 makes no mention of Johnson's pamphlet on the Falklands controversy of 1770–1 nor of Gibbon's great work.[6]

The *Decline and fall*, as Jonathan Shepard has pointed out above with reference to Byzantium, is not notable for its discussion of international relations. Yet there is much in it that is worthy of attention, and consideration of the discussion provides an opportunity for assessing Gibbon's attitudes in terms of both empire and enlightenment. In the course of the book, Gibbon considers empires of the mind, their rise and relationships, particularly Christianity and Islam, and his emphasis on the ideological dimension of power is valuable. In one respect, the theme of the Roman Empire collapsing because of internal political–cultural decay rather than external attack accords with the eighteenth-century, indeed timeless, preference for 'moral' history and history with a meaning. This is an exemplary tale with an 'enlightenment' moral: the customary diatribe against excess and corruption is given depth and direction by Gibbon's critique of the impact of monotheism. On the other hand, such a thesis permits Gibbon to avoid a detailed examination of the mechanics of warfare and international relations.

Yet the discussion of such relations in the book is by no means restricted to the decline and fall of the Roman Empire. There is also some consideration of the earlier rise of Rome, as well as the post-Roman states in the west, most interestingly the Norman kingdom

---

[5] H. M. Scott, 'The second "Hundred Years War" 1684–1815', *Historical Journal* 35 (1992), pp. 443–71 at p. 450.
[6] H. M. Scott, *British foreign policy in the age of the American Revolution* (Oxford, 1990).

of Sicily, but also, for example, republican Venice. The successive
eastern opponents of Byzantium, as Anthony Bryer has established
above, also receive distinctive treatment.

Gibbon distinguishes between two kinds of international
relations: those of defined and civilized states with each other
and those between barbarians and civilized states. The constant
pressure on settled peoples of migrant, mobile, fluid forces is one of
the many themes of the book. At times there is also a moral clash:
Gibbon was clearly receptive to the positive re-evaluation during
the Enlightenment of 'primitive peoples'. Thus, the enlightened
Catalan Jesuit historian J. F. Masdeu, whose work first appeared in
1781, presented a positive view of the primitive Spaniards, while
their Roman conquerors were seen as cruel and oppressive.[7] Leo
Damrosch is mistaken when he claims that Gibbon identified
'emotionally with the armies of civilization' and reserved 'his
deepest contempt for their barbarian opponents'.[8] In fact he
contrasted 'the untutored Caledonians glowing with the warm
virtues of nature, and the degenerate Romans polluted with the
mean vices of wealth and slavery'.[9] When Justin received
the embassy of the Avars, 'the servile adoration of the Byzantine
court' contrasted with 'the freedom and pride of a barbarian'.[10] In
southern Italy 'the superior spirit and discipline of the Normans
gave victory to the side which they espoused'.[11] In the seventh and
eighth centuries 'in Sardinia, the savage mountaineers preserved
the liberty and religion of their ancestors; but the husbandmen of
Sicily were chained to their rich and cultivated soil'.[12] The
Crusaders were defeated in Egypt not by 'the degenerate children
of the companions of Noureddin and Saladin', but 'by the arms of
their slaves or Mamalukes, the hardy natives of Tartary, who at a
tender age had been purchased of the Syrian merchants, and were
educated in the camp and palace of the sultan'.[13]

Barbarians were closer to the original state of man and this
increased their military potency:

---

[7] F. W. Alonso and G. C. Andreotti, 'On ancient history and Enlightenment: Two Spanish
histories of the eighteenth century', *Storia della Storiografia* 23 (1993), pp. 75–95 at p. 91.

[8] L. Damrosch, *Fictions of reality in the age of Hume and Johnson* (Madison, 1989), p. 122.

[9] *Decline and fall*, ed. Bury, I, p. 130. On this passage see most recently, L. Davis, '"Origins
of the specious": James Macpherson's Ossian and the forging of the British Empire', *The
Eighteenth Century* 34 (1993), pp. 132–50 at pp. 144–5.

[10] *Decline and fall*, ed. Bury, v, p. 3.   [11] *Ibid.*, v, p. 23.

[12] *Ibid.*, vi, p. 175.   [13] *Ibid.*, vi, p. 361.

In the state of nature every man has a right to defend, by force of arms, his person and his possessions; to repel, or even to prevent, the violence of his enemies, and to extend his hostilities to a reasonable measure of satisfaction and retaliation. In the free society of the Arabs, the duties of subject and citizen imposed a feeble restraint.[14]

Theirs was a 'state of society in which policy is rude and valour is universal'.[15] Nomadic peoples were even more martial, because in their marginal habitats it was possible to recover 'the first ages of society, when the fiercer animals often dispute with man the possession of an unsettled country'. In contrast, 'in the civilized state of the Roman empire the wild beasts had long since retired from the face of man and the neighbourhood of populous cities'.[16] The energy of the barbarians had a primeval quality: Gibbon compared the 'rapid conquests' of Monguls and Tartars 'with the primitive convulsions of nature, which have agitated and altered the surface of the globe'.[17]

Barbarians were difficult to deal with. The 'apparent submission' of the Caledonians 'lasted no longer than the present terror. As soon as the Roman legions had retired they resumed their hostile independence.'[18] The Chagan of the Avars 'was not inferior to the most civilized nations in the refinements of dissimulation and perfidy'.[19] Islam owed much to the military strength of the Arabs:

the arms of Sesostris and Cyrus, or Pompey and Trajan, could never achieve the conquest of Arabia; the present sovereign of the Turks may exercise a shadow of jurisdiction, but his pride is reduced to solicit the friendship of a people whom it is dangerous to provoke and fruitless to attack. The obvious causes of their freedom are inscribed on the character and country of the Arabs. Many ages before Mahomet, their intrepid valour had been severely felt by their neighbours in offensive and defensive war. The patient and active virtues of a soldier are insensibly nursed in the habits and discipline of a pastoral life.

Gibbon also focussed on specific military factors:

---

[14] *Ibid.*, v, pp. 358–9.
[15] *Ibid.*, vii, p. 2.
[16] *Ibid.*, i, p. 93. For a similar view, William Robertson, *The history of the reign of the Emperor Charles V. With a view of the progress of society in Europe, from the subversion of the Roman Empire, to the beginning of the sixteenth century* (3 vols., London, 1769; 1782 edn), vol. i, pp. 5–6.
[17] *Decline and fall*, ed. Bury, vii, p. 1.
[18] *Ibid.*, i, p. 129.   [19] *Ibid.*, v, p. 55.

When they advance to battle, the hope of victory is in the front; in the rear, the assurance of a retreat. Their horses and camels, who in eight or ten days can perform a march of four or five hundred miles, disappear before the conqueror; the secret waters of the desert elude his search; and his victorious troops are consumed with thirst, hunger, and fatigue in the pursuit of an invisible foe, who scorns his efforts, and safely reposes in the heart of the burning solitude. The arms and deserts of the Bedoweens are . . . the safeguards of their own freedom.[20]

Yet, Gibbon also focussed on a shift in favour of civilized society.[21] Civilization had led to science and 'cannon and fortifications now form an impregnable barrier against the Tartar horse';[22] although elsewhere in the book he noted the transferability of military techniques to barbarians: 'The despair of a captive, whom his country refused to ransom, disclosed to the Avars the invention and practice of military engines; but in the first attempts they were rudely framed and awkwardly managed.'[23] In the siege of Constantinople in 626, the Avars revealed 'some progress in the science of attack', although 'the powers of fire and mechanics were used with superior art and success' by the defenders.[24] In his account of thirteenth-century Mongol operations, Gibbon noted that Genghis Khan was able to employ Chinese engineers to besiege successfully the fortified towns between the Caspian and the Indian Ocean. Similarly, earlier Chinese knowledge of gunpowder did not prevent the Mongol conquest of China.[25]

Nevertheless, 'Greek fire', which Gibbon described in detail,[26] prefigured gunpowder in giving the Byzantine Empire a vital technological edge over its opponents. In the earlier Arab siege of 668–74 'the Saracens were dismayed by the strange and prodigious effects of artificial fire';[27] and in this and the second Arab siege of 716–18 'the deliverance of Constantinople may be chiefly ascribed to the novelty, the terrors and the real efficacy of the *Greek fire*', the use of which continued until gunpowder 'effected a new revolution in the art of war and the history of mankind'.[28]

Gibbon's argument that cyclical processes were not at work in

---

[20] *Ibid.*, v, p. 319.   [21] *Ibid.*, vii, p. 82.
[22] *Ibid.*, iv, p. 167.   [23] *Ibid.*, v, p. 56.
[24] *Ibid.*, v, p. 86.   [25] *Ibid.*, vii, pp. 9, 11.
[26] *Ibid.*, vii, pp. 10–11.   [27] *Ibid.*, vi, p. 3.
[28] *Ibid.*, vi, pp. 9, 12. For an emphasis on continuity in the practice of warfare from the 'tactically integrated army of Alexander . . . to the time of Napoleon', A. Ferrill, *The origins of war from the Stone Age to Alexander the Great* (London, 1985), pp. 7, 217–22.

the relationship with 'the savage nations of the globe . . . the common enemies of civilized society',[29] appeared justifiable in the eighteenth century, as such nations appeared unable to overcome the militarily superior forces of more 'civilized' societies and no such future eventuality seemed likely. A contrast between the more specialized and organized forces of essentially settled peoples and their more mobile often nomadic opponents of what Gibbon termed 'the pastoral world', could be seen in the struggles between the Turks and the Bedouin, Mughal India and invaders from Afghanistan, Safavid Persia and the same invaders, and Manchu China and the peoples of lands conquered between 1691 and 1760, such as the Khalkhas of Eastern Mongolia and the Dzungarians of Western Mongolia. Gibbon was apparently ignorant of the latter for he referred to the 'polite and peaceful nations of China, India and Persia, who neglected, and still neglect, to counterbalance' the 'natural powers' of 'barbarians' 'by the resources of military art'.[30] The more specialized forces generally enjoyed the advantages of numbers and firepower, although other factors could be decisive: Safavid Persia was overthrown at the battle of Gulnabad (1722) in large part because the Afghan forces were better led.

Whatever the situation between Asian powers, the success of the major European states in creating effective forces able to use concentrated and disciplined firepower in order to defeat opponents was notable in Gibbon's lifetime. The success of these forces against opponents armed with guns, such as the Turks in the Russo-Turkish conflicts of 1736–9, 1768–74 and 1787–92, was particularly significant and, to that extent, Gibbon's emphasis on gunpowder was somewhat limited. Superior technology was not the sole factor; a superiority in military technique, broadly conceived to include drill, cartography, logistic and financial institutions as well as tactics, which was more difficult to transfer or replicate than technology, resting as it did on the foundations of centuries of European social and institutional change, was also pertinent. In 1783 Russia was able to annex the Crimea: the Khanate of the Crimean Tatars was no more. Marshal Saxe drew attention to the broader context and drew a direct comparison between the Turks and the Gauls in his *Rêveries*: 'the number of years during which the Gauls were perpetually conquered by the Romans,

---

[29] *Decline and fall*, ed. Bury, IV, p. 164.   [30] *Ibid.*, VII, p. 6, IV, p. 166.

without ever attempting to retrieve their losses by any alteration in their discipline, or manner of fighting. The Turks are now an instance of the same.'[31]

For Gibbon, force was the crucial relationship between barbarian and civilized peoples: the means by which each put pressure on the other. Diplomacy had little role, because barbarians could not be trusted; although the ability by 'apparent firmness' to create an impression of strength was important, as with Julian's reception of the Avar envoy.[32] As mentioned above, Gibbon had little to say about Byzantine diplomacy, although the use of other tribes to attack those that posed threats was an important device and Gibbon does mention it.[33] Either the overwhelming force of a powerful empire was required to control, or, at least, restrain barbarians, or, thanks to the capacity of gunpowder to multiply force, this could be achieved by the smaller forces of individual modern European states. Gibbon did not work through the implications of states operating both in a competitive system of civilized polities and against barbarians, but he was clear that the former system was necessary to progress. The divided nature of Europe was presented as essential to the quality of governance, the number of independent forces was multiplied and 'in peace, the progress of knowledge and industry is accelerated by the emulation of so many active rivals'.[34] This had been prefigured in early-republican Rome, but, in contrast, Byzantium, isolated by language and arrogance, 'was not disturbed by the comparison of foreign merit; and it is no wonder if they fainted in the race, since they had neither competitors to urge their speed, nor judges to crown their victory'. This, in Gibbon's view, was not challenged until the Crusades when 'the nations of Europe and Asia were mingled . . . and it is under the Comnenian dynasty that a faint emulation of knowledge and military virtue was rekindled in the Byzantine empire'.[35]

Gibbon shared Robertson's view that 'imitation or cultural

---

[31] A. Fisher, *The Russian annexation of the Crimea, 1772–83* (Cambridge, 1970); B. W. Menning, 'Russian military innovation in the second half of the eighteenth century', *War and Society* 2 (1984), pp. 23–41; W. C. Fuller, *Strategy and power in Russia 1600–1914* (New York, 1992), pp. 158–66; V. Aksan, 'The one-eyed fighting the blind: mobilization, supply, and command in the Russo-Turkish war of 1768–1774', *International History Review* 15 (1993), pp. 221–38; J. M. Black, *European warfare 1660–1815* (London, 1994), pp. 15–16, 26; H.-M. Saxe, *Rêveries* (London, 1757), p. 47.
[32] *Decline and fall*, ed. Bury, v, p. 4.   [33] *Ibid.*, v, p. 21.
[34] *Ibid.*, IV, p. 166.   [35] *Ibid.*, I, p. 109.

transmission holds the key to growing European homogeneity'. This emphasis on progress through essentially competitive emulation is indeed one that can be found in modern historical work on early modern military history in the global perspective, most obviously that of McNeill and Parker.[36] Furthermore, Gibbon was correct to focus on the particular character of European history. Whereas many other populous, agrarian areas have tended to be under the control of empires, most obviously in China, northern India, Persia and the Near East, a crucial aspect of post-Roman European history has been its multipolar nature. This multipolarity has been challenged by quests for hegemony, and Gibbon discussed these in terms of the ambitions of barbarian invaders and of attempts to revive aspects of the Empire of the west, by, for example, Theodoric, Charlemagne and the Ottonians. Seeking to win the support of the Avars against the Gepids, Gibbon makes Alboin, king of the Lombards, declare that the reward would be 'inestimable: the Danube, the Hebrus, Italy, and Constantinople would be exposed, without a barrier to their invincible arms'.[37] Such hopes were ephemeral, but those who rather sought to recreate links with the Roman past did not impress Gibbon. Theodoric had qualities but 'wanted either the genius or the opportunities of a legislator' and thus failed to create the basis of a lasting power. Charlemagne similarly lacked 'the general views and the immortal spirit of a legislator, who survives himself for the benefit of posterity. The union and stability of his empire depended on the life of a single man.'[38] The medieval German emperors were 'unworthy successors' of Trajan and Constantine, and Charles IV, 'an elective and impotent magistrate', possessed the show but not the reality of power.[39]

Reviving imperial Rome, according to Gibbon's interpretation and presentation of the medieval emperors, which is a serious over-simplification of the political actions and aspirations of these rulers, was no longer an option. But for Gibbon, and the medieval

---

[36] K. O'Brien, 'Between Enlightenment and stadial history: William Robertson on the history of Europe', *British Journal for Eighteenth-Century Studies* 16 (1993), pp. 53–63 at p. 60; W. H. McNeill, *The age of gunpowder empires 1450–1800* (Washington, 1989), p. 1; G. Parker, *The military revolution. Military innovation and the rise of the West, 1500–1800* (Cambridge, 1988), p. 144.

[37] *Decline and fall*, ed. Bury, v, p. 6.

[38] *Ibid.*, IV, p. 187, V, p. 285.   [39] *Ibid.*, V, pp. 307–10.

emperors he discussed who sought no such revival, this reflected the strength of the post-Roman European system, for the multiplicity of states was maintained by a balance of power that matched in the international sphere the necessary disposition and operation of power within communities. Gibbon read this preference for balance back into the past. 'The firm and equal balance of the constitution' of republican Rome somewhat confusedly 'united' the character of three different elements: popular assemblies, senate and regal magistrate.[40] Again, 'legislative authority was distributed in the assemblies of the people by a well-proportioned scale of property and service'.[41] In contrast, Theodoric failed to join, through balancing, 'Goths and Romans',[42] while in eighth-century Rome the successful recreation of the 'rough model of a republican government', with its consultation and checks and balances, failed because 'the spirit was fled' so that 'independence was disgraced by the tumultuous effect of licentiousness and oppression'.[43] In south Italy the Normans created a 'military senate . . . chosen by the popular suffrage' on the basis of 'age, birth, and merit'.[44] The 'primitive government' of Venice 'was a loose mixture of democracy and monarchy'.[45]

International balance was also necessary. Theodoric 'maintained with a powerful hand the balance of the West . . . and although unable to assist his rash and unfortunate kinsman the king of the Visigoths, he . . . checked the Franks in the midst of their victorious career . . . the Alemanni were protected . . . an inroad of the Burgundians was severely chastised'.[46] In contrast, in the early fifteenth century, 'instead of prolonging the division of the Ottoman powers, the policy or passion of Manuel was tempted to assist the most formidable of the sons of Bajazet'.[47] The balance was presented as crucial to the maintenance of multiple statehood in western Europe.

Gibbon's use of the concept of the balance of power, however, raises several questions. The apparent precision and naturalness of the language of balance greatly contributed to its popularity in an age in thrall to Newton and mechanistic physics. However, the

---

[40] *Ibid.*, IV, p. 160. [41] *Ibid.*, V, p. 263.
[42] *Ibid.*, IV, p. 187. [43] *Ibid.*, V, pp. 263–4.
[44] *Ibid.*, VI, pp. 178–9. [45] *Ibid.*, VI, p. 382.
[46] *Ibid.*, IV, p. 186. [47] *Ibid.*, VII, p. 76.

notion offered little guide as to what criteria should be used to measure strength or assess intentions, while there was a central contradiction between the descriptive and normative possibilities of the theory. It was also unclear how regional balances were related to a general balance. Gibbon noted that 'by the departure of the Lombards and the ruin of the Gepids, the balance of power was destroyed on the Danube',[48] but, although Avar dominance in that region threatened Constantinople, it is unclear what the global significance of such regional balances was supposed to be. As with other concepts, these limitations in terms of analytical rigour did not remove the value of the balance of power as a political and polemical tool; indeed its very openness to interpretation made the concept more flexible and thus widened its use in discourse.[49] In his *The history of the Emperor Charles V. With a view of the progress of society in Europe, from the subversion of the Roman Empire, to the beginning of the sixteenth century*, William Robertson had earlier presented the 'balance of power' in the same favourable light. It was seen as a product of

political science . . . the method of preventing any monarch from rising to such a degree of power, as was inconsistent with the general liberty . . . that great secret in modern policy, the preservation of a proper distribution of power among all the members of the system into which the states of Europe are formed . . . From this era [the Italian Wars of 1494–1516] we can trace the progress of that intercourse between nations, which had linked the powers of Europe so closely together; and can discern the operations of that provident policy, which, during peace, guards against remote and contingent dangers; which, in war, hath prevented rapid and destructive conquests.[50]

Robertson's book, especially its closing sections, was an important source for Gibbon's thinking on international relations. The balance was crucial to the idealization of modern Europe by eighteenth-century historians as a peaceful system of interbalanced states.

Elsewhere in the *Decline and fall* Gibbon brings his precise mind to bear on looseness in explication by others, but this was not the case

---

[48] *Ibid.*, v, p. 53.
[49] J. M. Black, 'The theory of the balance of power in the first half of the eighteenth century: a note on sources', *Review of International Studies* 9 (1983), pp. 55–61.
[50] Robertson, *Charles V*, vol. I, pp. 134–5.

in his employment of the balance of power. More generally, there was some contradiction in his handling of such questions as the value both of divided authority within a state and of multiple statehood. Thus, Gibbon wrote of Italy in the late sixth century as 'divided and oppressed by a ducal aristocracy of thirty tyrants' adding that the threat of Frankish invasion led the Lombard dukes to renounce 'their feeble and disorderly independence; the advantages of regal government, union, secrecy, and vigour, were unanimously confessed'.[51] Gibbon also referred to 'the rival principalities of Benevento, Salerno, and Capua . . . the thoughtless ambition or revenge of the competitors invited the Saracens to the ruin of their common inheritance'. The failure to achieve 'a perfect conquest' of southern Italy led to continual calamity.[52] The Muslims of Sicily were also 'ruined by their divisions' to the advantage of the Normans,[53] while the disunity of Christendom made it fruitless to hope for the recovery of Constantinople:[54] having weakened classical Rome, Christianity was unable to provide the ideological fusion necessary to sustain Christendom as a successful multipolar system in the face of the Turkish advance. Acre 'had many sovereigns and no government', and was full of lawlessness and vice.[55] The urgings of Pius II for unity and activity against the Turks were ignored:

Regardless of futurity, his successors and the powers of Italy were involved in the schemes of present and domestic ambition; and the distance or proximity of each object determined in their eyes its apparent magnitude. A more enlarged view of their interest would have taught them to maintain a defensive and naval war against the common enemy; and the support of Scanderberg and his brave Albanians might have prevented the subsequent invasion of the kingdom of Naples.[56]

For Gibbon, therefore, the value of dispersed power, both within states and in the international system, depended on their political culture and ideology. The attitudes of ruling individuals or groups were of particular importance, as was their ability to command or secure domestic support, an ability that was not simply a function of constitutional systems. Thanks to Islam, in Arabia 'the hostile

[51] *Decline and fall*, ed. Bury, v, pp. 14, 21–2
[52] *Ibid.*, vi, pp. 167–8, see also p. 175.
[53] *Ibid.*, vi, pp. 176–7.   [54] *Ibid.*, vi, p. 207.
[55] *Ibid.*, vi, p. 364.   [56] *Ibid.*, vii, pp. 207–8.

tribes were united in faith and obedience, and the valour which had been idly spent in domestic quarrels was vigorously directed against a foreign enemy'.[57] Earlier, 'the empire of Rome was firmly established by the singular and perfect coalition of its members. The subject nations, resigning the hope and even the wish of independence, embraced the character of Roman citizens.'[58]

An ideology could be of value not only because it created, animated and bound together an empire, but also if it enabled a multipolar system to operate more successfully. Gibbon adopted such a perspective when considering contemporary Europe:

It is the duty of a patriot to prefer and promote the exclusive interest and glory of his native country: but a philosopher may be permitted to enlarge his views, and to consider Europe as one great republic, whose various inhabitants have attained almost the same level of politeness and cultivation. The balance of power will continue to fluctuate, and the prosperity of our own or the neighbouring kingdoms may be alternately exalted or depressed; but these partial events cannot essentially injure our general state of happiness, the system of arts, and manners, which so advantageously distinguish, above the rest of mankind, the Europeans and their colonies.[59]

It was scarcely surprising that Gibbon welcomed the Eden treaty of 1786, an Anglo-French commercial agreement that lowered tariffs, removed prohibitions and reflected an optimistic assessment of the possibilities of encouraging international understanding. He wrote to his friend Lord Sheffield:

As a citizen of the world, a character to which I am every day rising or sinking, I must rejoice in every agreement that diminishes the separation between neighbouring countries, which softens their prejudices, unites their interests and industry, and renders their future hostilities less frequent and less implacable.[60]

Accordingly, in the *Decline and fall*, Gibbon condemned the disruptive character and impact of irrational emotionalism and 'the wild democracy of passions':[61] the preference for self over society, the quest for glory. In terms of international relations, he clearly thought highly of Marcus Aurelius who detested war, 'as the disgrace and calamity of human nature', except when in 'the

---

[57] *Ibid.*, v, p. 396. [58] *Ibid.*, IV, p. 165.
[59] *Ibid.*, IV, p. 163. [60] *Letters*, vol. III, p. 61.
[61] *Decline and fall*, ed. Bury, v, p. 20.

necessity of a just defence'.[62] The failure of Julian's Mesopotamian expedition against the Persians led to a fine section contrasting the fate of the expedition and the hopes of its bellicose supporters:

They entertained a fond persuasion that the temples of the gods would be enriched with the spoils of the East; that Persia would be reduced to the humble state of a tributary province, governed by the laws and magistrates of Rome; that the barbarians would adopt the dress, and manners, and language of their conquerors; and that the youth of Ecbatana and Susa would study the art of rhetoric under Grecian masters.[63]

Justinian sought fame in 'the poor ambition of titles, honours, and contemporary praise'. He had 'the cold ambition which delights in war, and declines the dangers of the field'.[64] Tamerlaine 'followed the impulse of ambition'.[65] For Gibbon, true fame lay elsewhere. His general perception of international relations in terms of the personal views of rulers ensured that he adopted a moralistic attitude to their use of power; and this was extended to republics. Thus he wrote of Venice:

their zeal was neither blind nor disinterested; and in the conquest of Tyre they shared the sovereignty of a city, the first seat of the commerce of the world. The policy of Venice was marked by the avarice of a trading, and the insolence of a maritime power; yet her ambition was prudent: nor did she often forget that, if armed galleys were the effect and safeguard, merchant vessels were the cause and supply, of her greatness.[66]

Gibbon's personal preference was clearly for what could be described as an enlightenment view on international relations. The *philosophes* argued that national interests, if correctly understood, were naturally compatible, and that war arose from irrational causes, such as religion and the irresponsibility and self-indulgence of leaders, and from the nature of secret diplomacy.[67] Thus Gibbon

---

[62] *Ibid.*, I, p. 78.   [63] *Ibid.*, II, p. 525.
[64] *Ibid.*, IV, pp. 431–2.   [65] *Ibid.*, VII, p. 75.
[66] *Ibid.*, VI, p. 382.
[67] A. D. Hytier, 'Les Philosophes et le problème de la guerre', *Studies on Voltaire and the Eighteenth Century* 127 (1974), pp. 243–58; R. Niklaus, 'The pursuit of peace in the Enlightenment', *Essays on Diderot and the Enlightenment in honour of Otis Fellows* (Geneva, 1974), pp. 231–45; H. Meyer, 'Voltaire on war and peace', *Studies on Voltaire and the Eighteenth Century* 144 (1976); H. Mason, 'Voltaire and war', *British Journal for Eighteenth-Century Studies* 4 (1981), pp. 125–38; round table on ideas of war and peace in the eighteenth century, Eighth International Congress on the Enlightenment, Bristol, 1991.

presented the longest-lasting conflict in classical times in an unsympathetic, and simplistic, fashion:

the conflict of Rome and Persia was prolonged from the death of Crassus to the reign of Heraclius. An experience of seven hundred years might convince the rival nations of the impossibility of maintaining their conquests beyond the fatal limits of the Tigris and the Euphrates. Yet the emulation of Trajan and Julian was awakened by the trophies of Alexander, and the sovereigns of Persia indulged the ambitious hope of restoring the empire of Cyrus.[68]

He also referred to indulgence in the 'dream of conquest'.[69] The most influential work on international relations, Emmerich de Vattel's *Le droit des gens* (1758), stressed the natural law basis of international law and emphasized the liberty of nations as a feature of natural law relating to sovereign states. This entailed not the liberty to oppress others but the peaceful enjoyment of rights.[70]

Such views are echoed in Gibbon's thesis that territorial expansion was dangerous, not only for prudential reasons, namely that the state might become over-extended as a force within the international system, but also because it posed a threat to the character and culture of the governing order. Thus, Augustus' scepticism about the value of distant conquests was praised by Gibbon.[71] Trajan was criticized for seeking fame and military glory and his conquests seen as transitory,[72] and, in contrast, the prudent cession of territory by the more pacific Hadrian was praised.[73] More generally, 'the decline of Rome was the natural and inevitable effect of immoderate greatness';[74] a conventional view of the period.[75] Conquest had a similar effect on the Arabs:

Had the impulse been less powerful, Arabia, free at home, and formidable abroad, might have flourished under a succession of her native monarchs. Her sovereignty was lost by the extent and rapidity of conquest. The

---

[68] *Decline and fall*, ed. Bury, v, p. 39.
[69] *Ibid.*, v, p. 42.
[70] F. S. Ruddy, *International law in the Enlightenment. The background of Emmerich de Vattel's 'Le droit des gens'* (Dobbs Ferry, New York, 1975).
[71] *Decline and fall*, ed. Bury, I, p. 2.
[72] *Ibid.*, I, pp. 6–7.
[73] *Ibid.*, I, p. 7. On the generally defensive nature of imperial grand strategy, E. N. Luttwak, *The grand strategy of the Roman Empire* (Baltimore, 1976), pp. xi–xii.
[74] *Decline and fall*, ed. Bury, IV, p. 161.
[75] P. R. Ghosh, 'Gibbon's dark ages: some remarks on the genesis of the *Decline and fall*', *JRS* 73 (1983), p. 17.

colonies of the nation were scattered over the East and West, and their blood was mingled with the blood of their converts and captives. After the reign of three caliphs, the throne was transported from Medina to the valley of Damascus and the banks of the Tigris; the holy cities were violated by impious war; Arabia was ruled by the rod of a subject, perhaps of a stranger.[76]

The language used to describe the impact on the Mongols of their rule over China underlined the theme of the corruption of power: 'the Mogul army was dissolved in a vast and populous country . . . [Kublai Khan] displayed in his court the magnificence of the greatest monarch of Asia . . . His successors polluted the palace with a crowd of eunuchs, physicians and astrologers . . . One hundred and forty years after the death of Zingis, his degenerate race, the dynasty of the Yuen, was expelled by a revolt of the native Chinese; and the Mogul emperors were lost in the oblivion of the desert.'[77] The notion that conquest could lead to a dangerous over-expansion and then to implosion was a common one. It was applied by British writers concerned about the consequences of British colonial gains, but also in their discussion of foreign powers. Discussing in Parliament in April 1791 whether Britain should take action to prevent Russia from retaining her conquests from the Turks, the Foxite Samuel Whitbread claimed that the extension of Russian power to the south would weaken her, that large empires could not subsist and that if a Russian state stretching from the Pacific to the Balkans did sustain itself, it would have to devote its attention to domestic problems. Frederick, earl-bishop of Derry, had anticipated Whitbread's first point earlier that month, and the dangers of making gains from Poland and the Turks were pointed out by contemporary Austrian and Russian critics and have been supported in recent scholarship.[78]

Such notions were appropriate for commentators from a power not seeking European conquests. Similarly, many natural law theorists came from the federal states of the Holy Roman Empire,

---

[76] *Decline and fall*, ed. Bury, v, p. 396.
[77] *Ibid.*, vii, p. 19.
[78] *Cobbett's Parliamentary History of England from the Norman Conquest, 1066 to the year 1803*, ed. W. Cobbett (36 vols., London, 1806–20), vol. xxix, pp. 181–204; B. Fothergill, *The mitred earl* (London, 1974), pp. 137–8; H. Ragsdale (ed.), *Imperial Russian foreign policy* (Cambridge, 1994), pp. 83, 98, 356–7; D. Saunders, *Russia in the age of reaction and reform 1801–1881* (Harlow, 1992), *passim*, for example, pp. 12–13.

the United Provinces and the Swiss Confederation, with their stress
on legal relationships and their, in most cases, only limited interest
in aggression; while the *philosophes* came from a power that had
ceased to seek European territorial gains. The bold and acquisitive
aspirations and aggressive methods that had characterized French
policy for much of Louis XIV's reign or at the outset of the War of
Austrian Succession were not matched in Europe while Vergennes
was foreign minister (1774–87), nor, more generally, between the
1740s and the outbreak of the French Revolutionary War.

This viewpoint, which can be characterized as 'enlightened', had,
however, its limitations. Other than in terms of reprehensible
ambition, it offered little understanding of dynamic elements in
international relations, the scope of change and the attempt by
certain powerful rulers to match diplomatic developments to their
growing power. Thus, Montesquieu has been seen as displaying 'a
fearful resistance to change'.[79] Gibbon offered little guidance to the
processes at work in international relations, contemporary or past,
and his view of the balance of power was clearly that it was a
necessary reactive tool. He wrote of Charlemagne, 'At the head
of his veteran and superior armies he oppressed the savage or
degenerate nations, who were incapable of confederating for their
common safety.'[80] Aside from the balance, international order was
to be maintained because 'in war, the European forces are
exercised by temperate and undecisive contests',[81] while the
dissemination of gunpowder weaponry ensured that the European
powers 'stood on the same level of relative power and military
science'.[82]

These bland statements did not describe the international
relations of the eighteenth century. Far from being indecisive,
major changes could be sought, as in the plans for the partition of
the Habsburg inheritance in 1741, and achieved, as with Peter the
Great's conquest of Sweden's Baltic provinces. Although no
European power had a technological edge that might provide a
window of opportunity in 1710, the respective strength of the states
was such that they were not on the same level of power. Russia's

---

[79] M. L. Perkins, 'Montesquieu on national power and international rivalry', *Studies on Voltaire and the Eighteenth Century* 37 (1965), pp. 61–77 at p. 76.
[80] *Decline and fall*, ed. Bury, v, p. 285.
[81] *Ibid.*, iv, p. 166. [82] *Ibid.*, vii, p. 82.

dominance of both the Baltic and eastern Europe was clear, while the cooperation of Austria, Prussia and Russia in the First Partition of Poland in 1772 scarcely suggested that a balance of power was operating in a benign and temperate fashion. The British envoy in Paris claimed in 1774 that the triple alliance was 'a connexion so contrary to every political principle, a connexion begun in and supported by violence . . . every system is unhinged . . . we see the wisest courts act in direct contradiction to their essential natural interests'.[83]

Thus, while Gibbon was writing the *Decline and fall* the European international system appeared to be in a state of collapse, with nothing to prevent the partitioning powers from making new gains. Gibbon's view of the balance of power did not imply an equality of powers in Europe: it implied no more than a balance sufficient to prevent the re-emergence of a potential universal monarchy. From this point of view, the Partitions of Poland would not necessarily represent a threat to the balance of power, certainly not one comparable to the increasingly imperial ambition of revolutionary France from 1792 on; to some extent, indeed, the Partitions might be thought to have strengthened the balance. Yet they also reflected the role of unconstrained power in eighteenth-century international relations. Ignoring the complaints of the princes of Anhalt, Frederick II of Prussia sent in troops to obtain recruits, leading the Bavarian foreign minister to reflect in January 1773, 'it seems that the right of the strongest now determines all the moves of the great'. The growth and nature of Russian power were seen as particular threats. Whereas for Gibbon the 'europeanization' of Russia and her subsequent expansion was a matter of comfort, securing Europe, as it did, from fresh irruptions from central Asia – his geographical location of the threat to modern civilization; for many others 'Russia's adoption of the political culture of continental Europe rendered the new great power even more terrifying in foreign eyes'. Thus the process of cultural advance emphasized by Gibbon offered little reassurance because no balance of power operated in the benign fashion he suggested. In 1782 Catherine II won the hesitant support of the Emperor Joseph II for the 'Greek Project': the carving out of the Turkish dominions of a new eastern

---

[83] J. M. Black, *The rise of the European powers 1679–1793* (London, 1990), p. 127; W. C. Fuller, *Strategy and power in Russia 1600–1914* (New York, 1992), p. 90.

Roman Empire in favour of her second grandson born in 1779 and named Constantine.[84]

Given Gibbon's argument that a multipolar state system represented a major improvement on universal empire and that the balance of power was fundamental to the maintenance of this system, it is striking how he neglects the actual developments of the 1770s. As it turned out, the partitioning powers divided. Indeed, Austria and Prussia went to war in 1778–9 and came close to it in 1784 and 1790 – the weakness of the European system was readily apparent, and it was to collapse as a consequence of the Revolutionary and Napoleonic wars. Successive coalitions against France were defeated, the territorial and constitutional nature of the Low Countries, Italy and Germany were totally remoulded, the interests of third parties were arbitrarily handled by stronger powers, for example, at Campio Formio, Tilsit and, ultimately, Vienna, and by 1812 France had swollen to rule or dominate much of Europe.

Initially, this was in large part the consequence of a new ideology, that of revolutionary France, but with time this became softened by the exigencies, benefits and compromises of power. This accorded with Gibbon's presentation of international shifts, most obviously with the rise of Islamic power, but was not clear in his last years. Dining with Gibbon in Lausanne in May 1792, the diplomat John Trevor noted that his compatriot was 'more animated than usual', adding 'Even Mr. Gibbon who in general voit assez de sang froid seems to be alarmed at the temper of the times.'[85] The Paris that had lauded Gibbon on his visit in 1777 was swept aside. In his work Gibbon added to the 'civic humanist cycle' of decline through corruption, 'the Enlightenment's conception of the development of civilization' which is 'akin to Scottish scientific Whiggism'.[86] The former was presented as safeguarded in modern times by the balance of power, the latter by the distant nature of any threat

---

[84] These quotations in Black, *European powers*, p. 203 and H. Bagger, 'The role of the Baltic in Russian foreign policy, 1721–1773' in Ragsdale (ed.), *Imperial Russian foreign policy*, pp. 36–72 at p. 38.

[85] Trevor to Lord Malmesbury, 28 May 1792, Winchester, Hampshire County Record Office, Malmesbury papers vol. 169. I should like to thank the Earl of Malmesbury for permission to consult these papers.

[86] J. W. Burrow, *A Liberal descent. Victorian historians and the English past* (Cambridge, 1981), pp. 63, 113. See also J. G. A. Pocock, 'Gibbon's *Decline and fall* and the world view of the late Enlightenment', *Eighteenth-Century Studies* 10 (1977), pp. 287–303, reprinted in Pocock, *Virtue, commerce and history* (Cambridge, 1985), pp. 146–52.

from central Asia. However, Gibbon overlooked the way in which international relations were actually operating in Europe, while, in his eyes, civilization itself was soon to be challenged.

The French Revolution indeed vindicated Gibbon's suggestion that the stability and civilization of contemporary Europe might be threatened, although he minimized and misjudged the source of the threat when he wrote:

this apparent security should not tempt us to forget that new enemies and unknown dangers may *possibly* arise from some obscure people, scarcely visible in the map of the world. The Arabs or Saracens, who spread their conquests from India to Spain, had languished in poverty and contempt till Mahomet breathed into those savage bodies that soul of enthusiasm.[87]

Damrosch criticizes Gibbon for 'remarkable complacency',[88] but his was an understandable error: the threat to European civilization appeared remote precisely because there was no sense that it could come from within. Pocock has, however, suggested that Gibbon was fearful of an ideological threat from within civilized Europe: Joseph 'Priestle's blend of unitarianism, materialism, and millennialism ... the democratic fanaticism' he feared latent in English Dissent.[89] When the threat from within Europe materialized in the form of the French Revolution, the configuration of assumptions and prejudices that underlay British attitudes altered. The earl of Dalkeith thought the 'September Massacres' of 1792 in Paris outstripped 'the massacres of Rome in its most abandoned style'.[90] Once atheistic France had been identified with Antichrist, Catholics could appear as allies, and religion could seem crucial to social order.[91] Such a view of religion was not new, indeed it was a commonplace of clerical preaching and writing on government throughout the eighteenth century. Nevertheless, the Revolutionary crisis lent a new focus. Six weeks after Gibbon's death, additional instructions were sent to Robert Liston, envoy at Constantinople, that indicated that barbarism had been reinvented, sufficiently so for the British to present the revolution

---

[87] *Decline and fall*, ed. Bury, IV, pp. 164–5.   [88] Damrosch, *Fictions of reality*, p. 123.
[89] Pocock, *Virtue, commerce, and history*, p. 155.
[90] Dalkeith to Malmesbury, 29 September 1792, Winchester, Hampshire County Record Office, Malmesbury papers vol. 149.
[91] A. Robinson, 'Identifying the beast: Samuel Horsley and the problem of Papal Antichrist', *Journal of Ecclesiastical History* 43 (1992), pp. 592–607 at p. 607.

as a common threat, rather as Islam had been for Byzantium and Persia:

In all your conferences with the Ottoman Ministers you cannot too strongly impress upon their minds the dangerous tendency of the avowed principles of the present French government if the most absolute anarchy can be so called, where the miserable people, deluded by the specious pretence of liberty, groan under the most despotic tyranny. Your Excellency will explain to them that those principles aim at nothing less than the subversion of all the established religions and forms of government in the whole world, by means the most atrocious which the mind of man will ever conceive, by the indiscriminate massacre, as practised in their own devoted country, of all who were supposed to be averse to their system, without distinction of age, sex or condition, by sacrilege, plunder and devastation of private property, without the shadow of justice, and in a manner unexampled in the history of the most barbarous and savage nations.[92]

It would be foolish to criticize Gibbon for failing to judge the future were it not that he attempted just such a prediction in order to lend depth to his account of the contrast between contemporary and classical Europe, and, as G. M. Young pointed out with reference to Gibbon's account of Byzantine history, 'the errors of the great are more instructive than their triumphs'.[93] Gibbon's thesis of external threat was more relevant to the British position in India. India was vulnerable to invaders from Central Asia, most recently Nadir Shah, who, after conquering Persia, had defeated the Mughals at Karnal in 1739 and sacked Delhi; and Ahmad Khan of Afghanistan, who had defeated the Marathas at Panipat in 1761. As Britain's interests and power increased in India, she inherited these concerns. In 1787 John Shore, a senior official in Bengal and later governor-general of India, wrote to the then governor-general, Earl Cornwallis, about a great Central Asian dynasty, 'the House of Timur I believe is fallen never to rise again; unless a Nadir Shah should arise from the degenerate stock', adding in his next letter, 'the motions of an Asiatic despot are not to be tied by the strictest rules of reason'.[94] The same theme of the irrational nature of non-European power

---

[92] Additional instructions for Liston, 26 February 1794, Kew, Public Record Office, Foreign Office Papers 78/15 f. 46–7.
[93] G. M. Young, *Gibbon* (2nd edn, London, 1948), p. 156.
[94] Shore to Cornwallis, 3, 9 September, Kew Public Record Office (hereafter PRO) 30/11/122 f. 17, 20.

was struck in the same year by William Kirkpatrick, British Resident with Scindhia, one of the Maratha leaders. He wrote of a struggle involving Scindhia in terms that echoed much of Gibbon's history:

In the present case, when [the] conduct of either party is so little regulated by any fixed or steady principles of policy, and when so much depends upon a variety of contingencies which either do not occur or have not so much influence, in states further advanced in political and military knowledge, such conjectures are to be received with particular caution.[95]

Furthermore, the warfare between Indian rulers, with their vast, and in some respects exotic, armies, was apparently similar to many of the struggles described by Gibbon. Paradoxically his theme of civilization on the European model threatened the British position in India, for it largely entailed the adoption of military techniques and weaponry that were to cause the British many problems in the Second Maratha War of 1803. Any emphasis on external threat to the British Empire in India was, with the benefit of hindsight, misleading, for just as within Europe with the French Revolution, the challenge was to come from within: the Indian Mutiny and later the independence movement.

In the case of Europe the eventual overthrow of the Napoleonic empire by an alliance of European states can be used to argue that 'Gibbon's account of the superior political stability of modern Europe – one based upon nation-states, advanced commercial stability, the spread of property and the balance of power – proved perceptive'.[96] This is, however, problematic. Napoleonic France was defeated by other empires – Austria, Russia and Britain – and their allies, and neither Austria nor Russia were committed to Gibbon's account as just advanced. Indeed, it has recently been argued that the Vienna settlement 'rested not on balance of power but on hegemony',[97] especially those of Austria in Italy, Russia in eastern Europe and Britain on the oceans. This analysis is also valid for the pre-Revolutionary period, and Gibbon's failure to appreciate it reflected his essentially conventional, not to say unreflective, optimistic assessment of international relations.

[95] Kirkpatrick to Cornwallis, 13 June 1787, Kew PRO, 30/11/121 f. 60.
[96] R. Porter, *Gibbon* (London, 1988), p. 155.
[97] P. W. Schroeder, 'Did the Vienna Settlement rest on a balance of power?', *American Historical Review* 97 (1992), pp. 683–707 at p. 705.

A parallel criticism could be made of the *Mémoire justificatif* Gibbon wrote in 1778 in response to the French justification of hostility towards Britain. In this Gibbon made reference to the 'tribunal' of European opinion and suggested that had a foreign power seized the Thirteen Colonies from Britain 'l'Europe entière se seroit soulevée contre l'injustice'.[98] However, Gibbon wrote this piece as a supporter of the government and in response to the request of Cabinet members.

Another sphere in which the 'enlightened' notion of international relations was limited was that of transoceanic expansion, a field in which the 'satisfied' powers – Britain, France, Spain and the Dutch – were all active in the eighteenth century. In the half-century before the *Decline and fall* was published Britain had expanded at the expense of non-European powers in India and North America. Transoceanic activity was a theme of the early 1770s. In 1770–1 Britain had risked war with France and Spain as a result of a confrontation over the Falklands; in 1772–3 she had provided an indication of the global potential of European power with a successful campaign against the Caribs of St Vincent; and in India acquired Benares in 1775.

There was little direct echo of this in the *Decline and fall*. The Europeans' 'easy victories over the savages of the new world'[99] ensured that in the unlikely event of civilization collapsing in Europe before new barbarian inroads, it would be sustained 'in the American world'.[100] In an echo of this, Gibbon noted that Europe had been earlier protected by the naval weakness of an Asiatic power: 'if Chosroes had possessed any maritime power, his boundless ambition would have spread slavery and desolation over the provinces of Europe'.[101]

This process was not presented without criticism, but Gibbon was convinced of its general benefit:

Since the first discovery of the arts, war, commerce, and religious zeal have diffused among the savages of the Old and New World these inestimable gifts . . . every age of the world has increased and still increases the real wealth, the happiness, the knowledge, and perhaps the virtue of the human race. The merit of discovery has too often been stained with

---

[98] 'Mémoire justificatif', in Gibbon, *Miscellaneous works* (5 vols., London, 1814), vol. v, pp. 1, 25.
[99] *Decline and fall*, ed. Bury, vii, p. 82.
[100] *Ibid.*, iv, p. 166.   [101] *Ibid.*, v, pp. 71–2.

avarice, cruelty, and fanaticism; and the intercourse of nations has produced the communication of disease and prejudice. A singular exception is due to the virtue of our own times and country. The five great voyages, successively undertaken by the command of his present Majesty, were inspired by the pure and generous love of science and of mankind ... introduced into the islands of the South Sea the vegetables and animals most useful to human life.[102]

In his acceptance of the harshness of 'discovery', Gibbon revealed enlightened susceptibilities. His account was also eurocentric. Savages were to receive 'gifts'. Cook introduced pigs and possibly the white potato, as well as 'exotic weeds' to New Zealand. Leaving aside the issue of 'ecological imperialism',[103] it is clear that a 'present-minded' critique of Gibbon's account would emphasize the possibilities of a more multifaceted treatment of human happiness and progress and would contrast his relative openness to non-European religion with a failure to appreciate other aspects of the cultures of those he termed 'barbarian'.

It is legitimate to ask how far Gibbon's attitude to expansion of empire was such that a parallel between imperial Rome and contemporary Britain could be maintained. The theme of over-reach might have appeared extraordinarily prescient to a political order worried that the crisis of empire would not be restricted to the Thirteen Colonies, but that their loss would be followed by that of Canada, India and Ireland.[104] Gibbon attributed the strength of republican Rome in part to its ability to reconcile the conquered;[105] that was what the British eventually attempted with the attempt to end the American War of Independence by the Carlisle Commission of 1778 and with the move to assuage discontent in Ireland by granting the Irish Parliament legislative independence in 1782.

Yet Gibbon might appear as anachronistic in light of the renewed interest in territorial expansion that affected Britain after the American War. A new attitude in favour of conquest has been

---

[102] *Ibid.*, IV, p. 168–9. Compare John Matthews above, p. 17.
[103] A. W. Crosby, *Ecological expansion. The biological expansion of Europe, 900–1900* (Cambridge, 1986), pp. 228–30, 234.
[104] John Robertson emphasizes a contrast in Gibbon's views of Rome and Britain, below; see also J. M. Black, *British foreign policy in an age of revolutions, 1783–93* (Cambridge, 1994), p. 17.
[105] *Decline and fall*, ed. Bury, IV, pp. 161, 165.

presented as offering a new ideological support for territorial empire and this has been seen as becoming far more influential in Gibbon's last years, especially during the Third Mysore War of 1790–2.[106] Although the cause, course and consequences of the acquisitions were different, in Gibbon's last eight years Britain established colonies in the Andaman Islands, Australia, Penang and Sierra Leone, claimed Lord Howe Island and the Chatham Islands, made important gains in southern India and, by threat of war, established a right to acquire territory on the Pacific coast of modern Canada.

These were scarcely the actions of a sated power, nor of one ready to follow Augustus in setting bounds on its growth or of Hadrian in restoring gains. Yet attitudes similar to those of Gibbon were voiced. The India Act of 1784 declared that 'schemes of conquest and extension of dominion in India are measures repugnant to the wish, the honour, and the policy of this nation'.[107] Two years later, the third duke of Richmond, Master General of the Ordnance, had no time for the idea that Britain should acquire more sugar islands, as they would be 'more . . . than our number of people or riches can afford to cultivate . . . The protection of such distant possessions is always difficult for this country which has so few troops to spare.'[108] In 1787 Lord Thurlow, the Lord Chancellor, in the Lords 'reprobated any shadow of right to our settlements on the Mosquito Shore at any time and treated the soidisant subjects . . . as a set of buccaneers merely subsisting by smuggling, and hitherto uninterrupted rather by connivance than authority', a harsh view of 'informal empire'.[109] The following year 'the luminous pages of Gibbon' were cited by Sheridan when declaring that there was no parallel in the classical world for Warren Hastings' exactions and

---

[106] P. J. Marshall and G. Williams, *The great map of mankind. British perceptions of the world in the age of Enlightenment* (London, 1982), p. 157; Marshall, '"Cornwallis Triumphat": war in India and the British public in the late eighteenth century' in L. Freedman, P. Hayes and R. O'Neill (eds.), *War, strategy and international politics* (Oxford, 1992), pp. 60–74. C. A. Bayly, *Imperial meridian. The British Empire and the world 1780–1830* (Harlow, 1989), pp. 100–9 emphasizes the period of the Anglo-French conflicts that began in 1793.

[107] Quoted in B. B. Misra, *The central administration of the East India Company, 1773–1834* (Manchester, 1959), p. 32.

[108] Richmond to the Marquis of Carmarthen, Foreign Secretary, 26 March 1786, London, British Library (hereafter BL), Egerton Manuscripts 3498 f. 235.

[109] Carmarthen to Robert Liston, 9 April 1787, Edinburgh, National Library of Scotland, Department of Manuscripts 5546 f. 109.

aggression in Bengal,[110] a statement the book scarcely supported. In 1790 the earl of Fife noted, 'I have no ambition for extended dominions but only to manage what we have'.[111] Two years later, after some opposition politicians had been shown a draft of the royal speech, Lord Loughborough wrote to Pitt about the gains from Mysore:

It would be a satisfaction to many to find some distinct intimation that the value of these acquisitions was estimated rather by their importance as a safeguard to our old possessions than as an extension of territory, and that security not conquest was the object of our military operations.[112]

Yet there were contrary pressures. If, as in Australia and the Andaman Islands, no native state was acknowledged, then Britain could act in a bold fashion, taking advantage of established conventions relating to land seen as 'waste' or 'desert'.[113] A serious limitation on any defensive orientation was provided by the role of aggressive British merchants and officials, while a stress on the limited nature of British aspirations can be questioned by considering the extent to which the nature of British 'defensive' requirements had altered, with the expansion of empire, the experience of defeat in the American War of Independence and recent evidence of and fears concerning French imperial ambitions.[114]

Gibbon's portrayal of international relations was insufficiently detailed to enable him to probe such ambiguities in the classical world. He was, however, aware of similar pressures. Thus, in his account of republican Rome, Gibbon wrote

The most important resolutions of peace and war were seriously debated in the senate, and solemnly ratified by the people. But when the arms of the legions were carried to a great distance from Italy, the generals assumed the liberty of directing them against whatever people, and in

[110] P. Quennell, *Four portraits. Studies of the eighteenth century* (London, 1945), p. 125.
[111] Fife to William Rose, 7 May 1790, Aberdeen, University Library, Department of Manuscripts, 2226/131/817.
[112] Loughborough to William Pitt, 9 December 1792, Kew, PRO, 30/8/153 f. 71.
[113] W. E. Washburn, 'The moral and legal justifications for dispossessing the Indians' in J. M. Smith (ed.), *Seventeenth-century America: Essays in colonial history* (Chapel Hill, 1959), pp. 22–32; A. Frost, 'New South Wales as *terra nullius*: the British denial of Aboriginal land rights', *Historical Studies* 19 (1982), pp. 513–23.
[114] B. E. Kennedy, 'Anglo-French rivalry in India and in the Eastern Seas, 1763–93: a study of Anglo-French tensions and of their impact on the consolidation of British power in the region' (unpublished Ph.D., Australian National University, 1969), pp. 342–54.

whatever manner, they judged most advantageous for the public service. It was from the success, not from the justice, of their enterprises that they expected the honours of a triumph.[115]

This was stopped by Augustus and his successors who appreciated the danger of any subject gaining military fame.[116] Such a juxtaposition of success and justice was overly simplistic and reflected Gibbon's moral and moralistic concerns.[117] Thus, in the treatment of Theodoric, presented as 'the rare and meritorious example of a barbarian who sheathed his sword in the pride of victory and the vigour of his age', preventive defence was supported by just territorial claims:

He reduced, under a strong and regular government, the unprofitable countries of Rhaetia, Noricum, Dalmatia, and Pannonia ... His prudence could not safely intrust the bulwark of Italy to such feeble and turbulent neighbours; and his justice might claim the lands which they oppressed, either as part of his kingdom, or as the inheritance of his father.[118]

More generally, the moral approach of Gibbon's didacticism was such that in his treatment of international relations he focussed on the virtue of prudence and the prudence of virtue. This resembled other aspects of enlightenment discussion of international relations, for example the call for open diplomacy, or the radical thesis that it was necessary to transfer control over foreign policy from essentially bellicose, irrational and selfish monarchs, to the people who would be led by reason and would love peace.[119] Gibbon's views on the need for balance in domestic governance led to the same conclusion, but it did not offer a basis for the analysis of either contemporary or classical international politics.

The *Decline and fall* was critically and commercially successful, but Gibbon's ambivalence towards Christianity was such that he can scarcely be used to typify the values of his age. This was also true of his cosmopolitanism, opposition to war and martial glory, and disapproval of imperial expansion, although Dr Johnson had

---

[115] *Decline and fall*, ed. Bury, I, p. 62.
[116] *Ibid.*, I, p. 3.
[117] Peter Ghosh has stated 'the elementary truth that Gibbon was a moralist', 'Gibbon observed', *JRS* 81 (1991), p. 137, n. 37.
[118] *Decline and fall*, ed. Bury, IV, p. 185.
[119] R. Howe, 'Revolutionary perspectives on old regime foreign policy', *Consortium on Revolutionary Europe. Proceedings 1987*, pp. 265–75.

advanced these themes in his *Thoughts on the late transactions respecting Falkland's Islands*.[120] Like Johnson, Gibbon had 'an enlightened superiority to patriotic prejudice' and yet was also affected by a sense of national pride.[121] Arthur Young complained in 1787 that 'to reason with a British Parliament, when her noisy factious orators are bawling for the honour of the British lion, for the rights of commerce, and freedom of navigation; cost an hundred millions sterling . . . they are deaf to you'.[122] Gibbon's irony would have made short work of the claims of such 'patriots' had he been treating the British Empire, but, because his subject was distant and, in particular, foreign history, the irony of his authorial voice did not challenge national suppositions other than indirectly. Gibbon benefited from the popular interest that a sense of parallelism between Rome and Britain encouraged, but he kept them at a distance. Whereas Fielding in his *Journey from this world to the next* (London, 1743), which Gibbon praised in the *Decline and fall* as providing 'the history of the human nature',[123] used metempsychosis to make points that would have been direct, pertinent and barbed to contemporary readers, Gibbon does not, for example, criticize the purchase of army commissions or the affairs of the East India Company in his work and thus 'ransack antiquity and history'[124] to serve a present purpose that would have dated fast.

Certain commentators argued in this period that classical history should not be studied precisely because it was not pertinent. The anonymous writer of *Reflections on ancient and modern history* claimed that:

The best source of civil instruction must be searched for in examples not altogether so remote from our own times. The grand business of the Roman policy was only to contain their own dominions in order and

---

[120] Dr Johnson, *Thoughts on the late transactions respecting Falkland's Islands* (London, 1771). See J. M. Black, 'Johnson's *Thoughts on the Falklands*: a Tory tract', *Literature and History*, 2nd ser., vol. 1, no. 2 (1970), pp. 42–7.

[121] Burrow, *Liberal descent*, p. 122.

[122] A. Young, *Travels during the years 1787, 1788 and 1789* (2nd edn, 2 vols., London, 1794), vol. 1, p. 39.

[123] *Decline and fall*, ed. Bury, iii, p. 384 n. 13. Julian the Apostate, 'the only character in his history for whom Gibbon seems to feel some affection' (Young, *Gibbon*, p. 121), was used by Fielding as his narrator for much of his work. On this choice, B. A. Goldgar, 'Myth and history in Fielding's *Journey from this world to the next*', *Modern Language Quarterly* 47 (1986), pp. 241–3.

[124] *Whitehall Journal*, 6 November 1722.

obedience: on the contrary, the interests of modern communities depend entirely on the management of many neighbouring states, equal perhaps in power to themselves.[125]

In 1771 Philip, fourth earl of Chesterfield, wrote to Robert Murray Keith, then preparing himself for a diplomatic career, 'Let modern history be both your study and amusement; by modern history [I mean] from 1500 to your own time, from which era Europe took that colour which to a great degree it retains at this day, and let Alexander and Julius Caesar shift for themselves.'[126] Gibbon's utilitarianism was different: an exemplary tale that explained the history of Europe until it reached its contemporary state of multiple statehood and Mediterranean, particularly Balkan and Italian, decadence. He presented in a clear, narrative form, interesting people and events, dramatic occurrences and often theatrical details to the domestic reader. History as an exemplary tale was generally accepted because politics and morality were not differentiated, either on the individual or on the communal scale. The writer of *Reflections on ancient and modern history* complained that 'with modern writers everything is either vice or virtue'.[127] Lord Lyttelton, who devoted much of his life to his *History of the life of Henry the Second* (London, 1767), responded in 1772 to praise that 'it may be useful to the highest interest of mankind, by inculcating a right sense of morality and religion, which indeed I had at heart, above any other work, and without the hope of which I could not have gone through the drudgery of it with any satisfaction'.[128] Gibbon, more talented and imaginative though less politically experienced than Lyttelton, shared the peer's concern for morality. In his masterpiece, Gibbon discussed the beneficial consequences of the steady 'progress of arts and agriculture', and he clearly saw them as crucial to social development.[129] Nevertheless, Gibbon

---

[125] Anon., *Reflections on ancient and modern history* (Oxford, 1746), p. 23. For the situation in France see most recently C. Grell, *L'histoire entre érudition et philosophie. Etude sur la connaissance historique à l'âge des Lumières* (Paris, 1993).

[126] Chesterfield to Robert Murray Keith, 4 August 1771, BL Additional Manuscripts 35503 f. 197.

[127] Anon., *Reflections on ancient and modern history*, p. 26. A good example was Voltaire's anti-Catholic portrayal of recent Irish history. This has recently been criticized for its distortion of facts, G. Gargett, 'Voltaire and Irish History', *Eighteenth-Century Ireland* 5 (1990), pp. 117–39.

[128] Lyttelton to —, 5 April 1772, BL RP 2377ii.

[129] J. Clive, *Not by fact alone. Essays on the writing and reading of history* (New York, 1989), pp. 64–5.

found little place for them in his narrative. His was essentially a political account; the notion of rulership, governance and political life as moral activities were such that the sway of empire, both past and present, were seen in that light by both Gibbon and his readers.[130]

[130] I should like to thank Nigel Aston, Karen O'Brien, Roy Porter, Roland Quinault, John Robertson and David Womersley for their comments on earlier drafts of this essay.

CHAPTER 11

Gibbon's Roman Empire as a universal monarchy: the Decline and fall and the imperial idea in early modern Europe

John Robertson

It is not often emphasized how hostile Gibbon was to his great subject, the Empire of Rome. Yet his view of empires, stated in the opening sentence of the *Essai sur l'étude de la littérature*, was unequivocal: 'l'histoire des empires est celle de la misère des hommes'.[1] Rome horrified even as it fascinated him. As he wrote to his father on his arrival in the city in October 1764, with a spontaneity missing from the artfully crafted recollections in the *Memoirs*: 'whatever ideas books may have given us of the greatness of that people, their accounts of the most flourishing state of Rome fall infinitely short of the picture of its ruins. I am convinced that there never existed such a nation and I hope for the happiness of mankind that there never will again.'[2] Drawing attention to this passage, Arnaldo Momigliano observed that it revealed a Gibbon who was never the slave of his classicism, and whose history would become the story of how humanity had 'turned its back on Rome'.[3]

Gibbon's choice of the Roman Empire as his subject has received a number of persuasive explanations, none of which, it seems to me, has quite taken the measure of this hostility. Though the first to recognize that his choice required explanation, Gibbon's own attempt to provide one in the *Memoirs* was understandably mellow, a lineal account of personal intellectual development which left little scope for the reconstruction of the wider settings in which his work gained its purpose and originality.[4] Among modern

---

[1] Edward Gibbon, *Essai sur l'étude de la littérature* (1761), in *Miscellaneous Works*, vol. IV, p. 15.

[2] Gibbon to Edward Gibbon, Snr, Rome, 9 October 1764, in *Letters*, vol. I, p. 184.

[3] Arnaldo Momigliano, 'Preludio settecentesco a Gibbon', *Rivista Storica Italiana* 89 (1977), pp. 5–17 at p. 17.

[4] There was also an element of self-justification: David Womersley, 'Autobiography in time of Revolution: a new theory of the drafts of the *Memoirs*' in David Womersley (ed.), *Gibbon: bicentenary essays* (forthcoming: The Voltaire Foundation, Oxford).

explanations, the historiographical studies of Momigliano stand first: they point not only to the opportunities provided by imperial history for the writing of a new, modern form of history which combined narrative, philosophy and erudition, but also to the very contemporary interests in Oriental scholarship which drew Gibbon onwards and away from Rome.[5] A second explanation, developed notably by Hugh Trevor-Roper, underlines the significance of ancient Rome as Europe's earlier age of cultural greatness, and the consequent need to understand the long decline, from which modern Europe had only recently recovered. Naturally associated with this explanation is Gibbon's evident determination to combine ecclesiastical with civil history, and to implicate Christianity in the process of imperial decline. Understood in these terms, Rome's significance as a subject was of course widely recognized in the eighteenth century: but it was Gibbon who had the intellectual ambition, as well as the scholarship, to confront the problem as a whole.[6] Neither the historiographic nor intellectual explanations for Gibbon's choice of subject, however, can throw much light on his hostility to the Roman Empire as such. The aversion to Christianity, however deep it went, did not entail a hostility to the Empire. That hostility might be explained as a simple expression of moral outrage at the Empire's decadence and corruption: but the suggestion that the sceptical, ironic Gibbon was primarily a moralist is less than persuasive.[7] An additional, intellectually more

[5] Arnaldo Momigliano, 'Ancient history and the antiquarian' and 'Gibbon's contribution to historical method', both in his *Studies in historiography* (London, 1966), pp. 1–39 and 40–55; 'Gibbon from an Italian point of view' in G. W. Bowersock *et al.* (eds.), *Edward Gibbon and the decline and fall of the Roman Empire, Daedalus. Journal of the American Academy of Arts and Sciences* 105 (Cambridge, Mass., 1976), pp. 125–36; 'Preludio settecentesco a Gibbon'. This account of Gibbon's originality has recently been restated in a revised form by David Wootton, 'Narrative irony and faith in Gibbon's *Decline and fall*', *History and Theory*. Theme issue 33 (1994), pp. 77–105.
[6] H. R. Trevor-Roper, 'The idea of the decline and fall of the Roman Empire' in W. H. Barber (ed.), *The Age of the Enlightenment. Essays presented to Theodore Besterman* (Edinburgh and London, 1967), pp. 413–30; 'Gibbon and the publication of *The decline and fall of the Roman Empire*', *Journal of Law and Economics* 19 (1976), pp. 489–505. The pioneering and, until now, only full study of Gibbon in his eighteenth-century intellectual context was that of Giuseppe Giarrizzo, *Edward Gibbon e la cultura Europea del settecento* (Naples, 1954).
[7] The suggestion is advanced in passing by Peter Ghosh, 'Gibbon observed', *JRS* 81 (1991), esp. pp. 137 and n. 37, 143 and n. 80; but see now the same author's much more fully argued paper, 'Nature and neo-classicism in Gibbon: normative and universal components of his thinking' in Womersley (ed.), *Gibbon bicentenary studies*.

exacting explanation seems necessary. It is this that I wish to offer now, by an exploration of the ideas of empire current in early modern and especially eighteenth-century Europe.[8]

At first sight, the key to those ideas might seem to lie close at hand, in the crisis of a contemporary empire which Gibbon was ideally placed to observe. As he remarked more than once to Deyverdun, his life in the 1770s and early 1780s was the story of the decline of two Empires, the Roman and the British.[9] Yet what is striking is how little connection Gibbon appears to have made between them. Throughout the long American crisis his correspondence reveals almost no reflection on the issues.[10] In Parliament his loyalty to the ministry's stand in defence of the Empire rarely wavered; and he was happy to write as a government publicist to refute the French monarchy's charges against British policy, in the *Mémoire justificatif* (1779).[11] Still less was Gibbon engaged by developments in Ireland, characterized by the Genevan observer J. L. de Lolme as 'the British Empire in Europe'.[12] The lack of interest is the more remarkable in the light of Lord Sheffield's prominent involvement in the debate in the early 1780s over Ireland's commercial and constitutional relationship to Britain – a debate whose interest and importance historians still overlook. When Sheffield sent him a copy of his pamphlet in 1784 Gibbon commented only on its lack of style; a year later he denied having ever seen it, declaring that writing the decline of a great empire left him no leisure for the affairs of 'a remote and petty province'.[13] Gibbon's disengagement from the problems of the British Empire is accentuated by the comparison with David Hume, who by his

---

[8] A similarly conceptual approach to Gibbon is adopted by J. G. A. Pocock, for example in 'Between Machiavelli and Hume: Gibbon as civic humanist and philosophical historian' in Bowersock (ed.), *Edward Gibbon*, pp. 153–70; I am indebted to John Pocock for discussions of Gibbon and ideas of empire in particular.

[9] To Georges Deyverdun, 4 June 1779, and 20 May 1783, *Letters*, vol. II, pp. 218, 326.

[10] For example, his letters to J. B. Holroyd, the future Lord Sheffield, 31 October 1775, 11–13 August 1777 (from Paris), 2 December 1777, 9 December 1778, *Letters*, vol. II, pp. 91, 156–7, 167, 197. In the first and third of these, Gibbon characterized the British as engaged in the 'conquest' of America; but if the word carried a critical edge, he made no attempt to press home his attack.

[11] *Mémoire justificatif pour servir de réponse à l'exposé des motifs de la conduite du Roi de France relativement à l'Angleterre* (1779), in *Miscellaneous Works*, vol. V, pp. 1–34. See also to Lord Weymouth, 10 August 1779, *Letters*, vol. II, p. 224.

[12] J. L. de Lolme, *The British Empire in Europe* (London, 1787).

[13] To Lord Sheffield, 18 October 1784, 1 October 1785, *Letters*, vol. III, pp. 7, 35. Gibbon offered retrospective amends in the *Memoirs: Autobiographies*, Memoir E, pp. 334–5.

death in 1776 was declaring himself an American in his principles, and who had earlier remarked that Ireland deserved better treatment than that of a conquered province.[14] So dissociated in Gibbon's mind were the fates of the two empires, it is clear that the contemporary discussion of the British Empire offers us no shortcut to a better understanding of his view of the Roman. A longer route has to be followed.

It is my argument that an explanation of Gibbon's treatment of the Roman Empire should be sought in the context of a discussion of empire as 'universal monarchy' which goes back to the early sixteenth century, and the monarchy of Charles V. In what follows I shall outline the course of this early modern discussion, up to the contributions of Gibbon's immediate eighteenth-century predecessors, before briefly indicating how it may be seen to have shaped Gibbon's treatment of the Roman Empire in the *Decline and fall*. I hope that this may throw light on Gibbon's – insufficiently appreciated – hostility to the ancient Roman Empire, and also, in passing, on his comparative detachment towards the fate of the modern British Empire.

However unexpected the dynastic contingencies which brought Charles V his extraordinary collection of thrones and titles, it did not take contemporaries long to identify the historical and intellectual resources which would enable them to understand and even justify it. The precedent of ancient Rome was obvious immediately. Application of this ranged from the Spanish historian Pedro Mexia's *Istoria Imperial y Cesarea*, written in the form of biographies of the Roman emperors from Julius Caesar to Charles V, to Gattinara's subtler suggestion that Charles should treat his Italian states after the example of the Romans' client kingdoms.[15] Further support for Charles' great monarchy could

---

[14] Hume made his declaration of American principles to Baron Mure of Caldwell, 27 October 1775, *The letters of David Hume*, ed. J. Y. T. Greig (2 vols., Oxford, 1969), vol. II, p. 303; the comment on Ireland was in 'That politics may be reduced to a science' from *Essays moral and political* (1741–2), in *Essays moral, political and literary*, eds. T. H. Green and T. H. Grose (2 vols., London, 1898), vol. I, p. 103.

[15] Pedro Mexia, *Istoria imperial y Cesarea* (Seville, 1547), translated as *The imperial History: or lives of the emperors, from Julius Caesar, the first founder of the Roman monarchy*, by W. Traheron, corrected by Edward Grimston (London, 1623). On Gattinara's thinking: J. M. Headley, 'The Habsburg world empire and the revival of Ghibellinism', *Medieval and Renaissance Studies* (Chapel Hill, 1978), p. 109.

be found in the arguments developed to uphold the universal
authority of medieval emperors against the rival claims of the
papacy, and in the interpretation of Daniel's prophecies, as undertaken by the Lutheran Johann Sleidan in the *Quattuor summis imperiis*
(1556). But these arguments too referred prominently to ancient
Rome, and in the intensely classical culture of the Renaissance it
was natural to understand Charles V's monarchy as a re-creation of
the Roman Empire. Indeed, Charles would go further, the famous
emblem of the ship sailing beyond the Pillars of Hercules, with the
motto '*plus ultra*', indicating an ambition even more extensive than
that of the Romans.

There were good reasons, however, why Charles V's monarchy
could not simply be thought of as an 'empire'. One set of reasons
related to the terms on which Charles held the Spanish monarchy.
Jealous of the imperial title by which Charles ruled in Germany, the
Spanish denied him its use in their kingdoms; and after Charles had
divided his inheritance, Philip II and his successors perforce
acknowledged that the title belonged to the Austrian Habsburgs. In
any case neither Charles nor his heirs ruled the Spanish monarchy
as a single unified realm. The multiple kingdoms of which it was
composed were in principle of equal standing – '*aeque principaliter*';
by contrast, the territories in the New World were 'incorporated'
within the kingdom of Castile. As such those territories might be
termed 'provinces', but Spanish jurists like Solórzano Pereira
remained reluctant to use the corresponding term '*imperium*' to
characterize the monarchy overseas.[16] A second set of complications derived from the appropriation of the concept of empire
by individual monarchies, under the formula '*rex in regno suo est
imperator in regno suo*'. The most familiar expression of this is of
course in the Act of Appeals (1533); but the English monarchy was
a latecomer to the idea, which was first exploited on behalf of
the French and Neapolitan crowns in the early fourteenth century.
This usage of *imperium* is commonly, but inaccurately, viewed
as equivalent to a declaration of national sovereignty: it was
itself Roman in connoting the priority of civil over ecclesiastical

---

[16] J. H. Elliott, 'A Europe of composite monarchies', *Past and Present* 137 (1992), pp. 52–3; Juan
de Solórzano Pereira, *Política Indiana* (1647, Madrid, 1972), book IV, ch. 19, s. 37; book V,
ch. 16, s. 12.

jurisdiction, and the pretension to a unified territorial authority.[17] But its currency in so many kingdoms throughout Europe ensured that the seemingly Roman scale of Charles V's monarchy could no longer simply be characterized by reference to the concept of 'empire'.

In its place came the concept of 'universal monarchy'. While the Roman Empire continued to provide its archetype, the term 'universal monarchy' shed the accumulated associations of *imperium* to capture the sheer extent of the monarchies over which Charles and his Habsburg successors ruled.[18] In the course of the sixteenth century the new idea was elaborated by a number of sympathetic exponents. The most ambitious of these was the Neapolitan friar Tommaso Campanella, whose *Monarchia di Spagna* (written in 1600–1) combined the wisdom of astrology, prophecy and *ragion di stato* to signal the possibility of a universal monarchy under the Spanish Habsburgs. Less extravagant, and more plausible, was the interpretation of the idea offered by the original theorist of *ragion di stato*, the Piedmontese Jesuit Giovanni Botero, who represented universal monarchy as fitted rather for preservation than conquest, and as necessary to enable Christian Europe to meet the challenge of the infidel. Botero also gave the idea a maritime dimension, emphasizing the value of enclosed seas such as the Mediterranean for ensuring communication between the parts of a large monarchy, while providing an outlet, through the Straits, to the ocean.[19]

By no means all interpretations of universal monarchy were so favourable, however. Implicitly threatening the independence of every other monarchy or political community, the suggestion

---

[17] Walter Ullmann, '"This realm of England is an empire"', *Journal of Ecclesiastical History* 30 (1979), pp. 175–203; J. P. Canning, 'Law, sovereignty and corporation theory' in J. H. Burns (ed.), *The Cambridge History of Medieval Political Thought c. 350–c. 1450* (Cambridge, 1988), pp. 464–73; J. H. Burns, *Lordship, kingship and empire. The idea of monarchy 1400–1525* (Oxford, 1992), esp. ch. 3: 'Lordship and kingship: France and England'.

[18] Franz Bosbach, *Monarchia Universalis. Ein politischer Leitbegriff der frühen Neuzeit* (Göttingen, 1988), provides a recent, comprehensive account of the history of the concept from the monarchy of Charles V to the eighteenth century.

[19] Tommaso Campanella, 'Della monarchia di Spagna' (1600–1), published in Latin as *De Monarchia Hispanica* (Amsterdam, 1640), and in English as *A discourse touching the Spanish monarchy*, trans. by [Edmund Chilmead] (London, 1654; repr. 1660). Giovanni Botero, *Della ragion di stato* (1589), ed. by L. Firpo (Turin, 1948), book I, chs. 5, 7, 8, pp. 58–60, 63–8; and *Relationi del mare*, in *Aggiunte di Gio. Botero benese alla sua ragion di stato* (Pavia, 1598), pp. 81–95.

that Charles and his Habsburg successors enjoyed or aspired to universal monarchy was more often made in accusation than in commendation; and the consolidation of confessional divisions only intensified the vehemence of the accusation. The new concept thus lacked the positive evaluation which had attached to *imperium*, and the Roman model of empire ceased to command general admiration. The acquisition of a hostile connotation, however, did not diminish the currency of the idea: by their enemies even more than by the Habsburgs themselves, the pursuit of universal monarchy was regarded as the key to understanding European politics. Early in the seventeenth century an Italian observer, Trajano Boccalini, suggested that the threat had been exaggerated, and represented all Europe's monarchs as more alarmed by the emergence of leagues of many equal commonwealths, as among the Germans, the Swiss and the Dutch.[20] The proposition that such leagues might offer a viable alternative to large-scale monarchy, and thus obviate the threat of universal monarchy altogether, was to have an enduring future; but it did not displace the preoccupation with universal monarchy.

A more direct and comprehensive challenge to the hold of universal monarchy on the European political imagination was that of the great Dutch philosopher, Hugo Grotius (though significantly he owed much to Spanish jurists). To Grotius it was absurd that the conduct of states should be understood in terms of universal monarchy or the fulfilment of prophecies. But the alternative which Grotius offered in his *De jure belli ac pacis* was little less alarming. For his vision of a Europe of sovereign states presupposed that sovereigns stood to each other as individuals in the state of nature, with an almost unlimited right of pre-emptive defensive strike.[21] The possibilities of this doctrine as a cover for aggression and plunder were immediately exploited at the Habsburgs' expense by the leading Protestant war-lord of the age, Gustavus Adolfus of Sweden. But perhaps still more significant, as Richard Tuck and James Tully have recently argued, was the doctrine's application

---

[20] Trajano Boccalini, *I ragguagli di Parnasso* (1612–13), trans. by Henry, earl of Monmouth, as *Advertisements from Parnassus: in two centuries, with the politick touchstone* (London, 1674), pp. 138–46, 256–62.

[21] Hugo Grotius, *De jure belli ac pacis libri tres* (1625) in the series Classics of International Law: Carnegie Endowment for International Peace (2 vols., Oxford, 1925), book II, ch. 22, ss. 13–15; book II, ch. 1, ss. 2, 16; book III, chs. 4–8.

beyond Europe, on the oceans and continents where the Dutch and other Europeans now sought to trade and settle. By using the juristic ideas of rights to pre-emptive defence and to property in uncultivated land, Grotius and his English followers, Selden, Hobbes and Locke, were able to offer a range of justifications for the aggression of merchants and sellers towards the native peoples of Asia, Africa and America.[22]

Successful pursuit of maritime hegemony and colonial settlement would soon be thought of as constituting an 'empire of the seas'. But this new use of the term 'empire' was effectively detached by its foundation in Grotian natural law from the precedent of Rome, and was thus freed from an association with the adverse image of Rome as a universal monarchy. In short (and this is, at best, to simplify a very complex story), several of the most important arguments on which the modern concept of maritime, colonial empire was founded in the seventeenth century were already quite distinct from the terms in which the ancient, Roman model of empire had come to be understood, the terms of universal monarchy.

A continuing preoccupation with universal monarchy in Europe was in any case ensured by the aggression of Louis XIV. In a manner not seen since Charles V, the French king unashamedly avowed his aspiration to universal monarchy. So completely did he turn the tables on the Habsburgs that the most notorious of his publicists' works, Antoine Aubery's *Justes pretentions du Roi sur l'Empire*, was promptly re-issued in a Latin abridgement by the – presumably shocked – imperial librarian to ensure its widest circulation.[23] Heavyweight denunciations were soon forthcoming from imperial

---

[22] Richard Tuck, *Philosophy and government 1572–1651* (Cambridge, 1993), pp. 169–79, 190–201; and *Sorry comforters. Political thought and the international order from Grotius to Kant* (Oxford: forthcoming). James Tully, *An approach to political philosophy: Locke in contexts* (Cambridge, 1993): 'Rediscovering America: the *Two treatises* and aboriginal rights'. Disagreements between the English and Grotius, as in Selden's attack on the doctrine of the freedom of the seas, should not obscure their common use of natural rights arguments in justification of maritime and colonial policy.

[23] Antoine d'Aubery, *Des justes pretentions du Roi sur l'Empire* (Paris or Amsterdam, 1667); on its translation and abridgement by the imperial librarian as *Axiomata politica Gallicana* (1667), see Franz Bosbach 'Eine französische Universalmonarchie? Deutsche Reaktionen auf die europäische Politik Ludwigs XIV' in J. Schlobach (ed.), *Vermittlungen. Aspekte der deutsch-französosischen Beziehungen vom 17. Jahrhundert bis zur Gegenwart* (Berne, 1992), pp. 56–7.

publicists, notably Lisola and Leibniz;[24] but the most original responses to the threat which Louis was taken to represent came later, from Britain.

English public opinion had grown increasingly agitated by the apparent threat of a Bourbon universal monarchy since Louis' unprovoked invasion of the Netherlands in 1672.[25] As the crisis of the Spanish Succession came to a head in the 1690s, the threat was subjected to fresh analysis by a number of English and Scottish writers, including Charles Davenant and Andrew Fletcher. Taking the arguments of Mexia as his foil, Davenant explained that any universal monarchy naturally pursued conquest rather than peace, along with a monopoly of commerce throughout the world and the imposition of a uniform intellectual and cultural tyranny over its provinces. While the danger from France was greater than it had ever been from Spain, however, England now possessed the means to frustrate Bourbon ambition, since England already enjoyed its own, beneficent form of empire, an empire of the sea. On Davenant's account, a maritime empire was one fitted only for preservation, and as such it qualified England to act as guardian of the liberties of Europe.[26] Coming from Scotland, Fletcher could not be quite so sanguine. The frustration by English interests of the Scots' attempt to establish an overseas colony at Darien in 1698 suggested to him that a maritime empire such as England's might, after all, become a universal monarchy: rather than rely on English guarantees, Fletcher offered Europe a vision of peace founded on a general application of the idea of confederal leagues of equal commonwealths.[27]

24 [Franz von Lisola], *Bouclier d'estat et de justice. Contre le dessein manifestement découvert de la monarchie universelle* (Frankfurt-am-Main, 1667); G. W. Leibniz, *Mars Christianissimus* (1683), trans. and ed. by P. Riley in *The political writings of Leibniz* (Cambridge, 1972).
25 S. C. A. Pincus, 'The English debate over universal monarchy' in John Robertson (ed.), *A Union for Empire. Political thought and the British Union of 1707* (Cambridge, 1995).
26 Charles Davenant, *An essay upon universal monarchy* (1701), in *The political and commercial works of Charles Davenant*, ed. Sir Charles Whitworth (5 vols., London, 1771), vol. IV, pp. 1–41; on which: John Robertson, 'Universal monarchy and the liberties of Europe: David Hume's critique of an English Whig doctrine' in Nicholas Phillipson and Quentin Skinner (eds.), *Political discourse in early modern Britain* (Cambridge, 1993), pp. 357–61.
27 Fletcher's analysis of the threat presented by universal monarchy was developed in three of his works in particular: *Discorso delle cose di Spagna* (Napoli [i.e. Edinburgh], 1698); *A speech upon the state of the nation: in April 1701* (1701); and *An account of a conversation concerning the right regulation of governments for the common good of mankind* (Edinburgh, 1704), all reprinted in *The political works of Andrew Fletcher* (London, 1732).

It was Davenant's rather than Fletcher's view which prevailed after the Union of Scotland and England in 1707, and which set the terms in which British opinion understood the Peace of Utrecht, by which the Spanish War was ended in 1713. Although Bourbon rule in Spain was confirmed, 'the liberties of Europe' had been secured. What Utrecht established was a 'balance of powers', of which Britain, by its control of the seas, would be the natural arbiter. In due course these became the shibboleths of eighteenth-century British diplomacy, of which Gibbon was to demonstrate such a fluent command in his *Mémoire justificatif* as late as 1779. The danger of universal monarchy had happily been frustrated, but the possibility that it might return remained a necessary premise of understanding the European states-system.[28]

Before considering Gibbon's treatment of the Roman Empire in the perspective of this discussion, we need to look more closely at the ways in which it was taken up by his immediate eighteenth-century predecessors, whose works we know he read and reflected on. Particularly relevant are writings of Giannone, Montesquieu, Hume and Robertson. As a Neapolitan, Pietro Giannone was unusually well-placed to observe both the Spanish monarchy and papal Rome: his *Istoria civile del regno di Napoli* covered the history of the kingdom from the Roman Empire to the end of Spanish rule in 1707, according a prominent place to the kingdom's involvement in the conflict between emperor and pope across the Middle Ages. Montesquieu's first concern was naturally with the French monarchy, and with the example and legacy of Louis XIV. But visits to Italy (including Naples) and England in the later 1720s extended his interests in both the Spanish and the English monarchies. It was immediately on his return, between 1731 and 1733, that Montesquieu wrote the *Réflexions sur la monarchie universelle*, in which he explicitly addressed the question whether, in the present state of Europe, another people might repeat the Roman achievement of 'une supériorité constante' over all others. As we shall see, this work was closely related to the *Considérations sur les*

---

[28] H. M. Scott, '"The true principles of the Revolution": the Duke of Newcastle and the idea of the Old System' in Jeremy Black (ed.), *Knights errant and true Englishmen. British foreign policy 1600–1800* (Edinburgh, 1989), emphasizes the durability of British foreign policy assumptions, and the renewed concern over Bourbon aspirations to European predominance in the mid-eighteenth century.

causes de la grandeur des Romains et de leur décadence (1734), and Montesquieu originally intended to publish the two together. In the event he suppressed the *Monarchie universelle*, but incorporated much of its analysis in *L'esprit des lois* (1748). David Hume's views of universal monarchy and empire were developed in two collections of essays, the *Essays moral and political* of 1741–2, and the *Political discourses* of 1752, but he continued to make significant revisions to his arguments in the 1760s. Finally, William Robertson's *History of the reign of the Emperor Charles V* (1769) appeared just before Gibbon settled down to the Roman Empire, offering a detailed, 'philosophic' history of that enormous monarchy and its impact on the European political order.

What Gibbon will have found in the writings of these four authors were a series of arguments on the threat represented by universal monarchy, and one significant line of disagreement. In the first place, it was obvious to all four authors that the monarchy of Charles V had inaugurated a new age in European politics, which was best understood as a revival of the Roman model of imperial monarchy. From the vantage-point of Naples, Giannone commented particularly on the resemblance between the Spanish and the Roman monarchies in the manner of their rule.[29] In his *Monarchie universelle* (which Gibbon would not have read), Montesquieu had observed that, by comparison with the limited patrimonies which kings had been able to accumulate under the 'Gothic' form of government, Charles V's monarchy represented 'un nouveau genre de grandeur, l'Univers s'étendit, et l'on vit paroître un Monde nouveau sous son obéissance'.[30] But exactly the same point was made, with an explicit reference to the threat of universal monarchy, by Hume in his essay 'Of the Balance of Power' (which was accessible to Gibbon).[31] Robertson avoided the term universal monarchy, but had no doubt of Charles V's 'grand system of enterprising ambition' – or of the terror it inspired in Europe.[32]

29 Pietro Giannone, *Dell' istoria civile del regno di Napoli libri XL* (4 vols., Naples, 1723), vol. III, p. 544.
30 Montesquieu, *Réflexions sur la monarchie universelle en Europe* (1734), in Montesquieu, *Oeuvres complètes*, ed. Roger Caillois, Bibliothèque de la Pléiade (2 vols., Paris, 1951), vol. II, pp. 29–30.
31 Hume, 'Of the Balance of Power' (1752), *Essays*, vol. I, p. 353.
32 William Robertson, *The history of the reign of the Emperor Charles V. With a view of the progress of society in Europe, from the subversion of the Roman Empire, to the beginning of the sixteenth century* (3 vols., London, 1769), vol. II, p. 60; vol. III, pp. 128, 432, 436.

Both Montesquieu (in a passage also in *L'esprit des lois*) and Hume further commented on the subsequent renewal of the threat of universal monarchy by Louis XIV.[33] The idea was clearly still in active intellectual circulation, but to all four authors it carried an overwhelmingly negative charge.

There was also a broad agreement among the four authors that there had never been a serious prospect that universal monarchy would be established in modern Europe. As Montesquieu put it in the *Monarchie universelle*, such a thing had become 'moralement impossible'. Amplifying a remark by Giannone in his *Istoria civile* (and perhaps also following another Neapolitan, Paolo Mattia Doria), Montesquieu emphasized that the Spanish monarchy had incapacitated itself by its persistent misuse of the riches of the Indies. Not even Louis XIV, he added separately, had ever come close to enjoying the universal monarchy his enemies alleged he sought.[34] Both of these observations reappeared in *L'esprit des lois*, along with a new and more general argument that extensive, despotic monarchies were only possible in the East, where appropriate geographical conditions existed. The physical features of Europe placed natural limits on the extent of its monarchies, which should not be classified as 'despotisms'. Elsewhere in *L'esprit des lois* Montesquieu also revived and elaborated Boccalini's suggestion that leagues or 'républiques fédératives' were a viable alternative to monarchy. As Montesquieu understood it, modern Europe could well accommodate both forms of political order: taken together they made Europe 'une grande République', 'une nation composée de plusieurs'.[35]

Choosing his own terms, Hume reached the same conclusion. Europe had become a copy at large of what Greece was formerly in miniature, a grouping of distinct states mutually enriched by commerce and learning. The principle of the balance of power was

---

[33] Montesquieu, *Monarchie universelle*, section xviii, in *De l'esprit des lois* (Paris, 1748), book IX, ch. 7, *Oeuvres complètes*, vol. II, pp. 33–4, 375; Hume, 'Balance of power', *Essays*, vol. I, pp. 353–4.

[34] Montesquieu, *Monarchie universelle*, *Oeuvres complètes*, vol. II, pp. 19, 30–3. Spanish misuse of the wealth of the Indies was a recurrent Neopolitan theme: Giannone, *Istoria civile*, vol. III, pp. 544–5; Paolo Mattia Doria, *La vita civile* (3 vols., 1710; 3rd edn, Naples, 1729), part II, ch. 3, particella x: 'Del commercio in genere, e poi del presente usato in Europa', pp. 334–50. Montesquieu met Doria on his visit to Naples in 1728.

[35] Montesquieu, *L'esprit des lois*, book VIII, chs. 17–21; book IX, chs. 1–3, 7, 9–10, 16; book XI, ch. 19; book XVII, chs. 3–4; book XXI, ch. 22, in *Oeuvres complètes*, vol. II; also *Monarchie universelle*, in *Oeuvres complètes*, vol. II, pp. 21, 34.

now properly understood, and circumstances favoured its establishment. (Both halves of this proposition were important: a balance of power was always dependent on historical contingencies.) Hume's confidence that universal monarchy had ceased to be a present prospect grew still stronger in the 1760s – as did his alarm at the financial and political consequences of Britain's persistent refusal to admit this, attributing to the French monarchy an ambition it could no longer hope to realize.[36] In what was perhaps an echo of Hume's confidence, Robertson went so far as to suggest that the principle of the balance of power was already understood and operative at the time of Charles V's accession: the terror of his monarchy never had a real foundation.[37]

Between Hume and Montesquieu there was, nevertheless, one significant divergence. It concerned the supposed antithesis between maritime empire and universal monarchy. Montesquieu was confident that commerce was a beneficent force in international relations. It fostered 'les moeurs douces', and promoted a regard for justice and hence peace. England's particular aptitude for commerce, therefore, posed no threat to others in Europe. Even if 'a neighbour nation' – Ireland – had had to be reduced to dependence, England's empire of the sea was not an empire of conquest: no nation was better fitted to act as impartial arbiter of Europe's affairs.[38] Hume, like Fletcher, could not be so complacent. The determination of the British to regulate trade to their advantage constantly endangered the freedom of commerce which was so important a support of the balance of power. In the case of America, Hume came to believe, the British insistence on their trading monopoly would eventually have to be enforced by a territorial conquest.[39] It was not likely, therefore, that the

---

[36] Hume, 'Of the rise and progress of the arts and sciences' (1742), in *Essays*, vol. I, pp. 182–3; 'Balance of power', *ibid.*, pp. 353–5. On the development of his argument: Robertson, 'Universal monarchy and the liberties of Europe'.

[37] Robertson, *Charles V*, vol. I, *A view of the progress of society in Europe from the subversion of the Roman Empire, to the beginning of the sixteenth century*, p. 112; vol. III, pp. 431–2.

[38] Montesquieu, *L'esprit des lois*, book XIX, ch. 27 (on the 'empire de la mer' of the 'island' nation of England), *Oeuvres complètes*, vol. II, pp. 574–9; also book XX, chs. 1–2, 7, 12.

[39] Hume, 'Of the jealousy of trade' (1758), *Essays*, vol. I, pp. 345–8; and his letters to William Strahan, 26 October and 13 November 1775, *Letters*, vol. II, pp. 300–1, 304–5 (comments which may be read as an application of the argument of his much earlier essay, 'That politics may be reduced to a science' (1741), and as suggesting that America was being treated like Ireland. See note 14 above.).

distinction between maritime empire and universal monarchy could long be sustained.

On this issue it would seem that Gibbon was to follow Montesquieu, not Hume. The two Empires of Rome and Britain were quite different in character, and there was no reason to suppose that the fate of a maritime empire like the British should arouse the same alarm – or command the same intellectual commitment – as the fall of the great territorial empire of Rome. In concentrating on the latter, by contrast, Gibbon was heir to the assumption that Rome should be understood as a universal monarchy. An assumption which all four authors had shared, it had been more fully elaborated in a work by one in particular, in Montesquieu's *Considérations sur les causes de la grandeur des Romains et de leur décadence*. Read by Gibbon during his first stay in Lausanne, the *Considérations* no less than *L'esprit des lois* displayed that characteristic 'energy of style and boldness of hypothesis' for which Gibbon remembered Montesquieu in the *Memoirs*:[40] an outline of the work's argument provides the final element of the context in which I wish to set Gibbon's treatment of the Roman Empire.

Consistent with his conviction that a universal monarchy was now impossible, Montesquieu's emphasis throughout the *Considérations* was on the singularity of the Roman achievement of greatness, its difference from anything found in the modern world. The key to this difference lay in the specific circumstances and institutions of the Romans, which had fostered their distinct 'esprit général'. The institutional foundation of the republic had been the law requiring the equal distribution of land between the citizens, who thus had a common interest in the defence of their city. Given such equality, the ancient Romans had despised the pursuit of commerce and the arts; instead they cultivated the military virtues of fitness and discipline, never succumbing to the idleness of modern peacetime

---

[40] *Memoirs*, memoir B, p. 142, although a comparable reference in memoir C, p. 234, indicates that Gibbon was probably thinking of *L'esprit des lois*. That he did, however, read the *Considérations sur les Romains* in Lausanne is indicated by the quotation from it at the beginning of the essay on Caesar's histories: 'Remarques sur les ouvrages et sur le caractère de Salluste, Jules César, Cornelius Nepos et Tite Live', dated 1756, in *Miscellaneous works*, vol. IV, p. 408. Gibbon referred to the edition of Lausanne, 1750. See also Patricia B. Craddock, *Young Edward Gibbon: gentleman of letters* (Baltimore and London, 1982), pp. 89–92.

armies. They had also quickly mastered the art of naval warfare, but since primitive technology (in particular the absence of the compass) meant that this was little more than an extension of land war, it had required none of the resources now needed to attain 'the empire of the sea'.[41]

In any case the Romans had achieved their conquests as much by art as by force. It had been their constant policy to divide their enemies, as in Greece they had first subdued the Aetolian and Achaian Leagues with the assistance of Macedon, before obliging the latter to accept a humiliating treaty. Had Louis XIV been so ruthless, Montesquieu observed, he would have supported the restoration of James II only in Ireland, thereby ensuring that the one power capable of opposing his designs would remain divided.[42] The Romans did not even make peace in good faith: those who began as their 'allies' would be exploited until they had been reduced to the condition of subjects. 'Maîtres de l'univers, ils s'en attribuèrent tous les trésors; ravisseurs moins injustes en qualité de conquérants, qu'en qualité de législateurs.' Properly neither a republic nor a monarchy, Rome had simply become 'la tête du corps formé par tous les peuples du monde': its empire, Montesquieu insisted, was quite different from those subsequently founded by the German nations, in which vassals retained their independence.[43]

When such was the nature of Rome's rise to greatness, the passage from the republic to the principate was of secondary significance. However unedifying a spectacle, the civil wars begun by Sylla and continued by Pompey, Caesar and his assassins had not weakened Rome's Empire: a state in which all were in arms was even more formidable to its enemies.[44] It would be long before the Romans lost their characteristic ferocity: a populace which lived off distributions of corn would remain immune to the temptations – and the disciplines – of trade and manufactures.[45] Gradually, none the less, it became clear that the Empire was ruled as a tyranny.

---

[41] Montesquieu, *Considérations sur les causes de la grandeur des Romans et de leur décadence* (1734), in *Oeuvres complètes*, vol. ii, pp. 75–82, 87–9; for the concept of the Romans' 'esprit général', pp. 147, 193.

[42] *Considérations, Oeuvres complètes*, vol. ii, pp. 91–104. As usual Montesquieu alluded to Louis as 'un grand prince, qui a regné de nos jours'.

[43] *Ibid.*, ii, pp. 105–8.

[44] *Ibid.*, ii, pp. 120–36, esp. p. 129.   [45] *Ibid.*, ii, pp. 147–9.

Crediting Augustus with the decisive changes, Montesquieu emphasized his special talent for dissimulation: 'rusé tyran', he led them 'doucement à la servitude'. His shameless successors, Tiberius and Caligula, had only made the tyranny more open.[46] It was true that the Antonines had then provided a succession of genuinely virtuous emperors, bringing happiness as well as glory to the Roman people. But not even the Antonines had reversed the concentration of power in the hands of the emperor. Heirs to all the powers once distributed among the several magistrates of the Republic, the Roman emperors possessed an authority far more arbitrary than that enjoyed by any king in modern Europe. The only check which they were obliged to acknowledge was that exercised by their armies: if an emperor was unable to impose his authority on his soldiers, then indeed the empire might take on the aspect of an irregular republic, like the military aristocracy of Algiers.[47]

It was not tyranny which undermined the Empire, but, Montesquieu argued, its division as a consequence of the Emperor Constantine's wish to found a new Rome bearing his own name. Even though the Empire was already too large, it had been a body whose parts depended on each other: once severed, they had fallen separately.[48] The western Empire was the first to go. Left open to the barbarian hordes, its attempts to appease them by payment of tribute, or to recruit them into the Roman armies, had simply encouraged their invasions. Soon the emperors had abandoned the city of Rome itself to these conquerors.[49] Meanwhile the eastern Empire survived only as an enfeebled tyranny, in which the emperor was at the mercy of a court riven by faction and religious controversy. It had lingered on because Arab energies were consumed in the conquest of Persia, while the Latins were preoccupied with crusades.[50] Unlike Rome, Constantinople did become a centre of commerce, thanks to the silk trade and the Greeks' mastery of the sea. But if this brought immense wealth to the state, it only softened the process of decline, just as the treasures of the Indies sustained several of the weakest nations in modern Europe. There

---

[46] *Ibid.*, II, pp. 136–47.   [47] *Ibid.*, II, pp. 153–62.
[48] *Ibid.*, II, pp. 166–8.   [49] *Ibid.*, II, pp. 171–82.
[50] *Ibid.*, II, pp. 190–203. The Images controversy was the subject of Montesquieu's one sustained discussion of the role of religion in the decline of the Empire: his diagnosis concentrated upon the Greeks' failure to understand the limits of ecclesiastical and secular power.

were nations, Montesquieu remarked, which God indulged in the useless possession of a great empire.[51] Gradually but inevitably the eastern Empire contracted, until at its end it was like the Rhine when it reached the ocean, reduced to a mere stream.[52]

A similar conviction of the uniqueness of the Roman Empire as a universal monarchy may be seen to have shaped the *Decline and fall*. This is not to suggest, however, that Gibbon simply echoed or amplified Montesquieu's arguments. The references to the *Considérations* in the *Decline and fall* are predominantly critical, conveying a scholar's disdain for the philosopher's complacent attitude to his sources, and readiness to sacrifice chronological accuracy to sweeping generalization.[53] Far richer and more exact than Montesquieu's sketchy outline, Gibbon's narrative made possible a much more subtle treatment of their common theme.

The conviction that the Roman Empire was a universal monarchy pervades the *Decline and fall* from the very start, informing the construction and argument of the opening set of three chapters (over which we know that Gibbon took particular pains). The chapter titles themselves make the point. First comes 'The Extent and Military Force of the Empire in the Age of the Antonines'. This establishes the necessary association of the Empire with the maintenance of a large standing army: simply to defend what they had conquered, the Romans would have to preserve a superiority of both numbers and technique. The importance of the navy, by contrast, is played down.[54] The 'extent' of the Empire is then

---

[51] *Ibid.*, II, pp. 204–5.   [52] *Ibid.*, II, pp. 208–9.

[53] There are references to Montesquieu's *Considérations* in chapters 7 and 26 of the *Decline and fall*. In chapter 7 Gibbon quoted Montesquieu's 'ingenious, though somewhat fanciful' description of the Empire as an irregular republic, not unlike the aristocracy of Algiers, before going on to criticize Montesquieu for his reliance on the doubtful narrative of the Augustan History. The criticism in the final note (n. 136) to chapter 26 was still sharper, as Gibbon derided Montesquieu's inexactness in dating the settlement of the Goths within the Empire: *Decline and fall*, I, ch. 7, pp. 196–7 and notes 52–4, ch. 7; II, ch. 26, p. 640. Gibbon had earlier criticized Montesquieu's theory of general causes for overlooking the significance of particular facts in the *Essai sur l'étude de la littérature* (*Miscellaneous works*, IV, pp. 69–70).

[54] *Decline and fall*, I, pp. 9–18. Gibbon ended his assessment of Rome's military force by estimating its total establishment, by sea and land, to have been no more than 450,000 men: 'a military power, which, however formidable it may seem, was equalled by a monarch of the last century, whose kingdom was confined within a single province of the Roman Empire'. His note (n. 69) referred to Voltaire, *Siècle de Louis XIV*, c. 29, but added the reminder that 'France still feels that extraordinary effort'.

conveyed by a review of its provinces. Tracing a large circle northwards and eastwards from Spain before returning to the Mediterranean, the review ends at the Columns of Hercules, beyond which the Romans had not ventured (a point which Gibbon enforced by a mocking footnote at Voltaire's expense).[55] Gibbon's final judgment of the Empire's extent left no room for illusion. The number of its provinces and the strength of its emperors had encouraged the ancients to confound the Roman monarchy with the globe of the earth: they believed that it was universal. But a prosaic calculation of its length and breadth would have shown them that there was still plenty of room for barbarians.[56]

Chapter 2, on 'the union and internal prosperity' of the Empire under the Antonines, gives pride of place to the benefits which the Empire brought its subjects: religious toleration under sceptical, polytheistic magistrates, and scope for agricultural improvement, commercial exchange and a desirable measure of luxury. But the enumeration of benefits is repeatedly interrupted by reference to the disadvantages for which the union of the Empire was no less responsible. The first of these was the loss of any constitutional freedom in the provinces, followed by the generalization of slavery. The abandonment of conquest in favour of peace and prosperity necessarily undermined military commitment, while cultural uniformity led to intellectual enervation.[57] In chapter 3, 'Of the Constitution of the Roman Empire', the fatal consequences of these weaknesses are made clear. Moving abruptly back in time, the first half of the chapter is a systematic exposé of the political system of Augustus. Under a cloak of constitutionalism, the parvenu Augustus had established a cruel tyranny.[58] The decisive categories

---

[55] *Decline and fall*, I, pp. 19–27, and note 87 (which in the first edition was an endnote): 'M. de Voltaire . . . unsupported by either fact or probability, has generously bestowed the Canary Islands on the Roman Empire.'

[56] *Ibid.*, pp. 27–8. Reinforcing the point, one of Gibbon's manuscript alterations to the text of his copy of the fourth edition was an additional note 88, in which he remarked on the tendency for early geographers to exaggerate distances: d'Anville had shown the extent of the Mediterranean to be rather less than Ptolemy had thought. Once more drawing the obvious modern comparison, Gibbon added that 'Louis XIV once had occasion to say that he lost more land by the geographers than he gained by the generals' (*The history of the decline and fall of the Roman Empire*, vol. I, the fourth edition (London, 1781), p. 33: copy in the British Library, c. 135. h. 3).

[57] *Decline and fall*, I, pp. 29–59.

[58] Augustus' supposedly obscure origins were a recurring preoccupation of Gibbon's: *ibid.*, I, pp. 71–2; amplified in manuscript annotations to the fourth edition: *Decline and fall*, vol. I (fourth edition), p. 85.

here are Montesquieu's: the critical distinction is not between republican and imperial forms of government, but between (limited) monarchy and tyranny or despotism. From its inception under Augustus, Gibbon is arguing, the Roman Empire was an extended despotism – a universal monarchy in the full pejorative sense of the term.[59] Hence the profound ambivalence of his final, famous assessment of the Antonine Age. It may have been the age in which humanity was most happy and prosperous, but that was the result of the improbable contingency of the Antonines' own austere virtue. In its constitution the Empire remained a despotism; and since the Romans had deceived themselves into thinking that their Empire filled the world, the world became for them 'a safe and dreary prison'.[60]

As a despotism dependent on its standing army, the Roman Empire was also condemned to instability. Decadence, material and moral or cultural, was a necessary consequence of universal monarchy, and provided Gibbon with the leading theme of the *Decline and fall's* first three volumes. But as Gibbon had known from the outset, decline was not synonymous with fall: his problem was as much one of the Empire's survival as its decay. As he traced the course of crisis and recovery through the reigns of Severus, Diocletian, Constantine and Theodosius, a history took shape whose implications were, if anything, still more troubling than the 'simple and obvious' story of decline. What Gibbon found himself explaining was the capacity of a universal monarchy to renew itself, by shifting its centre, by devolving its authority upon subordinate Caesars, each with his own court, by a timely and ostentatious abdication (for which Gibbon compared Diocletian directly with Charles V) and an ensuing division of the Empire between east and west, and finally by harnessing the spiritual force of Christianity.[61] The last may indeed have eradicated all surviving traces of pagan tolerance and civic spirit; but its contrasting faces of enthusiasm and superstition were ideally fitted to revitalize and sustain a

---

[59] *Decline and fall*, i, pp. 60–74.
[60] *Ibid.*, pp. 76–84. The assessment of the Antonine Age is on p. 80. In the first edition the Roman world was a 'secure' rather than 'safe' prison.
[61] *Ibid.*, chs. 5 (Severus), 13 (Diocletian), esp. pp. 391–2 on the abdication ôf Diocletian, with an allusion to Robertson as the historian of Charles V; ii, chs. 17, 20 (Constantine); iii, ch. 27 (Theodosius).

universal monarchy. Whatever the degree of its internal corruption, such a monarchy could still endure: for the Empire to fall, the intervention of an external force was required, in the shape of the barbarians. Their appearance on the borders of the Empire finally exposed the self-deception at the heart of the pretension to universal monarchy, and their speedy conquests revealed the extent to which the Roman armies had lost the commitment on which their superiority depended.[62]

In the long run, however, the settlement of the barbarians in the western Empire would lay the basis of a new political system, one which Gibbon was confident would secure Europe against a recurrence of universal monarchy on the Roman model. The theme is taken up and displayed in volume v, chapter 49, in which Gibbon carries the reader from the controversy over images in the early eighth century to the issuing of the Golden Bull by the Emperor Charles IV in 1356. Astride his narrative lay Gregory VII's assertion of the papal claim to temporal as well as spiritual supremacy, the restoration of the Empire in the west by Charlemagne, and the conflict between the twelfth- and thirteenth-century papacy and the two Fredericks, 'the greatest princes of the Middle Age'. Yet Gibbon passes over these momentous events with striking brevity, and an apparently calm conviction that neither pope nor emperor was ever in a position to establish a universal temporal authority.[63]

If there was a moment when the balance between them was endangered, it was when Henry VI succeeded in uniting the German Empire to the kingdoms of Naples and Sicily.[64] But neither Henry nor his son Frederick II had capitalized on the opportunity, and the papacy had recovered its nerve in time to frustrate their ambition. Shortly after the death of Frederick II in 1250, Naples passed to the Angevins, while the end of the Hohenstaufen dynasty left the Empire in Germany resembling 'a monster with an hundred heads'. The phrase added a rhetorical flourish to Pufendorf's notorious image of the Empire as '*monstro simile*'; but Gibbon immediately made his argument precise by adding, after

---

[62] *Ibid.*, II, pp. 636–40, on the settlement of the Goths within the Empire under Theodosius.
[63] *Ibid.*, v, pp. 88–165.
[64] *Ibid.*, v, ch. 49, p. 162; cf. ch. 56, pp. 642–3.

Montesquieu, that 'the union of the Germans has produced, under the name of an empire, a great system of a federative republic'.[65] The ostentatious majesty with which Charles IV issued the Golden Bull in 1356 was thus but a mask for the emperor's weakness – a telling reversal of the modesty under which Augustus has hidden the secret of his 'absolute and perpetual monarchy'.[66] Gibbon stopped his *History* before the accession of Charles V; but his point had been made: 'There is nothing perhaps more adverse to nature and reason than to hold in obedience remote countries and foreign nations, in opposition to their inclination and interest.'[67] A universal monarchy such as the Roman Empire had once sought to impose had always been unnatural, and there had been no serious prospect of its renewal in the west.

Nominally, the eastern Empire had remained the heir to the universal pretensions of ancient Rome throughout the Middle Ages. But Gibbon never supposed that it had inherited the ambition of its predecessor. In his introduction to the final two volumes of the *Decline and fall*, he had made it clear that he expected the interest of Byzantine history to lie in its 'passive' connection to the revolutions which transformed the world during the Empire's long decline: his narrative was to have Mahomet, the Crusaders and the Great Khan, not the Greek emperors, as its active protagonists.[68] That judgment was confirmed in chapter 53, when Gibbon reviewed the extent and character of the eastern Empire in the tenth century. However spacious its provinces, the extent of the Empire only concealed its weakness. 'The vanity of the Greek princes most eagerly grasped the shadow of conquest and the memory of lost dominion.'[69] The military strengths of the Greeks were those of defence, not aggression. To defeat the more warlike Saracens and Franks they had relied on superior art and wealth: the

---

[65] *Ibid.*, v, pp. 164–6. Compare with Robertson, *Charles V*, vol. I, pp. 180–6, where the Empire is characterized as a 'regular confederacy', and pp. 376–80 note 41. Gibbon referred to Robertson's discussion, and to their common guide through 'the immense labyrinth of the *jus publicum* of Germany (M. Pffefl, *Nouvel abrégé chronologique de l'histoire et du droit public d'Allemagne* (2 vols., Paris, 1776) in his note 149). For Pufendorf's image: Severino de Monzambano [Samuel Pufendorf], *De statu imperii Germanici* (1667, 1684 edn), Cap. VI, section ix, p. 237; and for Montesquieu's concept, *L'esprit des lois*, book IX, ch. I, in *Oeuvres complètes*, vol. II, pp. 369–70.

[66] *Decline and fall*, v, pp. 167–9.

[67] *Ibid.*, v, pp. 159.   [68] *Ibid.*, v, pp. 1–7.

[69] *Ibid.*, v, pp. 468–70; compare Howard-Johnston above, pp. 53–77.

jealously-guarded secret of Greek fire, the ability to hire mercenary soldiers and the maintenance of a navy had ensured the Empire's long survival. The wealth of the Empire was due to its populousness, encouraged by an easy immigration policy, and to its commerce and manufactures, the monopoly of silk manufacture in particular. Advanced as these aspects of the Byzantine Empire might seem, however, Gibbon was careful to indicate their limitations. The primacy of the Greeks in silk manufacture was an accident of situation, and did not survive the capture and diffusion of the secret by the Saracens and the Normans. The wealth of the emperors had been accumulated by hoarding, a method, as Gibbon observed, which modern policy had rejected in favour of the use and abuse of public credit. The ships of the Greek navy were smaller in scale than their ancient predecessors, yet naval tactics remained unchanged from the time of Thucydides.[70] If, as Montesquieu had suggested, the Greek Empire offered an early example of the relatively unaggressive tendencies of a maritime, commercial empire, it did so, Gibbon would add, in a primitive, pre-modern form.

Internally, the eastern Empire had settled into a lifeless despotism. The emperors devoted themselves to superstitious ceremony, while their subjects never aspired even to the idea of a free constitution. The eastern Church could offer no countervailing power: Greek ecclesiastics were the subjects of the civil magistrate, and never succeeded like the Latin clergy in establishing the Church as an 'independent republic'.[71] The result was an abject spiritual and cultural uniformity, from which no Byzantine Athanasius could emerge to break the fetters of 'a base and imperious superstition'. Such a uniformity, Gibbon observed, was the antithesis of the happy mixture of union and independence – union of language, religion and manners, independence of governments and interests – which had proved so stimulating to the cities of ancient Greece, and which had since been reproduced, on a larger scale but in a looser form, among the nations of modern Europe. While the Empire of the Caesars had undoubtedly checked 'the activity and progress of the human mind', its very aggression had maintained some spirit of emulation among the Romans;

---

[70] *Decline and fall*, v, pp. 471–9, 496–508. [71] *Ibid.*, v, pp. 479–96.

under the Byzantine Empire, the Greeks merely languished in self-satisfied isolation.[72]

When the *Decline and fall* was completed, therefore, six volumes of historical narrative had lent their weight to the conviction that the threat of universal monarchy in Europe had disappeared with the fall of the Roman Empire. It was a conclusion of which Gibbon himself had been confident since 1772, when he drafted the 'General observations'. Written in close proximity to the first three chapters, these play a role in relation to the *Decline and fall* strikingly similar to that of Montesquieu's *Monarchie universelle* in relation to his *Considérations sur la grandeur des Romains*. There Gibbon met the anxiety that Europe might still be threatened with a repetition of the calamities which befell Rome with a two-fold assurance. Not only was Europe now a 'great republic' composed of a number of kingdoms and commonwealths, but there was no known barbarian threat; and if any should arise, America would preserve the civilization of Europe, while the simple arts of agriculture would gradually tame the new savages.[73] From the heights of such confidence, one can perhaps understand why Gibbon should have taken the loss of the British Empire in America so calmly, and have been so dismissive of the troubles of the 'remote and petty province' of Ireland. It was far more important that the dreadful prospect of universal monarchy, for which the Roman Empire had for so long been the standard-bearer, could now be exposed and discounted, enabling humanity at last to turn its back on Rome.

Unfortunately, of course, it was not to be so simple. As Gibbon lived long enough to begin to suspect, the great republic of modern Europe was not secure against a recurrence of extensive despotic empires. Just ten years after Gibbon's death, Napoleon was crowned emperor of the French, and effectively of Europe; within a hundred and fifty years Hitler had proclaimed the thousand-year Reich. Yet if these episodes challenge Gibbon's confidence in the

---

[72] *Ibid.*, v, pp. 508–18. Gibbon's comparison between ancient Greece and modern Europe was very close to Hume's in 'Of the rise and progress of the arts and sciences'. See above p. 258.

[73] *Decline and fall*, III, pp. 629–40. 'General observations on the fall of the Roman Empire in the west', on whose dating and composition: Ghosh, 'Gibbon observed', and see Cameron above, p. 36 and Ghosh, below, pp. 292–3.

end of empire in Europe, it should also be recalled that Europe would twice be saved from the east, if not by barbarians, then at least (as this is a not inappropriate moment to remember) by Slavs, and on the second occasion from the west as well, by Americans.[74]

[74] I am grateful to David Womersley for helpful observations on the first draft of this essay.

CHAPTER 12

The conception of Gibbon's History

Peter Ghosh

I

The key to an analytic understanding of Gibbon's *History* lies, as I have suggested,[1] in his much neglected *Essai sur l'étude de la littérature* of 1758–61. Here he posited a stratified model of the historical process, separating out 'determinate, but general causes' – which operated in the realm of 'manners, religion and all that comes under the yoke of opinion' – from the superficial sphere of 'particular causes'. Once we possess the theory of general causes, 'it allows us to see them governing the greatness and the fall of empires'.[2] Simple as it may sound, this was a conceptual achievement of immense significance. In the first place, the appeal to 'determinate, but general causes' allowed the historian to escape the snares both of rigid system building and of Pyrrhonism (that is, scepticism). Furthermore, although (as Gibbon noted) 'no one doubts the influence of these [general] causes',[3] the French *philosophes*' deployment of manners and religion was bland, since they were not adequately related to the detailed texture of particular events. Gibbon, however, was always conscious that the concrete establishment of that relation was one of the central problems of historical writing. For example, the high political narrative might run contrary to the current of profound forces, and 'it is when [general causes] produce their effects in the teeth of all the partial causes that one can bring into play, that they reveal themselves most strikingly'.[4] Thus Gibbon's ideas on stratification

---

[1] 'Gibbon observed', *JRS* 81 (1991), pp. 132–56, esp. pp. 138, 141, 146.
[2] *Essai sur l'étude de la littérature*, ch. LV. Translations from Gibbon's original French are my own.
[3] *Ibid.*, ch. 50 [MS draft numbering], Add. MSS 34880 f. 151.
[4] Ch. 55, Add. MSS 34880 f. 152; cf. ch. LV and, for example, *Decline and fall*, ed. Bury (2), V, p. 297. Allusion in the text to volumes I–VI of *Decline and fall* indicates the layout of the first

went beyond those of the *philosophes*, especially Montesquieu,[5] even if he modestly ceded to the latter the posthumous(!) honour of putting this idea into practice.[6] At the same time he also antici-pated many of the more significant modern conceptualizations of the historical process (Hegelian, Marxist, *Annaliste* etc.) whilst avoiding much of their rigidity. But though he is in many senses a father of modern historical writing, this, one of his greatest achievements, was not appreciated at the time. Even his most gifted readers, then and now, assumed that he was to be weighed (and usually found wanting) in the scales of eighteenth-century 'philosophy'.[7] Since his ideas are buried deep in the *Essai* and are

edition (1776–88) but references in the following notes are to the second edition of Bury (1909–14).

5 A rudimentary notion of stratification is implicit within the Enlightenment commonplace of *moeurs*; Montesquieu, in particular, was always feeling for a conception of profound causes. A striking passage in his *Considérations sur les causes de la grandeur des Romains et de leur décadence* (1734) contrasts the realm of Fortune with that of 'causes générales' (ch. 18), and this was Gibbon's starting point. However, Montesquieu never achieved a stable conception of stratification: hence his continued allegiance to the importance of individuals (Hannibal, Caesar, Trajan, Belisarius) at the expense of profound causes, and inability to explain Byzantium except as the product 'des troubles *sans cause* et des révolutions sans motifs' (ch. 22, compare section VII below). He had besides virtually no interest in 'secret' causes, nor in ruins and liberty, which were central to Gibbon. Montesquieu was a pioneer in many directions, but the effect of the *Considérations*, as of *L'esprit des lois*, is kaleidoscopic rather than orderly, or stratified. Gibbon was the first to give stratification full purchase throughout the specific texture of an historical account.

6 *Essai*, ch. LV.

7 All Gibbon's early readers discuss him as a broadly literary author. This implicitly separated him from 'philosophy', as is clear from the comparisons drawn between the first volumes of the *History* and Adam Smith's *Wealth of nations*: in Hume's words, the latter's work 'requires too much thought to be as popular as Mr Gibbon's' (19 March 1776, *Miscellaneous Works*, vol. II, p. 160). Indeed the *History* does not present a system of philosophy in the manner of either Smith or Hume's *Treatise*. Its contribution is decentralized and arises from reflection on particular cases: hence Strahan's view that the book 'abounds with the justest maxims of sound policy, which . . . *discover* your intimate knowledge of human nature, and the liberality of your sentiments'. (To Gibbon 8 October 1775, *ibid.*, vol. II, pp. 138–9, my emphasis.) The one palpable element of philosophy *en philosophe* lay in chs. 15–16, as Hume at least perceived (to Gibbon 18 March 1776, *Autobiographies* C, pp. 312–13), but appreciation of these chapters and their 'philosophy' was a minority taste away from the anti-clerical salons of Paris, and drew scant support in Britain even among 'philosophical' readers. In the nineteenth century Gibbon's apparent separation from 'philosophy' widened into a real or virtual denial of intellectual content *tout court*, exemplified in the verdicts of Coleridge, Guizot *et al.* (Ghosh, 'Gibbon observed', nn. 69, 122). Hugh Trevor-Roper has tried to reverse this tradition, by presenting Gibbon principally as the heir of Montesquieu and as the originator of a philosophical history which the former sketched: 'Gibbon and the pub-lication of *The decline and fall* . . . 1776–1976', *Journal of Law and Economics* 19 (1976), pp. 489–505; also, 'Edward Gibbon's *Decline and fall of the Roman Empire*' in *The Great Ideas Today* (Chicago, 1981), pp. 117–58. But this does not, I think, suffice. In his new guise

only fully expounded in its unpublished drafts,[8] we should not be surprised at such a response. None the less, Gibbon's intellectual originality lies here, in the realm of historical theory and practice, and any 'philosophical' consequence he enjoys stems primarily from his contribution to the revolution in the weight and status of historical method which was one of the great achievements of the Enlightenment.

The ideas of the *Essai* can be seen to be worked out twenty years later in the *History*. It is true that in a book which deliberately aspired to sell, Gibbon did not wish to trouble his readers with formal abstractions, but still the idea of stratification underlies its entire conception of causality. There are, first of all, quite explicit reminders, as when he compares 'the importance of laws and manners' to 'the transient intrigues of a court, or the accidental event of a battle'.[9] Beyond this it underlies and elucidates a whole series of tropes. Most familiar is the notion that the fate of the Empire '*seemed* to depend on the life and abilities of a single man': here is the last, superficial defence against inevitable tidal collapse.[10] Again, Gibbon's triumphant surmounting of the classical and Renaissance reliance on capricious Fortune, rests on a counter appeal to 'the deep foundations' of Roman greatness as against the surface mutability of 'the vicissitudes of fortune'.[11] His notion of

---

Gibbon appears essentially as an English-speaking outpost of continental 'philosophy', and, if he is a philosopher, as a derivative one. Neither his initial reception by readers (as above) nor the extent of his intellectual debt to Montesquieu will support this interpretation. Detailed analysis will confirm the truth of Gibbon's statement that his principal obligation to *L'ésprit des lois* lay in its stimulus to 'inquiry', so long as we understand this as a euphemism for 'criticism' along historical lines. (*Decline and fall*, ed. Bury (2), VI, p. 332 n. 147.) In short we must come back to Gibbon's own perspective: that his work *was* deeply connected with enlightened philosophical inquiry, but via its historiographical contribution (*Essai*, chs. XLIV–LV; cf. Ghosh, 'Gibbon observed', n. 68).

8 Published as an appendix to my 'Gibbon's first thoughts', *JRS* 85 (1995) pp. 148–64.
9 *Decline and fall*, ed. Bury (2), II, pp. 168–9; cf. I, pp. 173, 210, 238: 'a tedious detail of subordinate circumstances'; III, p. 128, IV, p. 176 'partial events', pp. 470–1, V, pp. 311, 322, VI, p. 72 etc.; *Journal*, 17 November 1762, 16 September 1763.
10 *Decline and fall*, ed. Bury (2), III, p. 139 (my emphasis); cf. (among many examples) *Journal*, 17 November 1762; *Decline and fall*, ed. Bury (2), IV, pp. 364–6; V, pp. 302–3.
11 *Ibid.*, IV, p. 172; 'the vicissitudes of fortune' (and variants thereon) is a constant trope, e.g. I, p. 3; II, p. 348; III, p. 377; IV, pp. 108, 126; V, p. 392; VI, p. 65 etc. For his conscious superiority over the Renaissance with its 'superstitious respect for the great names of antiquity', 'Common place book' (1755–?6), 'Italian language', Add. MSS 34880 f. 35b; *Essai*, chs. III–VI; *Journal*, 3 December 1763; *Decline and fall*, ed. Bury (2), III, p. 396 n. 42; VII, p. 335.

secrecy, of the 'secret and internal causes' of Rome's fall,[12] is also obviously reliant on the idea of a stratified historical process: secret causes are profound causes, the 'nice and secret springs of action which impel, in the same uniform direction, the blind and capricious passions of a multitude of individuals'.[13] As this statement (which is itself borrowed from the *Essai*)[14] makes clear, 'secrecy' has nothing to do with what is occult or random; rather, secret causes are general and massively predictable. They are only secret in the sense that most (but not all) contemporaries either fail to locate them or else act regardless.[15] Furthermore, it is only by reference to a stratified view of causation that we can excuse or comprehend the contortions of language and metaphor by which Gibbon sought to convey the process of decline and fall – as when we find that the Empire 'continued to languish under the mortal wound' inflicted by Constantine in creating the distinction between Palatines and Borderers.[16] 'Mortal' is out of place for such a slow-acting thrust, but if we substitute 'profound' the oddity is removed. In similar fashion, the alleged abandonment of defensive armour by the legions during the reign of Gratian is described as the 'immediate cause of the downfall of the empire'.[17] Now chronologically there is no immediacy since (in Gibbon's account) the western Empire will not fall for a century; but if we bear in mind that 'immediate' is one of his Gallicisms, meaning literally 'unmediated' and hence referring to causes operating directly in the higher or superficial sphere, his sense becomes clear.[18]

Stratified thinking is pervasive and such instances can be largely multiplied.[19] In the final analysis – notwithstanding Gibbon's

---

[12] *Decline and fall*, ed. Bury (2), II, p. 168.   [13] *Ibid.*, III, p. 196.   [14] *Essai*, ch. LXXIX.

[15] For example, *Decline and fall*, ed. Bury II, p. 450, III, p. 176, IV, p. 19.

[16] *Ibid.*, II, p. 189.   [17] *Ibid.*, III, p. 197.

[18] The famous accusation that Montesquieu, by an inexcusable error, had disguised 'the principal and *immediate* cause of the fall of the Western empire' relies on the same construction: *ibid.*, III, p. 139 n. 143.

[19] For example (1) the flouting of 'public opinion' is the flouting of a profound force, as defined in the *Essai*, ch. LV, cf. *Decline and fall*, ed. Bury (2), III, pp. 143, 232, *Journal*, 17 September 1763; (2) consistent with the *Essai*'s description of 'general causes', the term 'general' – as in 'General observations' (*Decline and fall*, ed. Bury (2), IV, p. 172) – often refers to workings at the profound level for example, *Decline and fall*, ed. Bury (2), I, p. 296, V, p. 283, VI, pp. 105, 462, VII, pp. 316, 329, although the bland usage where it means merely 'outline' or 'overall' is also common. (3) Stratification also pervades the *Memoirs*: 'From the general idea of a militia, I shall descend to the militia of England . . . to the state of the Regiment in which I served, and to the influence of that service on my personal situation and character' (*Autobiographies*, B, p. 178, cf. B, pp. 178–91).

distaste for such analysis – the fall of the Empire is of course due to profound forces, i.e. to internal, moral and religious decay, and the events of wars and policy are but the fluctuating, superficial register of the profound loss of Roman freedom and virtue. *If* he draws an antithesis when he states that 'the great body [of the empire] was invaded by open violence, or undermined by slow decay', it is a false one: violence on top goes *with* decay below or within.[20] Such is the thread behind the history of decline and fall, stated in a sentence. It is nearly, one might suppose, as 'simple and obvious'[21] as the decay of liberty itself – but legions of commentators would rebuke one for saying so.

However, the *History* is more than simple and obvious. Like a gorgeous coral, it is luminous and yet the product of a long series of accretions. Readily as we may grasp its stratified cross-section, it cannot be understood adequately without reference to its conception in the literal, genetic sense, that is as the result of an unbroken chain of intellectual events going back at least to the *Essai*, many of which are subsumed in the *History* itself. Never was there a work less fathomable, if construed simply as a 'text' in isolation.

II

The *Essai* was clear-cut in its insistence that the study of classical 'belles lettres' required both old fashioned erudition or precision in detail as well as a more modern 'philosophical', or as we might say 'conceptual' control: but it said nothing as to the form in which this ambition might be realized. Hence the significant fact that Gibbon's entire *oeuvre*[22] – written or projected – falls into two discrete categories. First, there are works which broadly resemble the *Essai*: short in length, aimed at a learned audience, eschewing literary and rhetorical construction, and centring on themes and problems. Such were his writings on demography, coinage, geography, chronology, classical religion, rituals and shows, literary form and the whole range of 'pièces detachées' which he was for ever collecting up in MS books. These impress both by the breadth of their subject matter and by their resemblance to modern learned articles. The latter feature is no teleological illusion since it stems

---

[20] *Decline and fall*, ed. Bury (2), II, p. 1; cf. III, p. 306.
[21] *Ibid.*, IV, p. 174.   [22] Except the *Memoirs*.

from the enormous influence exercised on Gibbon by that proto-
typical learned society, the French Academy of Inscriptions – better
understood under its familiar title, the Academy of Belles Lettres –
which had (and has) its own periodical publication, the *Mémoires*.
Had he been born a Frenchman and gained access to the Academy,
we can readily imagine him publishing frequently, maintaining a
firm theological and political scepticism, and perhaps becoming
Secretary to the Academy, without ever writing a narrative history.
Such after all was the life of Nicholas Fréret – '*le grand Fréret*', 'the
celebrated Fréret', the type of the Academicians he admired, and
to whom he paid one of his highest (though covert) tributes: 'It is
seldom that the philosopher and the antiquarian are so happily
blended.'[23]

Such 'academic'[24] writing came naturally to Gibbon. This could
not be said of his second set of projects, which centred on the
writing of formal, literary history. In a famous but casually read
statement in his *Memoirs* he stated: 'I *know*, by experience, that from
my early youth I aspired to the character of an historian.'[25] There is
no doubting the ardour of his aspiration: at the very moment the
Essai was being readied for publication in May 1761, Gibbon was
already casting about for possible themes for formal historical
'composition'. But still it was an aspiration rather than a certainty,
as may be seen by his confession at the time that he was unsure
whether he could sustain 'the part of an historian': 'I can only know
my powers by trying them; and in order to learn them I ought soon
to choose some subject of history, which may do me honour if well
executed, and which, in the case of an upset, will not cause me to

---

[23] Respectively *Miscellaneous works*, vol. III, p. 125; *English essays*, p. 136 n. 9; *Decline and fall*, ed.
Bury (2), I, p. 255 n. 90, a tribute repeated at IV, p. 462, n. 118, *Essai*, ch. VIII, *Miscellaneous
works*, vol. III, p. 56. A remarkable account in Gibbon's papers, the 'Catalogue des Divers
morceaux de M. Fréret inserés dans l'Histoire et les Mémoires de l'Academie des Belles
Lettres, distribués ici suivant l'ordre des matieres', Add. MSS 34880 ff. 84–85b, discloses
a species of rational devotion he accorded no one else. But we should not forget the many
other Academicians to whom Gibbon was significantly indebted – d'Anville, de la
Bléterie, de Guignes, Bougainville, Vertot, de la Nauze, Sainte-Palaye – and the roll call
of those he met and approved in Paris in 1763 was essentially that 'of the principal
members of the Academy of inscriptions' (*Autobiographies*, B, pp. 201–4, here p. 204). For
his standing order for the *Mémoires*: to [Becket] 8 May 1762, Bodleian MS Don. d. 137
f. 213.

[24] Although there is a lineal continuity between the eighteenth- and the twentieth-century
usages of this term, I confine myself to the former.

[25] *Autobiographies*, B, p. 193.

regret having spent too much time with a genre which was not my own.'[26]

To write 'history' was to aim high. It was a classical genre which had 'dignity' just as the great historians had 'majesty': the *Decline and fall* was, in Gibbon's own words, 'an important History'.[27] So it required more than the synthesis of philosophic viewpoint and erudite matter which was common ground between himself and the members of the Academy of Belles Lettres.[28] Above all, writing 'history' was a public act which required the power to appeal to a wide audience. It thus involved literary presentation; a portentous, and preferably sublime, subject; and it raised, too, the possibility of authorial fame – something to which, even in 1761, he did not pretend indifference.[29] But these demands involved Gibbon in difficulties. Any large-scale historical composition was bound to involve lengthy stretches of political and military narrative,[30] something he regarded with ambivalence or even hostility. Narrative was the stuff of classical histories and thus it was 'important'[31] by definition. However, like most 'enlightened' historians he detested war, which he considered could only be treated sympathetically within the framework of primitive society.[32] Again, both political

---

[26] 'Idée de quelques sujets pour une Composition Historique', 26 July 1761, Add. MSS 34880 f. 185; cf. *Autobiographies*, B, pp. 166–7.

[27] *Decline and fall*, ed. Bury (2), III, p. 389; *Journal*, 28 August 1762; *English essays*, p. 232; cf. Hugh Blair, *Lectures on rhetoric and Belles Lettres* (London, 1783), vol. II, pp. 259–61, 273, etc.

[28] It is of course absurd of Momigliano to present Gibbon as the sole author of this synthesis – how unGibbonian! D'Alembert himself perceived its possibility (*Encyclopédie*, art. 'Erudition'; cf. *Journal*, 26 April 1762) – as also to reduce the Academicians and others embodying this stance to the mere level of *érudits* (for example, Bayle, Le Clerc and the editors of the *Bibliothèque raisonnée*, cf. *Journal*, 21 March 1664). Momigliano supposed that the *Essai* effected this synthesis, but yet the *Essai* was written in defence of the Academy's viewpoint: *Autobiographies*, B, p. 167. Most surprisingly, he used the accolade to Fréret in the *History* as his epigraph but, even if Fréret is not named here, it is clear that Gibbon is referring to an Academician; A. Momigliano, 'Gibbon's contribution to historical method' (1954), repr. in his *Studies in historiography* (London, 1966), pp. 40–55, at pp. 40–4. Of course Momigliano realized the existence of flaws amidst the profound and durable insight of this early piece, but never attempted the reconstruction of his views this entailed: cf. A. Momigliano, *The classical foundations of modern historiography* (Berkeley, 1990), pp. 74–5; also his 'Eighteenth-century prelude to Mr Gibbon', *Gibbon et Rome* (Lausanne, 1977), p. 61. David Wootton's attempt to modify Momigliano's model by inserting Hume *vice* Gibbon is open to similar objections in principle and fact, 'Narrative, irony and faith in Gibbon's *Decline and fall*', *History and Theory*. Theme issue 33: *Proof and persuasion in history* (1994), pp. 77–105, section I.

[29] 'Idée de quelques sujets . . . ', Add. MSS 34880 f. 185; cf. *Autobiographies*, B, p. 175; E, pp. 333, 346; *Journal*, 7 December 1763.

[30] Cf. *Decline and fall*, ed. Bury (2), I, p. 255.   [31] *Autobiographies*, C, p. 278.

[32] *Decline and fall*, ed. Bury (2), I, pp. 249–50, III, p. 490, VII, p. 199; *Autobiographies*, B, p. 188.

and military narrative was part of the superstructure of 'particular causes' which, except in cases such as the battle of Tours in 732 where the substructure was entirely neutral,[33] did not generate or significantly affect the course of history. Finally, Gibbon was faced – as he repeatedly confessed – with a major stylistic problem: his immediate idols, Montesquieu and Tacitus, both cultivated density and brevity, which translated naturally enough into brief 'academic' utterances, but was hardly suited to be a popular style, sustainable over a long span of narrative.[34] Readers of Gibbon's last two volumes in particular will know how justified is his admission of their stylistic difficulty, and to what extent they still display 'a kind of obscurity and abruptness, which always fatigues, and may often elude, the attention of the reader' such as he had attributed to the *Essai*.[35] The *Memoirs* repeatedly betray his worries over literary style, indicating that, even after the *History* was complete, he knew he had not matched the ease, pace and clarity of his acknowledged master in narrative, Titus Livy.[36]

Given these difficulties, Gibbon's long agony before starting his narrative history; the tensile and imperfect structure of the *History* itself; and his refusal even to contemplate another such project after its completion, all become comprehensible. The *Decline and fall* was not the likely product of natural inclination, but was achieved (insofar as it was successfully achieved) against the grain. Gibbon was driven on to 'climb the summit' by that 'active virtue' which he exalted and by that love of fame (in its classical sense) which, as he confessed 'is the motive, it is the reward, of our labours'.[37] As a matter of fact, he was incapable of writing wholly out of character and the *History* falls somewhere between these two pure types of literary output. Although ultimately an attempt to write in

---

[33] *Decline and fall*, ed. Bury (2), vi, pp. 16–19. However, the 'neutrality of the substructure' must be understood in the context of the argument of section vii below.

[34] *Autobiographies*, B, p. 173, C, p. 278, E, p. 308; *Journal*, 16 September 1763.

[35] *Autobiographies*, B, p. 172; cf. E, p. 333 on volume vi of *Decline and fall*.

[36] 'No one admires the historical talents of Titus Livy more than myself – the majestic march of his narrative which causes events to succeed one another rapidly but without confusion or precipitancy, and the even, sustained energy of his style which seizes the reader from his cabinet so as to place him in the theatre', *Journal*, 24 October 1763. This was the ideal which Gibbon himself could never attain, his process of thought being far too complex cf. *Autobiographies*, A, p. 353; C, p. 278; E, p. 308; E, p. 337; R. Porson, *Letters to Mr Archdeacon Travis* . . . (London, 1790), pp. xxix–xxx.

[37] See *Autobiographies*, E, p. 349; *Decline and fall*, ed. Bury (2), ii, p. 37; 'Vindication' in *English essays*, p. 232 respectively; cf. *Decline and fall*, ed. Bury (2), i, p. 419, ii, p. 110, vi, p. 46.

the public, narrative manner, it is narrative shot through by the
suspensions of a scholarly, analytic, and 'academic' approach.
Indeed it is that mixture which makes the work so superior to its
contemporaries and essentially inimitable; but still its mixed
character stems from protracted and painful origins. To these we
turn.

III

In July 1762 Gibbon effectively halted the search for an ambitious
historical subject begun in the previous year. He allowed himself
two possible alternatives: *The history of the liberty of the Swiss* or *The
history of the Republic of Florence, under the Medicis.*[38] They were
alternatives with but one theme, the value of liberty, the comprehensive moral lesson that underlies all Gibbon's major works, not
least his Roman *History.*[39] However, at this date narrative history
remained an aspiration only because, as he well knew, it would have
to wait upon peace and then upon his Grand Tour. If we look
at what he did, rather than what he aspired to do, there is an
impressive continuity throughout the period 1756–65 (and indeed
1768–72). No doubt he read the modern historical narratives by
Hume, Voltaire and Robertson,[40] but it was only a background
preparation, and he seldom bothered to engage with them. The vast
majority of his time and serious reading was spent on classical
authors and subjects, whilst his insistence on going on Tour, something he had been planning since 1759,[41] was another reflection of
this interest. Leaving aside brief sketches for remote historical
projects, his literary production was almost exclusively classical and
in 'academic' format: in 1761–2 for example, we find the supplement
to the *Essai* on 'the System of Paganism', the *'extrait raisonné'* on
Hurd's Horace, and innumerable journal disquisitions on his
classical reading.[42] Predictably, therefore, on arriving in Lausanne

---

[38] *Journal*, 26 July 1762.
[39] The *Memoirs* certainly fall into this category, with their emphasis on the author's
struggles towards intellectual and moral independence: *Autobiographies*, F, p. 61 (cf.
Journal, 8 May 1762; *Decline and fall*, ed. Bury (2), IV, p. 10), C, pp. 274–5, 289–92, E, pp. 307,
327–47 *passim*; *Miscellanea Gibboniana* (Lausanne, 1952), p. 101.
[40] *Journal*, 11 February 1759, 13 August 1761, 2 November 1761, 28 August 1762.
[41] 'Idée générale de mon sejour à Paris' (1763), *Miscellanea Gibboniana*, p. 110.
[42] Chs. LVI–LXXVIII; cf. *Journal*, 11 January 1761; *English essays*, pp. 27–53; cf. *Journal*, 18 March
1762 respectively.

in May 1763 his first actions were to read Juvenal and to settle down to prepare what he commonly referred to as the *Recueil géographique*.[43] He also expanded his proposed stay in Lausanne from two or three to nine months because he had begun to consider the possibility of publishing the *Recueil* – the first small move away from the plans for narrative composition sketched out the previous year.[44] It is the most humdrum of his extended writings, being, as its title implies, a collection of materials on Italian localities culled from classical authors. Still it bears the hallmarks of the 'academic' approach. Its geographical premiss leads to a physical concentration on the *longue durée* at the expense of narrative, and it is peppered with analytic excursuses on such matters as Fréret's theories on primitive Italian migration and settlement.[45] Such was the unlikely soil from which the original conception of a Roman history – that is, a history of the city of Rome – grew.

What makes the Roman history quite unlike the Florentine and Swiss sketches was that here the narrative conception was *derived from* 'academic' and analytic studies on the topography, buildings and monuments of Rome. The latter were not tacked on, as a secondary division of the subject, as was the case with the narrative histories of his contemporaries.[46] Indeed without its physical basis the very idea which Gibbon first insisted upon, the history of 'the City',[47] would have had little purchase, since the history of 'Rome' was otherwise so hard to distinguish from that of the Empire.[48]

---

[43] Sheffield was not equal to interpreting the tangled MSS of the *Recueil*, and perpetrated the gross howler of elevating the title of its first section – 'Nomina gentesque antiquae Italiae' (Add. MS 34881 f. 121b) – to that of the whole. For its origins *Letters*, nos. 46, 50; *Journal*, 31 December 1763.

[44] *Letters*, nos. 44, 46, 50.

[45] *Miscellaneous works*, vol. IV, pp. 158–63.

[46] The nearest exception is Voltaire's *Le siècle de Louis XIV* (Berlin, 1751): arts and manners still come second to political narrative, but they make a second volume (out of two) rather than a mere tailpiece. Gibbon applauded this, but, equally pertinently, criticized Voltaire for separating out his topics 'as they are all connected in human affairs', *Journal*, 28 August 1762; cf. *Essai*, ch. XLIX.

[47] *Autobiographies*, C, p. 270.

[48] However Gibbon was always confident he could do this. Reading the fifth century *De reditu suo* of Rutilius Claudius Namatianus he noted that by this date Rome had lost the moral persona which had made her 'mistress of the provinces'; 'reduced to her physical idea, she represented nothing more than walls, temples and houses built on seven hills situated on either side of the Tiber' (*Journal*, 19 December 1763). That is, after the moral collapse of the heart of the Empire, a physical history was all that could or should be written; and the history he later conceived as the decline and fall of the Empire was in origin that of the separation of Rome from the provinces, a conception still visible in the

Serious interest in the city of Rome is clear from the first major item of academic reading he undertook at Lausanne in 1763, the fourth volume of Graevius' huge *Thesaurus antiquitatum Romanorum* (1694–9).[49] Along with several shorter works on the monuments and topography of the city, the most important item in the Thesaurus was Nardini's *Roma Antica* (1666), a book he pronounced 'excellent', and its author a 'friend'.[50] Turning to the section on Rome in the *Recueil*, which was written with close reference to Nardini,[51] we find the germ of the history of Rome is already in evidence. It begins with 'Ambitus, Moenia, et Portae' [Circuit, Walls and Gates] and continues with 'Miranda' [Things to Admire]: all of them buildings or monuments. From this exclusively physical basis Gibbon derived 'Aetates' [Ages], so that the Ages of the City were measured in the history of its buildings: either through the waves of building associated with Tarquin, Augustus and the emperors after Vespasian, or via waves of destruction – the Gallic invasion of the third century BC, Nero's fire, and the process of medieval ruin and decay. Interest in this last subject is also clear from his journal.[52] As yet Gibbon remained solely interested in building; he was not concerned to establish its link to the wider history of moral and social life. Thus military victory is not seen as the fruit of Roman virtue; it only 'furnished the occasion for the vow, the riches to build

---

History (*Decline and fall*, ed. Bury (2), VII, p. 218 and below p. 285). The idea for a 'History of the City' could also draw on the famous city histories with which Gibbon was familiar, notably Pietro Giannone's *Istoria civile del regno di Napoli* (2 vols., [The Hague?], 1753) and also F. S. Maffei's *Verona illustrata* (2 vols., Verona, 1731–2), which he read as part of his 'preparatory' work before 1773: *Decline and fall*, ed. Bury (2), III, p. 496, n. 55. But Gibbon was precise about his debt: the contribution of such books was only a remote one, *Autobiographies*, B, p. 143.

[49] *Journal*, 31 December 1763 (Johannes Georgius Graevius, *Thesaurus antiquitatum Romanorum* (Leiden, 1694–9)). He then used P. Cluvier's *Italia antiqua* (Leiden, 1624–9) for the rest of Italy, which did not impress so favourably (*Journal*, 7 December 1763); whilst his apportioning roughly as much labour to Rome as to the rest of the country indicates where his interest lay. He did not now read the other great guide to Roman monuments, A. Donati's *Roma vetus ac recens* (Rome, 1639), but was obviously familiar with it when he wrote 'Sur les triomphes des Romains': cf. *Journal*, 10 October 1763, *Miscellaneous Works*, vol. IV, p. 385 n. *. Presumably he obtained a copy in Rome, since there is no journal entry bearing on the point.

[50] *Journal*, 2 October and 29 October 1763.

[51] *Journal*, 15 October and 20 October 1763; 26–8 March 1764. Writing up his account of Rome at these two widely separate dates explains Gibbon's apparently unresolved indecision as to whether Rome should be the first (ch. 3) or the last (chs. 42–6) town treated in the *Recueil*, but its centrality was clear in either case, Add. MSS 34881, ff. 125b, 141–5b.

[52] *Journal*, 6 October 1763; cf. *Decline and fall*, ed. Bury (2), II, p. 278 and n. 49.

a temple, and the [plundered] works of art to adorn it'. Similarly 'the decadence of the arts' is relevant only for its impact on building styles, not as a symptom of corruption.[53] None the less, here is the origin of the projected history of the City, a full year before Gibbon's moment of inspiration in Rome in October 1764.

In a sense, then, that famous *séance* on the Capitol, brooding on the overlay of the Roman ruins by Christian building, was nothing new. We shall not underestimate the power of Gibbon's literacy in preparing him for what he would see: having read Nardini and Cluvier's *Italia antiqua*, he noted, 'wherever I may end up in Rome or Italy, I shall no longer be a stranger'.[54] By the same training he was a firm believer in the *genius loci*,[55] and he understood from reading Ammianus, the feelings of awe and sublimity which he should feel in the presence of Roman ruins.[56] Visualizing history in terms of successive strata of building – a striking demonstration of disinterest in political narrative – was commonplace with him, and the very idea that 'The cross was erected on the ruins of the Capitol' is one he expresses as early as 1758.[57]

Nevertheless, the physical presence of Rome and his musing on the Capitol – as he supposed, on the very site of the temple of Jupiter – did provide a new inspiration in October 1764, just as he

---

[53] *Miscellaneous Works*, vol. IV, pp. 222, 223.

[54] *Journal*, 13 October 1763; cf. *Letters*, nos. 60, 61. Ancient historians commonly emphasize Gibbon's dependence on literary sources, precisely because evidential expansion since his day has been so much concentrated in non-literary areas. However, despite a relative predominance of literary sources, the tendency of Gibbon's 'academic' work is insistently 'modern', showing a keen interest in coins and inscriptions for example, whilst the *History* is inconceivable without a physical and visual interest in monuments and ruins, even if his receptivity was enhanced by a cultural tradition which was partly literary, but also partly visual: see below, p. 312; cf. Ghosh, 'Gibbon observed', n. 143. Francis Haskell (moved by *his* disciplinary imperatives) comes close to breaching the received opinion, but is ultimately a victim thereof and of a concern with 'images', which embraces busts, pictures and ruins indiscriminately, *History and its images* (London, 1993), pp. 186–93.

[55] He supposed this conception to be common to pagan and Christian alike: 'All religions are local to a certain extent. The least superstitious of Christians would feel more devotion on Mount Calvary than in London', *Journal*, 16 July 1764; cf. *Autobiographies*, C, p. 267; *Decline and fall*, ed. Bury (2), II, p. 480 and n. 65; VII, p. 236; 'Common place book', 'Genii", Add. MSS 34880 f. 63b.

[56] *Miscellaneous Works*, vol. IV, p. 219; cf. Ammianus Marcellinus *Rerum Gestarum libri qui supersunt*, xvi. 10, ed. and trans. J. C. Rolfe (Cambridge, Mass., 1971), pp. 243–55.

[57] 'On erige le croix sur les debris de Capitole', *Essai*, first draft, ch. 67; Add. MSS 34880 f. 155; this is of course a common conception in the *History*, e.g. *Decline and fall*, ed. Bury (2), II, pp. 1, 484; IV, pp. 57, 112 n. 25; V, pp. 332, 476. See however, Ghosh, 'Gibbon's first thoughts' (above, n. 8) for the important differences between the views of 1758 and later, stemming from the shift in his religious position.

always claimed.[58] In 'Sur les triomphes des Romains', his only significant piece of writing while in Rome,[59] Gibbon noted that Romulus, the founder of the temple of Jupiter Feretrius, was followed by 'all those who afterwards entered in triumph [and who] came to adore the Jupiter of the Capitol'.[60] The triumph was not only a static or symbolic encapsulation of Roman military success and republican virtue, it was '*an institution which became from what followed the principal cause of the greatness of Rome*. Three hundred and twenty of these triumphs took her to that pinnacle of greatness which she occupied under the empire of Vespasian.'[61] Thus it was the temple of Jupiter which caused Gibbon to consider writing the wider history of Roman *esprit*. Its ruin and supersession suggested not only the essence of *romanitas* as a cradle of, and timeless norm for, 'civilization', but also a narrative idea: the succession and cessation of triumphs, of decline and fall in conjunction with the physical decay of the City. Since this was the kernel of the book he ultimately produced, and since it explains the silent abandonment of the statically and geographically conceived *Recueil* – a project to which he had been loyal only six weeks previously[62] – we may reasonably prefer his belief in the profound significance of that Roman evening in October 1764 to the quibbling of pedants who focus on the supposed or literal inaccuracies of the *Memoir* drafts at this point.

IV

I pass over the period 1765–8 with but two remarks. First, the seed planted in Rome was a frail one, a thought at the back of his mind.

---

[58] 'French autobiographical sketch' (1783) (printed by Patricia B. Craddock, *Edward Gibbon, luminous historian, 1772–1794* (London, 1989), p. 367; *Decline and fall*, ed. Bury (2), VII, p. 338; *Autobiographies*, C, p. 270.

[59] First begun 4 November 1763; completed 13 December. But even here he made use of a passage from his Lausanne Journal, compare *Journal*, 3 November 1763, Add. MSS 34880 f. 238. This conforms to the practice of re-using old material sketched in Ghosh, 'Gibbon observed', pp. 138–9, and which was an artistic commonplace before the modern fetish of originality *per se*.

[60] *Miscellaneous works*, vol. IV, p. 383.

[61] Add. MSS 34880 f. 220, original emphasis; cf. *Decline and fall*, ed. Bury (2), III, p. 262, 'the accumulated spoils of three hundred triumphs'. Gibbon's original French text is a loose, and (particularly in its emphasis) significant, remoulding of Montesquieu. Compare Gibbon's 'Ce fut l'origine des triomphes, *Institution qui devint dans la suite la Cause principale de la Grandeur de Rome*' with Montesquieu's *Considérations*, ch. 1.

[62] *Journal*, 30 August 1764; cf. *Letters*, no. 60.

At the time, the *séance* on the Capitol had been but part of a more comprehensive experience, and even in the *Memoirs* it is still only a tailpiece to the impact of 'the *eternal City*', ranging through time from episodes which long precede the *History* – 'each memorable spot where Romulus *stood*, or Tully spoke, or Caesar fell' – to the recent 'miracles of Rome', such as Raphael's Transfiguration and the architecture of St Peter's. Modern classicism, quite as much as ancient ruins, struck Gibbon as sublime.[63] Back in England, having abandoned the *Recueil*, he recurred with seemingly mechanical precision to the status quo of 1762 – poised between the Florentine and Swiss projects – and since he was once more in the company of his lifelong Swiss friend Georges Deyverdun the resolution of the dilemma was simple.[64] Secondly, since the resultant fragment of Swiss History was the product of a series of conscious planning going back to 1761, the psychological impact of its abandonment in 1768 can hardly be exaggerated. In the aftermath Gibbon regressed to the writing of academic 'pièces detachées', such as those which make up the MS essay book of 1768, the essay on the Cyropaedia, and the *Critical observations* on Virgil. Yet he remained anxious to achieve something more substantial than this. One piece in the 1768 essay book, the 'Recueil sur les Poids', evinces the hope that it might evolve, like the *Recueil géographique*, by process of sheer accumulation into a book.[65] His hesitant resumption of the history of *urbs Roma* after 1768 is best explained in this light, since its attractions were similar. It, too, took its origins in detached, apparently 'academic', 'remarks and memorials', but yet it might amount to so much more.[66] Having been burnt once by the flame of ambition, Gibbon hoped to achieve greatness by stealth.

We can trace the outlines of the 'History of the City' in some detail. This may seem a surprising assertion when it has left no manuscript remains, but, in addition to the writings of 1763–5 and

---

[63] *Autobiographies*, C, pp. 267–8 (draft C is the only detailed account we have) cf. D, p. 405; *Decline and fall*, ed. Bury (2), I, p. 288, II, p. 33, III, p. 500 and n. 67. His correspondence (*Letters*, no. 60) and the 'journal' entries made in December 1764, with their praise for *both* classical and post-Renaissance work all make the same point: G. A. Bonnard (ed.), *Gibbon's journey from Geneva to Rome* (London, 1961), pp. 236–51.

[64] *Autobiographies*, C, pp. 273, 276; cf. *Letters*, no. 71.

[65] *Miscellaneous works*, IV, p. 120. For a reconstruction of this period (insofar as it is not super-seded here) and the dating of MSS, see Ghosh, 'Gibbon's dark ages: some remarks on the genesis of the *Decline and fall*', *JRS* 83 (1983), pp. 1–23.

[66] *Autobiographies*, D, p. 412.

the quite detailed account given in the *Memoirs*,[67] we have a great, neglected resource: the extensive passages covering Rome in the *Decline and fall* itself. Here, typically, Gibbon did not so much abandon as overlay his original idea, and he was still insisting in volume VI (1788) that, 'In the first ages of the decline and fall of the Roman empire our eye is inevitably fixed on the royal city.'[68] Unless we bear in mind that original conception, the extraordinary architecture of the finished *History* is hardly comprehensible.

It was of course impossible to construct a continuous narrative of the 'History of the City',[69] but Gibbon was clearly able to sketch its decline and fall through a frieze-like succession of snapshots, which may plausibly be classified into distinct phases. These open with the late history of the senate and the Praetorians, which reveals their declining role in the making and unmaking of emperors. This phase was the closest Gibbon came to any sort of narrative continuity, as is evident from chapters 4–7 of the *History* which are made up of alternating Roman and provincial sections – a plan which highlights the original Roman focus and strongly suggests that Gibbon filled in the imperial 'gaps' later. After the hiatus marked by chapters 8–10 (on the Persians, the Germans and the barbarian incursions of the mid-third century) where Rome drops out of the picture entirely, we enter a new phase. Its history now centres on the ever rarer visits of provincial-born emperors, their triumphs and their buildings. Starting with Aurelian,[70] these visits are faithfully minuted. After the expiry of senatorial authority is formally pronounced,[71] there follows the assertion of a striking negative: that 'the most fatal though secret wound which the senate received from the hands of Diocletian and Maximian was inflicted by the inevitable operation of their absence'.[72] Nothing could be more expressive of an originally Rome-centred perspective. The last of the triumphs comes with Diocletian, and even ceremonial visits peter out in Constantine's studied insult 'to the Jupiter of the Capitoline Hill'[73] and Constantius' visit of 357. This terminus is marked by Gibbon sounding the full-toned note of awe

---

[67] *Ibid.*, C, p. 284. [68] *Decline and fall*, ed. Bury (2), VII, p. 218.
[69] Ghosh, 'Gibbon's dark ages', p. 16.
[70] *Decline and fall*, ed. Bury (2), I, pp. 321–3, 333–4. [71] *Ibid.*, I, p. 364.
[72] *Ibid.*, I, p. 369, although insistence on the importance of absence from Rome goes back at least to ch. 7 (I, p. 187).
[73] *Ibid.*, I, pp. 406–7; II, p. 328 respectively.

at Rome's monuments, and Trajan's column in particular: just as he had done in 1763 and would do again in the *Memoirs* nearly thirty years later.[74]

A third phase coincides with the 'period of the fall of the Roman empire'[75] and centres on the increasing openness of the City to barbarian invasion. When drafting the *Essai* in 1758 and also the 'General observations' in 1772, Gibbon had dated *imperial* collapse to the years after 395 under 'the degenerate successors of Theodosius',[76] – a chronology which coincided fairly enough with the sack of the *City* by Alaric in 410. By 1780, when writing volume III, he had revised the period of imperial collapse forward to the Goths' passage of the Danube in 376[77] but still, despite a now considerable time-lag, the sack of Rome remained the centrepiece of the volume: significant testimony to the inertial force of the original plan, which helps explain a loss of coherence as this tome 'deviated into . . . minute and superfluous diligence'.[78] Gibbon's first preparations can be seen in chapter 29 after the death of Theodosius; chapter 30 proclaims Alaric's designs on Rome and narrates both his first appearance before Rome in 404, and that of Radagaisus in 405 – which latter event we know to have been covered in the drafts for the 'History of the City'.[79] Finally, chapter 31 brings the narrative climax, preceded and long suspended by the sublime picture of the manners of 'the ETERNAL CITY',[80] which ranges over the full period of 620 years since Rome was last entered by the Gauls in 211 BC.

After this climactic effort, one is bound to feel that further brief accounts of the threats to Rome posed by Attila, Genseric and Ricimer are bathetic, and it seems clear from the overviews of imperial decline of 1758 and 1772, that if empire was all he had been writing about, Gibbon must have agreed. (Perhaps reflection along these lines underlies his later regret that volumes II and III were over-long?)[81] But when we recall the hybrid origin of the 'History of the City', whereby regard for the general, narrative perspective

---

[74] *Ibid.*, II, pp. 275–8; *Journal*, 26 September 1763; *Miscellaneous works*, vol. IV, p. 219; *Autobiographies*, C, pp. 267, 270.

[75] *Decline and fall*, ed. Bury (2), III, p. 73.

[76] *Ibid.*, IV, p. 174; cf. *Essai* draft, ch. 55, Add. MSS 34880 f. 152.

[77] *Decline and fall*, ed. Bury (2), III, p. 139 n. 143.

[78] *Autobiographies*, E, p. 324.   [79] *Decline and fall*, ed. Bury (2), III, p. 283, n. 88.

[80] *Ibid.*, III, pp. 304–25.   [81] *Autobiographies*, E, p. 324.

of the loss of liberty is offset by tenacious adherence to the more 'academic' idea of the *longue durée* as embodied in the persistence of the city itself – its buildings, rituals, shows, riots, demography, taxes, coinage and food supply – then the prolongation of the story after 410 becomes comprehensible.[82]

The accounts of these late invasions lead to a new phase in the history of the City. Paradoxically, because there is no effective western *Empire* after the invasions of Alaric, the city and senate of Rome become a more natural focus for the history of '*Italy*' – a term which becomes increasingly prominent after the death of Theodosius.[83] This contraction of horizons allows the original project to come more closely to the surface than at any time since chapter 7, as is evident from the frequent citation of sources, some of a very inferior stripe, known to have been associated with his work on the 'History of the City' before 1773: Baronius, Pagi, Sigonius, Tillemont, Muratori's *Antiquitates* and *Annali*.[84] Thus Gibbon permits himself extended episodes on Roman buildings, festivals and institutions: the Lupercalia, the senatorial trial and condemnation of Arvandus for misrule in Gaul – as if this were Cicero *contra* Verres – and Odoacer's restoration of the consulship.[85] A further explicit reference in the published text to the 'History of the City' is another symptom of the 'surfacing' of the original stratum.[86]

But from this point, as we enter the second half of the *History* (volumes IV–VI) and 'the darkest ages of the Latin world',[87] Rome's *longue durée* tends increasingly to become that of the reader. It is hard for Gibbon to produce new effects as he faithfully records Theodoric's or Narses' entries into Rome: three volumes after the knell of the triumph has been sounded with Diocletian in AD 303, he has, like a theatrical producer, to announce positively its last

---

[82] Elements supplementary to the original plan – such as Gibbon's longstanding interest in the barbarian nations (Germanic and Oriental), and the developing narrative of the eastern Empire – are also responsible, although the latter of these may derive via a progression from Old to New Rome.

[83] Cf. *Decline and fall*, ed. Bury (2), IV, pp. 28–9.

[84] *Autobiographies*, C, p. 284; cf. *Decline and fall*, ed. Bury (2), III, p. 495, n. 52, and chapter 36 *passim*; on Muratori see Ghosh, 'Gibbon's dark ages', n. 10 and 'Gibbon observed', n. 167.

[85] *Decline and fall*, ed. Bury (2), IV, pp. 21–2, 35–6, 42–5, 58–9 respectively; cf. II, p. 205 n. 185, IV, pp. 532–3, Add. MSS 34880 f. 157 and n. ‡ on Cicero.

[86] *Decline and fall*, ed. Bury (2), IV, p. 21 n. 52.

[87] *Ibid.*, IV, p. 216.

appearance in AD 554.[88] Unfortunately Italy is omitted from
Procopius' *De aedificiis*, which robbed him of the chance to survey
Rome's monuments and ruins in any depth at this date, and
although he writes at some length on the Gothic sieges of Rome in
the sixth century,[89] these tell us nothing of the life and history of
the city. Rather, they are episodes in military, not urban history,
digested (like so much else in volume IV) exclusively from
Procopius. By the end of the century Gibbon is reduced to the
bathos of 'Rome was again besieged'.[90] When, in accordance with
the original project, 'we again inquire into the fate of Rome' it
appears that in the time of Gregory the Great she 'had reached . . .
the lowest period of her depression', although there would seem to
be strong competition for this accolade a century later under Pope
Leo.[91]

One explanation for this bathos is that we are now trying to read
the 'History of the City' chiefly through the medium of volume IV of
the *History*, by some distance its most unsatisfactory component. It
is a plausible inference that had Gibbon persisted in writing the
'History of the City', he would have achieved a more satisfactory
organization and proportions. Fundamentally though, he was a
consciously and even exaggeratedly 'enlightened' historian, who
was not mealy-mouthed in stating that as the 'History of the City'
progressed beyond 476 it went through 'the darkness of the middle
ages'.[92] From such disenchantment springs not only bathos but the
curtailing of the entire history of Rome between the eighth and
fourteenth centuries to just half a chapter in the published
work (chapter 49). Over the years he repeatedly indulged in the
rhetorical trope of 'ten centuries of anarchy and ignorance', of
'the world awakening from a sleep of a thousand years'[93] – a
distinctly inflated view compared with Robertson's contemporary

---

[88] *Ibid.*, IV, pp. 202–4, 452; cf. I, p. 406.

[89] *Ibid.*, IV, pp. 332–47, 427–37; cf. IV, p. 264 n. 106 on Procopius.

[90] *Ibid.*, V, 22. We can infer little about the history of the city from chapter 22, the *tour de force*
on Roman law and manners, since, although the idea for such a project is implicit in the
Essai (ch. LII, cf. *Decline and fall*, ed. Bury, I, p. 137, n. 75 on Dio Cassius), ch. 44 was a new
composition in 1782: *Autobiographies*, E, p. 326 and below pp. 302–3.

[91] *Decline and fall*, ed. Bury (2), V, p. 32; cf. p. 281.

[92] *Autobiographies*, C, p. 284.

[93] *Decline and fall*, ed. Bury (2), IV, p. 130, *Journal*, 27 September 1762; cf. *Miscellaneous works*,
vol. IV, p. 430 (1756); *Decline and fall*, ed. Bury (2), I, p. 64; IV, p. 286, n. 160; VI, pp. 112, 416;
VII, p. 33.

estimate of only four centuries.[94] This emphasis derives of course from the centrality of the 'Renaissance of Belles Lettres' to Gibbon's historical outlook since his youth.[95] This was why the plan for the 'History of the City' ended in 'the ruins of Rome in the fourteenth Century'[96] – a goal kept in view in the finished *History* when, at its conclusion, we meet Petrarch who 'revived the spirit and study of the Augustan age'; he in turn stands at the head of a genealogy of Renaissance humanists which of course ends with Gibbon himself and his own 'pilgrimage' to Rome.[97]

Gibbon's 'primitive' streak needs emphasis, not only because of our reluctance to acknowledge it today, but because of its consequences. In the 'dark ages' after the fall of the western Empire the hybrid conception of the history of the City – a libertarian narrative theme within a physical urban context – ceased to operate. Gibbon had *no* general narrative conception for the later period;[98] only the physical and local context remained. This was the root of the enormous difficulties he would face with the second half of the *History* in the 1780s.

In particular he did not take the path marked out by the authors he read in his youth – most obviously Giannone's *Civil history of Naples*.[99] He did not seek to trace the transformation of Rome, the capital of the Empire, into Rome, the seat of the papacy. In his own insistent imagery, he was more interested in 'the ruins of the Capitol' than the erection of 'the triumphant banner of the Cross' upon them.[100] Yet their connection is palpable within the *History* itself. Although he set out in the 'General observations' of 1772 from the premiss that Christianity discouraged the traditional, active

---

94 William Robertson, *The history of the reign of the Emperor Charles V. With a view of the progress of society in Europe, from the subversion of the Roman Empire, to the beginning of the sixteenth century* (London, 1769): 'A view of the progress of society', vol. I, pp. 17, 19.

95 For example, *Essai*, ch. III; *English essays*, p. 47; *Journal*, 9 February 1764, review of Abbé Fleury.

96 *Autobiographies*, C, p. 284; cf. *Decline and fall*, ed. Bury (2), i, p. 63 n. 45.

97 *Decline and fall*, ed. Bury (2), VII, pp. 266, 338; *Autobiographies*, C, p. 266; cf. *Decline and fall*, ed. Bury (2), IV, p. 21, n. 52.

98 None the less, in chapter 49 and again in chapters 69–71, he can think of no better way to mark the passage of time than to trace the futile and false attempts to resurrect Roman liberty, which is effectively a confession of bankruptcy.

99 Giannone, *Istoria civile*. Gibbon's well-known reference to Giannone in the *Memoirs*, B, p. 143, is fully substantiated by the contents of his Lausanne 'Common place book' of 1755–?6, Add. MSS 34880 ff. 5–83 *passim*.

100 *Decline and fall*, ed. Bury (2), II, p. 1; see above p. 282.

virtues of *civil* society,[101] this did not preclude the Church from becoming an *ecclesiastical* home for, and successor to, republican virtue. Not only did the primitive Church constitute 'a distinct republic' within the Roman Empire,[102] but 'the safety of the [Christian] society, its honour, its aggrandizement, were productive, even in the most pious minds, of a spirit of patriotism, such as the first Romans had felt for the republic'.[103] For this reason, 'were it possible to suppose that the penetration of Decius . . . could foresee the temporal dominion which might insensibly arise from the claims of spiritual authority, we might be less surprised that he should consider the successors of St Peter as the most formidable rivals to those of Augustus'.[104] Alongside many continuities of detail, Gibbon perceived a substantial, religious continuity between paganism and Catholicism;[105] whilst the fact of papal succession 'to the throne of the Caesars', leading to the establishment of a Christian republic comparable in extent to the old Empire, based on similar manners and with a common jurisprudence, was also palpable.[106] The relationship of the papacy and the Empire formed, he said, 'the important link of ancient and modern . . . history.'[107] So *if* he had been trying to construct a link between them in this fashion, and his plan really had been to describe 'the triumph of barbarism *and religion*',[108] he knew precisely the road to take.

Yet despite this mass of textual potential,[109] Gibbon was never

---

[101] *Ibid.*, IV, p. 175.
[102] *Ibid.*, II, p. 129; cf. II, pp. 3, 334.   [103] *Ibid.*, II, p. 42; cf. II, pp. 38, 57, 110–11, 311–12.
[104] *Ibid.*, II, p. 121; cf. II, p. 384.   [105] *Ibid.*, III, pp. 226–7.
[106] *Ibid.*, II, p. 92, IV, pp. 86–7; cf. II, pp. 48–9.   [107] *Ibid.*, V, p. 286.
[108] *Ibid.*, VII, p. 321 (my emphasis). This quotation was first torn from context by Bury (*ibid.*, I, p. vii) and has sown confusion ever since. In context Gibbon was discussing the causes of the destruction of Roman monuments: 'In the preceding volumes of this History I have described the triumph of barbarism and religion; and I can only resume, in a few words, their real or imaginary connection with the ruin of ancient Rome.' Thus 'triumph' here was a triumph in the strict sense, that is of the entry of the barbarians and the papacy into the city, and their consequent physical impact. But, as is clear from this quotation alone, Gibbon did not rate this highly, allotting more importance to the medieval destruction wrought by demand for building stone and by 'the domestic hostilities of the Romans themselves' (*ibid.*, VII, pp. 322–9, at p. 326). It ought to be self-evident that neither the triumph of the papacy, nor of the barbarians, nor of 'barbarism' (for example, *ibid.*, VII, p. 98) are general interpretative themes in the *History*. For what the *History* is about after volume IV, see sections VI–VII below.
[109] All the precedent arguments are, of course, partial ones: thus the Church stood for passive obedience as much as civic freedom (*Decline and fall*, ed. Bury (2), II, pp. 76, 313–14, IV, p. 175), whilst the foundation of the papacy represented not simply the triumph but also the abuse of primitive Christianity (*ibid.*, II, pp. 42–3, 85–6 etc).

tempted to develop it. At a very early stage in the *History* (and evidently as a result of his work on the 'History of the City') he goes out of his way to debunk any real, that is, moral, continuity between Rome and the papacy. After describing the secular games of AD 248 in chapter 7, he comments: 'when the popish jubilees, the copy of the secular games, were *invented* by Boniface VIII, the crafty pope pretended that he only *revived* an ancient institution'.[110] The jubilees are thus a modern fruit of papal avarice, being intimately linked with the system of papal indulgences which lay at the root of the Protestant 'revolt' of the sixteenth century.[111] A similar hostility underlies other chance remarks on the papacy,[112] as we might expect given the centrality to his literary pantheon of writers such as Giannone, Fra Paolo and Pascal, who from youth on had defined his detached, moderate and enlightened pedigree.[113] But why, if all these authors had confronted the papacy in their work, did Gibbon effectively shun it? The obvious explanation for this renunciation (which he himself took for granted) is that, although he was in many things profoundly European, he was in others as profoundly English: the danger posed by the papacy and Catholicism was simply too remote to be worth confronting, and his emigrations to Protestant Lausanne would not change his perception.[114] Underlying all his historical projects was a 'simple and obvious' moral purpose. Thus he could remark of the gain and loss of constitutional liberty – itself a typically English point of reference – 'Both lessons equally useful.'[115] By contrast, there was no useful lesson to be derived from papal Rome and so it would hardly feature.

---

[110] *Ibid.*, I, 208 n. 72 (my emphases).   [111] *Ibid.*, VII, pp. 256–8.

[112] For example, *ibid.*, II, p. 148, cf. pp. 99, 113.

[113] For example, *Autobiographies*, B, p. 143; *English essays*, p. 254; *Decline and fall*, ed. Bury (2), VII, p. 104 n. 38.

[114] I adhere to the orthodox view that *English* anti-Catholicism in the eighteenth century was a trivial, not a mainstream pursuit. Another explanation of Gibbon's avoidance of the papacy is that this was an area rendered sensitive by his youthful conversion and consequently open to adverse critical comment. Still, the fragmentary remarks which appeared in the *History* were sufficiently explicit to offer an opening along these lines, even if critics preferred in fact to concentrate on his 'infidelity' (*English essays*, p. 268 notwithstanding: cf. *ibid.*, pp. 233, 272). Certainly, the idea that Gibbon's account of the papacy is 'a relatively benign one' is a misreading relying only on the conventional gentility of the close to chapter 70 (*Decline and fall*, ed. Bury (2), VI, p. 311): cf. J. G. A. Pocock, 'Edward Gibbon in history', *The Tanner Lectures in Human Values* (Salt Lake City, 1990), vol. XI, pp. 291–364 at p. 359.

[115] *Journal*, 26 July 1762.

It is probable that because he was confining himself to reconnoitring a 'History of the City', physical and local context remained sufficient for Gibbon, and the want of a large-scale conceptual and narrative structure for 'dark age' Rome did not press. In any event he persevered and 'almost grasped the ruins of Rome in the fourteenth Century' in the summer of 1772.[116] None the less, the conceptual void is plainly associated with the thin, formless and disconnected nature of his early studies for the period after 476.[117] But by a typical act of procrastination, he simply left this difficulty outstanding. Once he had settled his estate after the death of his father, the great concern was to begin a history, not to worry about how it might one day finish – a concern reflected by a giant step backwards in time. Thus the transition from the 'History of the City' to that of the Empire was marked by the 'General observations on the fall of the Roman Empire in the west' of 1772 which in turn led into the first draft of the opening chapters of the *History* as we know it.[118] The 'History of the City' was not so much abandoned as incorporated into the new work: like a Roman ruin itself, it supplied the substructure to Gibbon's intellectual triumph over the next ten years (1773–82). However, it also left enormous unresolved questions to face, should he ever get beyond AD 476.

V

By transferring from the history of the City to that of the Empire we are at once struck by the sheer increase in the scale of the undertaking. This was a striking index of resurgent ambition, and Gibbon would not have forgotten the twenty-year labour of Livy (which would parallel his own), nor the reward it secured: to become 'one of that small number of great men, whose very name is the fairest elegy that can be pronounced on him'.[119] All the same,

---

116 *Autobiographies*, C, pp. 284–5.   117 See Ghosh, 'Gibbon's dark ages', pp. 2–3, 16.
118 The matter of this paragraph is extensively discussed in Ghosh, 'Gibbon's dark ages' and also his 'Gibbon observed'.
119 'Remarques sur les ouvrages et sur le caractère de ... Tite Live' (1756), *Miscellaneous works*, vol. IV, pp. 422–34. 'When, on one side, we consider the greatness of the task and, on the other, the prodigious labours Titus Livy must have spent on [his history] to render it as perfect as it is, twenty years will not be judged ill-spent; on the contrary, we will admire the application of this author almost as much as his genius', *ibid.*, vol. IV, p. 423.

in the first three volumes many facets of the expansion arose easily from the original project, and in all probability the tendency towards 'insensible' expansion was one of the primary causes of the change of plan.

We saw, for example, that the early narrative made more sense when it became continuous, rather than being cut into 'Roman' segments. Again, as Gibbon admitted, consideration of the form of Roman government was inseparable from that of its seat,[120] and so the account of the new system of administration under Diocletian and Constantine is but a logical extension of his earlier work. Then the initial focus on Rome all too readily suggested a spotlit counter-focus on the 'SECOND or NEW ROME',[121] to say nothing of the east/west polarity which runs through the entire work. The famous description of Constantinople in chapter 17 clearly reflects this origin in its surface brilliancy and underlying coldness: the new town encloses only five, not seven hills; it is 'an artificial colony . . . raised at the expense of the ancient cities of the empire', but the old capital still maintains the supremacy 'due to her age, to her dignity, and to the remembrance of her former greatness' – qualities of which she can never, by definition, be deprived.[122] And by an extraordinary exercise of double standards, Gibbon refuses to give an account of Constantinople's buildings or monuments, even though such accounts form the core of his evocation of the awful sublimity of Rome.[123] Most important of all, the underlying libertarian theme was essentially the same as before, and the phases of the history of the City clearly suggest, and sometimes dictate, the outlines of the first three volumes as we have seen.

Beyond simple expansion, the history of the Empire also involved labours of integration, a process first begun in the 'General observations' of 1772. Gibbon's preparatory work before this was *not* simply confined to the City – a striking measure of his incoherence and uncertainty; rather, he carried out 'various studies' which were

---

[120] *Decline and fall*, ed. Bury (2), I, p. 407; II, pp. 168–213.
[121] *Ibid.*, II, p. 168.   [122] *Ibid.*, II, pp. 158–60; 164; 166 respectively.
[123] *Ibid.*, II, p. 163. Gibbon's argument that it would contravene the design of the *History* to give such a description is plainly fraudulent, and he *does* offer a description of the new town's buildings and monuments later in chapters 40 and 60 (IV, pp. 258–66, VI, pp. 427–30; cf. V, p. 142, VI, pp. 79–81), although the emotional coldness remains. It goes without saying that he eschews an account of Turkish building, VII, p. 210.

'directly or indirectly relative' to the final *History*.[124] The extra items were his work on Godefroy's commentary on the Theodosian Code, and an assessment of 'the causes and effects of the Revolution' effected by the rise of Christianity. The desire to include these supplies another obvious motive for the switch from the history of the City to the Empire; but whilst the evidence of the Code is absorbed in diffused fashion over much of the opening three volumes, the incorporation of religious history – strictly, of the church 'as subservient only, and relative, to the [state]'[125] – was a major and discrete expansion. This is apparent from the *de novo* composition of the very first chapters on Christianity (chapters 15–16),[126] as also from the complex (but superlative) integration of civil and ecclesiastical history in volumes II and III via multiple narrative strands, which stands in marked contrast to the simple linearity of the 'History of the City'. Finally, there are elements which are purely additional: most obviously the display in chapters 8 and 26 of the Near and Far Eastern learning on which Gibbon had prided himself since his teens, and which was a central focus for his reading in the *Mémoires* of the Academy of Inscriptions.[127]

In these respects embracing the imperial theme was deeply attractive: it allowed Gibbon to build in a large number of analytic and 'academic' components, exemplified by the famous analyses of

---

[124] *Autobiographies*, D, p. 412, C, p. 285.   [125] *Decline and fall*, ed. Bury (2), v, p. 261.

[126] *Autobiographies*, E, p. 308.

[127] Momigliano presents the quest for oriental learning as (a) principally novel and (b) a matter for experts: 'Eighteenth-century prelude to Mr Gibbon' in *Gibbon et Rome*, pp. 65–70. This is mistaken. Gibbon's enthusiasm stems from his youth (*c.* 1750) and was inspired by works written up to a century before: S. Ockley's *History of the Saracens* (London, 1708–18), B. D'Herbelot's *Bibliothèque orientale* (Paris, 1697), Pococke's *Dynasties of Abulpharagius* (1663), that is E. Pococke, *Grighor, Abu al-Faraj [Arabic] historia compendiosa dynastarum* (Oxford, 1663) (*Autobiographies*, F, p. 58, B, p. 121; *Decline and fall*, ed. Bury (2), v, p. 429, 335 n. 9), and Galland's *Les milles et une nuit, contes arabes* (1704–17) (*Autobiographies*, B, p. 118; *Decline and fall*, ed. Bury (2), v, p. 518 n. 231). Secondly, such learning was not confined to experts. This is clear from its audience, as the above examples (except Pococke) show, and from its intellectual centrality: the predominant aim of Enlightenment 'orientalism' (*pace* Edward Said) was to supply an escape for mainstream authors from the confines of a Christian, Eurocentric focus. It thus reflected part of a fundamental transition in European thought, and far exceeded the bounds of merely 'oriental' learning, appearing in popularizing sources such as the English *Universal history* (1736–66) (cf. *Autobiographies*, B, p. 120) and Voltaire's *Essai sur les moeurs*, that is, F. M. A. de Voltaire, *Essai sur l'histoire générale et sur les moeurs et l'esprit des nations, depuis Charlemagne jusqu'à nos jours* (7 vols., Geneva, 1756). That there was also an expert strand of oriental learning throughout the period, from the inquiries of the Academie des Inscriptions to those of Sir William Jones and D'Anquetil, goes without saying.

religion, monasticism and barbarian life. (Perhaps he could have gone further in this? The striking failure to include a systematic analysis of Roman law in the first three volumes may reflect inertial adherence to the more linear structure associated with the history of the city.)[128] On the other hand, the history of Empire exacted a high price, in that it involved a large amount of narrative coverage. But Gibbon did not repine at this challenge. From the first he was on guard against the longeurs or triviality of political and especially military narrative: 'The personal character of the emperors, *their victories, laws, follies, and fortunes*, can interest us no farther than as they are connected with the general history of the Decline and Fall.'[129] He seeks to woo the reader from the traditional Renaissance preference for narrative and military excitement, and portrays his analytic and static episodes as being themselves classically derived, from Tacitus. Their principal object, he claims, 'is to relieve the reader from a uniform scene of vice and misery':[130] a stark contrast to the Abbé Mably, a conservative classicist, who censured the first half of the *History* precisely because of its suspension of the narrative.[131] How often does Gibbon denounce, abbreviate or suppress 'the uniform and disgusting tale of slaughter and devastation'! and by evoking the pathos of war – 'in

---

[128] Note, however: firstly, that on some fundamental points Gibbon was wholly sceptical of the value of the Roman law codes as a source – accusing the civilians of servility to the emperors and of ignorance of the 'real nobility' of Rome (*Miscellaneous works*, vol. III, p. 187 n. *; cf. *Decline and fall*, ed. Bury (2), I, pp. 136–7, 147–8, III, 232 n. 10). This point is commonly overlooked. Secondly, his conception of the intellectual significance of Roman law was as part of an essentially *static* deposit, which passed from antiquity down to his own present. This chronology illustrates both his strength and weakness *vis-à-vis* the modern ancient historian, and also illuminates his placement of the chapter at this point. Thirdly, neither of these points, nor the interpretation outlined in chapter 44 itself (*ibid.*, IV, pp. 486–7, 533), suggest that if Gibbon had inserted a chapter on law at an earlier stage it would materially have altered his view of Roman government and morals. It is a fair inference from *ibid.*, III, p. 22 n. 62 that Gibbon always looked forward to writing a survey of Roman law whilst writing volumes I–III, but anyway he had mastered the Theodosian Code and Godefroy's commentary – the principal foundations of chapter 44 – before starting volume I. The English root of Gibbon's suspicion of Roman law is evident in his 'critical abstract' of Blackstone's *Commentaries, English essays*, pp. 59–87, here p. 59. For the rather different views on the part of ancient historians, cf. Averil Cameron pp. 48–9 and John Matthews pp. 25–6 above.

[129] *Decline and fall*, ed. Bury (2), I, p. 171 (my emphasis).

[130] *Ibid.*, I, p. 211.

[131] *De la manière d'écrire l'histoire* (Paris, 1783), p. 184; cf. Hugh Blair, *Lectures on rhetoric*, vol. II, pp. 270–1. Gibbon isolated the personal element in Mably's attack, putting it down as sour grapes; in this way he veiled the original but idiosyncratic nature of his procedure (*Letters*, no. 592, *Autobiographies*, E, p. 315 n. 33).

the miserable account of [which] the gain is never equivalent to the
loss'[132] – he revitalizes a subject which is otherwise the Achilles heel
of 'enlightened' historians and which in Voltaire for example, can
degenerate into bathos and farce.

These traits reflect upon the distance between Gibbon and his
historical contemporaries. Even Hume and Robertson were written
down in 1768 as part of 'the crowd of historians', who display 'a
simplicity satisfying to the spirit and who in avoiding details have
avoided difficulties'.[133] Of course Gibbon grew to know them better
after he wrote this,[134] but his respect for their history – as distinct
from their friendship and 'philosophy' – was always conditional.
The celebrated remark that 'I have never presumed to accept a
place in the triumvirate of British historians' was deeply evasive,
coming from a man who was 'too modest or too proud to rate my
own value by that of my associates'.[135] Intellectual pride sits alongside personal modesty here, marking Gibbon's consciousness that
he was never one of 'the crowd'; that his work and approach were

[132] *Decline and fall*, ed. Bury (2), VI, p. 425.
[133] *Miscellaneous Works*, vol. IV, p. 188; cf. *Journal*, 13 November 1761 on Hume; *Autobiographies*,
B, pp. 166–7.
[134] Still, Gibbon had been in correspondence with Hume before he wrote this, and correspondence was the basis of their friendship (*Letters*, nos. 78, 70, *Autobiographies*, C, p. 277
n. *). On the other hand, Robertson did not open a correspondence until ten years later,
in June 1777, despite a flattering reference to him in Gibbon's first volume of February
1776 (*Decline and fall*, ed. Bury (2), I, p. 241). His reluctance reflects the Scottish Moderates'
distaste for chapters 15–16: *Miscellaneous works*, vol. II, pp. 159–60, 200–1; *Letters*, no. 440;
Hugh Blair to Adam Smith, 3 April 1776, in E. C. Mossner and I. S. Ross (eds.), *The
correspondence of Adam Smith* (London, 1977).
[135] *Autobiographies*, E, pp. 312, 330. Although the classical image of the 'triumvirate' was
inimitably his own, Gibbon was none the less deliberate in tracing the triumviral
grouping back to Hugh Blair's *Lectures on rhetoric*: 'During a longer period, *English*
Historical Authors were little more than dull Compilers; till of late the distinguished
names of Hume, Robertson, and Gibbon, have raised the *British* character, in this species
of Writing, to high reputation and dignity' (vol. II, p. 285, emphases added). This was
plainly in accord with the Scots' project to integrate themselves with the English under
the 'British' label, a project which has deluded Linda Colley into believing that the
English accepted it and submerged their own identity in that of *Britons*: Linda Colley,
Britons: forging the nation, 1707–1837 (New Haven and London, 1992). Gibbon was gracious
to Robertson in private regarding the triumvirate, although even then he felt himself the
Lepidus (*Letters*, no. 592; cf. 677), but this must be offset by his interest in the particularly
English 'character of so singular a nation as we undoubtedly are' (*ibid.*, no. 77; cf. no. 43),
so that one central aim of the *Mémoires littéraires de la Grande Bretagne* was to 'study the
moeurs of the English' (sic) ('Avis au lecteur', p. v (London, 1768)). The glory he derived
from 'the name and character of an Englishman' (*Decline and fall*, ed. Bury (2), I, p. xlvi)
is well known; the principal accentuation of the (entire) *History* towards the English
reader, especially in the notes, less so. In Gibbon's own vocabulary, he wrote *both* as a
patriot and as a philosopher (cf. *ibid.*, IV, p. 176).

(as he said) 'exclusively my own', being less superficial, more learned, and less tied to narrative, allowing for a more sophisticated and extensive interweaving of profound, static and analytic components.[136] Such, in short, are the qualities which justify 'the vanity of authors who presume the immortality of their name and writings',[137] and which declare the first half of the *History* a classic in *our* day. It is the work of a great individual who is (no doubt unintentionally) demeaned by the tendency to merge him with one or another group of philosophers, Scottish or French. Contrariwise, he, like the French Academicians, exemplifies the sheer pervasiveness and variety of 'enlightened' attitudes in eighteenth-century Europe, qualities which are obscured if we confine our gaze to the *philosophes*.

VI

Of course the note of edification cannot be sustained. After 476 the foundation provided by the 'History of the City' and its libertarian theme disappeared (as we have seen) and there is no pendant to the 'General observations on the fall of the Roman Empire in the west', for the eastern Empire. So, having expanded his focus to take in the whole Empire, Gibbon was doubly overcommitted, in period and in scope, as regards the second half of the *History*. No wonder the 1776 Preface only committed him to go as far as 476.[138]

What, then, was to supply the lack of a general theme? Gibbon had rejected the papacy, but if he was serious in talk about connecting 'the ancient and modern history of the World',[139] the obvious secular route would have been to follow the fortunes of the western emperors along with the evolution of what Gibbon and his contemporaries called 'the feudal system',[140] perceived as the dominant European system of manners and social organization after 476. Indeed this might seem straightforward, given the prior existence of the striking essay, 'Du gouvernement féodal' of 1768, which interprets the evolution of western and central Europe from

---

[136] *Autobiographies*, E, p. 334. A striking symptom of Hume's greater reliance on narrative lies in his suggestion to Gibbon that the narrative from Commodus to Alexander Severus (*Decline and fall*, I, chapters 4–7) could have been filled out and expanded (*Autobiographies*, E, p. 308) – a microcosm of the different approaches pursued in their respective *Histories*.
[137] *Ibid.*, E, p. 349.   [138] *Decline and fall*, ed. Bury (2), I, p. xl.
[139] *Ibid.*, I, p. xli.   [140] For example, *ibid.*, I, p. 220, III, p. 495.

the fifth to the twelfth centuries along quintessentially Gibbonian lines. But he did not take this road. Even if we put aside subordinate objections such as ignorance of German, or distaste at seeming to rework Voltaire,[141] a history centred on the western emperors was something Gibbon had already rejected when he rejected the popes as a basis for operation: the one could hardly be taken without the other. Furthermore, the essay on feudal government is not (as was once asserted)[142] a reflection of Gibbon's interest in matters early medieval, but an explanation of why the 'dark ages' were dark; of why he did *not* share the medieval enthusiasms of previous generations of Frenchmen – Montesquieu, Du Bos, Boulainvilliers and Mably.[143]

Like his 'enlightened' contemporaries, Gibbon adhered to a normative belief in liberty as the parent of all good things: peace, toleration, wealth and the productions of human genius. To be sure, more subtle and significant paradoxes derived from this apparently simple theme. Above all there was the dilemma held to be of most relevance for modern times: that the progress of wealth and luxury, which were the fruits of liberty, might culminate in subverting it. But feudal society represented decline and fall of a wholly anomalous kind, whereby peoples originally free and savage – in this like the early Romans – 'became progressively more corrupt *without* becoming more civilized'.[144] Here the fruit of liberty was not virtue but anarchy and progressive servitude; the free nobility was destroyed and love of country collapsed, as did the idea of uniform law. These healthy elements were replaced by a parochial and fragmented society, organized on military lines, and devoted to warfare at the expense of town life, commerce and learning.[145] In short, the dark ages and feudal society – the history of barbarism as much as of papal religion – were detestable subjects for Gibbon.[146]

---

[141] *Annales de l'Empire depuis Charlemagne* (The Hague and Berlin, 1754), one of the first historical works by Voltaire that Gibbon read, takes an imperial route through medieval history with a full treatment of feudalism: 'Common place book', Add. MSS 34880 ff. 13b–15b.

[142] G. Giarizzo, *Edward Gibbon e la cultura Europea del settecento* (Naples, 1954); cf. Ghosh, 'Gibbon's dark ages', pp. 1–4.

[143] *Miscellaneous works*, vol. III, p. 143.

[144] *Ibid.*, vol. III, p. 190 (my emphasis); cf. *Decline and fall*, ed. Bury (2), IV, p. 129 n. 66: 'We are continually shocked by the union of savage and corrupt manners.'

[145] *Miscellaneous works*, vol. III, pp. 183–202.

[146] Cf. *ibid.*, vol. III, p. 282; *English essays*, p. 174; *Decline and fall*, ed. Bury (2), VI, p. 465.

But, as with the papacy, he did not feel the need to confront them, because England was the one country in Europe where feudal society was held to be quite extinct – a fact reflected by the striking omission of England from his essay, despite its avowedly European scope.[147] The famous remark in the *History* that the 'fierce giants of the north broke in, and . . . restored a manly spirit of freedom; and after the revolution of ten centuries, freedom became the happy parent of taste and science'[148] is founded on a gigantic ellipsis, the omission of 1000 years. 'Du gouvernement féodal' explains why that period was usually too painful to contemplate and why, even when writing in French, Gibbon could convey an essentially English message.[149] As he would point out in the *History*, his standpoint here was that of 'an impartial stranger', even if, in thus flaunting an English identity, he was incapable of purging a Gallicism in his style.[150]

So he remained without a general conception equivalent to that of decline and fall to sustain the continuation of the *History* after 476. The outline descriptions he does offer are effectively fictions, and their character is scarcely disguised: measured on the libertarian scale of the first three volumes, 'the empire of the East . . . subsisted one thousand and fifty-eight years in a state of premature and perpetual decay',[151] that is, it had no history at all. Put another way, the only link between the two halves of his great work lies in the words of the title, and Gibbon did not scruple to own this.[152] But the process whereby the later volumes *were* generated remains a richly revealing commentary, albeit as much on Gibbon's weakness as his strengths, and no assessment of the author or his *History* can omit it.

---

[147] *Miscellaneous works*, vol. III, pp. 190, 193.

[148] *Decline and fall*, ed. Bury (2), I, p. 64.

[149] Conformable to Gibbon's general constancy of opinion and the practice of re-using material, the ideas and language of 'Du gouvernement féodal' surface at *ibid.*, I, pp. 383–4; cf. *Miscellaneous works*, vol. III, p. 199; *Decline and fall*, ed. Bury (2), IV, pp. 130–52; V, pp. 304–5, 325–7, VI, pp. 14, 102–5; cf. *Miscellaneous works*, vol. III, pp. 190, 196, 202.

[150] *Decline and fall*, ed. Bury (2), IV, pp. 130–1; he was plainly thinking of the French '*étranger*' that is, 'foreigner', since he was obviously not a 'stranger' to France or these thinkers. See *ibid.*, V, pp. 277–9 for sustained employment of this Gallicism.

[151] *Ibid.*, III, p. 378; cf. V, p. 180 'the fate of the Greek empire has been compared to that of the Rhine, which loses itself in the sands before its waters can mingle with the ocean' (a borrowing from Montesquieu, *Considerations*, ch. 23); *Decline and fall*, ed. Bury (2), VII, p. 33: Constantinople, whose decline is almost coeval with her foundation . . . '

[152] *Autobiographies*, E, p. 325; cf. *English essays*, p. 163, *Decline and fall*, ed. Bury (2), VI, p. 537.

The origins of volume IV, which might loosely be subtitled 'the Age of Justinian, Seen through a Reading of Procopius',[153] go back to the 'History of the City'. When first looking at sixth-century Rome, Gibbon inevitably had recourse to the principal Byzantine writers on the Gothic wars: hence the citation of Procopius as early as chapter 2 of the final *History* and of Agathias in chapter 8.[154] This early reading prepared the way for the Preface of 1776, where Justinian was already allotted a position of prominence, albeit only as part of a projected history of the period 476–800 which would be as comprehensive in geographical scope as the first three volumes (where the Roman Empire is habitually referred to as 'the world').[155] But over time this broadly focussed conception was eroded in favour of a more linear one, based on the idea of chronological 'series' – precisely the reverse process to that undertaken in the first three volumes. By the end of volume III (written in 1779–80) the plan of the future volume IV (of 1782–4) is clearly in view: 'The majesty of Rome was faintly represented by the princes of

---

[153] Cf. *Decline and fall*, ed. Bury (2), IV, pp. 224–6.

[154] *Ibid.*, I, p. 55 n. 95, p. 219 n. 28. All Procopius' major works are cited by chapter 13; cf. Add. MSS 34882 ff. 108–115b, an index listing the first citations of sources in the *History*, and including several early citations of Byzantine materials. There were other routes which, like the history of the city, drew Gibbon to the outer limits of Byzantine history and the inner sanctum of its source materials. Firstly, any classical author is reliant not only on Byzantine transmission of Roman texts, but also Byzantine compilations therefrom: a strong expression of continuity. Typically, in a 1758 draft for the *Essai* Gibbon cites from a Byzantine version of Dio Cassius, Add. MS 34880 f. 152. Secondly, such continuity was natural to the seventeenth-century *érudits* who bulked so large in Gibbon's reading and mental horizons: their work extended seamlessly from the Roman through to the Byzantine Empire, most obvious in that of Ducange, 'the Tillemont of the middle ages' (*Decline and fall*, ed. Bury (2), VI, p. 79 n. 32; cf. VI, pp. 10 n. 18, 441 n. 29), and they also produced editions of major Byzantine authors from Procopius onwards (*ibid.*, IV, p. 224 n. 14, VI, p. 66 nn. 5, 7). Thirdly, interest in Near Eastern history, which he saw as dominated by essentially continuous characteristics and thus without chronological limits, led him to suggest (in the 'Mémoire sur la monarchie des Mèdes' of 1768) a history of the Sassanid dynasty in Persia (AD 226–633), 'fondée sur la combinaison des écrivains Persans et Arabes avec les historiens de l'église et du bas empire' (*Miscellaneous works*, vol. III, p. 77 n. *). Everywhere – in Roman, ecclesiastical and 'Oriental' history – his interests narrowly abut Byzantium, but do not centre on it. We see then why he might come to regard it as a 'passive' focus (*Decline and fall*, ed. Bury (2), V, p. 182); why he found its identity so elusive, being unable to decide whether it was Roman, Greek or Oriental; why his account of it is thus a relative failure; but why it is simplistic merely to pose the question as to whether Gibbon was 'in sympathy' with Byzantine history or not. In principle at least, he held that no historical subject was to be judged 'on its own terms'; all were subordinate to universal standards: cf. Averil Cameron, James Howard-Johnston and Anthony Bryer above, pp. 37–8, 53–5, 101–2.

[155] For example, *Decline and fall*, ed. Bury (2), I, p. 89, II, p. 277, III, p. 246, V, p. 33; cf. *Miscellaneous works*, vol. IV, p. 127.

Constantinople, the feeble and imaginary successors of Augustus. Yet . . . the history of the *Greek* emperors may still afford a long series of instructive lessons and interesting revolutions.'[156] In its final guise volume IV contracted significantly in time-span (from 800 back to *c.* 630), thereby jettisoning Charlemagne and his forebears from the original scheme of 1776. Within the shortened period, it then focussed heavily on the linear, narrative series of the Byzantine emperors, which derived from an essentially linear series of sources beginning with Procopius. This led to a second major omission – Mahomet and the rise of Islam – although these subjects are frequently anticipated in the text.[157]

The implication is clear: confronted by a conceptual vacuum after 476 – a dividing line which gave him pause until the day he crossed it[158] – Gibbon suffered a collapse, regressing back to elementary notions of linear chronology. Of course, the discussion of chronology which had occupied some of the best minds in Europe in the century and a half preceding his birth was far from trivial,[159] and his own training in chronology was deeply creative. It taught him what he claimed history, or even literacy, as a whole should do: to 'exalt and enlarge the horizon of our intellectual view', so that this could embrace whole eras and millennia.[160] Such an expansion of view into *all* areas of the past, however remote, lay at the core of the revolution in historical perspective effected in the Enlightenment and prepared the nineteenth-century impact of geology and biology on time horizons. It also fostered relativity of viewpoint and, by a blank admission of 'the narrow space of history and fable' within

---

[156] *Decline and fall*, ed. Bury (2), IV, p. 171; cf. 105; Gibbon was aware, too, that the sixth-century pattern of Byzantine intervention in Italy, to shore up the western Empire, originated in the reign of Leo (457–74), which also occurs at the end of volume III (*ibid.*, IV, pp. 31–40).

[157] *Ibid.*, IV, p. 414, V, pp. 43, 79, 102, 173–4. The omission is damaging because the events of Heraclius' reign are split between chapters 46–7 (volume IV) and 52 (volume V), and become essentially two separate histories, one from a Byzantine and one from a Muslim point of view and sources. With fractures of this kind there cannot be said to be a focus of any kind, not even a 'passive' one.

[158] *Autobiographies*, E, p. 325; cf. *Decline and fall*, ed. Bury (2), VII, pp. 1 n. 1, 308 n. 102. However, his reading of the Greek classics during this interval clearly allowed for resumption of a *Greek* (and thus Byzantine) history, since utilization of apt local and classical parallels was an essential Gibbonian device used to enliven the narrative, *Letters*, no. 592; cf. *Decline and fall*, ed. Bury (2), IV, pp. 233, 242, 269 n. 117, 278–9, 295, 297, 298 n. 20, 313 n. 39, etc.

[159] F. E. Manuel, *The eighteenth century confronts the gods* (London, 1959); also his *Isaac Newton, historian* (London, 1963); A. Grafton, *Joseph Scaliger*, vol. II (London, 1993).

[160] *Decline and fall*, ed. Bury (2), V, p. 259; cf. IV, p. 286 n. 160; *Autobiographies*, B, p. 121.

'the boundless annals of time',[161] raised problems about historical induction and perspective which even today we hardly confront and, being ourselves such a short way along the road of historical record, cannot pretend to solve. But alongside these lofty perspectives, chronology also pointed to the humdrum computation of linear series. This was necessary of course as the bedrock of narrative,[162] but it was also liable to abuse: either by the tracing of genealogical descent for its own sake (a pursuit in which Gibbon revelled promiscuously),[163] or, in extreme form, the construction of pseudo-narrative via the annalistic assemblage of material year by year. Such was the method of many of the authors who made up Gibbon's original post-476 reading: Tillemont, Muratori, Baronius, Pagi, even Voltaire's *Annales de l'Empire*. In regressing back to simple narrative uninformed by a more general movement of manners and morals, and in relying on a base concept of linearity – a series without substance[164] – Gibbon was for once the slave, not the master, of his erudite heritage.

He could not continue thus. In the winter of 1782–3 he made a special effort to compensate, which gave rise to chapter 44, the famous chapter on Roman mores as deduced from the law codes.[165] This is indeed the *tour de force* it was intended to be, but it has little organic connection with the text that precedes it, as Gibbon virtually conceded at its opening: 'The laws of a nation form the most instructive portion of its history; and, although I have devoted myself to write the annals of a declining monarchy, I shall embrace the occasion to breathe the pure and invigorating air of the republic.'[166] Relief at his escape from the Byzantine 'annals' back

---

[161] *Decline and fall*, ed. Bury (2), IV, p. 462, VII, p. 317; cf. I, p. 215, VI, p. 32.

[162] This is in itself a fundamental – or elementary – point which literary theorists of 'narratology' and some historians seem not to understand, for example, L. Stone, 'The revival of narrative', *The past and the present revisited* (London, 1987), ch. 3.

[163] Gibbon was conscious of ambivalent feelings here. The standard objections to pride of birth were obvious to him – and in that sense he was quite unlike French aristocratic investigators such as Boulainvilliers – but they were offset by the evidence of what he took to be universal historical induction (even if in fact this had more to do with his local, English situation): that there was an innate interest in the subject common to all men, and that a free nobility was essential to constitutional balance 'in almost every climate of the Globe, and in almost every form of political society'. See *inter alia, Autobiographies*, A', pp. 417–19, A, pp. 354–5; *Miscellaneous works*, vol. III, p. 187 n. *; *Miscellanea Gibboniana*, p. 106; *Decline and fall*, ed. Bury (2), II, pp. 174–5, III, pp. 306–18, V, pp. 288–90, VI, pp. 466–74, VII, pp. 258–64.

[164] *Decline and fall*, ed. Bury (2), VII, p. 234.

[165] *Autobiographies*, E, p. 326.   [166] *Decline and fall*, ed. Bury (2), IV, p. 471.

to an analytic mode and into early Roman history is palpable. Justinian supplies the occasion, not the substance, of the chapter, and Byzantium is as much an afterthought or appendix to its picture of Roman manners and morals, as the chapter is to the volume. The failure to integrate the narrative and analytic modes in volume IV is so gross as to recall what were the worst (in this respect) of the standard Enlightenment narratives, such as Hume's, where token sections on laws and manners remain subject to strict apartheid. However, since there was no unifying interpretative focus, this was almost bound to happen, and chapter 44 (or chapter 47, an analogous case)[167] is no more than a temporary, albeit glorious, stop-gap. Only a radical solution could be adequate to the problem Gibbon faced.

He achieved this by effectively terminating the Roman history with volume IV. Volumes V–VI (chapters 48–71) are in most essentials a new and different book and, in this sense at least, we may speak of a 'transformation' in the later part of the *History*.[168] As he admitted when introducing it, he found later Byzantine history so uninviting, so lacking in either a moral foundation or moral lessons, that he 'should have abandoned without regret the Greek slaves and their servile historians'.[169] How close he came to doing this is apparent from the 'many designs and many tryals' he canvassed for the continuation of the *History* at this date.[170] These include the manuscript entitled 'Outlines of the history of the world', dateable to 1784,[171] a concise survey of salient events

---

[167] Unlike chapter 44, chapter 47 was not simply a special effect, but an obviously central part of sixth-century Byzantine history, already anticipated at the end of volume III (*ibid.*, IV, p. 105). But like chapter 44, and unlike the parallel chapters in the volumes II and III, it fails to intersect with the secular narrative and becomes simply a free-standing entity, which Gibbon emphasizes by treating it as an exemplar of the theological *longue durée* and deducing its impact down to the seventeenth century. Of course chapter 47 bears obvious similarities to the treatment of Arianism in chapter 37 § II (volume III) and chapter 54 on the Paulicians (volume V) in taking a theological controversy as its focus: but chapter 37 remains essentially integrated within the theme of 'decline and fall', whilst, within the much looser structure introduced in volume V, chapter 54 does not seem anomalous.

[168] Cf. D. Womersley, *The transformation of 'The decline and fall of the Roman Empire'*, Cambridge Studies in Eighteenth-Century English Literature and Thought 1 (Cambridge, 1988) for a different view from a literary perspective.

[169] *Decline and fall*, ed. Bury (2), V, p. 182.

[170] *Autobiographies*, E, p. 332.

[171] Add. MSS 34880 ff. 239–59b; cf. Ghosh, 'Gibbon's dark ages', appendix I. There I preferred 1784 as its date but allowed some room for 1781–2. The latter date is, however, at variance with Gibbon's anticipations at the end of volume III (written in 1780), with the Preface of 1 March 1782, and with the French sketch of his life penned in the summer of 1783, which

principally in European history between 800–1500 with a mild west European bias. The inference must be that he was looking to see if the materials available for historical composition here were any more favourable than those he might encounter by taking the Byzantine or broadly 'Eastern' route. In that case he would have started a new book, in name as well as in substance. However, there is no reason to suppose the 'western' prospect looked any rosier then than it had done when writing 'Du gouvernement féodal' sixteen years before,[172] and in fact he decided to continue under his original title.

Considered simply as a *pis aller*, there were good reasons for this. As we saw, volume IV was written in anticipation of Mahomet and the rise of Islam and would have looked hopelessly vulnerable had that not been met. Then there remained one part of the later history of Rome which resonated powerfully with Gibbon: the recovery of the ruins of classical Rome from the fourteenth century, a scene which of course took him back to his original moment of inspiration.[173] He did not want to lose this. Finally, we can hardly underestimate Gibbon's commercialism. The man who altered a supposititious reference to Louis XVI in the 'General observations' to please the Paris booksellers,[174] knew full well that many of those who had bought the earlier volumes of the *History* would feel committed to completing their sets, to say nothing of the near impossibility of repeating the runaway success of 1776 with a wholly new project.[175] So the trappings of continuity were maintained: volume V begins with a chilly reminder of volume IV, one chapter tracing the succession of Byzantine emperors through 600 years 'in regular series'[176] and another covering the western popes and emperors in similarly linear fashion; volume VI closes with its remarkable evocation of the city and ruins of Rome.[177] But between these outer limits a new and extraordinary plan is offered whereby,

---

consistently imply untroubled adherence to a Byzantine or 'Eastern' route after 476 (see n. 156 above, *Decline and fall*, ed. Bury (2), I, p. xli, Add. MSS 34874 ff. 130–1 respectively). Thus we must opt for the obvious solution: that Gibbon only faced up to the intellectual chasm confronting him when he absolutely had to, in 1784; cf. *Autobiographies*, E, p. 332.

[172] Gibbon upholds the *relative* inferiority of the west to Byzantium through to the end of the Crusades: *Decline and fall*, ed. Bury (2), VI, pp. 71–2, 102, 462–6. All his judgments on 'medieval' civilizations are of this relativistic variety.

[173] *Ibid.*, IV, p. 21 n. 52; VII, p. 338.   [174] *Autobiographies*, E, p. 324 and n. 48.

[175] *Ibid.*, E, pp. 311, 322–4, 337–9; *Letters*, no. 498.   [176] *Decline and fall*, ed. Bury (2), V, p. 183.

[177] Ghosh, 'Gibbon observed', section V.

although Byzantium is admitted to be of little interest in its own right, still it 'is *passively* connected with the most splendid and important revolutions which have changed the state of the world'.[178] Exactly how vulnerable Gibbon felt this construction to be, may be gauged both from the defensive tone of its introduction in the *History*, and from the *Memoirs*, where he summons the Abbé Mably to its defence: a notable gesture whether we consider the coolness of their personal relations or the relative distance between their views.[179]

Gibbon never did find a replacement for that unity of theme which elevates his first three volumes; rather he made a virtue out of necessity and allowed authorial freedom to become his (dis)organizing principle. The alleged basis of volumes v–vi was that of 'groupping [sic] . . . by nations'.[180] But while it is true that he tried, in a notional effort at system, to cover all the peoples who impinged on Byzantine history, nationality offered little firm standing ground. The term 'nation', though much in evidence, had no stable meaning for him and could signify races, nations or tribes: ethnic, legal or cultural units. The appeal to nationality was thus a fig-leaf of system covering a desire to embrace choice historical episodes. When Gibbon says 'the FRANKS', he really means the western emperors and the popes; 'the LATINS, the subjects of the pope, the nations of the West' are the Crusaders; and 'the ARABS or SARACENS' are a label for Mahomet and the rise of Islam.[181] A diet of plums forms the substantial basis of the final volumes, representing a most powerful expression of its fragmentary character and abjuration of a master narrative.

Bereft of a central design as his anchor and reference point,

---

[178] *Decline and fall*, ed. Bury (2), v, p. 182.
[179] *Autobiographies*, E, p. 334 and n. 54. This might be read as a joke at the expense of the latter-day Cato, but E, p. 314 n. 32 rules out that delicious possibility. The passage Gibbon refers to in Mably is a fleeting and eminently conventional reference to the Empire after Constantine: 'Vous ne trouverez plus que quelques princes qui méritent d'être connus, et l'histoire ne doit s'occuper alors que des barbares qui détruirent bientôt le nom romain', *De la maniere d'écrire l'histoire* in *Oeuvres completes* (London, 1789), vol. xii, p. 388. This will hardly bear the significance he attaches to it, not least because the barbarians in question could well be Western. Mably's classicism was of a more 'Ancient' variety than Gibbon's, reflected by his demand for precisely that unity of plan which eluded Gibbon in volumes v–vi (of the *Decline and fall*, ed. Bury (2), vi, p. 389, cf. p. 363) and by his ideas on narrative: p. 295 and n. 131 above.
[180] *Autobiographies*, E, p. 332.
[181] *Decline and fall*, ed. Bury (2), v, pp. 183–4.

Gibbon's otherwise consistent repetition of practices employed in the first three volumes necessarily appears in a new light. The historian had not changed, only his predicament. With only a 'passive' focus, the self-proclaimed right to vary the length of coverage was subject to no control except that of personal judgment: 'nor can *I refuse myself* to those events which . . . will interest a philosophic mind' (such as his own).[182] Reference to interesting 'circumstances' – though a part of his plan from the very first page of the *History* – and the recounting of fables with a moral also come to seem looser and more anecdotal. There is continuity, too, in the incorporation of Near and Far Eastern learning in the text: yet although our perspective on decline and fall is always 'remote' when in China,[183] due to the absence of a firm centre the impact of Zingis is more centrifugal than that of Attila. Another index of authorial freedom is Gibbon's presence in the text as cicerone. He converses throughout the *History* with '*his friends*',[184] but his presence becomes doubly necessary in the last volumes, given their complex and wholly personal scheme of organization and the bewildering transitions it engenders: 'After pursuing above six hundred years the fleeting Caesars of Constantinople and Germany, I now descend, in the reign of Heraclius, on the eastern borders of the Greek monarchy'; 'From the isle of Sicily the reader must transport himself beyond the Caspian Sea to the original seat of the Turks or Turkmans.'[185] Not surprisingly the guide is sometimes afraid of having lost his party: 'The reader has not forgot . . . '?[186] This is not a psychologistic disorder (as American writers continue to suppose)[187] whereby Gibbon somehow conflated

[182] *Ibid.*, VII, p. 1 (my emphasis); cf. V, pp. 182–3, VI, p. 135, VII, p. 11 etc. Another element of caprice occurs in chapter 51, when he proposes that his account of the seventh-century Muslim conquests will focus on countries 'included within the pale of the Roman empire' (V, p. 428). In fact the countries involved are covered roughly evenly except Syria, a focus which has nothing to do with Rome, but (as so often) reflects profusion of source material – Al Wakidi's separate history of the conquest of Syria, largely reproduced in Ockley's *History of the Saracens*, vol. I, pp. 21–342; cf. *Decline and fall*, ed. Bury (2), V, p. 442 n. 53.
[183] *Decline and fall*, ed. Bury (2), III, p. 74, VII, p. 1.
[184] *Autobiographies*, E, p. 346; cf. *Decline and fall*, ed. Bury (2), I, p. xlvi; Ghosh, 'Gibbon observed', n. 106.
[185] *Decline and fall*, ed. Bury (2), V, p. 332; VI, p. 233.
[186] *Ibid.*, VII, p. 65.
[187] Lest any doubt remain, Gibbon's grasp of a normal subject-object relation is clear from those remarks which acknowledge the separate identity of the reader and of the subject matter, however egotistical the historian may appear: 'nor can I check [the Arabs']

himself with his subject: that would be to contravene the essential principle of philosophic detachment, the belief that the historian could and should be the impartial spectator of events in the remote past. Rather it is testimony to the idiosyncrasy of the proceeding – a far cry from the severe adherence to 'design' at the outset – and it infuriated those readers (such as Horace Walpole) who looked to trace some form of coherent evolution from the ancient to the modern world.[188] Finally, this view of the last volumes as but a tenuously linked set of plums might seem to be confirmed by the terms in which Gibbon habitually described them. As he wrote encouragingly to his publisher Cadell in 1786, 'The last three volumes . . . contain a larger period of time, and a far greater variety of events.'[189] Colour, splendour and relative superficiality were now to be preferred to the 'minute diligence' of volumes II and III, and he appealed unashamedly to what was 'splendid and important', 'memorable', 'rich', 'various', 'rapid' and 'romantic'.[190]

In these ways, the final volumes mark a return to concerns from his youth, and Gibbon was aware of a continuity: 'before the age of sixteen I was master of all the *English* materials, which I have since employed in the chapters of the Persians and Arabians, the Tartars and Turks'.[191] In 1761, near the beginning of his search for a great historical subject, he had considered that of Richard *Coeur de Lion* in the Holy Land. Then he had rejected it, being repelled by Richard's redneck qualities: like Commodus, he had the 'ferocity of a gladiator', thus typifying the savage and superstitious futility of the Crusades. Yet he had been attracted by the presence of Muslim

victorious career . . . ' *ibid.*, v, p. 183; cf. VI, pp. 1, 63; VII, p. 218; Ghosh, 'Gibbon observed', n. 106 *contra* L. Braudy, *Narrative form in history and fiction* (London, 1970); D. P. Jordan, *Gibbon and his Roman Empire* (London, 1971); Craddock, *Edward Gibbon, luminous historian*; Roy Porter, *Edward Gibbon: making history* (London, 1988), Conclusion.

[188] To Lady Ossory, 10 February, 8 November 1789, in W. S. Lewis (ed.), *Horace Walpole's correspondence* (London, 1939–83), vol. XXIV, pp. 39–40, 79. This is the obvious explanation for the paucity of the impact made by Gibbon's final volumes on subsequent European historiography noted by Bryer, above, p. 115.

[189] *Letters*, no. 638; cf. no. 677.

[190] *Decline and fall*, ed. Bury (2), V, pp. 182, 332; VII, p. 338; *Autobiographies*, E, p. 332; for 'romantic', for example, *Decline and fall*, V, pp. 184, 211, 248, 487, 502; VI, p. 181, 469, 473; VII, p. 69 etc., but note, too, many earlier usages: for example, *Miscellaneous works*, vol. III, p. 106 (1768), *Decline and fall*, ed. Bury (2), I, pp. 239, 397; II, p. 402; III, p. 409. None of this, however, implies any reversal of his hostility to warfare or military narrative, and abridgement of such narrative in volumes V–VI is far more brutal than before. For example, V, p. 43; VI, pp. 305–6, 338; VII, pp. 13, 187 n. 50, 205 etc.

[191] *Autobiographies*, B, p. 121.

sources and by the appeal of the story 'on its marvellous side.'[192] So, twenty-five years on, he would allow himself some pages on the subject, and in reproducing these tales of derring-do – albeit from the Muslim sources – he wondered if he had not succumbed to the charms of romance: 'Am I writing the history of Orlando or Amadis?'[193] The closeness of the later text to romance, to Tasso, the Arabian Nights, and the innumerable neo-classical and historicist plays which were one of Gibbon's passions – Johnson's *Irene*, Marmontel's *Belisaire*, Racine's *Berenice* and Voltaire's *Mohammed* and *Tancrede* – is also continually in evidence.[194] On this reading, then, the man who had climbed to the summit in 1781[195] now sought gracefully to descend, no doubt assisted by his boon companion: the charming, able, feckless, lazy Deyverdun. The last two volumes of the *History* supply a logical (and even a literal) transition to the projects of late middle age, such as the *Antiquities of the House of Brunswick*[196] – comparable in length to an 'episode' in volumes v and vi – or the character portraits of 'eminent persons in art and arms, in Church and State' since the reign of Henry VIII. Here 'rich

---

192 Add. MSS 34880 f. 185, cf. *Miscellaneous works*, vol. v, p. 488. But again, Gibbon's weakness for expounding the marvellous is just as clear in the early volumes of the *History*, e.g. *Decline and fall*, ed. Bury (2), I, pp. 472–3 (a striking parallel).

193 *Decline and fall*, ed. Bury (2), VI, pp. 364–9, at p. 367. Of course, irony and affection are mixed in equal amounts here, and we should remember that it was a common technique of Gibbon's to tell miraculous or fabulous stories in full, only subverting them by delicate and indirect means. Amadis de Gaule [?Wales] was a mythical prince of chivalry in Spanish romance, first translated into French by Herberay des Essarts (1540–8), and so of much the same period as *Orlando furioso* (1516). It remained popular in the contemporary French version by Mlle. de Lubert (1750) and into the nineteenth century through the English translation of Robert Southey (1803).

194 A sample of the profusion on offer in volumes v–vi: *Decline and fall*, ed. Bury (2), v, pp. 294 n. 74, 347 n. 43, 391 n. 150, 454 n. 75, 518 n. 231; VI, pp. 15, 36, 41 n. 98, 90 n. 66, 273 and n. 10, 292 n. 56, 298, 323 and n. 166, 456–7, 505 n. 69, 518 n. 21; VII, pp. 3 n. 4, 73 n. 77, 97 n. 21, 99 and n. 26, 168 n. 7, 179 n. 31, 195 n. 74; cf. Geoffrey Keynes (ed.), *The library of Edward Gibbon: a catalogue* (London, 1980): see under 'Comedies', 'Tragedies' and major playwrights. It should be stressed that the former is but a small fraction of Gibbon's use of literary sources throughout the *History* – Tasso could have the same effect on him as Homer (*Decline and fall*, ed. Bury (2), I, p. 249) – and, secondly, that his reasons for such usage did not include subverting the boundaries between history and fiction: hence a stout regard for 'truth', and distaste for those who abused 'the privilege of fiction' (*Decline and fall*, ed. Bury (2), III, p. 44). When the Germans chose to assail the usage of literature in history under the flag of *Quellenkritik*, it was not so much an index of the technical weakness of previous practice, as of changing assumptions about the fixity of human nature and of a deliberate repudiation of literature as a source: the Rankean 'revolution' cost historical writing quite as much as it gained.

195 Cf. *Autobiographies*, E, p. 349.

196 *Decline and fall*, ed. Bury (2), VI, pp. 201 n. 75, 516–17; VII, p. 311 n. 110.

display' and public 'importance' are of the essence, but in no case did Gibbon intend to return to full dress historical composition.[197]

VII

But this cannot be our last word unless we accept that Gibbon, in reaching for what was 'splendid', had 'turned aside from . . . the more useful parts of history',[198] and thus that he had abandoned the stratified conception of the historical process. Yet in fact this conception is invoked as profusely as ever, and the last two volumes are not simply drama and romance by other means. If they lack formal integration, there remains a sense in which they are written on a unitary principle – that of *negative reference* to Rome – an idea which, by definition, was present to him from the first. In Gibbon's language, the later *History* was bound to be splendid and rapid because there was so little solid, Roman usefulness to convey, and this absence supplied a uniform feature even to what was splendid and various. If Byzantium was the 'passive focus', the supremely durable culture and civilization of Rome supplied its absent centre.

In choosing to write with a Near Eastern focus Gibbon felt himself to be writing largely about primitive societies whose deep foundations were simple – principally that combination of freedom and military prowess which he saw as intrinsic to 'the definition of a pastoral nation'.[199] However, they lacked the 'more solid and permanent' benefits of law and policy, trade and manufactures, arts and sciences; and so, despite the accidental benefits of what Max Weber was to call booty capitalism, 'a private citizen in Europe is in possession of more solid and pleasing luxury than the proudest emir'.[200] There was thus little or no 'complex machinery' of civilization to describe, and the historian's focus was pre-eminently

---

[197] *Letters*, no. 826; cf. no. 765.
[198] *Decline and fall*, ed. Bury (2), I, p. 173.
[199] *Ibid.*, VI, p. 147. Compare chs. 9, 26 with V, pp. 28, 283 (Lombards), pp. 335–49 (Arabs), VI, pp. 103–5 (Franks), pp. 145–8 (Hungarians), pp. 186–7 (Normans), p. 268 (Turks), VII, pp. 1–7 (Moguls and Tartars), where Gibbon draws attention to the generic similarity; on the shift in the final volumes towards a 'barbarian' focus, *Autobiographies*, E, p. 332, *Letters*, no. 677.
[200] *Decline and fall*, ed. Bury (2), IV, p. 180; V, p. 337 respectively; but the idea is clearly expressed in chapter 3 already (I, pp. 87–8). Of course Gibbon held that the same was true of Greece and Rome 'in their primitive ages', when 'a war was determined by a battle' (*Autobiographies*, B, p. 179).

superstructural. For example, the basis of the Muslim caliphate lay in the unchanging character of the Arab 'rovers of the desert', who enjoyed 'perpetual independence' and 'continued to unite the professions of a merchant and a robber'.[201] Given this free and fluid substratum, Gibbon might then ask of Mahomet (and of the author of the *Essai*): 'Does it seem incredible that a private citizen should grasp the sword and the sceptre, subdue his native country, and erect a monarchy by his victorious arms? In the moving picture of the dynasties of the East, a hundred fortunate usurpers have arisen from a baser origin, surmounted more formidable obstacles, and filled a larger scope of empire and conquest.'[202] So it proves repeatedly; most strikingly in the case of Zingis and Timour, 'whose rapid conquests may be compared with the primitive convulsions of nature, which have agitated and altered the *surface* of the globe'.[203]

The same may be said of the Crusades, the central episode of volume VI just as the rise of Islam was in volume V. Here Gibbon attacked the Scots, and particularly Robertson, even while protesting his public and private regard for them. They upheld the long-term significance of the Crusades as part of the progress of European society out of barbarism.[204] Gibbon rejected this smooth teleology, preferring a view which, on the face of it, he had derived from Voltaire in 1756: the Crusades were a burial ground for millions and thus the only benefit accruing was the accidental one whereby the 'Gothic edifice' tended to undermine itself.[205] Typically, however, he had supplied a structural foundation for this,

---

[201] *Decline and fall*, ed. Bury (2), V, pp. 460, 339, 384 respectively.

[202] *Ibid.*, V, p. 419.

[203] *Ibid.*, VII, p. 1 (my emphasis); cf. V, p. 322, *Miscellaneous works*, vol. III, p. 70. In accounting for 'the decline and fall of the empire of the caliphs', Gibbon pointedly refers (*Decline and fall*, ed. Bury (2), VI, p. 53) to the 'obvious' and 'visible' causes thereof: all that was not (quite) obvious or visible here was the lack of a deep foundation, so that the caliphate could be overthrown easily and within a timescale which was trivial by Roman standards. Thus its fall only 'seemed' to resemble that of Rome, *Decline and fall*, ed. Bury (2), VI, p. 51.

[204] *Ibid.*, VI, p. 465, cf. p. 394 n. 33; Robertson, 'A view of the progress of society in Europe', *Charles V*, vol. I, pp. 22–30; Adam Smith, *An inquiry into the nature and causes of the Wealth of nations*, eds. R. H. Campbell and A. S. Skinner (Oxford, 1976), vol. III, ch. 3, p. 406. Hume, however, takes the more simple, Voltairean view, *History of England*, ed. W. B. Todd (Indianapolis, 1983), vol. I, pp. 234–40, 365–94 *passim*. Thus Roy Porter's suggestion that the last two volumes present Gibbon's account of the recovery of the West seems to me quite mistaken, as if they were some sort of long-winded re-run of Robertson, *Edward Gibbon*, p. 146; cf. Pocock, *Tanner Lectures*, pp. 293, 311, 330, 358–9; see also n. 224 below.

[205] Entry 'Croisades' in 'Common place book', Add. MSS 34880 f. 54b, citing Voltaire, *Abregé de l'histoire universelle depuis Charlemagne jusqu'à Charles Quint* (London, 1753); cf. *Essai sur les moeurs*, ed. R. Pomeau (Paris, 1963), ch. LVIII.

in the long-standing 'aversion of the Greeks for the Latins', which arose from that familiar triad of profound forces: manners, language and religion. Being profound, it had endured over centuries. In chapter 60 he traced it to the time of Constantine, but he could have gone back to the opening of the *History*; indeed the pointed description of the Crusaders as 'Latins' makes the same point.[206] If we bear in mind Arab 'aversions' as well, the true character of the Crusades emerges: as an 'essentially superficial' episode where the confused, triangular clash of 'nations' yielded no durable consequence. Above all, the Latins learned nothing from the 'more polished' Greeks and Arabs. By taking Constantinople in 1204 they gained access to the single most precious repository of classical tradition; but instead of this triggering a renaissance of classical *belles lettres* – a movement which the west was only capable of sustaining some 200 years later – 'the most important effects' of the Crusaders' savage fanaticism 'were analogous to the cause'. In other words, the reign of superstition and darkness was renewed.[207]

Rome supplied the essential contrast to both 'the transient dynasties of Asia'[208] and the bloody flounderings of the Latins. Gibbon had always believed that durability was its unique feature: 'Of all the empires, that of the Romans arose the most slowly and was sustained the longest.'[209] Predictably, then, the caliphate (for example) far outstripped the 'timid maxims' of victorious Rome in its rise – even in its military operations it dispensed with Roman art and labour[210] – but as a result, 'We should vainly seek the

---

[206] *Decline and fall*, ed. Bury (2), VI, p. 381; cf. I, pp. 41–3; VI, p. 299.

[207] *Ibid.*, VI, p. 464; cf. pp. 95–105, 429–30; for Gibbon's belief in the subsequent importance of Greek learning to the Renaissance of letters, VII, pp. 119–37.

[208] *Ibid.*, VII, p. 82.

[209] 'Du gouvernement féodal' (1768), *Miscellaneous works*, vol. III, p. 194; cf. *Decline and fall*, ed. Bury (2), I, p. 31. The Chinese Empire might be a remote exception to Roman primacy in this respect: *ibid.*, V, p. 438.

[210] *Decline and fall*, ed. Bury (2), V, p. 450. For Gibbon durable civilizations based on towns and buildings had a natural affinity with military technology or 'science', and also with greater skill in siege warfare (where technology is pitted against buildings, and so requires an understanding thereof). The innovations of civilized powers – Greek fire or gunpowder – might be leaked to pastoral barbarians (*ibid.*, VII, p. 85), but the inferiority of the latter in this respect is marked to the end: at the siege of Constantinople in 1453 the Muslims depend on the technical advice of Christians, and even their strokes of genius rely on the brute 'strength of obedient myriads' to make up 'the deficiency of art' (*ibid.*, VII, pp. 187, 192). Thus in Gibbon's hands warfare is no longer just the narrative of the surface vicissitudes of fortune, but part of the struggle of civilization against barbarism; and to suppose that '[barbarian] military technology is not much different from that of the legions' is a fundamental misconception: Pocock, *Tanner Lectures*, p. 320.

indissoluble union and easy obedience that pervaded the government of Augustus and the Antonines.'[211] Here we see how truly ambivalent Gibbon's original tribute to the latter had been.[212] While it is common today to emphasize this as an early notice of Rome's moral decay, we altogether overlook his positive conception of its immense inertial mass, even when decadent. The durability of Rome, as a carrier of the complex machinery of civilization, is symbolized by Gibbon's favourite image of it as a building: 'the solid fabric of Roman greatness', 'the firm edifice of Roman power' as compared, for example, to 'the hasty structure of [Mahomet's] power and religion'.[213] For this reason the subjects of the final volumes confess their inferiority in the presence of classical ruins. When, for example, Musa, one of the Muslim conquerors of Spain, 'beheld the works of Roman magnificence, the bridge, the aqueducts, the triumphal arches, and the theatre of the ancient metropolis of Lusitania [Merida],' he commented: '"I should imagine . . . that the human race must have united their art and power in the foundation of this city: happy is the man who shall become its master!"'[214] Mastery was not worth much in an era when 'the conquests of an age' might be 'lost in a single day',[215] but Musa's inadequacy was as nothing to the blindness of the Athenians of Gibbon's own day, 'who walk with supine indifference among the glorious ruins of antiquity'.[216] Here again it is impossible to doubt the profound significance of Gibbon's vespers on the Capitol in 1764, that first great revelation of 'the majesty of ruin'.[217]

Of course it is not only ruins which shadow the last volumes of the *History*. 'The wealth of Lydia . . . [and] the splendour of the Augustan age' survive in books as much as in ruins,[218] and by this

---

[211] *Decline and fall*, ed. Bury (2), v, pp. 427, 524.

[212] *Ibid.*, I, pp. 85–6.

[213] On Roman 'fabric': *Decline and fall* 1776 Preface ('Roman' is misprinted as 'human' in modern editions, cf. *Decline and fall*, ed. Bury (2), I, p. xxxix); I, p. 31; III, p. 128, IV, pp. 107, 173, V, p. 281; cf. v, p. 500. From the image of Rome as a 'fabric' or 'edifice' derives the idea of her (metaphorical) 'ruins': for example, II, p. 451; III, p. 351; IV, p. 18; V, p. 281, *Autobiographies*, C, p. 284. On 'hasty structures' and 'baseless fabrics': *Decline and fall*, ed. Bury (2), v, p. 423; cf. v, p. 500; VI, p. 87.

[214] *Decline and fall*, ed. Bury (2), v, pp. 509–10.

[215] *Ibid.*, v, p. 499.

[216] *Ibid.*, VI, p. 508; cf. I, p. 54 (chapter 2) already. Not surprisingly Gibbon regarded the Arab 'rovers of the desert' (v, p. 460) as intrinsically second-rate builders: v, pp. 434–5, which repeats *Miscellaneous works*, vol. III, p. 70.

[217] *Decline and fall*, ed. Bury (2), VII, p. 138.   [218] *Ibid.*, VI, p. 260.

means, too, classical norms are applied to barbarian and Greek cultures. Alongside the steady drip of the footnotes – where Mariana 'seems to vie with . . . Livy', whilst 'Falcandus has been styled the Tacitus of [twelfth-century] Sicily; and, after a just, but immense, abatement . . . I would not strip him of his title'[219] – there are set-piece pronouncements of classical supremacy. The whole circle of Muslim and Byzantine literature and science comes under a judgment, which is exquisite in its mixture of grandeur and scruple: 'I *know* that the classics have much to teach, and I *believe* that the Orientals have much to learn.'[220] Negative reference to the durable civilization of Rome prepares, finally, its gradual recovery or renaissance in volume VI. As we have seen, the Crusaders were damned (with an implicit hindsight) for being incapable of this, but in the fourteenth century the day dawns for 'the *monuments* of art', for 'the disciples of Cicero and Virgil', and then for the majesty of Roman ruins, which, under the liberal eye of Manuel Chrysolaras, 'restored the image of [Rome's] ancient prosperity'.[221] In this way the theme of 'resurrection' is established, well before the fall of Constantinople in 1453 (in chapters 60, 61, 66, 67), and the 'return from the captivity of the new to the ruins of the ancient ROME' in chapters 69–71 appears as a real conclusion, not a mere consolatory epilogue.

So the author of the last two volumes of the *History* did not change his spots. Confronted by the problem of a perceived vacuum in civilization after 476, Gibbon did not tamely abandon the stratified idea of history but drew virtue from necessity: the very fact of that vacuum and the lack of a durable civilization became the deep background for his work. Yet in casting a balance, we must note, too, what Gibbon would not or could not do. By fixing his attention

---

[219] *Ibid.*, V, p. 502 n. 200, VI, p. 227 n. 145. Explicit comparisons may be multiplied, for example, II, p. 67 n. 178, V, p. 428 n. 11, VI, pp. 358 n. 67, 482 n. 19, VII, p. 150 n. 26, and the theme further expanded if we consider Gibbon's award of the 'classic' *imprimatur*, or his stylistic preferences, which apply even to the literature of his own day (III, p. 45, VI, pp. 10 n. 21, 441 n. 29). Of course he has another standard of judgment, besides the classical: that of authenticity, honesty and fidelity to nature, which was the source, for example, of his approval of Joinville and Villehardouin (VI, pp. 374, 406 n. 68). But for Gibbon nature and classicism are complementary, showing that his classicism is not lifelessly imitative like that of Byzantium, but expansive and modern or rather timeless: see Peter Ghosh, 'Gibbon's timeless verity: nature and neo-classicism in the late Enlightenment' in D. Womersley (ed.), *Gibbon bicentenary studies* (Oxford, forthcoming).

[220] *Decline and fall*, ed. Bury (2), VI, pp. 34–5; cf. pp. 67–9, 105–14.

[221] *Ibid.*, VII, p. 122 (my emphasis).

on what was Roman, either directly or by contrast, he did not treat post-Roman societies by standards intrinsic to themselves, and he had little or no scope to lay the alternative foundations of a post-Roman modernity. In this profound sense he remained, quite voluntarily, within the confines of a normative Renaissance classicism. For him the modern progress of European civilization really only began with the rebirth of classical antiquity, and if it was subsequently transcended, it was only by a more comprehensive (less exclusively political) classicism. So Rome was indeed 'ETERNAL', and classicism, being normative, hardly required historical explanation. Thus, despite the vast theatre of time and space traversed by the final volumes, he offered only a few unsatisfactory and contradictory hints as to how its recovery might have originated. He adhered to the idea that in the West competition within a European federation was a mainspring of progress, and he allowed too for the importance of Christianity:[222] but these foundations had been in place since the fall of Rome and were as much to do with causing the thousand year 'dark ages' as overcoming them. As a result the Crusaders, for example, could be both 'civilized' – such was the fruit of the obscure 'tide of civilization' which ebbed and flowed of its own volition – and also savage fanatics.[223] There was a history, not *of* but *out of* barbarism to be written here, but Gibbon was not the author. Robertson's contemporary 'View of the progress of [western] society' was, as a piece of historical writing, threadbare compared to Gibbon's; but still it bore on this question which, broadly, the *History* did not.[224] In historical method Gibbon was an original and very much a 'modern'; but the conceptions he served thereby retained palpable links to the party of the 'Ancients'.[225]

---

[222] On federalism: *ibid.*, IV, pp. 176–8; VI, pp. 113–14; VII, pp. 121–2; on Christianity, see, for example, VI, pp. 171–3.

[223] *Ibid.*, VI, pp. 423, 465.

[224] Treatment of the medieval Holy Roman Empire supplies another telling contrast: for Robertson this is tried and largely found wanting by the criterion of 'progress', whereas for Gibbon the standard of comparison is ancient Rome. Hence his account ends with what is, relatively speaking, a paean to Augustus: compare *Decline and fall*, ed. Bury (2), V, pp. 325–31 and Robertson, *Charles V*, vol. I, pp. 173–86.

[225] *Seventy-five years on*, all Gibbon's technical sympathies lay with the 'moderns' in the original quarrel, Wotton and Bentley (*English essays*, pp. 112–13; *Decline and fall*, ed. Bury (2), IV, p. 473 n. 14; V, p. 484 n. 144; VI, p. 33 n. 78; VII, p. 79 n. 70; *Autobiographies*, E, p. 323 n. 46), even if residual sympathy for Temple, the leading 'Ancient', and retention of some components of his view can also be detected (*Decline and fall*, ed. Bury (2), VII, p. 156 n. 39,

In the east, the proper sphere of the later *History*, these conceptions also worked against him, albeit in different ways. He
understood, of course, that the Turks were a fixture in his own day,
so it followed that, whereas Zingis 'had broken the fabric of . . .
ancient government' throughout much of the Near and Far East,
the Turkish case was different: 'The massy trunk was bent to the
ground, but no sooner did the hurricane pass away than it again
rose with fresh vigour and more lively vegetation.'[226] But having
been driven to acknowledge the existence of a profound substructure, 'the massy trunk', Gibbon's ability to realize it was so
limited that he described the Janissaries twice in the attempt.[227]
His failure with Islam was yet greater in scope. He supposed that
a pure, philosophical theism was frequently the product of
simple and even barbarous societies – Magian Persia, primitive
Christianity, the religion of Zingis,[228] as well as that of Mahomet –
but a corollary of this was that 'philosophic simplicity alone', without the aid of popular custom and superstition (or as we would say,
ritual), was insufficient to root a religion.[229] By this standard the
establishment of Islam was not only '*insensible*, since it [was] not
accompanied with any memorial of time or place, of persecution
or resistance' but *inexplicable* since, in their religion 'The
Mohammedans have uniformly withstood the temptation of the
senses and the imagination of man' over the course of twelve

Autobiographies, B, p. 105). However, the *Essai* remains Gibbon's definitive pronouncement: the quarrel trivialized and so subverted a liberal or modern study of the ancient
world, ch. vi and n. *. Behind this lay the belief which is visible throughout the *History*:
that the primary distinction was not between Ancient and Modern but between
civilization *in toto* and barbarism. Given that Modern civilization was essentially the same
thing as that of the Ancients, it showed that classical culture and values were, if rightly
interpreted, a modern and expansive programme; so setting, or comparing, one against
the other was not only trivial and futile, but profoundly damaging. Cf. the judicious
remarks of Joseph Levine, 'Ancients and Moderns reconsidered', *Eighteenth Century
Studies* 15 (1981), pp. 88–9, where he is more mindful of the wisdom of Solomon than in
Humanism and history (London, 1987), chapter 7, where he makes Gibbon 'half an Ancient'.

226 *Decline and fall*, ed. Bury (2), vii, pp. 74–5; cf. vi, p. 259.

227 *Ibid.*, vii, pp. 33–4, 82–5; this is but a slight advance on i, p. 26 where the Turkish empire
of his own day is dismissed as forming 'the arbitrary divisions of despotism and ignorance'
– suggesting that, as Gibbon himself would have supposed, enlightenment and detachment were easier to achieve in the remote past than in areas still clearly connected to the
present. Given his persecution of Voltaire as a Turcophile in the footnotes of volume vi,
we may suspect that the latter, minus Gibbon's classicizing, Eurocentric baggage, was the
more detached (*ibid.*, vii, pp. 146 n. 15, 196 n. 75, 211 n. 114; cf. v, p. 391 n. 150!).

228 *Ibid.*, i, p. 216; ii, p. 7; vii, p. 4 respectively.

229 *Ibid.*, ii, pp. 59–60; vi, p. 132.

centuries.[230] In short, Oriental history could not simply be written on the principle of negative reference to Rome eked out by the assumptions of conjectural history as to the unchanging manners of pastoral nations.

VIII

There are, of course, other characteristics of the *History* I have not mentioned, which also typify and unify its various parts. One is the relativistic detachment of the author who, much as he relied on the thematic unity supplied by Rome, could also experience it as 'a safe and dreary prison'.[231] Hence his longing for the multifarious freedom of the last two volumes and a wider opportunity to display judicial even-handedness between all comers. A second is encyclopaedism. The *History* was an attempt at a universal compendium of knowledge, as personal in format as Bayle's *Dictionary*. Given that its wealth of material so largely outstrips the ability of readers (at any date) to absorb it, we should not labour its omissions overmuch; it is its sheer inclusiveness which most often frustrates our efforts to describe or understand it. All the same, it was an encyclopaedia based on the distinctive, and to that extent restrictive, lines adumbrated in the *Essai*: a comprehensive gathering of modern knowledge from an ancient, or rather classicizing, point of view. As long as we remember *both* the classical and the modern foci of 'the historian's eye', our judgments on his work – which may lie open, as he suggested, to the 'superior science' of barbarous posterity[232] – will at least emanate from a tribunal Gibbon himself would have recognized as legitimate.[233]

---

[230] *Ibid.*, v, pp. 519, 420 respectively; cf. vi, p. 242; the instant persuasive effect and pure meritocracy of Islam are further occasions for surprise, v, pp. 516–17; cf. vii, p. 84.

[231] *Ibid.*, i, p. 90.

[232] *Ibid.*, vii, p. 135.

[233] I am most grateful to Jill Lewis, Oswyn Murray and Paul Cartledge for reading and commenting on this paper.

CHAPTER 13

Winston Churchill and Gibbon

Roland Quinault

Winston Churchill decided to read *The decline and fall of the Roman Empire* at the age of twenty, in 1895. At that time he was a cavalry subaltern at Aldershot and he thought it would be more agreeable to read Gibbon than to pile up statistics.[1] His resolve was strengthened by the advice of his old headmaster at Harrow: 'Gibbon is the greatest of historians, read him all through.'[2] Churchill began reading Dean Milman's eight-volume edition of *Decline and fall* in the summer of 1896. He was then posted, with his regiment, to Bangalore, in India, where he read Gibbon lying on his champoy during the after lunch siesta:[3]

I was immediately dominated both by the story and the style. All through the long listening middle hours of the Indian day, from when we quitted stables till the evening shadows proclaimed the hour of Polo, I devoured Gibbon. I rode triumphantly through it from end to end and enjoyed it all. I scribbled all my opinions on the margins of the pages and very soon found myself a vehement partisan of the author against the disparagement of his pompous-pious editor. I was not even estranged by his naughty footnotes. On the other hand the Dean's apologies and disclaimers roused my ire.[4]

Churchill also read Gibbon's autobiography, before concluding what he described as 'a delightful companionship of six months

---

[1] Randolph S. Churchill, *Winston S. Churchill*, vol. 1, Companion, part 1, *1874–1896* (London, 1967), p. 585: W. S. Churchill to Lady Randolph Churchill, 31 August 1895.

[2] R. S. Churchill, *Churchill*, vol. 1, Companion, part 2, *1896–1900*, p. 682: J. E. C. Welldon to W. S. Churchill, 28 September 1896.

[3] Martin Gilbert, *Road to victory: Winston S. Churchill 1941–5* (London, 1986), p. 666: Marion Holmes, diary, 28 January 1944.

[4] Winston S. Churchill, *My early life* (London, 1943 edn), p. 125.

with Gibbon'.[5] He then moved on to Macaulay, but soon concluded that he was 'not half so solid as Gibbon'.[6]

Winston's interest in Gibbon was prompted by the example of his father, Lord Randolph: 'Someone had told me that my father had read Gibbon with delight; that he knew whole pages of it by heart, and that it had greatly affected his style of speech and writing.'[7] Winston attributed his father's sonorous sentences to Gibbon's influence.[8] Randolph had learnt long passages of *Decline and fall* when he was an undergraduate at Merton College, and his accurate knowledge of the book was noted by the Oxford History examiners, who included E. A. Freeman.[9] Lord Rosebery noted that Gibbon was Randolph's main literary passion, not only at Oxford, but until his death in 1895.[10] Rosebery himself greatly admired the subtle irony of *Decline and fall*.[11] In 1894, Rosebery and three members of his Liberal Cabinet – Bryce, Morley and Trevelyan – joined the committee which organized the Gibbon Commemoration.[12] The committee was officially non-partisan, but it was initiated by an active Liberal, Oscar Browning, and its membership had a strong Liberal bias.[13] A. V. Dicey, Leslie Stephen, St John Brodrick and Frederic Harrison (who gave the memorial address) had all contributed to *Essays on reform*, the 1867 'Bible' of Oxbridge radicalism. Many of the Liberals on the committee, including Frederic Harrison, were positivists who were sympathetic to what they understood to be Gibbon's anti-clericalism and love of liberty.[14]

Winston Churchill had been brought up as a Tory, but soon after reading *Decline and fall* he described himself as a Liberal in all but name.[15] He was certainly influenced by Gibbon's liberal views on

[5] R. S. Churchill, *Churchill*, vol. I, Companion, part 2, p. 746: W. S. Churchill to Lady Randolph Churchill, 31 March 1897.
[6] R. S. Churchill, *Churchill*, vol. I, Companion, part 2, p. 714: W. S. Churchill to Welldon, 16 December 1896; p. 733: W. S. Churchill to Lady Randolph Churchill, 18 February 1897.
[7] Churchill, *My early life*, p. 125.
[8] Winston S. Churchill, *Lord Randolph Churchill* (London, 1907 edn), p. 26.
[9] T. H. S. Escott, *Randolph Spencer-Churchill* (London, 1895), pp. 46–7.
[10] Lord Rosebery, *Lord Randolph Churchill* (London, 1906), p. 35.
[11] The Marquess of Crewe, *Lord Rosebery* (2 vols., London, 1931), vol. II, pp. 378, 383, 494.
[12] *Royal Historical Society, Proceedings of the Gibbon Commemoration 1794–1894* (London, 1894), pp. 10–12.
[13] Royal Historical Society Archives (University College, London), 1894 Gibbon Commemoration minute book.
[14] Cf. the chapters by David Womersley and John Robertson above.
[15] R. S. Churchill, *Churchill*, vol. I, Companion, part 2, p. 751: W. S. Churchill to Lady Randolph Churchill, 6 April 1897.

several issues, such as slavery. In *Decline and fall*, Gibbon observed that the Roman Empire had been stained by the existence of 'an unhappy condition of men who endured the weight, without sharing the benefits, of society'.[16] In 1898, when Churchill argued with some aristocratic friends, he entrenched himself around the slogan 'No slavery under the Union Jack'.[17] Gibbon's liberal influence on Churchill was most apparent in the religious sphere. When Churchill was reading *Decline and fall*, he attacked the early religious movements of Christ, Mahomet and Buddha because they had been attended with 'deluges of blood and floods of theological controversy' which had diminished 'the sum of human happiness and prosperity'.[18] Churchill later observed that his reading of Gibbon and Lecky's *History of Rationalism in Europe* had established in his mind a predominantly secular outlook.[19] Lecky was a great admirer of Gibbon and a member of the 1894 Commemoration committee.

Gibbon's unhappy time at Magdalen College, Oxford, recounted in his autobiography, may have encouraged Winston's critical response to his brother Jack's decision to study at Oxford:

It has long been the home of bigotry and intolerance and has defended more damnable errors and wicked notions than any other institution – with the exception of the Catholic Church –under the sun. But I do not think your amiable and rational spirit is likely to be soiled by religious narrow mindedness.[20]

A year later, Winston again attacked Catholicism and religion in a Gibbonesque way:

As a rationalist I deprecate all Romish practices and prefer those of protestantism, because I believe that the Reformed Church is less deeply sunk in the mire of dogma than the Original Establishment. We are at any rate a step nearer Reason . . . Catholicism – all religions if you like, but particularly Catholicism – is a delicious narcotic. It may soothe our pains and chase our worries, but it checks our growth and saps our strength. And since the improvement of the British breed is my political aim in life,

---

16 *Decline and fall*, ed. Smeaton, I, p. 39.
17 Churchill, *My early life*, p. 216.
18 R. S. Churchill, *Churchill*, vol. I, Companion, part 2, p. 714: W. S. Churchill to Welldon, 16 December 1896.
19 Churchill, *My early life*, p. 129.
20 R. S. Churchill, *Churchill*, vol. I, Companion, part 2, p. 858: W. S. Churchill to J. Churchill, 13 January 1898.

I would not permit too great indulgence if I could prevent it without assailing another principle – Liberty.[21]

Gibbon had claimed that the Catholic clergy had preached doctrines of patience and pusillanimity – thus ensuring that 'the last remains of the military spirit were buried in the cloister'.[22]

When Churchill returned from India to England, in 1897, he stopped off in Rome, 'The imperial city around which my reading for so many months has centred.'[23] His Gibbon-like 'musing in the ruins of the capitol' prompted him to contemplate whether the British Empire would suffer a similar fate. On his return to England he witnessed the imperial celebrations of Queen Victoria's Diamond Jubilee and then gave his first political speech:

There were not wanting those who said that in this Jubilee year our Empire had reached the height of its glory and power, and that now we should begin to decline, as Babylon, Carthage and Rome had declined. Do not believe these croakers, but give the lie to their dismal croaking by showing by your actions that the vigour and vitality of our race is unimpaired and that our determination is to uphold the Empire . . . and carry out our mission of bearing peace, civilisation and good government to the uttermost ends of the earth.[24]

Gibbon had justified the Roman Empire in similar terms:

Whatever evils either reason or declamation have imputed to extensive empire, the power of Rome was attended with some beneficial consequences to mankind . . . Under the protection of an established government, the productions of happier climes, and the industry of more civilized nations, were gradually introduced into the western countries of Europe; and the natives were encouraged by an open and profitable commerce, to multiply the former, as well as to improve the latter.[25]

This passage reflects the influence on Gibbon of Adam Smith, whose *Wealth of nations* was ordered by Churchill after he had finished reading *Decline and fall*.

[21] R. S. Churchill, *Churchill*, vol. II, Companion, part 2, *1901–07* (London, 1967), pp. xxvi–xxvii: W. S. Churchill to Ivor Guest, 19 January 1899.
[22] *Decline and fall*, ed. Smeaton, IV, p. 106 (chapter 38).
[23] R. S. Churchill, *Churchill*, vol. I, Companion, part 2, p. 749: W. S. Churchill to Lady Randolph Churchill, 6 April 1897.
[24] R. S. Churchill, *Churchill*, vol. I, Companion, part 2, p. 774: W. S. Churchill to the Bath Habitation of the Primrose League, 26 July 1897.
[25] *Decline and fall*, ed. Smeaton, I, p. 52.

In his first book, *The story of the Malakand Field Force*, published in 1898, Churchill imitated Gibbon's language, syntax and sentiments:

The philosopher may observe with pity, and the philanthropist deplore with pain, that the attention of so many minds should be directed to the scientific destruction of the human species; but practical people in a business-like age will remember that they live in a world of men – not angels – and regulate their conduct accordingly.[26]

Churchill was highly annoyed when his uncle, Moreton Frewen, rewrote sentences which he had directly modelled on Gibbon.[27] Nevertheless Churchill thought that Gibbon, though 'stately and impressive', was not so easy to read as Macaulay.[28] So when Churchill wrote his next book, *The River War*, he tried to combine 'The staccato antithesis' of Macaulay with 'The rolling sentences and genitival endings' of Gibbon.[29]

Churchill was influenced not only by Gibbon's style, but also by his subject. Churchill's first four books described imperial frontier wars: a theme which looms large in *Decline and fall*. Churchill, like Gibbon, regarded these frontier wars as struggles between the forces of civilization and barbarism. On the title page of *The story of the Malakand Field Force*, he quoted Lord Salisbury: 'They (frontier wars) are but the surf that marks the edge and the advance of the wave of civilisation.'[30] Churchill alleged the Mohmand tribe on the north-west frontier of India lived in a state of degraded barbarism. He thought that they were foolish to attack the British Empire, which Daniel Webster had described as superior in military force to imperial Rome at the height of its power.[31] Churchill acknowledged, however, that the frontier tribesmen had a well deserved reputation for courage, tactical skill and marksmanship.[32] He attributed their defeat to the superior resources, discipline and technology of both the British and Indian troops. He

[26] Winston S. Churchill, *The story of the Malakand Field Force: an episode of frontier war* (London, 1990 edn), p. 208.
[27] R. S. Churchill, *Churchill*, vol. I, Companion, part 2, p. 899: W. S. Churchill to Lady Randolph Churchill, 25 March 1898.
[28] R. S. Churchill, *Churchill*, vol. I, Companion, part 2, p. 726: W. S. Churchill to Lady Randolph Churchill, 21 January 1897.
[29] Churchill, *My early life*, p. 225.   [30] Churchill, *Malakand Field Force*, p. iii.
[31] *The Daily Telegraph*, 8 October 1897.   [32] *The Daily Telegraph*, 16 November 1897.

thus echoed Gibbon's comments on the superiority of the Roman legions and the important role played by the auxiliaries.[33]

Churchill's views on British imperial frontier policy echoed Gibbon's views on Roman imperial frontier policy. Gibbon applauded Augustus for advising his successors to confine the Roman Empire within natural geographical limits. He observed that Hadrian and the Antonines maintained the dignity of the Empire, not by enlarging it, but by seeking the friendship of the barbarians beyond the frontiers.[34] Similarly, Churchill believed that the Himalayas were the natural frontiers of British India and that punitive expeditions beyond the frontier had only a temporary effect on the tribesmen: 'They have been pacified, not subdued; rendered hostile, but not harmless. Their fanaticism remains unshaken. Their barbarism is unrelieved. Some have been killed, but these fertile valleys will in a few years replace the waste of war. The riddle of the frontier is still unsolved.'[35] Churchill's pessimistic views about the north-west frontier of India echoed those of Gibbon about the Roman Empire's northern frontier along the Rhine and the Danube. Churchill opposed a further extension of the imperial frontier on both financial and moral grounds.[36] He thought that 'silver makes a better weapon than steel' since trade and subsidies would expose the tribes to the 'softening and enervating influences of civilisation'.[37] Thus he followed the frontier policies of Augustus and Hadrian as described and endorsed by Gibbon.

Churchill believed that the fanaticism of the tribesmen was increased by their Islamic faith – an observation Gibbon had made in his chapters on Mahomet and his followers.[38] Churchill contrasted the superstitious and unquestioning faith of the tribesmen with the civilizing influence of the Indian government which sapped the strength of superstition.[39] In *The River War*, Churchill again drew on Gibbon when he compared the exploits of the Mahdi in the Sudan, with those of Mahomet in Arabia. He claimed that the Mahdi was more successful in his lifetime than Mahomet had been. But whereas Mohammedism had only been opposed by decadent

---

[33] *Decline and fall*, ed. Smeaton, I, pp. 1, 10, 15–16.   [34] *Ibid.*, I, pp. 3, 9.
[35] *The Daily Telegraph*, 6 December 1897.   [36] Churchill, *Malakand Field Force*, p. 213.
[37] Churchill, *Malakand Field Force*, p. 215; Winston S. Churchill, 'The ethics of frontier policy', *The United Services Magazine* (1898), p. 509.
[38] Churchill, *Malakand Field Force*, pp. 3–4; *Decline and fall*, ed. Smeaton, v, pp. 257, 293.
[39] Churchill, *Malakand Field Force*, pp. 6–7, 25.

governments, Mahdism had come into conflict with western scientific civilization.[40] Churchill described the defeat of the Mahdists by the Anglo-Egyptian army at the battle of Omdurman as 'the most signal triumph ever gained by the arms of science over barbarians'.[41]

Churchill's assessment of the confrontation in the Sudan between the forces of barbarism and civilization was not entirely to the advantage of the latter:

What enterprise that an enlightened community may attempt is more noble and more profitable than the reclamation from barbarism of fertile regions and large populations? . . . Yet as the mind turns from the wonderful cloudland of aspiration to the ugly scaffolding of attempt and achievement, a succession of opposite ideas arises. Industrious races are displayed stinted and starved for the sake of expensive Imperialism which they can only enjoy if they are well fed. Wild peoples, ignorant of their barbarism, callous of suffering, careless of life but tenacious of liberty, are seen to resist with fury the philanthropic invaders, and to perish in thousands before they are convinced of their mistake.[42]

When Churchill submitted the manuscript of *The River War* to his fellow war correspondent, G. W. Steevens, the latter observed: 'Your philosophic reflections, while generally well expressed, often acute and sometimes true, are too devilish frequent.'[43] Yet Steevens himself wrote articles about the British Empire, under the pseudonym 'The new Gibbon', which Churchill thought could have been taken straight from the pages of *Decline and fall.*[44]

As a young soldier, Churchill must have been struck by a passage in Gibbon's autobiography, relating to his service in the Hampshire militia:

A youth of any spirit is fired even by the play of arms and in the first sallies of my enthusiasm I had seriously attempted to embrace the regular profession of a soldier. But this military fever was cooled by the enjoyment of our mimic Bellona, who soon unveiled to my eyes her naked deformity. How often did I sigh for my proper station in society and letters![45]

[40] Winston S. Churchill, *The River War: an account of the reconquest of the Sudan* (London, 1951 edn), p. 34.
[41] Churchill, *River War*, p. 300.
[42] Churchill, *River War*, pp. 9–10.
[43] Quoted in Charles K. Webster, 'The chronicler' in Sir James Marchant (ed.), *Winston Spencer Churchill servant of Crown and Commonwealth* (London, 1954), p. 134.
[44] Churchill, *My early life*, pp. 227–8.
[45] *Autobiography of Edward Gibbon as originally edited by Lord Sheffield* (London, 1972 edn), p. 106.

Churchill, like Gibbon, soon tired of army life and set his sights on authorship and Parliament. In 1899 he resigned his commission and returned to England to stand as a Conservative candidate at Oldham. In his election address he declared that the consolidation of the Empire and the preservation of its frontiers from aggression was the most formidable task facing Lord Salisbury.[46] He claimed that after the victory in the Sudan and the subsequent Fashoda incident, foreigners no longer regarded Britain as a power that was bound to fall as Rome had done.[47] Churchill was defeated on that occasion, but he was returned for Oldham at the general election in the following year.

During his early years in Parliament, Churchill kept up his historical interests by writing a two-volume biography of his father, in which he referred to Lord Randolph's precise and intimate knowledge of Gibbon.[48] Churchill had read Gibbon's remark that his eight years as an MP had given him a sense of civil prudence – 'the first and most essential virtue of an historian'. Churchill probably also shared Gibbon's view that 'the winter hurry of society and parliament' improved his mind and composition.[49] Certainly Winston's service with the Oxfordshire Yeomanry recalled Gibbon's service in the militia.

In the Edwardian period, Churchill criticized those imperialists who wanted to pile up armaments, taxation and territory.[50] In his review of Seebohm Rowntree's *Poverty. A study of town life*, Churchill quoted Gibbon and pointed out, with Gibbonian irony, that the urban poor were unable to find adequate housing, despite the size of the British Empire.[51] In 1909, he declared that the greatest danger to the British Empire came, not from foreign threats like the 'Yellow peril', but from the growing cities and decaying villages of Britain: 'It is there you will find the seeds of Imperial ruin and national decay – the unnatural gap between rich and poor, the divorce of the people from the land, the want of proper discipline

---

[46] R. S. Churchill, *Churchill*, vol. i, Companion, part 2, p. 1032: 24 June 1899.
[47] Robert Rhodes James (ed.), *Churchill speaks: Winston S. Churchill in peace and war. Collected speeches 1897–1963* (1981), p. 26: speech at Oldham, 24 June 1899.
[48] Churchill, *Lord Randolph Churchill*, p. 26.
[49] Gibbon, *Autobiography*, pp. 179, 185.
[50] R. S. Churchill, *Churchill*, vol. ii, Companion, part 1, p. 104: W. S. Churchill to Moore Bayley, 23 December 1901.
[51] B. S. Rowntree, *Poverty. A study of town life* (London, 1901). R. S. Churchill, *Churchill*, vol. ii, Companion, part 1, pp. 107, 111.

and training in our youth.'[52] Gibbon had similarly highlighted the internal socio-economic problems of the late Roman Empire and had attributed the decline of the Roman army to the gradual diminution of discipline and training.

In 1909 the rejection of the Liberal budget by the House of Lords prompted Churchill to attack the hereditary character of the upper chamber. His claim that most men of genius had come from the people recalled Gibbon's remark that the descendant of a king was less truly noble than the offspring of a man of genius, whose writings had a lasting value.[53] Churchill's observation that Christianity had first been preached by poor and humble men also echoed Gibbon's famous comment about a pure and humble religion.[54] When Churchill became Home Secretary, in 1910, he decided that prisoners should be provided with good reading, such as Gibbon and Macaulay. He conceded that convicted murderers would not have enough time to read Gibbon, but considered him ideal for those convicted of robbery with violence, arson and rape.[55] Churchill's policy had unexpected results, for although *Decline and fall* influenced one Dartmoor convict more than any other book, it also turned him against all religion.[56]

Churchill concluded his only novel, *Savrola*, with this sentence:

> But the chronicler, finding few great events, other than the opening of colleges, railways, and canals, to recount, will remember the splendid sentence of Gibbon, that history is 'little more than the register of crimes, follies and misfortunes of mankind'; and he will rejoice that, after many troubles, peace and prosperity came back to the Republic of Laurania.[57]

Churchill's belief in Gibbon's thesis – that war is the stuff of history – was confirmed by his own experience of colonial wars and the First World War. 'The story of the human race is war', he wrote in 1924, claiming that there had never been peace except for brief and precarious interludes.[58] But Churchill believed that peace could be

---

[52] W. S. Churchill (ed. Cameron Hazelhurst), *The people's rights* (London, 1970), p. 139.
[53] Churchill, *Collected speeches*, p. 182: speech at Burnley, 17 December 1909; Gibbon, *Autobiography*, p. 3.
[54] Churchill, *Collected speeches*, p. 182; Gibbon, *Decline and fall*, ed. Smeaton, I, p. 430.
[55] Violet Bonham Carter, *Winston Churchill as I knew him* (London, 1965), p. 187.
[56] Raphael Samuel, *East End underworld: chapters in the life of Arthur Harding* (London, 1981), p. 274.
[57] Winston S. Churchill, *Savrola* (London, 1915 edn), p. 260.
[58] Winston S. Churchill, 'Shall we all commit suicide?' in *Thoughts and adventures* (London, 1947 edn), p. 184.

better preserved if the victors dealt leniently with the vanquished. In this respect he echoed Gibbon who had considered the emperor Severus 'the principal author of the decline of the Roman empire' because he was despotic and unmerciful to his defeated opponents.[59] Churchill, by contrast, always sought reconciliation with the defeated enemies of Britain. After the First World War he suggested the words 'In Victory: Magnanimity' for a war memorial inscription and the phrase became one of the morals which prefaced his volumes on the Second World War.

In Churchill's account of the First World War, *The world crisis*, he noted that the evidence of history showed that states and empires rose to splendour and then declined.[60] By 1929, Churchill felt gloomy about Britain's prospects and he looked back, with nostalgia, to the long era of Victorian peace, prosperity and progress which he described as 'the British Antonine Age'.[61] Gibbon had described the Antonine era as 'The period in the history of the world, during which the condition of the human race was most happy and prosperous.'[62] Gibbon believed that modern Europe was safe from attack from barbarians since 'before they can conquer, they must cease to be barbarous'.[63] By 1925, however, Churchill feared that modern methods of warfare had created a new situation – morally as well as militarily:

In barbarous times superior martial virtues – physical strength, courage, skill, discipline – were required to secure such a supremacy; and in the hard evolution of mankind the best and fittest stocks came to the fore. But no such guarantee exists today. There is no reason why a base, degenerate, immoral race should not make an enemy far above them in quality, the prostrate subject of their caprice or tyranny, simply because they happened to be possessed at a given moment of some new death-dealing or terror-working process and were ruthless in its employment.[64]

Churchill's fears that modern barbarians could overthrow modern Romans were soon to be realized.

Churchill's hostility to Hitler and the Nazis was clearly justified by a passage in *Decline and fall*: 'History which undertakes to record the transactions of the past, for the instruction of future ages,

[59] *Decline and fall*, ed. Smeaton, I, p. 123.
[60] Winston S. Churchill, *The world crisis 1911–18* (London, 1937 edn), p. 19.
[61] Winston S. Churchill, *Great contemporaries* (London, 1937), p. 95.
[62] *Decline and fall*, ed. Smeaton, I, p. 78.
[63] *Ibid.*, IV, p. 110.   [64] Churchill, *Thoughts and adventures*, pp. 189–90.

would ill deserve that honourable office, if she condescended to plead the cause of tyrants, or to justify the maxims of persecution.'[65] Gibbon criticized the absolute power of the Roman emperors and observed that even the benevolent Antonines 'must often have recollected the instability of a happiness which depended on the character of a single man'.[66] Churchill echoed this comment when he spoke about Hitler:

One thing that has struck me as very strange, and that is this resurgence of the one-man power after all these centuries of experience and progress . . . we must strive to frame some system of human relations in the future . . . which will no longer leave the whole life of mankind dependent upon the virtues, the caprice or the wickedness of a single man.[67]

Churchill described Nazism as 'a barbarous paganism, which vaunts the spirit of aggression and conquest'.[68] He developed the barbaric analogy in a passage of *A history of the English-speaking peoples*, written in 1939:

If a native of Roman Britain was still alive . . . he would find a settled government and a sense of belonging to a world-wide empire . . . He would have the same sense of belonging to a society which was threatened and to an imperial rule which had passed its prime. He would have the same gathering fears of some sudden onslaught by barbarian forces armed with equal weapons to those of the local legions or auxiliaries. He would still fear the people across the North Sea, and still be taught that his frontiers were upon the Rhine.[69]

Churchill thought that historians would be baffled, a thousand years hence, if the British Empire was destroyed, for he believed that it could still save civilization.[70] He wanted the free states to unite and create a constabulary force which 'barbaric and atavistic forces' would respect.[71] Thus Churchill sought to emulate the example of the Antonine emperors who, in Gibbon's words, had preserved peace by 'a constant preparation for war'.[72] Churchill

[65] Gibbon, *Decline and fall*, ed. Smeaton, II, p. 11.
[66] *Ibid.*, I, p. 78.
[67] Winston S. Churchill, *Into battle* (London, 1945 edn), p. 128: 8 August 1939.
[68] Churchill, *Into battle*, p. 50: 5 October 1938.
[69] Winston S. Churchill, *A history of the English-speaking peoples. Volume I: The birth of Britain* (London, 1974 edn), p. 31.
[70] Winston S. Churchill, *Arms and the covenant* (London, 1938), pp. 465–6: 24 March 1938.
[71] Churchill, *Into battle*, p. 36: 2 July 1938.
[72] *Decline and fall*, ed. Smeaton, I, p. 9.

acknowledged that modern weapons made the dictators the greatest threat to peace and progress since the Mongol invasions and that in the past 'the light of civilised progress' had often been extinguished. Nevertheless he believed that the civilized powers could avert the barbarian onslaught if they showed foresight and determination.[73] Two months before the outbreak of war, Churchill predicted that, after a severe struggle, democracy and civilization would triumph and resume their onward march.[74] His comments echoed one of Gibbon's conclusions: 'Ages of laborious ascent have been followed by a moment of rapid downfall ... Yet the experience of four thousand years should enlarge our hopes and diminish our apprehensions ... it may safely be presumed that no people, unless the face of nature is changed, will relapse into their original barbarism.'[75]

Churchill hoped that if the British Empire came to an end, it would not be by a gradual process of dispersion and decay, but by a supreme exertion in the cause of freedom and right.[76] That supreme exertion came when Churchill was made prime minister in 1940. By then, what he termed 'the long night of barbarism' had descended on the occupied peoples of Europe.[77] Churchill also deployed language redolent of Gibbon in his famous speech on the Battle of Britain:

Upon this battle depends the survival of Christian civilisation ... and the long continuity of our institutions and our Empire ... if we fail, then the whole world ... will sink into the abyss of a new Dark Age ... Let us therefore brace ourselves to our duties, and so bear ourselves that, if the British Empire and its Commonwealth last for a thousand years, men will still say, 'This was their finest hour.'[78]

Gibbon had familiarized Churchill with a thousand-year empire which had long outlasted its finest hour. Churchill strengthened the dark ages analogy when he described London as a 'strong City of Refuge [which] enshrines the title-deeds of human progress and is of deep consequence to Christian civilisation'. Similar comments about Constantinople had been made by Gibbon.[79] He noted that in 677, when Constantinople was besieged by the Muslims, the spirit

---

[73] Churchill, *Into battle*, p. 59: 16 October 1938.   [74] *Ibid.*, p. 116: 28 June 1939.
[75] *Decline and fall*, ed. Smeaton, IV, p. 111.   [76] Churchill, *Into battle*, p. 100: 20 April 1939.
[77] *Ibid.*, p. 212: 19 May 1940.   [78] *Ibid.*, p. 234: 18 June 1940.
[79] *Ibid.*, pp. 248–9: 14 July 1940; *Decline and fall*, ed. Smeaton, IV, pp. 105–6.

of the people was 'rekindled by the last danger of their religion and empire' and they defeated the invaders by the novel use of Greek fire.[80] In 1940 it was the novel use of radar which enabled Britain to defeat the *Luftwaffe*.

Churchill declared that even if Britain was occupied then the fleet would carry on the fight, with the Empire across the seas, until the new world liberated the old.[81] His prediction had been fore-shadowed by Gibbon: 'Should the victorious barbarians carry slavery and desolation as far as the Atlantic ocean, ten thousand vessels would transport beyond their pursuit the remains of civilized society; and Europe would revive and flourish in the American world, which is already filled with her colonies and institutions.'[82] Nevertheless, Churchill was confident that the Axis powers could be defeated in Europe. At the start of 1941 he observed that the decline and fall of Mussolini's new Roman Empire would not take a 'future Gibbon' as long to write as the original work.[83] Hitler's failure to defeat Soviet Russia created a new totalitarian superpower in Europe. Gibbon had regarded Russia, under Catherine the Great, as part of civilized Europe, but Churchill did not regard the Soviet Union, under Stalin, in the same light. He thought that 'It would be a measureless disaster if Russian barbarism overlaid the culture and independence of the ancient states of Europe' which he regarded as the parent continent of civilization.[84]

Churchill thought that the peace and civilization of Europe could best be preserved, after the war, by uniting the democratic nations. In this respect, he again followed in the footsteps of Gibbon, who had suggested that the European nations 'might confederate for their common defence' and to preserve their common heritage:

It is the duty of a patriot to prefer and promote the exclusive interest and glory of his native country: but a philosopher may be permitted to enlarge his views, and to consider Europe as one great republic, whose various inhabitants have attained almost the same level of politeness and cultivation . . . the system of the arts, and laws, and manners, which so

---

[80] *Decline and fall*, ed. Smeaton, v, pp. 386–7.   [81] Churchill, *Into battle*, p. 223: 4 June 1940.
[82] *Decline and fall*, ed. Smeaton, IV, p. 109.
[83] Winston S. Churchill, *The unrelenting struggle* (London, 1942), p. 58: 9 February 1941.
[84] *Decline and fall*, ed. Smeaton, IV, p. 110; W. S. Churchill, *The Second World War. Volume IV: The hinge of fate* (London, 1951), p. 504: W. S. Churchill to the Foreign Secretary, 21 October 1942.

advantageously distinguish, above the rest of mankind, the Europeans and their colonies.[85]

In his post-war speeches calling for European unity, Churchill emphasized Europe's unique contribution to world civilization. He referred, not only to the Christian and classical heritage, but also to 'the critical spirit of rationalism' which he had first encountered in Gibbon. He sought to recreate in Europe the security and freedom of movement which had characterized the Roman Empire at its zenith, but based on democracy, not slavery.[86] He did not want Europe to imitate the enforced unity of the Roman Empire which Gibbon thought had been 'purchased by the loss of national freedom and military spirit'. Churchill presented the idea of United Europe as a moral, cultural and spiritual conception and he sought to promote classical studies as an important unifying influence.[87]

Churchill's remembrance of Gibbon was still evident during his second premiership. In 1953 he recited from memory the opening lines of the fourteenth chapter of Decline and fall:[88] 'The balance of power established by Diocletian subsisted no longer than while it was sustained by the firm and dexterous hand of the founder.' Gibbon described the long period of tension which followed Diocletian's abdication as 'a suspension of arms between several hostile monarchs, who, viewing each other with an eye of fear and hatred, strove to increase their respective forces at the expense of their subjects'.[89] This was a topical passage in 1953, when the Cold War was in progress and Churchill was trying, without much success, to revive the wartime understanding between East and West. He again recalled Gibbon in his speech to the 1954 Tory conference – his last as party leader:

I feel we may be sure that a respectful verdict will be granted to our Government by history. And even if we are not mentioned we may console ourselves with the reflection that history has been described by Gibbon as 'little more than a register of the crimes, follies and misfortunes of mankind'.[90]

---

[85] Decline and fall, ed. Smeaton, IV, p. 107.
[86] Winston S. Churchill, Europe unite (London, 1950), p. 82: 14 May 1947.
[87] Churchill, Europe unite, p. 80: 14 May 1947; p. 326: 12 May 1948.
[88] Lord Moran, Winston Churchill: the struggle for survival 1940–65 (London, 1966), p. 478: diary entry for 8 August 1953.
[89] Decline and fall, ed. Smeaton, I, p. 383.
[90] Winston S. Churchill, The unwritten alliance (London, 1961), p. 183: Blackpool, 9 October 1954.

Gibbon's *Decline and fall* had a profound effect on Churchill for a variety of reasons. He read the work when he was young and his ideas were unformed – except by his father's speeches which owed much to Gibbon. He was not a scholar of the late Roman Empire and in India he was far removed from intellectual companions and other works on the same subject. Thus Churchill brought to his reading of Gibbon no textual skills or contextual knowledge. In this respect, his approach to *Decline and fall* was relatively uncritical and markedly different from that of the contributors to this volume. Nevertheless, Churchill wrote extensive marginal comments on the text which criticized the remarks of the editor, Dean Milman. It is not clear if Gibbon was also criticized by Churchill, since his annotated copy of *Decline and fall* has not been located.[91]

Churchill's admiration for *Decline and fall* may have partly reflected his ignorance of the subject, but he was certainly able to appreciate Gibbon's literary merits. Lord Moran claimed that Churchill was impressed, not by what Gibbon said, but by how he said it.[92] Certainly *Decline and fall* provided Churchill with a model for his own writing: vivid historical narrative, ranging widely over period and place and enriched by analysis and reflection. Yet Churchill recalled that he was dominated, not just by Gibbon's style, but also by his story.[93] His appreciation of *Decline and fall* was enhanced by both the relevance of the work to his own experience and the concordance of Gibbon's outlook with his own.

Gibbon's preoccupation with the military aspects of the decline of the Roman Empire had an obvious attraction for Churchill, who was trained as a soldier to defend the British Empire and who thought that war consisted of 'the same tunes, played through the ages'.[94] Gibbon's stress on the fickleness of military fortune may help to account for both Churchill's pessimism about the military outlook after two world wars and his optimism when confronted by apparent defeat in 1940. Gibbon's emphasis on the importance of moral force was echoed in Churchill's observation that victory in

---

[91] Churchill, *My early life*, p. 125. I should like to thank the Rt Hon. Winston S. Churchill, MP, for his help in trying to locate his grandfather's copy of *Decline and fall*.

[92] Moran, *Winston Churchill*, p. 830.

[93] Churchill, *My early life*, p. 125.

[94] Winston S. Churchill, *In the balance* (London, 1951), pp. 306–7: 4 July 1950.

war was not solely determined by material factors.[95] Likewise, Gibbon's approval of the consolidation of the Roman frontier effected by Augustus and Hadrian encouraged Churchill's opposition to the further expansion of the British Empire.

Churchill supported the British Empire largely for Gibbonian reasons. Gibbon had admired the civilization of imperial Rome, but had condemned its despotic political system.[96] Churchill believed that the British Empire was a civilizing force which was free from the taint of Roman despotism. He regarded Parliament and the electoral system as the guarantor of national and imperial freedoms and he justified British rule over non-British peoples by reference to practical improvements in their quality of life. When Churchill became leader of the Conservative party, in 1940, he declared that Britain was the only nation in the world which had combined liberty with empire.[97] Liberty was more apparent in Britain than in the non-white parts of the Empire, but the whole British Empire was liberal by comparison with the current Nazi, Soviet and Japanese regimes.

In *The River War* Churchill noted that each generation was so preoccupied with the present that it was indifferent to the past, and even 'the tremendous crash of the Roman Empire is scarcely heard outside the schools and colleges'.[98] But Churchill was the exception who proved his own rule. For he read *Decline and fall* in the barracks, at Bangalore, and to such purpose that half a century later he triumphantly reasserted Gibbon's faith in liberty, civilized values and the progress of humanity.

---

[95] Churchill, *World crisis*, p. 677.
[96] Roy Porter, *Edward Gibbon: making history* (London, 1988), p. 139; and see John Robertson above.
[97] Churchill, *Into battle*, p. 293: 9 October 1940.
[98] Winston S. Churchill, *The River War: an historical account of the reconquest of the Soudan* (2 vols., London, 1899), vol. I, p. 11.

Epilogue

J. W. Burrow, Rosamond McKitterick and Roland Quinault

When contemplating the varieties of empire invoked in Gibbon's *Decline and fall* and discussed in this book, a number of themes have emerged. Given the scale and complexity of Gibbon's achievement, John Matthews has suggested that it be seen not so much as a search for a cause of decline as an investigation of a sequence of circumstances; we should think of the concept of decline and fall as a classical trope rather than as an analytical tool.

While there is much to recommend such a view, one might wish to make an exception of the first twelve chapters, in which the trope of decline does also seem to incorporate an underlying formula of the kind, which, following the work of Pocock,[1] we have learned to call Machiavellian: a people, corrupted by conquests and luxury, loses its virtue and with it its liberty, handing over its defence to barbarian auxiliaries who sell the empire to the highest bidder. This theme, classic, as Pocock has shown, in eighteenth-century political analysis and rhetoric, appears in Gibbon less frequently thereafter, though it tends to recur whenever there is a discussion of the relation of conquered peoples to their conquerors. Such a relation is one in which each is fatal to the other: Goths and Vandals are subject in turn to corruption by their corrupt Roman subjects, Arabs by Persians, Mongols by Chinese, while the Turks come to play, in relation to the Arabs, a role analogous to that of the Praetorian Guard in Rome; Gibbon himself explicitly noted the parallels.[2] Yet Gibbon's admiration of strength led to inconsistencies, most notably in his discussion of the deposition of the last Roman emperor in the west by the military commander

---

[1] J. G. A. Pocock, *The Machiavellian moment* (Princeton, 1975).

[2] *Decline and fall*, ed. Bury, III, p. 95; V, p. 484; VI, p. 48; VII, p. 20.

Odoacer. While expatiating on the disgrace to Rome and its weak citizens which this coup represented, Gibbon nevertheless manages to convey a sense of new beginnings as well as continuities, with a shrewd assessment of political realities.

If we add, as a feature of the Romans' own corruption, according to Gibbon, their orientalization – inevitably intensified with the removal of the capital to Constantinople – there is a further contemporary eighteenth-century resonance, pointed to by Jeremy Black: Gibbon deployed to the full the eighteenth-century trope of 'oriental luxury' and 'effeminacy', and their potentially corrupting effects, which sometimes emerged as a somewhat paranoid element in late eighteenth-century rhetoric in, for example, the suspicion of nabobs, the trial of Warren Hastings and the opposition to Fox's India Bill.

These basic ingredients are present and powerful in Gibbon and they are at times embodied in something like a formula of corruption and hence decline, but they do not unify or overmaster the work as a whole. One rather puzzling feature of the *Decline and fall* has hitherto been thought to be the 'General observations' (chapter 38). These Observations are not altogether coherent in themselves and appear only rather loosely related to the body of the text and thus, arguably, somewhat alien, as a simplification and abridgement, to its spirit and to the subtlety and density of Gibbon's narrative. John Matthews, however, has suggested that the 'General observations' should be thought of as a pointer forward (albeit not always noticeably followed up), rather than as a retrospective summary of the opening volumes. Averil Cameron reinforces this in her observation that the intention of the history after the 'General observations' is explicitly altered but was more the product of organic growth as a consequence of further reading in the Greek sources than of a preconceived scheme or clear concept of decline and fall, with the deliberate arrangement of the later parts as a series of portraits of 'nations' exterior to Byzantium – 'the new peoples to whom the torch was to pass' – rather than as a continuous chronological narrative. From our vantage point, of course, many of these new peoples were part of and gradually transformed the Roman heritage rather than being in any way separable from it. Much of this is actually clear from the *Decline and fall* but Gibbon did not present it as such nor did he follow to its logical conclusion his idea of the 'torch' passing. Thus the effect of his work has been to highlight the 'decline and fall' of Rome and to underplay the emergent empires.

It is clear from the chapters in this book nevertheless that, across two centuries, modern scholars in different fields still seem able to engage with Gibbon's work. Even when they disagree, they treat him as a colleague and therefore, not surprisingly, sometimes an erring one. The later part of the work, the principal focus of most of the chapters above, appears to show to some no notable faltering in judgment any more than in style. As both Averil Cameron and Peter Ghosh show, however, there is evidence of a fracture of sorts, a reappraisal and reordering of how Gibbon was conceiving the work on which he was engaged, with a less concentrated focus in the later books which required a different kind of justification. Whatever the variations in the appraisals of Gibbon's scholarship by the authors of this book, they follow no clear chronological trajectory, at least as far as the Byzantine Empire is concerned.

A major theme of the book has been Gibbon's use of his sources. Seldom has Gibbon's use of original sources, across a substantial part of the whole range of *Decline and fall*, been subjected to such scrutiny. Bury examined them for his edition of the work, but he was a single scholar; in Bury's notes within his 'implacable square brackets' can be found the state of scholarship as it was earlier this century, deployed in the assessment of Gibbon's scholarly authority. In the chapters of this book, notably those of Matthews, Cameron, Wood, Shepard, Howard-Johnston and Bryer, there has been a sustained and extensive, if inevitably exemplary rather than comprehensive, attempt to assess Gibbon the scholar from the perspective of the late twentieth century. The attempt itself constitutes a tribute to Gibbon's enduring presence and fascination for scholars as well as a salutary tweak to the consciences of those eighteenth-century historians who approach Gibbon, not as an earlier inquirer in their own field, and a colleague across the centuries, but through an interest in eighteenth-century British and European culture and historiography. The uneasy conscience of the would-be historians of historiography derives, or should derive, from the knowledge that, whatever one may be able to contribute by some knowledge of genre and contemporary political intellectual and historiographical context for the work, one has often no means of one's own to judge exactly how the past historian, especially one whose work covers so vast a field as Gibbon's, has re-shaped, capitulated to, selected shrewdly, arbitrarily, or anachronistically from, the primary sources available to him.

The latter point is to be stressed in the light of John Matthews' suggestions concerning the most obvious technical weakness of Gibbon's work being evident in his lack of understanding of the principles of source criticism, notably in his treatment of the Augustan history. Averil Cameron, moreover, highlighted the degree to which Gibbon found himself faced by problems of organization and interpretation, in her demonstration of how Gibbon found a means both of preserving the finality he had created in his account of the fall of the western Empire and of resolving the contradictions presented by Justinian's reconquest of the West and his overhauling of Roman law by reducing them to questions of personal moral character, just as his sixth-century source Procopius had done. In his analysis of Gibbon's account of the middle Byzantine period, James Howard-Johnston makes it clear that some of the distortions are a consequence not only of Gibbon cutting himself off from such vital sources of information as the hagiography and documents emanating from the apparatus of government but also of an overhasty, selective and apparently superficial reading of the narrative sources at his disposal. Gibbon therefore failed to realize the degree to which Byzantium had reverted to the Roman republican model he apparently prized so highly. On the other hand, these same sources were tapped more efficiently for what they might yield concerning other peoples – Slavs, Bulgars, Hungarians and Rus – and their conversion to Christianity; on eastern Europe Gibbon's sources were few but his judgment good. Yet even Jonathan Shepard's positive assessment of Gibbon is tempered by his own subtle exposition of the *De administrando imperii*; it suggests that Gibbon simply did not wish to moderate his indictment of the Greeks despite his discernment of a link between the conversion of barbarian rulers and the cultural advance of those rulers and their peoples. If Gibbon neglected some categories of source, he made innovative use of others. Anthony Bryer, for instance, reminds us of Gibbon's concern with material culture and his enormously valuable discussions, notably of the Ottomans and the later Byzantine Empires. In this instance especially, Gibbon was able to pander to his audience's taste for the oriental and exotic: the tale of Tamerlane's caging of the Turkish ruler Bajazet, for example, was one of the best known in the seventeenth and eighteenth centuries, celebrated in many paintings, plays and operas.

The discussion of the successor states to the Roman Empire in the west similarly illustrates Gibbon's by turn cavalier and perspicacious treatment of his sources. In his reading of Gregory of Tours' *Historiae*, as Ian Wood points out, Gibbon displays a strange mixture of credulity and condescension. He appears to have treated his narrative sources as reliable quarries for facts, rather than as histories like his own, interpreting the past with their own purposes in mind. Certainly he wrote more credulously about the Franks than about any other people and took at face value the querulous moralizing of many early Christian writers about Gaul as well as Italy. Yet, as Ian Wood argues, Gibbon had a purpose in his account of the Franks: while he underestimated the significance of Roman titles and the survival of Roman institutions for the barbarian world, he made a connection between the development of feudal government (as it was understood in the eighteenth century) and the end of Roman rule in the west which is still being debated today. Further, Gibbon made a deliberate attempt to reclaim the history of the Franks under the Merovingian rulers from its political exploitation by the pre-Revolutionary *philosophes*.

The papers examining Gibbon's use of his sources in various contexts are, for an eighteenth-century historian, at once reassuring and disconcerting. It is reassuring to have such authoritative and expert help from colleagues on precisely the kind of point on which one feels most ill-equipped, but disconcerting because of the emergence of a significant amount of disagreement over the general estimation of Gibbon's engagement with his primary sources. Gibbon could not have guarded himself against the *Historia Augusta*, for example, without being a quite different kind of scholar from the one he was. It is entirely intelligible, more-over, if not absolutely necessary, that he should have followed an acknowledged secondary authority like Giannone on early medieval Italy, especially one whose predilections he found sympathetic. Gibbon as a scholar could be, in a sense, only as good as the sources he trusted and the secondary authorities he chose to read or to which he had access. The critical spectrum running from the esteem of Anthony Bryer for Gibbon's work on the later Byzantine Empire to Rosamond McKitterick's low estimate of Gibbon on the Carolingian period, however, seems wide indeed.

A Gibbon inferior to and negligent of the scholarship of his contemporaries for the western medieval, and especially Carolingian, section of his history as Rosamond McKitterick suggests, is a problem of another sort. Given that elsewhere it appears that Gibbon's reputation for thoroughness and scholarly insight is not without foundation, why should Gibbon, in his treatment of the Franks, fall below the normal level of eighteenth-century scholarly attainment? Distaste hardly seems a plausible explanation, given his much more frequently expressed contempt for Byzantium. That Gibbon should treat a subject perfunctorily because he knew it has been treated more thoroughly by others seems foreign to his normal care for his reputation for comprehensiveness; his overtly expressed feelings of weariness with the minutiae of scholarship are peripheral and jocular.[3] Admittedly, as he found in his abortive project for a history of the Swiss, he could do nothing to remedy his ignorance of German. Perhaps the answer lies in our comments earlier concerning Gibbon's intentions for volumes IV–VI, and, as John Matthews, Averil Cameron and Peter Ghosh have implicitly indicated, in the structure of the account of the western Empire after the fifth century as a whole.

Estimations of Gibbon's handling of his sources within the chapters by Ian Wood and Tom Brown in particular become entangled with that of his treatment of the 'barbarians'. The question was raised whether his view of the barbarians changed over time. Judging from the comments of Tom Brown and Anthony Bryer, there is certainly a contrast, but this may have more to do with geography than chronology. That is, the contrast is between west and east rather than between earlier and later Gibbon. It is true that the one notorious error in his treatment of the Goths, namely, his determination to make them pastoral nomads, is derived, as Tom Brown points out, from his assimilation of them to the categories of Scottish sociological history, the history of Civil Society. It is an assimilation to which the eastern barbarians portrayed by Gibbon submit more meekly than those of the west, but Gibbon was determined to present them in this light. One has surely to take into account the influence of the elegiac neo-classical topos which inevitably colours his account of the invasion of Italy. Though he exonerated them from destroying Rome, the Gothic

---

[3] For example, *ibid.*, IV, p. 187 n. 59.

warriors 'insulted' by their presence the ground which had known Virgil and Catullus. The Arabs and Turks occupied still more ancient sites of classical civilization, but Gibbon was already too old, too much an Augustan, to be swept away by the new neo-Hellenic enthusiasms of the later eighteenth century; ancient Greece never meant for him what Rome did and Greece had become associated with a form of Christianity more alien than Roman Catholicism. Of course Gibbon never travelled there, but one must strongly suspect that even had he done so the call of the muezzin from the minarets around St Sophia would have made a less profound impression than the friars chanting in the temple of Jupiter; Gibbon was, after all, sympathetic to the Iconoclasts and not without approval of Islam.

Mention of places, and of the associations by which, for Gibbon, they were made sacred or by which they were overlaid, raises another question, that of Gibbon's relations to past civilizations and their remains through his visual sense. This is related, on each side, so to speak, to two other connected but not identical issues: his aesthetic tastes and, important for his qualities as an historian, his relation to things in the sense of tangible objects. Anthony Bryer rightly draws attention to the significance of the latter: to his feeling for the importance of dimension and location, of the sheer concrete presence of things and of the obligation and even pleasure of accuracy about them. It has given us much enjoyable pedantry or better than pedantry in the footnotes to the *Decline and fall*, and also its set-piece descriptions of the Coliseum, of the buildings of Rome as first seen by Theodoric, and the account, partly derived from Adam, of the palace of Diocletian.[4] Gibbon is both epigrammatically abstract and at times arrestingly concrete. It is entirely appropriate, even apart from the popularity of the topos, that he should situate the conception of the *Decline and fall* among *things*.

Gibbon's own precise aesthetic tastes are rather more elusive, unless one assumes them to be merely conventionally English

---

[4] Robert Adam, *Ruins of the palace of the emperor Diocletian at Spalato* (London, 1764). Gibbon, of course, was not the only one to be inspired by Adam's book, as is clear from Benjamin West's portrayal of 'Agrippina landing at Brundisium with the ashes of Germanicus' (Yale University Art Gallery, New Haven), painted in 1768, where the palace in the background is obviously based on plate VIII in Adam's book, depicting the side elevation of Diocletian's palace: see Helmut von Erffa and Allen Staley, *The paintings of Benjamin West* (New Haven and London, 1986), pp. 44–6 and catalogue no. 133, pp. 179–80.

and Augustan. They are not irrelevant to his endorsements and disparagements; in fact, they are to a significant degree the same. Ciceronian Latin was one touchstone; classical architecture decorum which could assimilate Mannerism but not Byzantium (St Peter's but not St Mark's) seems to be another. We have been reminded by Tom Brown of Gibbon's apparently wilful shunning of Ravenna on his Italian tour, and his view of St Mark's Square was damning.[5] But one has to suspect that historical and cultural association meant more to Gibbon than visual perception as such. The famous description of the terrace at Lausanne marking the completion of the Decline and fall in the Memoirs[6] is moving but classically, even perhaps conventionally, serene rather than sublime in the sense defined by Gibbon's friend Burke. It seems noteworthy as well as prophetic that in Florence, on his way to Rome, it was the busts of Roman emperors, not the glories of the Renaissance, that held his attention. 'The historian of the Roman Empire' seems already unconsciously in charge.

The latter part of the book takes us more emphatically to the eighteenth century; to Gibbon's wrestling with the huge, intractable problem of the architecture of his great work charted by Ghosh and to eighteenth-century attitudes, particularly of course, Gibbon's own; to the rival concepts of universal empire and of the balance of power (alternative versions of potential international stability) presented by Robertson and Black. Gibbon's own allegiance was given, clearly, to the notion he develops towards the end of the Decline and fall of modern Europe as a 'great republic' of nations, whose emulation and the strenuousness it fosters, not necessarily warlike but also cultural; as one of the chief preservatives of modern civilization against the stagnation and forfeiture of liberty which had overtaken the ancient world. It is an idea with, as Robertson points out, notable antecedents in European thought, with Montesquieu and Hume as carriers and the long-lived antithesis of 'Europe' not merely to 'oriental effeminacy' but also to 'Chinese' stagnation. From one point of view, it can be seen as a projection onto the cultural life of a community of nations of classically-derived Whig notions of constitutional balance. The most famous invocation of 'Chinese stationariness' is, of course, a nineteenth-century one, by John

---

[5] Letters, vol. I, p. 143.   [6] Memoirs, ed. Bonnard, p. 180.

Stuart Mill in *On liberty*. Mill surely derived it, not, in view of his hereditary antipathy to it, directly from the Whig constitutional tradition, nor from the eighteenth century, with whose political thinking he seems unfamiliar, but primarily from Guizot's *Lectures on the history of civilization*. The notion there that the energy of Europe derived from a conflict or competitions of powers, though Mill seems unaware of it, comes surely directly from Gibbon, whose *Decline and fall* in its French edition had, of course, been edited by Guizot.[7]

The narrative of this transmission of Gibbon into the mainstream of nineteenth-century liberal thought has not been properly worked out and remains largely neglected,[8] but mention of it is a reminder that the subsequent cultural influence of the *Decline and fall* is part of our own history as well as of our historiography and sense of history. This is vividly exemplified in Roland Quinault's tracing of the significance, for Winston Churchill's sense of history and of the historic encounters of his own age, of his devoted reading of Gibbon. The historian of the Roman Empire, one has to conclude, was not useless to the articulation of national defiance at a moment quite as critical as some of those which figure in the *Decline and fall*.

[7] F. Guizot, *Histoire de la décadence et de la chûte de l'empire romain* (13 vols., Paris, 1812): J. S. Mill, *Essays on French history and historians. Collected works*, vol. xx, ed. J. Robson (Toronto, 1977), p. 270.
[8] See, however, J. W. Burrow, *Whigs and Liberals. Continuity and change in English political thought* (Oxford, 1988), pp. 116–24.

Index

342